ROBOTS – OUR FUTURE PARTNERS?!

A Sociologist's View
from a German and Japanese Perspective

von

Miriam J. S. Leis

Tectum Verlag
Marburg 2006

Tag der mündl. Prüfung: 14. Dezember 2005
Erstreferentin: Prof. Dr. Karin Knorr Cetina
Zweitreferent: PD. Dr. Kay Junge

Leis, Miriam J. S.:
Robots – Our Future Partners?!
A Sociologist's View from a German
and Japanese Perspective.
/ von Miriam J. S. Leis
- Marburg : Tectum Verlag, 2006
Zugl.: Konstanz, Univ. Diss. 2005
Umschlagabbildung: Autorin
ISBN –10: 3-8288-9134-9
ISBN –13: 978-3-8288-9134-0

© Tectum Verlag

Tectum Verlag
Marburg 2006

I would like to express my gratitude to the following persons and institutions for their support and time for discussions and interviews

Dr. Ramin Assadollahi,
Dipl.-Ing. Rainer Bischoff,
Mr. Axel von Borstel, Dr. Augustin Bredenfeld,
Mrs. Karina Friedrich
Dipl.-Inf. Birgit Graf
Honda Motors Co., Ltd.
Dr. Kuniaki Kawabata, Dr. Johanna Kissler, Prof. Dr. Karin Knorr-Cetina,
Mr. Michael Lyons, PhD
Pfr.. Dr. Holgar Müller, Pfr.. E. Hübler-Umemoto
Dr. Tetsuya Ogata,
Dr. Alexandru Preda,
Mr. Joachim Recksiek,
Ms. Yumiko Sano, Mr. Kiyoshi Sawamura, Dipl.-Ing. Christoph Schaeffer,
Mr. Christopher Scholtz, Mr. Shinichi Shinkawa,
Dr. Stefan Stein, Mr. Junji Suzuki,
Mr. Sam Takashima,
Prof. Dr. Naoto Umemoto,
Prof. Dr. Ipke Wachsmuth

…and special thanks to my friends at *www.aibo-freunde.de*
…and to my parents and all my friends who have supported me
and have shown interest in my idea(l)s !

Contents

I.0 Preface: Fast Changing Times	i
I.1. Why Should a Sociologist Write about Robotics?	I
I.2 Personal Motivation for choosing a Topic about Robots and for doing a Comparison Study between Germany and Japan	II
I.3 Research Questions	IV

PART I

1.0 Visions	1
1.1 From Zoë to ASIMO– A Brief History of Robots	4
1.1.1 Ancient Myths	5
1.1.2 The Creation of Artificial Entities from a Christian Perspective	7
1.1.3 Non-humans and Artificial Entities from a Japanese Perspective	9
1.1.4 Religious Factors Overestimated?	12
1.1.5 Dolls and Puppets in Japanese Thought	15
1.1.6 The Flourishing Age of Early Automata	17
1.1.7 Frankenstein, Sandman and Philosophical Questions	19
1.1.8 Automata in Japan	22
1.2 Industrialization	27
1.2.1 Japan's Modernization Process	28
1.3 The Robot	32
1.3.1 Robots in Japanese Fiction and Literature…	33
1.3.1.1 Happy Birthday "Astro Boy" !	35
1.3.1.2 Mecha-Animé and the Gundam Universe…	40
1.3.2 The Robots are Coming	42
1.3.3 Defining "Robot"	43
1.3.4 First Real Robots	52
1.3.4.a) Excursion: Killed by a Robot?	53
1.3.4.b) Excursion: Failsafe Laws?	53
1.3.4.c) Excursion: Robot Shows	56
1.3.5 Why do we want robots?	57
1.3.5 a) Excursion: Robot Economy	64

PART II

2. (MA)CHI(N)E	67
2.1 What is (Wo)man?	67
2.1.1 Man, Machine or (Ma)chi(n)e ?	70
2.1.2 La Mettrie, Minsky, Moravec and the End of Humanity?	70
2.1.2.a) Short Reflection: Losing Ground in Virtual Worlds	77
2.1.3 The shift towards a "mechanistic" view of humankind	80
2.1.3 a) Excursion: What a Difference a Chip makes	82
2.1.4 Downgrading and Upgrading: Restoring the Vanishing Borders	83
2.1.4.a) Short Reflection II: Was God just a mediocre engineer?	87
2.2 Res Cogitans and Res Extensa - The Mind enters the Machine............................	87
2.2.1 Ever Failed a Turing Test?	90
2.3 The (Un)limited Animal	93
2.3.1 The Evolution of a *Cyborg*	96
2.3.2 Reflections on Technology and Society	99
2.3.2 a) Reflection: Fast and Ubiquitous	99
2.3.2 b) Reflection: No Serviceable Parts Inside	101
2.3.2.c) Reflection: The *Techno*-Paradox	103
2.4 Where to Place Artifacts?	107
2.4.1 The "Blade Runner Complex" and the Elimination of "Quasi-Objects"	107
2.4.2 A Note on "Actor Network Theory"	112
2.4.3 On Replacing Elements in a Network	121
2.4.4 The Placement of Subjects and Objects in Germany and Japan	123
2.4.4.1 Fuzzy Logic and Fuzzy Objects - A Short Introduction to the Concept	124
2.4.4.2 A Note on Statistics and "Fuzzy Set Theory"	127
2.4.5 Survey & Results	129
2.4.5.1 Preliminary Results	131
2.4.5.2 Interpretation	133
2.4.6 A Note on Anthropomorphizing	136

PART III

- 3.1.1 Japan – The *Robot Kingdom* !? — 143
- 3.1.2 Observations — 149
  - 3.1.2.1 Germany – The Robot Kingdom !? — 149
  - 3.1.2.2 Germany – The Robot Kingdom ?? — 155
  - 3.1.2.3 Japan – The Robot Kingdom ! — 158

- 3.2 Robot-Related Interest Promotion — 162
  - 3.2.1 Public Events — 163
  - 3.2.2 Robodex 2003 (held from 03.04.2003 to 06.04.2003) — 164
  - 3.2.3 Kansai and Kyushu: Japan's hubs for Robot development — 166
  - 3.2.4 Japan's Robotic Celebrities — 171
  - 3.2.5 Japan – Inside the Robot-Toy-Kingdom — 173

- 3.3 Robot Pets — 180
  - 3.3.1.1 AIBO — 182
  - 3.3.1.2 The History of AIBO — 183
  - 3.3.2 AIBO from a Sociologist's View — 189
    - 3.3.2.1 AIBO-Community — 189
    - 3.3.2.2 AIBO Life Style Phenomenon — 190

- 3.4 German and Japanese Robot-Research — 194
  - 3.4.1 Walking Humanoids — 194
  - 3.4.2 Comparison Study: Germany and Japan — 198
    - 3.4.2.1 "Form Follows Function" vs. "Function Follows Form" — 198
      - 3.4.2.1 a) Short Reflection III: The Art of Robotics — 203
    - 3.4.2.2 Concept Comparison — 204
  - 3.4.3 Partner Robot — 213

- 3.5 Explanations — 218
  - 3.5.1 Robotics and Demographic Factors — 218
  - 3.5.2 Explaining the "Robot Kingdom" — 221
    - 3.5.2.1 Attitude towards technology — 221
    - 3.5.2.2 From Ships, Cars and Consumer Electronics to Environmental Technology Robots and Animé — 226
    - 3.5.2.3 The "Cherry Blossom Effect" — 229
    - 3.5.2.3 From *Zen* to *ASIMO* and Back - In Search of Japan's Self-Identity — 231
    - 3.5.2.5 Nihonjinron — 232
    - 3.5.2.6 "Nihonjinron-Effect" as Self-Fulfilling Prophecy — 234
    - 3.5.2.7 Nihonjinon – Or Why the Robot is Japanese — 235
    - 3.5.2.8 Reanalyzing "*Tetsuwan Atomu* — 236

3.5.3 Why the Robot fits into the Japanese Culture	243
3.5.3.1 The Group - "Closed Circuit"	244
3.5.3.2 Harmony	244
3.5.3.3 Conformity, Ritualism and the Group	244
3.5.3.4 Public Behavior and Observing Rank	247
3.5.3.4 a) Excursion: A Note on accepting ones Position	249
3.5.4 Reflection: Robots as Role Models?	251
3.6 Personal Robots	253
3.6.1 Indications	254
3.6.2 Human-Robot Relations	257
3.6.3 A Further Note on Human-Object Relations as a Compensatory Resort	260
3.6.4 Shut-Ins and Loners	262
3.6.5 Robots to Care for - Robot Assisted Therapy	264
3.7 Reflection	266
PART IV	269
4.1 About Social Sciences and Robotics	269
4.1.2 Mind Without History	271
4.2 Natural and Artificial Intelligence	272
4.2.1 "Intelligent" Artifacts?	272
4.2.2 What is Intelligence?	274
4.2.3 Artificial Intelligence	277
4.2.4 Programmed for All (Im)practical Purposes	281
4.3 Phenomenology, Neuroscience and Robotics	284
4.3.1 Action Schemes	290
4.3.2 Towards a Robot-Phenomenology	296
4.3.2.1 Why do robots (still) fail at simple tasks	297
Takamanya – Or Managing Without Understanding	298
4.3.3 "Cultural OS	301
4.3.3.1 Running on the Wrong Program	304
4.3.3.2 Excursion: The Phenomenology of Problem-Solving	309
4.4 The use of Robots for Social- and Psychological Studies	311
4.4.1 Communication	312
4.4.2 Language	321
4.4.3 E-Motions	324

Bonus: Excerpt from *"Sayako"*	337

References and Information

References	340
German and Japanese Robot Projects in Brief	D- 1
List of Acronyms and Abbreviations	D-11
A.1 Work and Methodology	A 1
A.1.1 A note about using generalized expressions	A 1
A.1.2 A note about terms and definitions	A 2
A.2 A note about my methodological approaches	A 2
A.2.1 Goal of the study	A 2
A.2.2 Generating and testing hypothesis	A 3
A.2.3 Data and Observations	A 4
A.2.4 Interviews and discussions	A 8
A.3 German Summary	A15
A.4 Interview Summaries & Survey Data	S 1

(The names of some interviewed persons ("Amerigo", "Misenus", "Arvalis" and "Aoki") have been changed for this published version; pseudonyms have been computer generated)

A.4.1 Mr. Shinkawa (Robosquare Fukuoka, Robot Edutainment Center Japan)	S 1
A.4.2 Rev. Dr. *Amerigo* (Pastor, Protestant Church in Germany)	S 5
A.4.3 M. *Misenus*. (Former nursing-care worker in Germany)	S 8
A.4.4 Dipl.-Ing. Graf (Researcher at Fraunhofer IPA / Germany)	S17
A.4.5 Rev. *Arvalis* (Pastor, German Protestant Church in Japan)	S21
A.4.6 Prof. *Aoki* (Japanese Humanities Professor)	S26
A.4.7 Mr. J. Suzuku (Engineer at Mitsubishi Heavy Industries)	S30
AIBO Survey Data & Evaluation	S36

Preface: Fast Changing Times

Although impressive, today's robot technology is still rather comparable to the Wright brother's Flyer-3 than to an Airbus A380. But if one thinks about the fact that it took much over one million years to invent the airplane and only one hundred years to develop the first practical motor-powered aircraft into the state of the art A380, it looks as if the idea is born, its pace of progress may be rapid. This observation gets even more obvious if looking at the development of computers, information technology, biotechnology and robotics. In face of these fast changing times it is assumable that some of the data provided in this book will soon be historical records, outdated and overtaken by reality…

Even in the rather short time from April 2003 to April 2005, where I was writing on my thesis, there have been numerous developments in the field of robotics and Artificial Intelligence, where latest scientific achievements include improvements in pattern recognition and machine learning, energy-efficient biped walking, human-machine interaction and the fusion of biological neurons with computer chips. One also gets to recognize the increasing efforts being done in the areas of marketing and public relations in regard to robots. This is especially obvious in Japan, where in the two years from 2003 to 2005 much publicity has revolved around Honda's ASIMO and Sony's QRIO (formerly known as SDR-4XII), where more than a dozen new robots have been presented to the public or even went on sale, and where robots belong to the protagonists of the Aichi Expo 2005. Some visionaries predict that by the year 2050 Artificial Intelligence will have reached the level of human intelligence, or that at least that humanoid robots will stand the chance of defeating a human team in a soccer match. Regardless of how realistic such predictions may look, the tendency seems to be clear: the process of building robots has been initiated and will be very likely to be continued, possibly with ever-increasing pace. Mechatronic toys have already entered numerous children's rooms, perhaps shaping the minds and attitudes of future generations, influencing their perception of technology and humanity. And many politicians, researchers and economists already predict that the robot-industry will turn into the equivalent of today's automobile industry. In this respect I consider it important to cogitate about the impact thinking and acting machines could have on human society.

Clearly, the age of the artificial human is dawning; may it be in form of biotechnology, robotics / Artificial Intelligence, or the fusion of the biological with the artificial – Cyborg technology - welcoming anticipations awaited by the growing number of Transhumanists.

I.1. Why Should a Sociologist Write about Robotics?

Why should a social scientist choose to write about a topic like robots, some mechatronic machinery still rather associated with factory halls and hostile environments? Some even demand that non-humans should be excluded from the field of sociology by default. But with building robots, humans have begun to create artifacts in their own image; artifacts that some day are hoped (or feared) to think and act just like a human being. If planning to build such artifacts, wouldn't it represent a paradox if one excluded them from a social scientist's consideration?

The trend is obvious. Robots are already leaving the factory halls and quite literally set foot onto public places, offices and even our homes. Great efforts are being put into the research about making human-robot interaction easier and in equipping robots with some human traits that even include emotions. In this sense the existence of the robot also raises new questions about the position of humankind. Will the increase in human-machine interaction, while at the same time some suggest a decrease in human-human interaction, lead to postsocial relations; this means new relationships being tied between humans and objects[7]?

Especially in Japan, robots are said to comprise a huge percentage of future consumer goods; that is in a country, where an increasing number of people is already shifting their prime relationship to consumer goods and away from other humans; a general observation already made by Jean Baudrillard.[8]

Sociology and robotics represent complementary sciences, where both can learn from each other: roboticists may get helpful insights in regard to understanding how humans manage tasks like learning, problem solving, understanding, communication and making sense of their surrounding, whereas robots may provide valuable objects to social scientists for testing social theories.

Above this, robotics is a highly interdisciplinary field, comprising disciplines

---
[7] refer to Knorr Cetina, 1997 and Callon, 1986
[8] Refer to Baudrillard, 1981

spanning from information science, engineering, physics, mathematics, biology, neurosciences and psychology to economy, social sciences, cultural studies, linguistics, philosophy and even religion. And the insights having been gained through this study are not limited to the case of robotics. Actually one could also replace the "robot" by something else, to show how historical, socio-cultural, political and economic environments may shape and influence the development, fate and acceptance of inventions and ideas.

I.2 Personal Motivation for choosing a Topic about Robots and for doing a Comparison Study between Germany and Japan

Although being a social scientist (political scientist and sociologist) by training, I am (and have always been) greatly interested in natural sciences and technology; and have therefore chosen to specialize in sociology of science and technology, social interaction and communication theory, science policy and game theory. I also liked to maintain the connection to space exploration, Information Technology, computers, Artificial Intelligence, "Virtual Reality", biotechnology and even quantum mechanics in my term- and examination papers.

Although I was studying in Germany, nonetheless the news about Japanese robot developments like *P3* (Honda 1997), *AIBO* (Sony 1999), *SDR-4XII* (Sony 2000)[9] and *ASIMO* (Honda 2000) has even reached me half a world away. While working on my *Magister* thesis about country specific differences in legislation regulating embryonic stem-cell research I got deeply involved with the question in how far socio-cultural, political and economic conditions may influence a country's practices in the area of research and development. This led me to the question: why does Japanese robot research get so much more media attention

---
[9] Later known as "Qrio". Just before of publishing thius book, in late January 2006 Sony has announced that their projects on *AIBO* and *Qrio* will be discontinued.

than German robot research? Since I was also interested in robotics, I decided to tackle this topic in my dissertation thesis.

Being a German national who lived in Tokyo since the age of three, I considered it only reasonable to include a comparison between Germany and Japan in relation to possible differences in research strategies and public acceptance concerning robots. As I have discussed the issue with German friends, I was surprised to hear that almost all of them showed a somewhat negative attitude towards the idea of robots. Maybe, so was my first hypothesis, can the origin for this be traced back to differences in cultural socialization. But since Germany and Japan have much in common, especially in regard to their involvement in World War II, the miraculous post-war recovery catapulting both countries to top positions on the economic landscape, recent economic setbacks, and the demographic development of declining birthrates and the graying of society, I found it even more interesting to get behind the reasons why Japan's interest in promoting robot technology seems to be so much greater than Germany's.

Miriam J.S. Leis (Konstanz, Tokyo, Saipan April 2003 – April 2005)

I.3 Research Questions

Research questions: As I have found out that robotics, as well as sociology, are quite interdisciplinary fields, I decided on dividing my thesis into four parts, each concentrating on a different focus.

In the beginning was neither the word, nor the deed, but the question; and it was the questions being posed that guided me through my analysis in the quest for finding explanations.

Part 1: The History of Robotics in a Nutshell

Questions:
- Where and when did the idea of building "robots" originate?
- What (socio-cultural, religious, historic, economic) circumstances have shaped the attitude towards robots / robotics in Germany and Japan, and can there be found differences between the two countries?
- How is a robot being defined, and are there differences in regard to the definition between Japan and Germany?
- Where, when and why have the first industrial robots been deployed and what were the socio-economic consequences of this?

The first and introducing part of my thesis traces the history of the idea about (human-made) artificial entities, life-imitating automata and robots, as they are described in Eastern and Western mythology and literature, and were finally put into practice through mechanics and engineering. The analysis takes into account religious, socio-cultural, historical, political and economic factors, and depicts similarities as well as differences between German and Japanese attitudes, concepts and products of mind.

Part 2: Humans, Machines and Society

Questions:

- How did mankind's view about humanity change in face of the increasing progress being made in science and technology (including biotechnology, (computer) engineering, Artificial Intelligence and robotics)?

- Can the increasing number of artifacts that already share some traits with their human creators still be regarded as a *"pure object"* (Latour, 1995) or commodity?

- Do Japanese and Germans look at objects (and robots) in the same way?

Since humans are producing an increasing number of artifacts that share some qualities with their human creators, the question arises, where to place such entities in our world. Can they be granted entry into human society and be considered in social analysis, or will they remain excluded per definition, as it is the stance of classic sociology? Are there differences in how Germans and Japanese tend to regard objects or even integrate them into human society?

In my view, closely related is also the question about how to regard humankind: as just being some kind of organic machine or as something that can never be artificially (re)created? Paradoxically, through progress being made in modern science and technology, the human is ever more referred to as a machine, whereas machines are equipped with an increasing number of human-like characteristics.

Part 3: Robots – Our Future Partners?! A Comparison between Germany and Japan

Questions:

- Why is Japan and not Germany being called the *"Robot Kingdom[10]"*?
- What is the difference between the German and Japanese perception about the idea of robots leaving the factory halls and beginning to enter our everyday lives?

- What are the main differences between German and Japanese robot-research concepts?

- What is behind Japan's *"Robot-Kingdom"* image?
- Why do Japanese seem to embrace the idea of having robots around in such a positive fashion?

- Does there exist unique circumstances which could have led to Japan's perceived fondness for robots?

The third part of my thesis represents the main analysis. According to my observations Japan seems to be much more interested and involved in conducting and promoting (non-industrial) robot technology than Germany. This is insofar puzzling since Germany belongs to the world's top producers of complex high-tech machinery that is even exported to Japan. Also if taking a closer look at robot related research and development being conducted in Germany, one could not say that their technological standard considerably lags behind that of Japan. In some areas German robot research may even be more progressive than their Japanese counterpart, although both countries emphasize different aspects in their development. What seems to be clear is that Japan puts much more effort into public interest promotion about their robots. Whereas in Germany the idea of robots leaving the factory halls and entering a human's everyday life is still rather looked at with skepticism, in Japan the idea of robots

---

[10] A term originally coined by Frederik L. Schodt in his book *"Inside the Robot Kingdom. Japan, Mechatronics, and the Coming Robotopia"*. (Schodt, 1988)

serving as mankind's "friend and partner" tends to be embraced with quite positive expectations. In my view, it's not only the robot that is engineered, but also the image about Japan being the *"Robot Kingdom"*. So what might be the reasons for Germany's skepticism and Japan's displayed enthusiasm? What is really behind the *"Robot Kingdom"*? These are just some of the questions being analyzed from a multidimensional perspective by also critically reviewing classic explanations like Japan's animistic religion and the popularity of the fictitious robot hero *"Tetsuwan Atomu"*.

Finally I will note on possible future outlooks. What will the human-robot future hold for us? Can the increasing number of (maybe homophobic) people being preoccupied with the artificial ("communication robots", computers, "Virtual Reality") be seen as an indicator for the growing ills of human society and the decline in human-human relations?

Part 4: Towards a Robot-Phenomenology

Questions:

- How can the disciplines of social science and robotics profit from each other?

- What are the differences between Artificial Intelligence and human intelligence, between human emotions and (simulated) *"e-motions"*?

- How to evaluate the statement that there are no fundamental differences between human and artificial intelligence?

The fourth and final part of my thesis will deal with questions and thoughts which I think are of interest for both, sociologists and researchers in the area of robotics and Artificial Intelligence. I derive from the question why today's robots still have problems with tasks that seem simple to humans. For finding an answer to this question it is important to uncover how and why humans are able to manage coping with these supposedly simple tasks, something where neuroscientists and phenomenologists arrived at similar conclusions, although from different and even complementary perspectives. Not to underestimate is the aspect of a human's socio-cultural embeddedness that helps a person in structuring ones environment. Artificial Intelligence is still a mind without history.

Does there exist a fundamental difference between artificial and genuine intelligence, or is the difference only gradual, depending on the current stand of technology? Can everything be solved through programming? And in how far can one speak of a human's socio-cultural programming? If a simulation would be indistinguishable from its genuine counterparts, can it be argued that both are the same – at least for all practical purposes?

I also will note on the question about the future of humans and robots in the context of human-object / human-non-human relationships.

---

[20] I'm referring to the „*Innsbruck Experiment*".

PART I
0101000001100001011100100111010000100000000110001

The History of Robotics in a Nutshell

1.0 Visions

We, at least those fortunate people having the luck to live in a so-called (post) industrialized country, are living in a time where reality is beginning to overtake science fiction. Looking at the gadgetry of the original *Star Trek* series (mid 1960s), I guess my office-space is better equipped than the starship's bridge. Quantum-states are being "teleported" from one atom to another[20], endangered species are being cloned and the creation of chimera, genetically engineered creatures consisting of human and non-human DNA represents rather a legal than a technological problem. Mice can be remote-controlled over the computer by manipulating electronic signals in their brains[21] and computers are able to detect a human's brain activity and let him/her control a cursor on a computer screen only through "the power of thought"[22]. Real people, among them some of my friends and relatives, are walking on the streets with implanted electromechanical devices, but I consider it being rude calling them *cyborgs,* because the term somehow possesses a negative overtone. After having flown around the world in much less than 80 *hours*, I'm surfing the internet, yesteryear's dream described by Will F. Jenkins in a story called *"A Logic Named Joe"* (Will F. Jenkins 1946[23]), dive deep into the forerunner of William

---

[21] This experiment has been conducted by there research team around the bio-engineer Sanjiv Talwar at the State University of New York. Similar experiments have been successfully conducted at Duke University (US) with a monkey being able to control a robot-arm only through its neural activity.
[22] I'm referring to an experiment conducted at University of Tübingen / Germany to help paralyzed people control symbols on a computer screen and someday maybe a robot (as shown on *nano*, a German TV science-magazine).
[23] The story is mostly published under his pen name of Murray Leinster

Gibson's *"Cyberspace"*[24]. In the edge of my second computer screen sits an avatar of a small robot reminding me on today's appointments, and occasionally I chat with computers about philosophy (or is it a human being trying to trick me?). Some people call outer space their workplace and a few minutes ago, in the news, I heard about bold plans to make space flights available to the general public. Still too expensive, but as it has been with most things – except crude oil – prices will come down. I have seen robots walking and descending staircases just like humans and robotic android heads imitating human emotional expressions. Meanwhile I have switched off my *AIBO* robot-dog, still wondering if it (she?) is *"Three Law Safe*[25]*"* (only joking). I just couldn't really concentrate on my text, because she (it?) seems to be somehow restless today.

Until quite recently, robots, the main subjects of my work have been confined to the realms of myths and science fiction, and later to factory halls, but are now beginning to enter everyday life. Myths and legends as well as science fiction are not just entertainment. They are more than that. Through all times they reflected the hopes and fears of humankind. They are attempts to provide answers to the most essential questions: who are we? Where do we come from and where are we going to?

Isaac Asimov once defined science fiction as follows:

> *"Modern science fiction is the only form of literature that consistently considers the nature of*
>
> *the changes that face us, the possible consequences, and the possible solutions"*[26].

---

[24] As described in William Gibson's "cyber-punk" science-fiction novel *Neuromancer* (first published in 1984)
[25] I'm referring to the famous "Three Laws of Robotics" envisioned by the scientist and science fiction author Isaac Asimov in his robot stories.
[26] found on: http://www.panix.com/~gokce/sf_defn.html (found in May 2003)

And Ray Bradbury, author of "*Fahrenheit 451*"[27] said this about science fiction:

> "*Science fiction is really sociological studies of the future, things that the writer believes are going to happen by putting two and two together.*"[28]

I, as a sociologist and science-fiction enthusiast agree with Bradbury's statement that science fiction is indeed a form of "sociological studies of the future", exploring the social consequences by projecting today's trends. While engineers are mainly occupied with the question about if and how it will work, it's the writers, philosophers and social scientists that will be left with the question if and how it will work for humanity. They grasp the trends and anticipations and help us reflecting. They close the circle of checks and balances. They provide us with a look into our future – or one possible future. It's not mainly about if the portrayed technology will actually work, but rather a question about what kind of *consequences* a certain technological trend could entail.

Therefore I have decided on introducing you to the idea of man-made human-like entities which are nowadays commonly known as robots by combining the history of technology and scientific ideas with the history of philosophy, myths and science fiction. I will take you onto a journey through time and humankind's ideas, hopes and fears.

---

[27] The story plays in a world, in which books are banned and burned. Montag, a fire-fighter one day asks himself why people are rather willing to die than give up reading their books. Montag starts reading books himself and becomes guardian of literature and knowledge himself.
[28] found on: http://www.panix.com/~gokce/sf_defn.html (found in May 2003)

1.1 From Zoë[29] to ASIMO[30] – A Brief History of Robots

Many people tend to call every non-living object which somehow seems to act autonomously, i.e. without any (visible) human interference a robot (this also includes purely mechanical and remote-controlled devices). Even on the instruction-manual for a replica construction-kit of the famous Japanese "tea-carrying *Karakuri*[31] doll", a purely mechanical clock-work automaton from the *Edo*-Period (1603-1867) it says: *"The Tea-Serving Robot Developed in the Edo-Period"*.

Picture:
Replica of the Japanese
„Tea Carrying Automata"
(*Karakuri-Ningyō*) from
the Edo-Period

Photo: Miriam JS Leis, 2003
author's own collection

And if I look for synonyms for the term "robot" in the dictionary integrated into *MS-Word* it gives me "automaton", "machine" and "android[32]" (for "android" it gives me "zombie" – who has programmed this?). On the other hand some people restrict the usage of the term "robot" to a machine that *works* for a human on command and therefore exclude a whole array of "robots" purely built for entertainment, education and communication purposes, as "companions" or "pets"[33]. For reasons I will explain later, I suggest to use a

---

[29] A picture drawing mechanical android from the 19th Century.
[30] Humanoid robot developed by Honda Motors Co., Ltd. / Japan, debuted in the year 2000
[31] The Japanese term *Karakuri* means the mechanism that drives a machine
[32] Android = Automata in human form.
[33] Special thanks to my friends at the German AIBO-Community with whom I had discussions about this issue.

rather broad definition of the term "robot", which does not a priori induce a certain purpose for which they might be built.

But before I'll come to the real robots of today and provide you with a more technical definition, I will use the terms "robot" (in inverted commas) and automaton as synonyms, describing any form of artificial entity displaying some human or animal traits and take you on a journey through ancient myths, fantastic literature and the high-flying ideas of the Age of Enlightenment – how it all began.

Looking at it from this perspective it is quite remarkable that the idea of "artificial (wo)men" dates back at least to ancient Greek mythology and can be followed through medieval tales and legends, narrations from the time of European Romanticism up to modern science fiction, cutting through many cultures ranging from Orient to Occident.

1.1.1 Ancient Myths

Since many centuries humankind has already dreamed of building artificial human-like entities. Indeed, with Prometheus, Daedalus and Hephaestus the idea of "robots" can be traced back to ancient Greek mythology dated around 750 BC. It was Prometheus/Titan who created humans out of clay and despite interdiction gave them the fire (which means technology), causing the punishment of Zeus. This story is nearly paradigmatic in regard to questions about mankind's dealings with technology and its consequences. One of the earliest mythological "roboticists"[34] is said to be the Greek god Hephaestus, who has created different autonomously agitating entities like Talos, a giant made of metal to guard the island of Crete, hence the word *"automatoi"* (Greek: to move by itself).

---

[34] A term coined by the science-fiction author and scientist Isaac Asimov

Also in the ancient Jewish tradition, dating back to around 500 CE or even earlier, there exist many stories about the creation of artificial entities. One classic example of the creation of man-made human-like entities is the *Golem*, already mentioned in the Jewish *Kabbalah*, a collection of mystic knowledge that has been revealed to saints of ancient times and passed on orally for centuries[35]. Although the exact time concerning the origin of the *Kabbalah* remains disputed, the first written accounts appeared during the first and second century CE, whereas the most influential texts appeared in the 12th century CE. The *Golem* is described as a kind of mindless and soulless slave with human shape, formed out of clay, who comes into existence only through magic rituals and the recitation of formulas carried out by humans and not through the life-giving breath of God[36]. Therefore the *Golem*[37] remains the antithesis to *Adam*, who is seen as the entity created by the will of God and not the will of man[38]. Interestingly, especially if looking at the Jewish rejection of statues and idols, in Judaism originally the creation of a *Golem* was not associated with sin, but rather with the mystic experience of the deep secrets of life. There are many legends around the *Golem*. One of them that exists in many variations, is the legend of Rabbi Jehuda Loew who is said to have created a *Golem* in 1580 to protect the Jews living in Prague (coincidentally also the place where the term robot originated) against pogroms. Some of the legends, mainly the later ones which got increasingly ambivalent, end with the *Golem* becoming uncontrollable, finally beginning to destroy the city and representing a danger to mankind[39]. The *Golem* could only be deactivated with a trick, for example by taking away the

---

[35] The Golem also appears in the *Agadah*, a collection of legends and similes and occurrences of ethic character, dating back to the time between the 5th century BC and the 1st century CE. Further resources about the *Golem* can be found at:
http://www.atomick.net/fayelevine/pk/golem00.shtml, site accessed July 2004

[36] Some Jewish sources even suggest that *Adam* was a *Golem* until God fitted him with a soul.

[37] Hebrew: "unformed substance"

[38] It has only been the later stories and comments around the *Golem* which have seen this act of creation by humans in a rather negative way.

[39] e.g. refer to the story collection: *"The Golem Remembered, 1909-1980: Variations of a Jewish Legend"* (Goldsmith, 1981).

"*aleph*" on the *Golem's* inscription on its forehead and therefore changing the magic wording from "*ameth*" = truth to "*meth*" = death[40], which faintly reminds me on flipping an electronic switch from "I" to "O". (In the *Kabbalistic* tradition it is believed that the Hebrew letters of the alphabet contain the deep secrets about creation. Anagrams and exchanges of alphabetic symbols are often used for coding and decoding mystic messages; not that absurd an idea if one considers the genetic code.)

1.1.2 The Creation of Artificial Entities from a Christian Perspective[41]

Especially in the Christian tradition there has always been a sense of interdiction associated with the human creation of artificial "life" (and the artificial creation of human life), where the trepidation of God's chastisement lurks behind every attempt[42]. The creation of artificial "life" is related to the devil's deeds. As the legend goes, the medieval Saint Albertus Magnus once has created a walking and talking android (mechanical man) which was later destroyed by a fearful Thomas Aquinas who considered this entity as the work of the devil; and also doctor Faustus' ability to create artificial life (homunculi), as it is described in Goethe's classic literary work "*Faust*", has been granted by the devil.

---

[40] Even in the Japanese movie "*Innocence*" (Mamoru Oshii), a similar reference has been made.

[41] An interesting source for obtaining overview information about world religions, which I have used for obtaining general data about *Christianity*, *Shinto* and *Buddhism* can be found at: http://www.bbc.co.uk/religion/religions/

[42] I have also come across such findings during the research I conducted for my *Magister* thesis about an inter-European comparison about the legislation concerning embryonic stem cell research. Although stem cell research is different from robotics, and clerics I asked about these two technologies did not see any immediate relations between them, historical records and even comments made by Christian clerics (among them two Christian pastors I have interviewed; refer to part II of my thesis and the data provided at the appendix) reflect the uneasiness with the idea of creating human-like artificial entities, i.e. (humanoid) robots, especially in regard to questions of humanity (refer to part II of my thesis).

The predominating idea in Christianity, especially during medieval times, was that only God is able to create out of nothing (*creatio ex nihilo*). Mankind, so the belief, could merely rearrange God's creation. This idea has been relativized since the Renaissance, where the act of human original creativity and ingenuity has been heralded and where the arts and sciences were now practiced independently from the religious context. In Europe the peak of this development has been achieved during the Age of Enlightenment, where scientific ideas even began to supersede Christian religious believes, and where the construction and enjoyment of mechanical automata portraying humans and animals has been of immense popularity. But with the increasing pace of scientific and technological achievements, voices criticizing a mentality that everything may be explainable and achievable through the progress made in natural science and engineering have also arisen.

Even today, although nearly everybody is excessively using it, in Christian countries technology in general is often still viewed with a sort of suspicion, following the widespread Christian interpretation that Adam and Eve were expelled from paradise after eating from the "tree of knowledge" (gaining knowledge and with it technology) and therefore infecting humankind with the "original sin"[43]. Especially when it comes to the artificial (re)creation of life, may it be in form of genetic engineering or in building human-like machines, Christian patterns of thought are still said to put restraints onto the enthusiasm. Especially in Germany the Christian criticism in regard to genetic / biological engineering is very apparent, much greater than concerns about robotics, where religious institutions very rarely comment on.

But in my view the fault does not lie in the technology per se, but in the questionable human intentionality about what to do with it. One can use fire to keep persons alive or to burn them, build machinery to help and destroy humans and basically the same kind of technology is being used for creating splendid

---

[43] This is one common interpretation, the other one refers to demonizing the female

fireworks to enjoy people or for constructing guns and canons to kill them. Maybe the religious statements were meant as a warning since humans tend to lack the necessary foresight in regard to the consequences their initiated actions might have, as today's environmental problems again seem to demonstrate. It's just like Goethe's "*sorcerer's apprentice*" knew well enough to initiate a process, but lacked the knowledge about how to stop it as it became dangerous. Technology also serves as an amplifier of human actions, magnifying both, constructive and destructive intents.

1.1.3 Non-humans and Artificial Entities from a Japanese Perspective

For the Japanese case, the situation about creation, artificiality and sin looks quite different from the Western counterpart. Japanese culture and thought has predominantly been shaped by her unique traditional belief-system of *Shinto*[44] (literally meaning "way of gods") along with Buddhist and Confucian idea(l)s imported from China and Korea. Shinto has no founder, no commandments, no doctrines and knows no heaven nor afterlife[45] and has no concept of an "original sin". It mediates a positive and optimistic attitude towards *this* life, *this* world, the present - the now and here. This may also be of influence for the Japanese's willing and unproblematic acceptance of new ideas and technology. Whereas in Christian tradition the world is rather seen as a test with hardships and everything new is judged in regard to possible negative consequences and evokes concerns about punishment in the afterlife, the Japanese, not being under this load, have more freedom and fun just experimenting with it. Although not in

---

[44] For an excellent introduction to Shintoism you may refer to Ernst Lokowandt *"Shinto"*, 2001
[45] At least not in the interpretation as we find it in the Christian tradition, coupled to the idea of heaven, hell, sin, judgment and resurrection. In the Shinto tradition it is believed that the dead become *kami*, whereas under specific circumstances some dead may also become haunting ghosts. But overall the emphasis is directed towards *this* life.

the direct context of religious attitude, Lokowandt (Lokowandt, 2001) provides an example about television: while in (Western) Europe the introduction of television called sociologists and psychologists on the plan who were concerned about the present and future of family life, child development and social communication, the Japanese embraced the technology rather unprejudiced and continued living their lives as before while the television-set is running in the background[46]. So, why should ones curiosity about building human-like robots be not explored to its whole extent?

Kami, the "gods" or rather "spirits" of *Shinto*, are no abstract, omnipotent entities like the God of Judeo-Christian-Islamic tradition. *Kami* are vulnerable and can even die (like the goddess *Isanami* who died after giving birth to the god of fire[47]) and also enjoy life and entertainment. As the Japanese legend of *Amaterasu* and *Sosanoo* goes, it has only been through a grandiosely arranged entertainment show that the offended sun-goddess *Amaterasu* left her hiding place in a cave out of curiosity, and herewith saved Japan (and the whole world) from everlasting darkness[48]. *Kami* have feelings and share much of humankind's traits and even faults. Also unlike the Judeo-Christian-Islamic tradition in Shinto there exist no clear qualitative distinction between animate and inanimate matter and between man and *Kami*. *Kami* may reside not only in living things, but also in objects like stones, mountains, phenomenon like earthquakes and storms, or just in any object with a certain degree of awe-inspiring and impressive features, which also include dolls, automata and robots. In *Shinto* the clear distinction between god(s), (wo)man and objects is missing. This is even amplified as Japan lacks the concept of clearly distinguishing between the Western concepts of subject and object, an interesting observation to which I will return later in my analysis. And in *Shinto* there is simply no-one discouraging humans in trying to reconstruct nature.

---

[46] Refer to: Lokowandt 2001, p. 69-70
[47] A collection of Japanese legends, including the legend of *Isanagi and Isanami* and that of *Amaterasu* and *Sosanoo* can be found in: Schultz, Berndt (Ed.), 1979.
[48] ibid.

Besides *Shinto*, Buddhism has also been influential in Japan. As it is typical for Buddhism, by entering Japan it absorbed elements of the persisting *Shinto* tradition and has developed itself into a uniquely Japanese form. Although Buddhism originally promoted a world-denying philosophy, which stands in contradiction to the world-affirming *Shinto*, in Japan the latter orientation has prevailed. Japanese Buddhism, especially with its main sects of *Pure Land*, *Zen* and *Nichiren*, has been transformed into a life-embracing religion, concerned with worldly matters and guidelines for actual life. The transcendental dimension of Buddhism has found its new place mainly in the domain of arts, aesthetics and ethics.

Buddhism doesn't have the concept of a god(s) and the question about the creation of (wo)man and the world is omitted[49]. Scholars are still in dispute if Buddhism shouldn't be rather considered as a "way of life" than a religion (of course it depends on which aspect of Buddhism one considers, how religion might be defined and which criteria is being used as integral components of religion). Also Buddhism teaches that "will" and "ego" are just illusions and that there is no significant difference between living and non-living entities[50]. Hence Buddhism encourages respectful behavior also towards both, animate and inanimate matter.

At *Hotoku-ji*, a Buddhist temple on the Japanese island of *Shikoku*, there even exists a robotic monk, which most of the time sits still in meditation (yes, maybe Masahiro Mori[51] is right and robots can attain Buddhahood), and when its sensors detect an approaching worshipper it chants a *sutra* (Buddhist prayer / sermon). The installment of this robot had such emulating effects that a

---

[49] Although in many Buddhist cultures there exist legends about the creation of the world, these are mostly due to the blending of Buddhism with pre-Buddhist local religions.
[50] Refer to the Buddhist Sutra of the "Non-Dwelling Mind" and a (contemporary) sermon / commentary at: http://www.jaysquare.com/ljohnson/basic.html (found in November 2004)
[51] Author of the book "The Buddha in the Robot" (Mori, 1999)

neighboring *Shinto* shrine has also deployed its own robot[52]. So, what is a robot more in this colorful universe?

1.1.4 Religious Factors Overestimated?

In some writings (e.g. Schodt, 1988 : p. 195 - 212) and newspaper articles dealing with the seeming fondness of Japanese people for robots and the rather skeptical stance of Europeans, religious traditions (Christianity vs. *Shinto*) are often cited as the main explanatory factor. It is an acknowledged fact that values greatly influence the thoughts and actions of a people; and that such values are often rooted in ones religion or belief-system. Whereas Karl Marx thought that religious beliefs were the result of economic circumstances, Max Weber argued the other way around and did numerous analyses about the relationship between religion, society and economy. His most famous work in this context may be *"The Protestant Ethic and the Spirit of Capitalism"* (1904 – 1905)[53], where he proposes that the ethics of Puritanism, stressing humbleness, education and hard work as a symbol of devoutness, contributed to the Western rise of capitalism. Later Weber did similar analysis in regard to China (Buddhism and Confucianism) and India (Hinduism).

However I would say that the popularly proposed direct and short-circuited relationship between religious thought (*Shinto*, Buddhism and Christianity) and the people's attitude towards robots may be overstated or just put too simplistic. If looking at industrial robots, a field in which Japan and Germany belong to the world's leading countries, German concerns did not come from religious institutions, but rather from worker's unions. Since the topic of the now-emerging coming of non-industrial robots still does not belong to the issues of main popular interest in Germany, Christian religious institutions rarely

---

[52] The information was taken from an article of the Japan Information Network from May 28, 1999, found at htt://jin.jcic.or.jp/trends/article/990528ev_index.html
[53] Weber, 1958 [1904 – 1905]

comment on related subjects. Also, as far as I am informed, though it has been greatly featured in the media, it has just been a rumor that representatives from the Japanese automaker and robot-builder Honda Motors Co., Ltd. allegedly went to the Vatican in the 1990s to consult about the construction of a humanoid robot. And why should a Christian (society) has anything against a user-friendly type of machine which is designed to provide some useful services, whereas at the same time "sinful" behavior like abortion or couples living together out of wedlock may be tolerated?

Nonetheless in my discussions with two German Christian clergy(wo)men[54] about their Christian view concerning the creation of human-like robots, both expressed similar concerns, namely that such an act would lead to a self over-estimation of mankind's abilities in regard to technology, and that the preoccupation with technology and technological artifacts may cause a loss and devaluation of humanity and communication between humans. They both have warned against comparing robots with human beings and stated that the lack of German interest in giving robots a human-like form may indeed be explainable through the country's Christian tradition and the association of creating human-like entities with sin. But on the other side, interestingly, a Japanese Christian theologian and humanities professor teaching at Ferris University / Japan, told me a different story[55]. As it is the case with many Japanese, the respondent is a fan of *"Tetsuwan Atomu"*, a popular Japanese fictional human-like robot figure. He especially appreciates the human aspect in a robot. In his view the creation and programming of robots presupposes *human* experience and reflects a respectful attitude towards a human's creativity. Also to him the aspect of robots possibly substituting for humans has not been regarded as a realistic concern.

---

[54] Special thanks to Rev. Arvalis (Evangelical Church in Japan) and Rev Dr. "Amerigo", Reichenau / Germany for sharing their time for a discussion / interview with me about the topic regarding (humanoid) robots
[55] Special thanks to Prof. Aoki for sharing his time for a discussion with me about the topic regarding (humanoid) robots

For that it could be a short-circuited conclusion if one would directly attribute Germany's assumed lack of public interest in robots (an assumption which is still to be (re)analyzed) to the country's Christian heritage.

On the other side it is often stated that especially the *Shinto*- and to some extent also the Buddhist belief systems are the *cause* for the Japanese's positive stance towards robots. It is said that because Japanese are able to "regard robots as possessing a soul" they have developed a fondness for these artificial creatures, an argument which has also been confirmed through various interviews and discussions I had with Japanese engineers, PR-representatives and even Christian theologians. But in my view, I see no immediate logical causality why it should be that way. The same argument could also be used to postulate a contrary hypothesis: if robots are thought of as *Kami*-possessing entities in an animistic way, they could also evoke even more fear. And indeed as an acquaintance working in Japan told me, in this country it is common practice that machinery is offered water and food in order to keep the residing *Kami* from causing accidents. In my view *Shinto* and Buddhist influences rather have an impact on how robots are *regarded* and *treated* by humans than providing an answer to the question about *why* they are being built. I think the *why* is the same *why* for Japanese as it is the *why* for Westerners: mainly curiosity.

As I will outline in a more detailed way in the following chapters I regard religious aspects rather as indirect variables, influencing a people's views about mankind's position in the world and attitudes towards economic, technological and social matters. In other words, people may not simply criticize or foster the creation of (humanoid) robots or similar artifacts just because such an act would be against the will of God or because such an entity may be regarded as possessing a kind of soul. As far as I know, the Christian Bible doesn't explicitly forbid the creation of artificial life-simulating entities by humans. And although not prohibiting the artificial recreation of nature, *Shinto* and Buddhism also don't encourage such acts. Religious aspects may certainly have an influence on how one and the same act and its possible consequences are perceived: as honoring human creativity or as testimony for mankind's arrogance; as seeing the human aspects in the machine or as disrespecting human life; as playful entertainment or as fostering a materialistic world view. Religious aspects constitute only one factor in a society's complex patterns alongside historical circumstances, economic experiences, political considerations and the people's choice how to interpret, and in how far to follow religious teachings. And as a matter of fact, it has been in Christian Europe, where during the 17th to 19th century the most sophisticated, realistic life-imitating automata, the forefathers of today's robots have been created; and it has been in Christian North America where the first real robot was invented and where some of today's most intelligent robots like *Kismet*[56] have been created.

1.1.5 Dolls and Puppets in Japanese Thought

> *"nothing is sadder than a puppet without a ghost"*
> [from *"Ghost in the Shell"*[57]]

Dolls (the Japanese word for "doll" and "puppet" *ningyo* (人形) literally means "human shape") are treated with much respect in Japan. There even exist *Shinto* shrines and Buddhist temples[58] that perform ritualistic funeral ceremonies for old dolls. Generally, old and worn off dolls are brought to shrines, temples and museums instead of being thrown away. And at the *Nagashi bina* ceremony, dolls are offered to a local *Shinto* shrine and sent along a river in small boats in

---

[56] Robot developed at the Massachusetts Institute of Technology (MIT) with the ability to detect and interpret human intentions to a certain degree and display (simulated) emotional behavior
[57] Animé movie by Mamoru Oshii, 1995
[58] In Japan Shintoism and Buddhism have merged in many ways

order to carry away the troubles of their owner. An engineer at Mitsubishi Heavy Industries / Japan, who is now working on a robotics project, told me in a personal interview[59] that Japanese consider it cruel if someone treats a doll in a disrespectful manner. There are stories in Japan about mistreated dolls cursing, and about well-treated dolls helping their owners, whereas most of them concern the spirits residing in the dolls. One legend of another kind is about a prince called *Kaya* who has built a child-sized doll that helped to irrigate the fields during droughts. Unlike one would imagine, it has not been a mechanical android working in the fields, but just a standing doll which was constructed in such a way that if one poured water into a jar it was holding, the liquid was running over its face and gathering in the fields. Since people enjoyed watching it, they came and brought water along to put it into the jar and through this irrigated the fields. In a way this story nicely reflects the Japanese' tendency to combine entertainment and fun together with pragmatism, something that persists up to the present day and can be found for example in today's concepts for Japanese surveillance robots which combine entertainment with observation functions.

Although in the past times dolls were thought of as possessing some kind of spiritual abilities in many countries, this tradition is still quite predominant in much of Japan. In Japanese contemporary science fiction dealing with the topic of artificial entities, of which Mamoru Oshii's *"Ghost in the Shell"* (1995) and *"Innocence"* (2004) belong to the most prominent, the question about the spirit or ghost in the doll, android and machine is especially central.

In many countries all over the world, especially in Asian and Africa, it is believed that dolls possess some special intrinsic qualities which make them fascinating and fearful at the same time. Maybe this is because they just too much resemble a human being?

---

[59] Conducted on Nov. 17, 2003 at Mitsubishi Heavy Industry Headquarters / Tokyo

1.1.6 The Flourishing Age of Early Automata

Records based on fact and not legend indicate that around 1495 during the Renaissance, Leonardo da Vinci has designed and perhaps even built the first humanoid automata based on the time's knowledge about the human anatomy. The first android (automata in human form) from which there exist evidence that it has been actually built during the first half of the 16th century was a creation by Hans Bullmann from Nürnberg / Germany. With progresses in scientific knowledge and mechanical engineering, especially during the *Age of Enlightenment* (from the 17th century to the 18th century) mankind got a step closer to the real creation of artificial (wo)men. These ancestors of modern robots have been clock-work mechanical automata. Early automata, mainly used for entertainment purposes, have been constructed according to the mechanisms used in clocks, brought to motion by cog-wheels, strings and weights[60]. Especially in Europe one can find many sophisticated examples for such life-simulating automata, which have been very popular particularly during the 18th century. They reflect mankind's attitude of their time and the peoples' optimistic believe in science and progress.

In the first half of the 18th century Vaucanson constructed mechanical androids (machines that resemble the looks of a human) which played musical instruments, and it is even said that he constructed a mechanical duck with the capability, besides movement, to "eat" and "digest" food, although later it has been suggested that some cheating was involved in the latter case. Another cheat, Kempelen's *"Chess Player*[61]*"* built in 1769 (in fact the automaton was operated by a human, but its real working mechanism has only been found out about 70

---

[60] I have even built some replica of early Japanese automata myself, which was quite enlightening in regard to learning about the mechanisms.
[61] Also called „Chess Turk" or German: „*Schachtürke*"

years later[62]) has nonetheless stirred the imagination of many philosophers with early considerations about Artificial Intelligence. Jacquet-Droz's 18th century mechanical writing android and Edison's mass-produced "Talking Doll" (a phonograph has been put inside a doll) made around 1890 that proofed not to be very popular[63], are just a few examples for a new form of life-simulating entertainment products[64]. But maybe those mechanists have driven their striving for perfection to the extreme, landing in what Japanese roboticist Masahiro Mori calls the "Uncanny Valley" (Mori, 1999). His thesis states that an (artificial) entity arouses uneasiness if it *nearly* resembles a human being, but somehow lacks tiny nuances to get through as a real human[65]. Sigmund Freud attributed *"Das Unheimliche"* (The Uncanny) to a human's uncertainty about the question if the encountered entity is alive or not alive – or for that case a human or an automaton[66].

Despite all admiration, fascination and Age-of-Enlightenment-optimism, a growing number of people inspired by the philosophy of Rousseau and the emerging movement of romanticism (especially in England and Germany), began expressing their uneasiness about the idea of artificial humans and life-imitating automata. This new line of thought is especially apparent in the dark Gothic and Romantic literature (e.g. in the works of Mary Shelley and E.T.A. Hoffmann).

---

[62] refer to: http://www.hnf.de/presse/pressemitteilungen/2004/maerz/2503_04_schach_presseinformation 2.html (article found on March 13, 2005)
[63] Refer to: Wood, 2002 p. 113 ff.
[64] Refer to: "Living Dolls" (Wood, 2002), which gives an interesting and very informative overview about automata and mechanical dolls from a historical perspective.
[65] Refer to Mori, 1999
[66] Freud, Sigmund: The Uncanny (1925)

Reaching the Uncanny Valley?

Android head and torso of a robot created by engineers at Tokyo University of Science

(photo by Miriam J.S. Leis at *Robodex 2003*", Yokohama 2003)

1.1.7 Frankenstein, Sandman and Philosophical Questions

In Europe new discoveries in natural sciences, anatomy, mechanics and the physical existence of real automata has stirred the imagination and concerns of writers and philosophers alike.

In 1818 a more "scientific" (and less mystical) version of the *Golem*-legend has been written by Mary Shelley. The story's title is *"Frankenstein"* and the narration brought together aspects from discoveries in 18th century anatomy (especially through the experiments by Luigi Galvani who demonstrated that dead muscle can be brought to motion through the application of electricity) with classic fears about artificial entities finally running amok. Indeed, the monster created by Victor Frankenstein from dead body parts and brought to life, now through scientific methods instead of magic[67] (a modern version of the *Golem*-motive), has finally killed some of his family members and beloved ones. But if one looks attentively to the story, it has not been the fault of a bad "monster", but rather the reaction of this "monster" towards the people who created it as a sentient being and then denied him (it ???) living in human dignity[68]. But since then this theme, often distorted to the flat plot of "man creates monster and monster kills man", the *"Frankenstein-complex"* as Isaac

---

[67] Although the story does not tell anything about the process itself
[68] Retrospective, in view of the mid 19th century practice of publicly displaying deformed human beings as attractions (e.g. the "Elephant Man"), so-called "Freak Shows", the story also gets a new dimension of social criticism. But in view of the historical time-line it is very unlikely that Mary Shelley has been influenced by such public displays.

Asimov has once called it[69], has established itself predominantly in much of the Western fantasy and science-fiction literature dealing with man-made human-like entities. Above this, such patterns seem to have gotten imprinted into the "cultural memory" of Western thought when dealing with the ideas of creating robots or cloning human beings, as contemporary movie productions like *"Blade Runner, "The Terminator"* and *"The Matrix"* indicate.

The existence of real automata resembling human traits and performing human actions also initiated philosophical debates, as the example of the discussions around Kempelen's 18th century chess-playing (*"Chess Turk"*) "automaton" demonstrate [70]. Questions arose about the possibility if an automaton can actually think. And if so, what will be the difference between it and a human being? A kind of philosophical circle arose: if (wo)man is defined by his/her ability to think, as Descartes' famous quote implies: "I think, therefore I am", what then would be a thinking machine. And if thinking machines exist, what then is man? Another disturbing concern associated with the *"Chess Turk"* and other *real* automata has been that of mankind's arrogant act of transgressing the border between life and death, between real and unreal. This has also been a main topic of consideration in the stories by the German romanticist and all-round-talent E.T.A. Hoffmann (1776 – 1822). In his narrations *"Die Automate"* (1814) and the more famous one *"Der Sandmann"* (1817) Hoffmann reflects on the existence of such automata combined with social criticism. In his work *"Der Sandmann"*, topics have been hinted that are today as prevalent – and to some disturbing – as they have been in the past: what is the difference between man and machine? How can one distinguish between real humans and artificial entities? Is a communication between humans and machines possible, a question which is still discussed in numerous debates

---

[69] Asimov / Frenkel, 1985
[70] I would like to thank Dr. Stein, curator at the Heinz Nixdorf MuseumsForum in Paderborn / Germany for providing me interesting information about the *"Chess Turk"*. Also refer to: http://www.hnf.de/presse/pressemitteilungen/2004/maerz/2503_04_schach_presseinformation 2.html

hovering around the topic of the so-called *"Turing Test*[71]*"*. Another issue that has already been expressed in stories like *Pygmalion* and *Der Sandmann*, and which is still of predominant concern for some of my German friends when talking about the coexistence between humans and artificial entities, deals with the danger of preferring the artificial over the natural.

In *"Der Sandmann"* E.T.A. Hoffmann tells, in a literarily unique manner[72], the story of Nathanael, a young man plagued with madness and delusions, who falls in love with a woman, Olimpia[73], who in fact is an automaton (which sounds like a faint allusion towards the story of the sculptor Pygmalion, who falls in love with one of his statues and gets disappointed). This happening is about to doom Nathanael's whole life. Through his obsession with Olimpia he totally forgets about his mistress Clara and his beloved mother, nearly kills Clara and finally commits suicide. The narration is too complex to analyze in the context of my work (which is not literature critique), but nonetheless there are some aspects which I find worth mentioning in the relation of society, automata and philosophy: first one has to take a look onto the socio-historical background of the story. At the time of its origin (1816/17), there had been a real boom of displaying automata and mechanical androids (human-like automata) in public. Romanticism (ca. 1790 – 1840 [74]) was beginning to establish itself as a counter-movement against the scientific, mechanistic, materialistic and positivistic attitude of the Age of Enlightenment. Nathanael embodies Romanticism while his mistress Clara, described as cold-rational, prosaic and emotionless [75] (although possessing some traditional feminine attributes), symbolizes the Age of Enlightenment. In some aspects it even seems unclear, if Clara herself is an

---

[71] Refer to Part II of my thesis

[72] I don't want to go into details about literary studies and would like to refer to an extended array of secondary literature of which some titles can be found in the literature list of his book.

[73] The choice of the name evokes a whole array of associations with the Olympus, Greek mythology, Prometheus, Hephaistos and Pandora.

[74] The named dates of the beginning and end of epochs vary in different sources.

[75] "...Clara wurde deshalb von vielen kalt, gefühllos, prosaisch gescholten...", cited from E.T.A Hoffmann „Der Sandmann" (Hoffmann, 1998. [1816 / 17])

android. The automaton Olimpia as a fake imitation of life is surrounded by an air of insanity, eeriness, destruction and deception. Its association is negative. In a way Olimpia also symbolizes *Rococo*, the time's way of life practiced by many of Europe's aristocrats. In the world of *Rococo*, not only the automata-entertainment flourished, but also society adapted a way of life characterized by stiff, artificial, unnatural and automata-like behavior.

1.1.8 Automata in Japan

More than it is the case in Europe, in Japan the association between early clock work-automata, so called *Karakuri*[76]-dolls, and modern robots, is portrayed as very significant. As it has been the case in Europe, in an interesting co-incidence, the creation and display of human-shaped moving clockwork automata was very poplar in Japan during the 18th Century, although the contacts between Japan and foreign countries was quite limited during Japan's self-imposed "isolation-period" from 1633 to 1855, whereas in many depictions Japan's extend of isolation during this time has been exaggerated. Japan held trade relations with China, Korea, the Ryukyu-Kingdom (present day Okinawa) and the Netherlands. Dutch traders and the German scholar, Phillip Franz von Siebold (who was later expelled from Japan due to an incident with the *Bakufu*[77]), have also contributed much to raising the popularity of western sciences (especially natural sciences and medicine) in Japan[78].

Much of Japan's early know-how about mechanical technology, together with other things like administration, Buddhism and the writing system, originated in ancient China, Asia's equivalent to what Greece and Rome have been for European civilization. Especially during the time between the mid-6th to the mid-9th century A.D., the Japanese were eager to learn from the Chinese. But

---

[76] The term can be roughly translated into „a mechanism which produces some effect".
[77] The Japanese term for the *Shōgun's* administration, the *Shōgunate*.
[78] Refer to Johannes Barth: *Edo*, 1979, who provides an interesting and quite detailed insight into Japan's Edo period.

most of the contribution for the sophisticated 18th Century Japanese *Karakuri*-dolls came from analyzing European clocks left behind by Christian missionaries who entered Japan in the mid 16th century, but later were expelled during the fist half of the 17th century. The Japanese quickly mastered to get behind the mechanisms of the clocks and built doll-like automata, which can probably be attributed as Japan's first successful attempt of "re-engineering". One of the most famous Japanese examples for such an automaton is the so-called "Tea-Carrying Doll" created in the 18th century[79]. If one places a tea cup on the saucer the doll carries, it moves forward and stops when the cup is taken from the saucer. If the cup is replaced onto the doll's saucer, it moves back to its original position. In this way the "Tea-Carrying Doll" has not just been an object for display. It was also used in social interaction settings to "break the ice" between present parties. Many *Karakuri*-dolls were also used during religious festivities and were kept as treasures of the local communities. Today, Japanese *Karakuri*-dolls are still hugely celebrated in Japan, praised as a symbol of Japan's manufacturing tradition and are even regarded as "early robots": ASIMO's ancestor as the cover picture of the book "Japan's Creative Thinking" (JETRO, 2001) suggests.

But if looking at the automata, there seem to be differences between the European ones and Japanese *Karakuri*, which also may reflect different philosophies. In contrast to their realistic-looking, life-imitating European counterparts, Japanese *Karakuri* somehow appear less sophisticated, more doll-like and artificial. Also the movements of the *Karakuri* seem stylized and apparently mechanical. Nobody would mistake such an automaton for a human being. In fact, if looking at Japanese rituals and artistic performances such as *Noh* (a traditional form of Japanese theatrical performance dating back to the 14th century), one could rather mistake the people for automata. And indeed, as I

---

[79] I have assembled replicas of the *"Tea-Carrying Doll"* and the *"Bow-Shooting Boy"* available as construction-kits myself and made some observations.

have watched an ancient Japanese imperial court performance on TV, I first mistook the performers with their white painted faces and slow, abstract, mechanical and totally synchronized movements for artificial entities.

While in Western theatrical performance the expression of emotions is often done in a rather realistic or even exaggerated way, in Japanese traditional performing arts emotions are portrayed in a quite minimal and abstracted way, a technique Bertold Brecht called "Aesthetic Distancing". In a way this represents the same philosophy as there is in *Zen*-Buddhism (introduced to Japan around the 7th century), which promotes uncovering the *essence* of nature through minimal means and the artificial reproduction of this *essence* as a practice of meditation. *Noh* performers wear masks that are often described as possessing neutrality in expression, somewhat frozen in a state of neither alive nor not-alive, neither sad nor happy; and actors use a minimum of stylized movement and gestures[80]. *Noh* is the abstraction of human emotions as a doll is the abstraction of a human being. *Noh* performers do not use different masks to express different emotional states. In *Noh* masks differences in emotional expression, ranging from sadness to happiness, are achieved through (small) variations in the mask's angle and inclination, yielding an astonishing effect through changes in light reflection and shadows. An extensive study about the *"Noh Mask Effect"* has been conducted by Michael Lyons et al. (2000), who kindly provided the following pictures[81].

---

[80] Refer to Nakanishi and Komma, 1998 for an introduction to *Noh* and *Noh* masks with many pictures.
[81] Michael Lyons, PhD is senior researcher at the ATR Media Information Science Labs / Japan, who conducts research in the area of analyzing human expressions (gestures and facial expression) also in the context of human-machine interaction. For more information refer to: http://www.mis.atr.jp/~mlyons/

Noh masks in different vertical viewing angles:
left: - 30°   center: 0 °   right: + 30°

picture: courtesy of Michael Lyons
ATR Intelligent Robotics and Communications Labs Kyoto, Japan
(Refer to: Lyons, Michael et al., 2000 (a study about *"The Noh Mask Effect"*))

Whereas especially the faces of European automata look quite realistic, with some of them even possessing the ability of eye- and mouth movement, the heads of *Karakuri*-dolls are rather doll-like, static and abstract, reminding on *Noh* masks, and normally don't consist of movable eyes or mouths. Maybe the Japanese' tendency towards stylized, arranged and convention-oriented behavior, including the perfect bow in front of a customer and the correct way of presenting and receiving business cards has its roots in the overemphasis on ritualistic perfection in the *Shinto* tradition. And indeed, after seeing the Japanese humanoid robot *ASIMO* (created by Honda Motors) standing in a row with people during a company's celebration, it barely stood out.

Another very popular form of traditional entertainment in Japan is *Bunraku*[82], a puppet theatre. Although these are puppets and no automata, the mentioning of *Bunraku* nonetheless may be of interest here. In contrast European countries, where the puppet plays are rather associated with children's entertainment *Bunraku* is an art form for grown-ups[83]. As Japanese Professor Aoki told me in a discussion, although the puppeteers are not hidden from the stage and some

---

[82] Refer to Oga et al., 1986 for an introduction to *Bunraku* with many pictures
[83] As far as my observation goes, this tendency of puppet-plays being also directed towards adults looks like being an Asian phenomenon, which I have observed in Japan, China, Malaysia, Thailand, Vietnam and Indonesia.

don't even wear a black facial veil, the audience is able to totally shut out the existence of the human controllers, only concentrating on the harmonic movements of the puppets. The same observation has also been stated by Mr. Suzuki, engineer at Mitsubishi Heavy Industries, who told me in an interview about Japanese robotics, that the people watching *Bunraku* don't regard the puppeteer, but only concentrate on the appearance, movement and characteristic of the doll. In the same way, as it has been said by both, Japanese can forget about the inside of a robot. Mr. Suzuki also told me, that surprisingly (at least to me) in Japan statistically elderly people and women show a higher degree of affinity towards robots than younger people or men. The reason for this, he told me, lies in the fact that those people rather don't see the technology behind a robot, but only its appearance.

Paradoxically, if compared to the stiff, highly abstract and automata-like human *Noh*-performances and *Karakuri* dolls, the puppets of *Bunraku* possess many degrees of freedom, enabling them to perform vivid movements (including movement of the eyes, eyebrows and mouth) and giving them a wide palette of emotional and lifelike expressions.

Once again, Japanese traditional arts suggest that to their cultural thinking, the borders between animate and inanimate are not clearly distinct.

x Replica of Japanese *Karakuri*: "archer" / "bow-shooting boy"

Photo: Miriam JS Leis, Konstanz 2005 (Author's own collection)

"*The writer, the first android*", automata by Louis Jaquet-Droz

Photo : courtesy of Jean-Jacques Luder - www.automates-

1.2 Industrialization

With the beginning of the *Industrial Revolution* initiated in Great Britain around 1760, which then spread all over Europe and beyond, not only Western society was (re)shaped throughout the 19th century and beyond. In Germany and Japan the industrialization process has entered rather late, around 1840 in the first case and around 1880 in the latter.

By substituting animal- and manpower through machinery, new possibilities – and problems arose. It enabled the mass production of commodities, making goods available at cheaper prices. A new definition of time arose and new classes of oppressor and oppressed were formed. Pauperism and grave human misery occurred through the mechanization of the production process. Industrial mass production has made traditional manufacturing unprofitable, forcing workers to seek jobs in the industry. Since in the industry machines growingly substituted for human labor mass unemployment resulted. As it is the case with every commodity available in excess amounts, human labor became cheap and the human being prone to exploitation by those in possession of the means of production (Marx). Those people "fortunate" enough to find work in the industry had to adapt to the precision and clockwork of the machinery. The machine shifted from the entertainment automata to the dominator over man's freedom. In this context it is no wonder that a great discontent against machinery arose and ideas like Marxism have evolved.

The problem of the human having to adapt to the pace of machinery has also been a popular subject in the science fiction literature of the early 20th century that includes works like *"The Machine Stops"* (E. M. Forster, 1909), *"R.U.R."* (Karel Čapek, 1920 / 1921), *"We"* (Yevgeny Zamiatin, 1924[85]), and Fritz Lang's famous film *"Metropolis"* (1926).

---

[85] Although this book describes a society run like a huge machine, where every human is issued a serial number and logic has replaced imagination and arts, it can also be interpreted

1.2.1 Japan's Modernization Process[86]

As already mentioned before, due to her "isolation policy" from 1633[87] to 1867, which limited the contact with foreigners to a few trade relations with China, Korea and Dutch merchants, Japan did not only have little practical experience with the Western ground-breaking technologies (although the Japanese were quite interested in theoretical material about Western sciences which was brought along by Dutch merchants) but also missed out the important philosophical and social movements that came to life during the Age of Enlightenment, evolving in- and spreading through the whole European continent to North America. Nonetheless, as it has been the case in Europe, Japanese culture also flourished during the 17th to 19th century, making great advances in urbanization, scientific applications, manufacturing, economy, education, administration, arts and literature, although Western-style mass industrialization, rationalization and the use of then-modern technology in the military did not occur. In Japan iron-manufacturing was also limited. In 1853, despite Japan's "isolation policy", two American ships, the so-called *"Black Ships"* landed in *Uraga* (near the Japanese capital Edo, now Tokyo), although all foreigners permitted to land in Japan were only allowed to do so on the small artificial island of *Deshima*. The ship's commander Commodore Matthew Perry demanded in a letter from US president Fillmore that Japan had to open the country and establish trade-relations with America. Perry threatened that unless Japan complies, military force would be used, leading to war. Uncertainty over the real strength of the foreign fleet divided the Japanese elites into those willing to comply in order to avoid a war and those who strictly rejected compliance regardless of the costs. Although the information coming from the few Dutch merchants on *Deshima* was rather sparse, the Japanese knew that European

---

as a critique on socialism and totalitarian regimes, one reason why the book has been banned in Russia / The Soviet Union until 1988.
[86] Most of the historical data has been obtained from the Tokyo-Edo Museum / Japan and the history book *"Das japanische Kaiserreich"* by John Whitney Hall, 1968.
[87] Some sources also speak of 1635

countries have made great progress in the usage of technology (e.g. steam-driven ships that moved independently from the wind) and especially weaponry, causing the Japanese to assess their chances to win as rather slim. In this context a growing number of people voiced criticism against Japan's isolation policy and demanded the country's opening in order to take advantage of the foreign technological know-how to strengthen the nation. But to give in to the Americans sounded like resignation. The Americans returned with a big fleet and again stated demands, which were hard to chew for the Japanese and included unequal terms in favour for the Americans. The governing *Shōgunate* was in a knotty situation, since it would lose face in giving in as well as in risking a war. So the *Shōgun* decided to shuffle-off the problem to the Japanese Emperor, who throughout the *Edo*-Period was considered rather as spiritual leader than possessing actual power. Now his approval should provide some god-given legitimacy to the decision of Japan's concessions to the Americans. Officially the decision for Japan's opening was portrayed as a means to strengthen Japan's (military) position, but in reality it brought about economic decline, rising prices and social instability.

The arrival of the *"Black Ships"* led to quite confusion in the country and domestic disputes. Above this, in 1855 a strong earthquake struck the Japanese capital *Edo* (now Tokyo) leading to epidemics, and skyrocketing prices for rice and other goods resulting in riots and discontent with the *Shōgunate's* government (*Bakufu*) and the call for renewal. Finally, in 1867[88] this led to the fall of the *Shōgunate* and the dawning of a new era initiated by an Emperor who chose *"Meiji"* (= enlightened rule) as the title of his reign.

After having ended the *Tokugawa* reign, the new *Meiji* government initiated a bold program under the title of *fukoku kyohei,* meaning both: a wealthy country and a strong military. Japan's main goal was to change the unequal terms of the treaty signed with the Americans to a symmetric one. Therefore it was thought

---

[88] Some sources speak of 1868. I'm referring to the data obtained at the „Edo-Tokyo Museum" / Japan.

that Japan should demonstrate that it is indeed a civilized country, not different from the Western nations. With this one may say that the attitude which could be called "Japan's race against the future" had begun. Foreign experts, especially from Germany, Great Britain and France, have been called upon the plan to provide advice in areas of politics, administration, education, economics, science and the military field. In education, much emphasis has been laid upon engineering and natural sciences, something which is still predominant today. Everything was now designed around the idea of quick modernization, and industrialization. The Westernization plans of the *Meiji* Emperor went so far, that he considered modernizing or even abolishing the century old Japanese *Sumō* wrestling (an ancient form of Japanese wrestling deeply associated with *Shinto* rituals, that was especially popular during the Edo period) since he thought that such archaic practices would not fit into the picture of a Western-oriented progressive country. *Sumō* has not been abolished and Japan managed to combine tradition with progress in a unique way that today for many foreigners is fascinating and confusing at the same time: old temples next to skyscrapers (I have even seen old temples grounds fitted with an escalator). And today in Japan's age of industrial robots, traditional hand-made manufacturing, the remnants of the "dual economy" concept[89], is still honored as part of Japanese culture worth saving.

In Japan industrialization and technology happened without going through the whole maturing process as it has been the case in Europe and the US. But this does not mean, as it is commonly depicted in superficially written history books about Japan, that Japan's industrialization process was unproblematic and without social problems, an argument often used as an explanation for the Japanese' tendency to embrace new technology, including robots and massive automation without much hesitance[90]. Living standards for farmers and workers

---

[89] The parallel existence of modern, efficient industry and small, often privately run manufacturing business, which often also serve as suppliers for the industry.
[90] I'm referring to documents displayed at the Edo-Tokyo Museum / Tokyo, Japan

remained poor or even worsened, and the gap between rich and poor grew constantly deeper. It may have been only due to Japan's continuing feudal mentality, the people's high regard towards Confucian virtues like loyalty and obedience towards ones superior (hierarchical structure) and the people's readiness to accept ones fate and position, that Japanese workers possessed a comparatively high threshold of endurance in regard to bad living conditions. But also in Japan socialist and Marxist-inspired movements have formed. Especially in the outgoing 19th and early 20th century Japan was hit by strikes and massive worker's protests against bad living conditions, but they were soon crushed by government forces and laws against worker's uprisings were installed. Nonetheless such movements remained in existence, but their protests have gradually shifted towards other problems like air pollution, bad housing conditions and price increases. Until today, Japan's worker's unions and the Socialist Party have never gained such momentum as it has been the case in Europe.

Japan was a fast learner, quickly grasping the concepts of foreign technology and using them to her own advantage. Looked upon Japan's development through this perspective it is no wonder that this country has the image of having exercised excessive re-engineering. Today there are great efforts being undertaken to get rid of this re-engineering-image by providing information campaigns like the TV-documentary show "*Project X*" to present the Japanese' invention spirit.

The second trauma involving Japan's confrontation with superior foreign technology has occurred when the country was hit twice by an atomic bomb in Hiroshima and shortly after this in Nagasaki, and was forced by foreign powers to capitulate in World War II. Strangely, in Japan this had not led to the expected aversion towards nuclear energy. To the contrary: Japan has a great number of nuclear reactors throughout the country and comparatively little (public) criticism ever surfaces. Even if there occur accidents like at the Fast

Breeder reactor *"Monju"* (1995), or more recently in 1999 at the *Tokaimura* nuclear fuel plant, they seem to be "officially forgotten" after a few days.

1.3 The Robot

The term "Robot" actually has its origin in a science fiction play called "R.U.R.", the acronym for *"Rozuma Univerzalni Roboti"* (Rossums Universal Robot) by the Czech novelist Karel Čapek (Čapek 1920). In the Czech language, the word *"robota"* describes "forced labour". Although the robots in R.U.R are not mechanical and made of metal, like the machines we nowadays call robots, but genetically engineered organic human-like man-made entities [91] (like those *"Replicants"* in *"Blade Runner"*), the word "robot" has established itself for generally describing a whole array of non-biological man-made artifacts as a subset of machines with the ability of performing tasks and manipulating objects in a three-dimensional environment. The play "R.U.R." mirrors the historical experiences of human exploitation through the industrialization process. But this time it is not the humans who revolt against capitalists. Instead it is the "machines" themselves being exploited by man that rise up against their masters. In R.U.R. the classic ambivalent attitude between fear and fascination of humans about robots (and artificial human-like entities) is depicted. As expected, the robots finally got superior to their human creators, rebelled against being held in slavery and started to destroy the human race.

This kind of plot - man creates robot and robot kills man - has been the blueprint for much of the science fiction ever since, including more temporary creations like *"2001 – A Space Odyssey"* by Arthur C. Clarke (1968), where the

---

[91] I guess the reason for this is that the idea of mechanical manufacturing / engineering and with it the possibility of building mechanical "robots" has been there earlier than the idea about genetic engineering

intelligent computer *HAL*[92] kills some of the crew members who were planning to deactivate it[93], *"Blade Runner"*[94] (1982) *"The Terminator I – III"* (1984, 1991, 2003), *"Robocop"* (1987), , *"The Matrix"* (1999) and *"Animatrix"* (2003), *"I, Robot"* (2004) and even the Japanese animé *"Innocence"* (2004) by Mamoru Oshii. The dream finally turned into a nightmare – the nemesis for mankind's thoughtless actions.

1.3.1 Robots in Japanese Fiction and Literature
Autonomous Robot Heroes and *Tetsuwan Atomu*

Actually, although I have asked Japanese acquaintances about this, I am not aware of any major pieces of older Japanese literature which deals with considerations about humans and automata, as it has been the case in Europe with narrations like Hoffmann's *"Der Sandmann"* or *"Die Automate"*.

In contrast to that, the idea of robots looks like being an integral part of Japanese popular culture portrayed in lots of films and "literature", mostly *manga* (Japanese comics) and *animé* (Japanese cartoons) since the early 1950s. If turning on the TV in Japan during 6 PM or on a weekend's morning, one can choose from a whole universe where robots belong to the protagonists ranging from *"Gundam"*, *"Bidaman"*, *"Get Ride! AM Driver"*, *"Transformers"*[95], to reruns of the classics *"Arale-chan"*, *"Doraemon"*, *"Giant Robo"* and of course *"Tetsuwan Atomu"*[96] (now I can finally catch up with everything I missed during

---

[92] It is interesting that if you take the acronym HAL and replace it with the next letter in the alphabet you get IBM; a faint allusion to *Kabbalistic* practices?

[93] Actually the computer just executed the task it has been programmed for and the killing of the crew members was just the logical choice.

[94] Based o the Novel "Do Androids Dream of Electric Sheep" by Philip K. Dick

[95] All aired on "TV Tokyo"

[96] Due to the specifics of the Japanese language and script it is actually written as "Tetsuwan Atomu". Outside Japan the series is known as "Astro Boy". It never aired in Germany. When in the following I talk about *Tetsuwan Atomu"* I'm referring to the series as a whole. When I'm speaking about *"Astro Boy"* I refer to the robot-character.

childhood...). As Japanese Professor Aoki told me about his childhood experience in Japan, during the 1960s actually one only had the choice between two productions of television entertainment for children: *"Tetsuwan Atomu"* (1963) and *"Tetsujin 28-Go"* (1963)[97], both about robots. And having asked Japanese people working in the field of robotics, either as engineers, in governmental service or public relations[98], they all told me that *"Tetsuwan Atomu"* has been a great influence for deciding on their career. I have heard that other persons got similar answers when asking Japanese robot-enthusiasts about their biography. *"Tetsuwan Atomu"* or *"Astro Boy"* how this character is known outside Japan, that even appeared on a Tokyo tourism commercial from the Tokyo Metropolitan Government, shown nearly every morning around 6:42 A.M. on CNN Europe[99] can be regarded as a Japanese national symbol that is more than just an *animé* figure. In the following I will tell you more about this friendly robot, *soaring high in the sky[100]*.

---

[97] Both animé are based on manga first published in the early 1950s (Japan)
[98] I have heard this in personal interviews conducted at *Robosquare* Fukuoka, Mitsubishi Heavy Industries and TEPIA
[99] In October and November 2004
[100] The first words from the lyrics of the title song (English version)

1.3.1.1 Happy Birthday "Astro Boy" !

Today is April 7th. 2003 [101], I'm in Japan and there's a reason to celebrate in this country. It's the "Birthday" of the fictive science fiction robot-figure *"Astro Boy"* from a *manga* created by Osamu Tezuka in 1951 as a comic story. In the 1960s the first animated series of *"Tetsuwan Atom"* was shown in Japanese television. It was also the first Japanese *animé*[102] aired in the US and gained a somewhat international recognition (but not in Germany[103]), although not being able to catch up with the huge popularity inside Japan.

On this day even the English Newspaper "The Japan Times"[104] printed a huge picture of the *"Astro Boy* birthday celebration" on the title page next to "the war in Iraq" and "SARS" with an extended story on page 2. There was a birthday-parade in *Takadanobaba* / Shinjuku ward in Tokyo, where according to the story *"Astro Boy"*, the good-hearted, helpful and idealistic hero-robot was created in a laboratory. The fictional figure even got the status of an official resident in Niiza-city / Saitama-prefecture in Japan, the location, where a new *"Tetsuwan Atomu" animé*-series is being created[105]. Discotheques in Tokyo have arranged special *"Astro Boy"* birthday parties. At the train-station of *Takadanobaba* they have even changed the melody indicating arriving and leaving trains to the title song of *"Tetsuwan Atom"* and school children are learning the text and melody in their music lessons. Even down-to-earth robot-

---

[101] Without going into too deep a speculation, just would like to clue that the date April 7th may not be an arbitrary choice: in Japan April represents new beginnings (fiscal years, school years and employment contracts normally start in April) and seven is considered a lucky number in Japan.
[102] Japanese animation films
[103] Although in Germany the interest in Japanese animé is rising, especially among older children and teenagers, and some animé are even aired on television (e.g. *Pokémon*, and *Yi-Gi-Oh!* and *Gundam* on a small private channel), *Tetsuwan Atomu* is generally unknown there.
[104] The Japan Times, April 7th. 2003, p.1 and 2
[105] With this *Tetsuwan Atomu* shares this special status with a seal called *"Tama-chan"*, while human foreigners are protesting in Japan, since getting residential status is extremely difficult for them.

scientists I met, as well as politicians, attribute their interest in robotics to this character. A representative from *"Robosquare"* Fukuoka / Japan told me in an interview that the mayor of Fukuoka is a fan of *"Tetsuwan Atomu"* and therefore shows much personal interest in supporting the *"Robosquare"* project and plans to develop Fukuoka into one of Japan's major hubs for robot-technology. To Westerners this may sound like archaeologists attributing their job to their fondness for Astérix or an employee at the labor ministry admitting that (s)he got inspired through *Donald Duck*.

In connection to the "birth" of *"Astro Boy"*, this famous Japanese "goodhearted" animé-robot, the so-called *"Atom Dream Project"* has been initiated throughout Japan. This project is insofar unique, as it combines elements of this *manga / animé* series with actual activities in robot research, development, interest-promotion and merchandizing. The variety of *"Tetsuwan Atomu"*– related goods is already uncountable and I have not discovered anything in Germany that may match the Japanese situation. The only German product which might be somewhat comparable to *"Tetsuwan Atomu"* in regard to popularity may be *"Asterix"*. Since much of the Japanese' *"Tetsuwan Atomu"*-mania is also due to nostalgia and the remembrance of Japan's technological and economic rise, they have now created a new *"Tetsuwan Atomu"*-series which would more appeal to the *Gameboy-*, *Play-Station-* and *Nintendo*-used younger generation to "pass on the inspiration to the next generation" as I have once heard it during a commentary on Japanese television.

One special edition of a *"Tetsuwan Atom"* - manga (now on display at the Heinz Nixdorf MuseumsForum in Paderborn / Germany) consists of cartoon-stories combined with popular-scientific explanations about robot technology matching the particular story. These include product descriptions and explanations about engineering and functionality, like a chapter about the

ZMP[106]-walking algorithm used for biped robots like *ASIMO* or *QRIO*. There has also been a television-broadcast on May 2nd. 2003 on the Japanese semi-state-run TV channel NHK about the latest developments in Japanese robotic-research, drawing parallels between the abilities of actual robots and *"Astro Boy"*, just as it has been done in the special-edition manga. The outlay of the program that has been sponsored by some of the biggest Japanese companies belonged to the field of *edutainment* (a mixture of **edu**cational and enter**tainment** elements) and was held throughout positive in regard to robots, without even the slightest hints of concerns or even ambivalence. Quotes like *"robots as mankind's friend"* or *"the 21st. century will be the century of communicative and human-oriented robotics"* may summarize the tenor of this. A similar edutainment-film started on July 1st. 2004 at *MeSci*, the Japanese National Museum of Emerging Science and Innovation. The film revolves around the question: "Why are people building robots as models of human beings?[107]" –and indeed, Japan is taking this task quite seriously. Again *"Astro Boy"* has been the center figure, providing the fuel for Japan's high-flying dreams for robotics, hoping that some day robots will turn out to be just like their favourite animé-hero.

The far-reaching and inspiring impact of *"Tetsuwan Atomu"* is also reflected in the so-called *"Atom Project"*, which has been proposed by some Japanese researchers in the area of robotics and Artificial Intelligence. They are seeking governmental support for a huge utopian 30-year project with the final goal of developing a robot "with the mental, physical and emotional capacity of a 5-year-old human"[108], estimated to cost a total of 50 billion yen[109] per year (= 1 500 000 000 000 YEN = 14 150 526 238 US$ for the total span of 30 years).

---

[106] ZMP = Zero Movement Point. The *Manga* seems to have contained data similar to that mentioned in Sugihara et al., 2000
[107] The original Japanese title has been:
"人は、なぜヒト型ロボットを作るのだろう。。。？"
[108] http://www.aaai.org/AITopics/newstopics/cognitive1.html and
http://www.japantimes.co.jp/cgi-bin/getarticle.pl5?nn20030820b8.htm (on August 20, 2003)
[109] 50 billion yen = 400 707 606.55 EUR = 460 054 060.06 US$ (rate: 10.11.2003).

Even more notable is that in my view the arguments about economic revival and useful side-effects deriving from such a project sound rather like a justification and not a cause for such high-flying plans (the same also applies to the *Apollo-Project*[110]). According to my latest information it has not yet been decided on this, but the possible rejection would rather be due to the price tag and the current economic and fiscal situation in Japan than because of technical or even ethical concerns. As far as I know (current) Japanese Prime Minister Koizumi, who quite frequently shows up accompanied by some robot, I guess he would give his o.k. if money wouldn't matter. I wonder what will come out of this in view of President Bush's bold plans for Lunar-bases and manned flights to Mars (according to NASA estimates dated 1997, a manned flight to Mars would cost between $ 30- to 40 billion[111]), which suffered a huge setback in face of the Columbia space shuttle accident in 2003, and in face of China's new successful space program.

As it is the case with most comics, manga and animé, the stories of *"Tetsuwan Atomu"* are rather simple: there's a problem, or people are in distress and in a *Super Man*-fashion this child-sized robot appears and saves the day. But there are also passages, where questions about right and wrong and matters about humanity are concerned. Often *"Astro Boy"* turns out to be the "more human" of them. And indeed, the robot is portrayed as quite human: it – or he – learns, grows (although not physically) and also has his own problems and difficulties in "life". There also exist robot-critics, who don't want *"Astro Boy"* being around, but most of them can be convinced that humans and robots can live side-by-side in peace and harmony. Although *"Astro Boy"* possesses enormous strengths (100 000 HP), in a fashion similar to the famous robot-laws of Isaac Asimo's stories, this robot never harms a human being. As it is typical for Japanese robot-animation, robots almost never directly fight humans. If they

---

[110] Although the Apollo-Project has also to be regarded in its political context.
[111] = 40 000 000 000 US$

fight, generally they fight only other robots or just represent some form of high-tech vehicle piloted by human controllers (e.g. *Gundam*).

Surprisingly I did not find that much Japanese stories about autonomous robots like "*Tetsuwan Atomu*" as one would expect. The more renowned ones are *Dr Slump / Arale-chan* (by Akira Toriyama, creator of "*Dragon Ball*"), a collection of somehow weird stories about the adventures of a strong but somehow dim-witted robot resembling a 13-year old girl and its creator who invents a lot of odd and peculiar gadgets. The other, more classy series and Japanese export hit, *Doraemon* (known as *Ding Dong* outside Japan) by Fujiko F. Fujio is about a robot-cat from the 22nd century who comes to a 20th century family in order to help changing or improving the future by its ability of producing a whole array of useful and futuristic gadgets out of its "magic pocket". Interestingly the story first appeared in 1969 in a magazine for elementary school children, but has gained many grown-up fans ever since. The Japanese Toyama University even offers a non-credit course registered as "*Doraemon's World*", where students are made to analyze the scenes, science and background data of the animé[112]. Newer animé productions increasingly focus on either *Cyborgs* (hybrids of machine and (wo)man) or follow the tradition of human-controlled / remote-controlled robots, which started with shows like "*Tetsujin 28-go*" (1963) and "*Mazinger-Z*" (1972) and developed into the genre of so-called mecha-animé.

---

[112] Refer to: The Japan Times: May 16, 2004 (Online Edition)

1.3.1.2 Mecha-Animé and the *Gundam* Universe

The other Japanese animé still enjoying huge popularity is *Gundam* (1979 by Sunrise / Bandai)[113]. Although it's also about "robots", it's quite different from *"Tetsuwan Atomu"* and it is regarded as the most important works of mecha-animé[114]. Unlike *"Tetsuwan Atomu"*, *Gundam*-"robots" do not represent autonomous units, but rather fighter-vehicles piloted by humans, grand machines that evolved out of so-called "powered suits", wearable technologies to amplify human capabilities, somewhat comparable to the *ATAT* vehicles in *"Star Wars ̄ The Emipre Striks Back"*[115]. The initial story of *Gundam* is about humans who fled from the overcrowded and polluted earth to establish a new life in space colonies. Since the agreement on leadership for the new Space Colonies has proven difficult, the different colonists have decided on resolving the leadership question through fights between so-called *Gundam* machines piloted by human fighters. In a plot, that somehow gets one reminded on *Star Wars*, a *Dark Gundam* is located, which is about to turn *Gundam* fighters via genetic contamination into slaves of his Dark Army. The *Gundam* fight now turns from a fight over leadership into a mission to safe earth and the colonies, where now the pilots not only have to proof their fighting abilities, but also their skills of mental discipline. In *Gundam* it are rather the characters than the "robots" (or rater fighter vehicles) that stand in the center of the story, a

---

[113] A very good explanation about the whole *Gundam* universe is presented at the *Mobile Suit Museum* (part of the Bandai Museum) located in Matsudo / Japan. Some of the information about *Gundam* is taken from the museums guide book. The term *"Gundam"* derives from a fictional alloy called *"Gundarium"*.

[114] Short for "mechanical animé", which summarizes a whole array of Japanese animé involving robots and machines. The stories often play in a setting of attack, defence and fighting. As is has been the case with *Gundam*, its forerunners like *Tetsujin 28-go* (1963) and *Mazinger-Z* (1972) have also been remote-controlled / human-piloted "robots". Interestingly these hight-tech "mechas" often fight with archaic weapons like swords, knives and spears.

[115] Real examples for power assist suits are CAM from General Electric (US), the Power Assist Suit developed by the Kanagawa Institute of Technology (Japan), I-foot by Toyota (Japan) and the HAL-3 suit, short for Hybrid Assistive Limb, an exoskeleton for walking assistance developed at the Tsukuba University (Japan).

tendency which got even more apparent in the later productions (especially in *Gundam Wing*, a story about 5 teenaged human *Gundam*-fighters who undergo a personal and social transformation from machine-like soldiers into caring and responsible human beings)[116].

Whereas at the beginning *Gundam* has not proven that popular, its success started after the TV-series was turned into a motion picture. Now there exists a whole "*Gundam* Universe" with an already innumerable amount of different series (e.g. "*Mobile Suit Gundam*", "*Double Zeta Gundam*", "*Gundam F-91*", "*Gundam Force*", *Gundam Seed*", "*Gundam Wing*" etc., and a whole array of *Gundam* films produced for video clubs (OVA)).

A number of other productions inspired by the *Gundam* stories followed suit, whereas my observations reveal that in later productions of *mecha-animé* thoughts about the frontiers and distinctions between (wo)man and machinery and the topic of the cyborg became more central. Besides Oshii's works that I have already mentioned, *Bubblegum Crisis* (1987) and *Evangelion* (1995) belong to the most (internationally) renowned creations of this genre.

Bandai action-figure of battle-damaged „*Gundam*"
(author's own collection)

Photo: Miriam JS Leis, Konstanz

---

[116] Interestingly, in many "*Mecha Animé*" like *Gundam* and *Evangelion*, the human pilots guiding the machines are portrayed as being socially problematic, withdrawn and outsiders.

1.3.2 The Robots are Coming

Throughout history mankind has always dreamed of – and feared – the creation of mechanical devices used as substitutes for human labor; leading to a first breakthrough with the advent of the "Industrial Revolution" initiated in Great Britain around 1760. The development and usage of complex machines driven by steam and later electricity substituting for human or animal power and labor has been of great influence in regard to productivity, trade and economics, but also in regard to politics and philosophy throughout Europe and beyond. A second breakthrough happened in the 20th century. New models have been developed in the area of control theory and self-regulation systems for machines. Cybernetics has been introduced to describe regulation mechanisms in machines *and* biological organisms (Wiener 1961 [1948]), which also had influences on developments in the area of robotics. But only the invention of so-called ICs or integrated circuits, thin silicon chips consisting of millions of small interconnected semiconductor devices made possible the construction of microprocessors. Without those, such ubiquitous gadgets like personal computers, cell phones, memory cards, so-called "intelligent household appliances" and modern robots would be unthinkable. ICs can be counted among humankind's most influential technological inventions, having brought about the so-called "Digital Revolution" (now all information can be stored in a digital form), which in turn has shaped most of mankind's modern form of business, economics, communication and even language, lifestyle, leisure activities and philosophy. The "Digital Revolution" has helped Japan and later other Asian countries to rise to top positions on the economic landscape, but also increased the gap between rich and poor people and nations. It has brought along new forms of security – and crime. It has made our lives easier – and more complicated. It has enhanced communication-flow – and anonymity. And the IC has made possible the development of what we now call robots.

While early automata and machines can be described as only possessing qualities of *Res Extensa* to use the Cartesian terminology for describing the non-thinking, mechanical aspect of (wo)man, ICs have made it possible to put the quality of *Res Cogitans*, the "thinking aspect" into machines. A whole branch of Information Science and Computer Engineering has devoted itself to creating such Artificial Intelligence (AI[117]).

x

1.3.3 Defining "Robot"

As with every definition, there also seem to be problems and some kind of "fuzziness" in regard to what we should define as a robot and what not. It seems that there exist as many suggestions about what a robot may be as there are robots out there. Even the simpler question about how to *distinguish* an automaton from a machine and a machine from a robot isn't that easy to answer. To illustrate to which kinds of problems certain definitions may lead, I will give you an example:

A simple automaton can be run even without computer/microprocessor control, although most modern automates (e.g. ticket vending machines) are controlled by a computer and according programs. Let's look onto how a simple automaton works. First it is in a certain system-condition until it registers an input, e.g. an inserted coin and/or a signal if the user presses a button. Then it checks on its new system-condition and reacts with a certain output according to its internal structuring (e.g. it ejects the ticket, or lets us know that we have to add additional 50 cents). After having finished all steps, it returns back to its original condition. So far so good. I'm standing around, being in a certain condition. My friend calls me and tells me to come to point A, which I interpret

---

[117] Some also denote it as A.I., but I followed the suggestion of my computer by omitting the points.

as an input that has changed my original condition. I check on my new condition, i.e. do I have time and do I know where point A is. Then I activate my "program" and walk to point A (a very complex program, indeed), the output if you like. According to such a definition I'm an automaton – at least in certain situations. Some say (although others don't) that a robot is defined through its number of DOFs (degree of freedom) which describes, very simply put, the possibilities of a robot's joint movements necessary to reach specified areas in three-dimensional space[118]. I fulfil this criterion, too, which upgrades me from a simple automaton to a robot? There's another important aspect which is regarded important for the definition of a robot: being reprogrammable. But what is meant by (re)programmable? "Me *walking* to point A" can be translated into computer language and put into a program. One can also rewrite the program into "me *running* to point B", retranslate this into a language I understand and I will be able to run to point B instead of walking to point A when my friend calls me again. So I can be reprogrammed? We have to add another important criterion to this: "living" vs. "not living". I'm alive, but the automaton or robot is not alive, just like you won't seriously consider your automobile or computer as being alive. It's an artifact and it only works if we activate it, and it only carries out the tasks according to our construction and programming[119] (even if it does not perform according to our instructions, the reason can always be found in human error of the engineer/programmer). "Being alive" sounds like a simple definition, but the more I think about it, the more "fuzzy" the concept gets in modern times, as the vivid discussions around stem-cell research proof. Or just consider a person in a Hospital's ICU

---

[118] A more detailed explanation is available at: http://www.robotics.utexas.edu/rrg/learn_more/low_ed/dof/ ; you may also refer to some books about engineering, e.g. Hering, 2002.

[119] Even in the case of sophisticated robots that have some kind of "evolution programming" and are able to develop differently according to our interaction input (AIBO or PINO are such examples), which leads to a certain degree of wanted unpredictability in performance over time, these reactions and development options are also part of the construction and programming.

connected to life-support machines. Without this perfect symbiosis between man and machinery that takes over the functions of biological organs keeping up homeostatic processes, the patient might quite certainly die. What does "being alive" mean in such a case? How should such entity be called – a *cyborg*? And what if this entity is unconscious?

Let's take a look at some official definitions of a "robot", which can be found in different sources and encyclopaedia:

According to the *Robot Institute of America* a **robot** is defined as a:

> "[r]eprogrammable, multifunctional manipulator designed to move material, parts, tools, or specialized devices through various programmed motions for the performance of a variety of tasks"

(Robot Institute of America 1979)[120].

In the Cambridge Dictionary the following can be found:

> **robot**
> noun [C]
> a machine used to perform jobs automatically which is programmed and controlled by
> a computer
> Some types of robot can walk and talk, but they cannot think like humans. Robots are commonly used in factories to assemble machinery such as cars.
>
> (disapproving) If you describe someone as a robot, you mean that they do things
> in a very quick and effective way but never show their emotions.
> She plays the piano like a robot - perfectly but without any feeling.

(http://dictionary.cambridge.org/)

x

---

[120] definition and information found on: http://www.frc.ri.cmu.edu/robotics-faq/1.html#1.1

x

The Oxford English Dictionary defines "robot" as an:

"apparently human automaton, intelligent but impersonal machine..."

On http://www.jeffbots.com/dictionary.html I found the following:

1. A mechanical device that sometimes resembles a human being and is capable of performing a variety of often complex human tasks on command or by being programmed in advance.

2. A machine or device that operates automatically or by remote control.

3. A person who works mechanically without original thought, especially one who responds automatically to the commands of others.

The Australian Robotics and Automation Association provides the following definition about what a robot might be[121]:

- It possesses some form of mobility
- It can be programmed to accomplish a large variety of tasks
- After being programmed, it operates automatically

According to the official norm ISO/TR 8373-2.3 which is nearly identical to the European norm EN775, an *industrial* robot is defined the following:

> "A robot is an automatically controlled, reprogrammable [122] multipurpose, manipulative machine with several reprogrammable axis, which may be either fixed in place or mobile for use in industrial automation applications."
>
> English version from: http://www.ziplink.net/~rourked/robointr.htm

---

[121] Refer to: http://www.ethicsweb.ca/robots/whatisarobot.htm

[122] This means the actions / motions of the robot may be changed without physically altering the robot (annotation by MJSL)

The Japan Industrial Robot Association (JIRA), by omitting the "Industrial" now renamed to "Japanese Robot Association" (JARA[123]) does not provide an official definition, but distinguishes between six classes of robots[124]:

1. *Manual Manipulator:* Handling equipment that has no program and is guided directly by its operator.

2. *Fixed Sequence Robot:* Handling equipment with a fixed programmed sequence which enables it to perform a certain task. Reprogramming it to do other tasks is quite difficult and expensive.

3. *Variable Sequence Robot:* The same type as described in 2., but with the difference that it
   can quite easily and quickly be reprogrammed to do other tasks

4. *Playback Robot:* The motion-sequence is once demonstrated by the operator and is recorded in the robot's memory device. With this saved information, the motion-sequence can be repeated as often as needed.

5. *Numerical Control Robot:* It works analogue to the robot described in 6, but with the difference that the motion-sequences is inputted numerically over keys, switches or data carriers.

6. *Intelligent Robot:* This is the most advanced kind of robot. Over a diverse array of sensors it is capable of adapting its program operation to changes in regard to the object to be manipulated and the environment

(http://www.enas.de/roboter_definition.htm)

---

[123] They probably opted for JARA, because JRA is already used by the Japan Racing Association

[124] Found on: http://www.enas.de/roboter_definition.htm (July 2004), my own translation of the German description (a detailed explanation can also be found in the handbook "*Steuern und Regeln*", refer to "Further Readings" under the category "Robotics, AI, Engeneering, Cybernetics" listed under references.

Such differences in definition-standards, of course may lead to incompatibilities in regard to comparisons and statistics between different countries (e.g. Japan and Germany). Machines which fall into the robot category 1 (and maybe 2) according to the Japanese definition are not defined as robots if applying the ISO/TR or EN norms. Therefore if not taking this into consideration the number of robots installed in Japan would be overestimated. And indeed, one has to be careful with the comparison of data between Germany and Japan in regard to industrial robots if there exist unclarity about which definitions have been used as a basis.

It is interesting that many of the non-legal / non-technical definitions of the term "robot" can also be applied to humans in a figurative way, describing a person who does ones task perfectly but without emotions. From this it can be concluded that a robot is associated with attributes like precision, perfection and the lack of emotions.

In my project I have concentrated on *non*-industrial robots. Therefore definitions used for *industrial* robots have to be altered. By orienting myself on the legal ISO/TR and EN norms and after studying some engineering handbooks I have constructed the following definition for my analysis in regard to non-industrial robots[125]:

---

[125] For the sake of simplicity and since this will not be an essay about engineering, I omit detailed aspects about sensor-feedback control etc., which are often named in engineering handbooks, e.g. Hering, 2002. (For further technical information refer to "Further Readings": Robotics, AI, (Bio)mechanics, Enginering, Cybernetics in the references list, especially the listed book "Steuern und Regeln")

> A robot is a reprogrammable mechatronic[126] device, consisting of mechanical and electronic components, whose actuators[127] and movements are controlled through a computer or some other form of electronic data processing and memory devices. A robot is able to perceive and process data from its environment and perform movements without direct physical human interference, although it may be controlled through remote-control devices, vocal, visual or other forms of commands. In contrast to a computer which only processes and transforms information, or virtual agents, a robot is capable of moving around and performing tasks in a 3-dimensional[128] environment.
>
> (Miriam JS Leis, 2003)

The reason why I have decided to chose a rather wide definition is because I did not want to fix it on specific tasks (e.g. "moving materials" or "performing human tasks") nor assign specific attributes (e.g. (not) human like, (not) intelligent, (not) being able to think).

What has been important to me when constructing this definition was the ability to distinguish a robot from the following:

- living organisms
- string puppets
- purely mechanical automata
- simple machines like a "classic" vacuum cleaners, washing machines, TV-sets etc.
- computers
- virtual agents and avatars

---

[126] The term "mechatronic" was formed in Japan by fusing the words "mechanical" and "electronic", which has been widely adapted Western engineering jargon.

[127] A motor or transducer that converts electrical, hydraulic, or pneumatic energy into motion. Examples are cylinders, servo-motors or rotary Actuators. (For further technical information refer to "Further Readings": Robotics, AI, (Bio)mechanics, Enginering, Cybernetics in the references list)

[128] actually 4 dimensions, if you also consider time

But I wanted to leave some freedom in regard to its functions and abilities.

x

"*A robot is a reprogrammable mechatronic[129] device, consisting of mechanical and electronic components, whose actuators[130] and movements are controlled through a computer or some other form of electronic data processing and memory devices.*" This distinguishes it from living organisms, string-puppets, (early) mechanical automates and machines like common household appliances that sometimes represent some kind of borderline case, since they often have computers / microprocessors integrated (and are able to perform actions in 3-dimensional space without the direct physical interference by a human), but are rather difficult to reprogram in order to perform new actions.

"A robot is able to perceive and process data from its environment and perform movements without direct physical human interference, although it may be controlled through remote-control devices, vocal, visual or other forms of commands." I have left out the commonly used term "autonomous" on purpose and replaced it by being *"able to perform tasks without direct physical human interference"*, because the meaning of "autonomy", especially in the relation to "being programmed" can lead to manifold difficulties. But a robot can also be programmed to initiate certain actions upon vocal or visual commands (gestures) or electronic signals (remote control). The aspect of perceiving and processing data from its environment is regarded as an important implement that distinguishes robots from artifacts like automated toys which only play back predefined sequences regardless of the external conditions.

---

[129] The term "mechatronic" was formed in Japan by fusing the words "mechanical" and "electronic", which has been widely adapted Western engineering jargon.
[130] A motor or transducer that converts electrical, hydraulic, or pneumatic energy into motion. Examples are cylinders, servo-motors or rotary Actuators.

"In contrast to a computer which only processes and transforms information, or virtual agents, a robot is capable of autonomous physical movements and performing tasks in a 3-dimensional environment." A robot is able to move and /or manipulate objects in a three dimensional world (let's forget about Einstein for a while) through direct physical contact. This distinguishes it from a computer, which can only manipulate data, but is incapable of physically performing operations on objects. Of course a computer is commonly used to *control* a robot's movements.

Robots as a sub-set of machines can again be classified into different sub-sets (although some categories may overlap like robots being used for professional or non-professional services, or research platforms which may be used in the service sector):

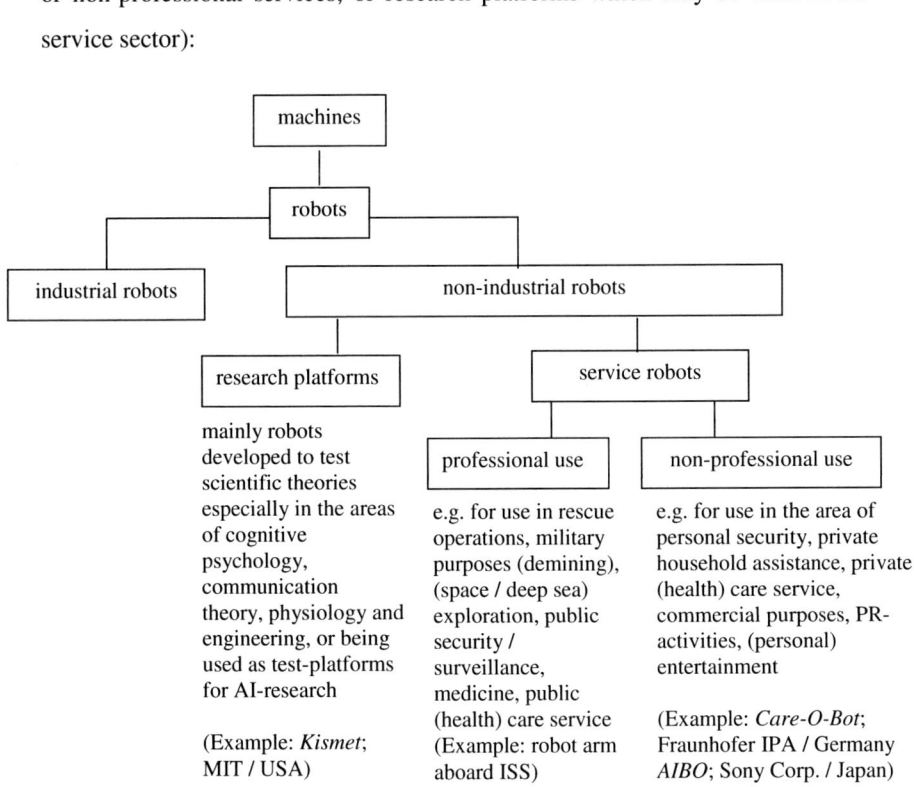

	machines	
	robots	
industrial robots		non-industrial robots

research platforms	service robots	
	professional use	non-professional use
mainly robots developed to test scientific theories especially in the areas of cognitive psychology, communication theory, physiology and engineering, or being used as test-platforms for AI-research	e.g. for use in rescue operations, military purposes (demining), (space / deep sea) exploration, public security / surveillance, medicine, public (health) care service	e.g. for use in the area of personal security, private household assistance, private (health) care service, commercial purposes, PR-activities, (personal) entertainment
(Example: *Kismet*; MIT / USA)	(Example: robot arm aboard ISS)	(Example: *Care-O-Bot*; Fraunhofer IPA / Germany *AIBO*; Sony Corp. / Japan)

1.3.4 First Real Robots

The first patent for a robot in the sense of a computer-controlled manipulation-device was obtained by George C. Devol, Jr. in 1954[131] and further developed by Joseph Engelberger. In 1962 General Motors Corp. was the first company to install a robot. Japan imported the first industrial robot from the US in 1967 and in 1971 Daimler-Benz (now DaimlerChrysler) deployed the first robot in Germany. Since these early developments (industrial) robots have been built for a wider commercial usage. They are employed mainly in the industry (automobile, steel, chemical etc.), but also in the fields of space and deep sea exploration, and are commonly assigned to do tasks too dangerous, too hard, too complicated, or too monotone for human workers. Since then the development of robots increased rapidly, their skills and sensory abilities have been improved ever since and with them their fields of deployment, ranging from simply welding metal over disarming ammunition to usage in the medical field. But their deployment has always been seen with ambivalence, at least in the West. This ambivalence manifested itself in knowing on the one hand that robots make our lives easier, but on the other hand their existence was also associated with fear. Fear about losing ones job due to automation. Fear about losing control. Even fear that robots may harm people.

At first the US has been the sole leader in robot technology. In 1968 *Unimation* (US) licensed its robot technology to *Kawasaki Heavy Industries Ltd.* (Japan). This was the starting point for Japan's successful entrance into the robot market, which by now produces about half of the world's industrial robots. Japan started to develop her own robot technologies (like the invention of the *Scara* arm by the Yamanashi University / Japan in 1979) and a whole array of companies began specializing in this field, having resulted in about 40 Japanese companies dominating the world market in industrial robot development and

---

[131] Refer to Asimov / Frenkel: Robots, 1985. P. 15

manufacturing, which has especially been the case during the booming 1990s. Today Japanese manufacturers of industrial robots experience increasing competition, this time particularly from Europe, where Germany and Italy belong to the dominating actors.

1.3.4.a) Excursion: Killed by a Robot?

The Japanese Kawasaki-worker Kenji Urada was the first person "killed" by a robot, in July 1981, because he has disregarded safety protocols[132]. In much of the media however the fault was rather attributed to the robot instead of the human who acted carelessly (or the persons who have built or programmed the robot). But "killing" implies intentionality, and intentionality means the existence of what we call a "conscious mind", something still far beyond the realm of today's robot technology. So the robot could only have "killed" the worker if it had been a deliberate act, out of self-interest or self-defence, which has absolutely not been the case here. Maybe we are anthropomorphizing on the wrong side!? What is also interesting is my observation that this incident led to more discussion and controversy in the West than in Japan, where the accident had happened.
x

1.3.4.b) Excursion: Failsafe Laws?

Also in science fiction the concerns about the safety and control of robots has become an important topic. Two major constants are typically connected to a robot's characteristics in science fiction: their lack of emotions and the potential danger they represent for mankind because of their physical (and often mental) superiority. The topic concerning a robot's mental superiority and even

---

[132] This incident is described quite dramatically as "murder" at:
http://www.mjwilson.demon.co.uk/crash/56/monitor.htm (article found in May 2003).

emotional abilities has established itself extensively in science fiction creations ever since the usage of computers has opened the door for equipping robots with some form of seeming intelligence, or at least providing that illusion.

In most of the early science fiction robots were described as "the other", and as being dangerous, emotionless, potentially uncontrollable and representing a menace to mankind. A "paradigmatic shift" came through the scientist and author Isaac Asimov who has created an anti-thesis to this negative view[133]. In his stories "*I, Robot*" (Asimov 1950) he invented the so-called "Three Laws of Robotics" (later he added law zero) as a kind lead motive and red thread that can be traced through nearly all of his robot-stories:

Law Zero:[134] A robot may not injure humanity, or, through inaction, allow humanity to come to harm.

Law One[135]: A robot may not injure a human being, or, through inaction, allow a human being to come to harm, unless this would violate a higher order law.

Law Two: A robot must obey orders given it by human beings, except where such orders would conflict with a higher order law.

Law Three: A robot must protect its own existence as long as such protection does not conflict with a higher order law

Also in the recent movie "I, Robot" (2004), loosely based on Isaac Asimov's novel, the "three laws" play a central part for the storyline. (For some reason there was no "Law Zero" in the story. If it would have been implemented, the problem portrayed in the film would not have occurred, except through accident).

---

[133] It was also Isaac Asimov who has in his stories coined the term "robotics" as a science about the construction and maintenance of robots. It has also been the stories of Isaac Asimov which have inspired Joseph F. Engelberger (who together with George C. Devol, Jr. has founded the robot firm Unimation) to get interested in robots. As a matter of fact his stories have also influenced me in regard to considering robotics from a sociologist's perspective.

[134] Law Zero from: http://utenti.lycos.it/seldonweb/isaac_asimov_uk_home.htm

[135] All except law zero from the story *Runaround* in *I, Robot* by Isaac Asimov, 2001 [1950]

Although Isaac Asimov may have invented these "laws" to make robots seem less threatening, ironically with his invention he may even have aroused some greater concerns about machines possibly posing a threat to mankind, this time not only through malfunction, but through their artificial reasoning - why else should they be restricted by laws? Asimov's "laws" have not only inspired other science fiction authors, but also some fairly down-to-earth-scientists working in the field of robot research who see them as an integral guideline for programming, preventing their artificial creations from getting uncontrollable like many *Golems*. But as Rodney A. Brooks, Professor of Computer Science and Director of the Artificial Intelligence Laboratory at MIT, has mentioned, today's robots still lack the perceptive capabilities of being able to obey these "Three Laws" [136]. But humans would possess the necessary perceptive capabilities to obey the Ten Commandments (or similar guidelines) and nonetheless often enough chose not to do so. What hopefully keeps robots from harming humans are only some sophisticated fail-safe-mechanisms built into them[137] – or just cutting their energy supply. In this sense robots are still much safer to deal with than humans.

(Perhaps) God created man in His own image. After a while man created machines in his own image and then machines will create machines in their own image (not that absurd if one considers that in fully automated Japanese factories robots are already building other robots).

---

[136] Refer to Brooks, 2003 (p. 72 ff)
[137] Also in regard to the technological aspects for a robot's safety mechanism refer to Schraft, Rolf Dieter et al. : 2004, p. 30 ff.

1.3.4.c) Excursion: Robot Shows[138]

"Any sufficiently advanced technology is indistinguishable from magic"

[Arthur C. Clarke]

I got the fortunate opportunity to see "life"-performances of robots in Japan on so-called robot shows, a popular form of entertainment in this country. By watching it, I wondered if this was how the people felt in the 18th century when seeing the wonders of early automata. People, from child to Grandma, flock around the stage, craning their heads, staying behind the barrier-markings. The barrier and the stage as the physical demarcation-line between the inaugurated experts with their artifacts and the spectators reminded me on Durkheim's division of the world into the "holy and the profane" (Durkheim: 1994 [1912]). Of course, according to the friendly hostess, the barriers are not there to protect the people from the robot, but to prevent the robot from getting confused or damaged by curious people getting too close ("it's very expensive, so people should be careful" was the explanation to a spectator who wanted to get closer to the action).

If not having known about today's stand of technology, I might well have wondered if it's all a fake. Of course the walking and stair-climbing *ASIMO*[139] is not a disguised 6-year-old in an astronaut's costume, and *QRIO*[140] dances without human interference, although its movements are programmed and stored on a patented memory device. And on hearing *ASIMO*'s motors and actuators, it faintly sounded like breathing, leaving me with the question if they have tuned it that way on purpose. But as Arthur C. Clarke once said: "Any sufficiently advanced technology is indistinguishable from magic."

---

[138] I am summarizing the observations I have made at a *QRIO*-demonstration at the Japanese exhibition *"Project X 21"* and an *ASIMO*-performance presented at the Japanese National Museum of Emerging Science and Innovation (MeSci).
[139] Biped humanoid robot developed by Honda Motors Co., Ltd. / Japan
[140] Biped humanoid robot developed by the Sony Corporation / Japan

Most people already know their mechatronic star and applause on its entry. In contrast to what is presented at trade-fairs, the robot show's programme mainly consists of entertainment elements, letting the robots perform songs, dances and a small chat with the moderator. During the show people express their astonishment and how cute they find the robots. Afterwards they try to imitate the *ASIMO-walk* which has seemingly already overtaken the *Moonwalk* in popularity.

Dancing is a main feature in such shows. To most humans, dancing is associated with life and creativity. In Hoffmann's *"Der Sandmann"* Nathanael dances with the automaton Olimpia, but her dancing is unnatural, since it is too perfect, making the dance to a kind of "Turing Test" to distinguish between the natural and the artificial. In contrast to Europe, in Japan there has been no tradition of ballroom-dancing or dancing in pairs. Traditionally, most Japanese dances are performed in groups, where all participants replicate the same prescribed, abstract movements, making modern *"Para Para*[141]*"* dances quite suitable for robot-programming. Paradoxically and maybe wisely, one often can find purposefully programmed imperfection at the robot's performance, letting it sing a wrong tune or dropping a fan during an Asian dance, later apologizing for the error, giving the machine some human traits…

x

1.3.5 Why do we want robots?

It is still heard that robots are responsible for our unemployment problems we are currently facing. But just take a closer look: are robots really to blame for our current problems of unemployment and economic problems? As it has been written about in a German News Magazine, especially for the time in the 1970s

---

[141] As I have heard on an airliner's music-channel, the *"Para Para"* dances, consisting of mechanical-seeming movements have become popular in Japan through the introducing tunes of the song *"Take On Me"* by *a-ha*.

to 1980s, at least for Western Europe and the US it has been an undeniable fact that the installation of robots in the production process has led to unemployment especially in the industrial sector[142]. However, in my view much of it has also been a result of an adaptation-lag, as with time new job opportunities in the areas of Computer- and Information Technology and maintenance have opened and the service sector has been expanded, partially compensating for the arisen problems. Nowadays it is unimaginable for an accounting office, for example, to get along without computers and modern automated office equipment. Today another problem seems to be more urgent than robotization: the export of manufacturing jobs to foreign countries like China and Vietnam or East European nations with low labor- and production costs. And just take a look at who is doing the dirty, dangerous and difficult jobs: it's mostly either immigrant workers or robots.

As I have already mentioned, since early times mankind has been fascinated by the idea of creating "living" artificial human-like entities, either through magic or engineering. May it be Golems, homunculi, automata or robots; the main purpose for their creation is to serve man and obeying the command of its human master. But there has also been another tradition, that of dolls and cogwheel automata which merely served the intention of entertainment. Following this line, there can also be distinguished to main categories for (future) deployment of non-industrial robots: service and entertainment (although the sets don't have strict binary boundaries and many robots are planned to serve both ends). It is reasonable to assume that the consequences for the human work-force will be different in both cases.

Let's start with analyzing the question why people build robots to work for them. I have found four main reasons:

---

[142] Refer to "Der Spiegel", No.6, February 8. 1982, p. 144 ff

1. Robots are being used to do jobs **too dangerous** for humans to perform, like defusing bombs, working in contaminated areas or in outer space / deep sea.

2. Robots are being used *because* of **scarce human resources**; if nobody can be found to take away your garbage or clean your house you can either do it yourself or let a robot do this for you.

3. Robots are being used, because they can perform tasks much **faster** and much **more precise** than humans.

4. Robots are being used, because on the long run they are **cheaper** than human workers.

In regard to points 1 and 2, people won't have to fear for their jobs, either because it would be nearly impossible for humans to perform these jobs without risking their lives, or because there's simply nobody willing to do these jobs anyway. Since with the passage of time, the world has become more dangerous (nuclear facilities, chemical factories, progresses in space- and deep sea exploration) and safety laws have become much stricter, the demand for such robots will be on rise. In the latter case robots will contribute to the positive effect of creating new jobs for engineers, programmers (and sociologists?!) and boost the economy.

Points 3 and 4, especially point 4 are more critical. But let's begin with number 3: In the so-called capitalized world, competition runs the economy, something which becomes even more pressing in the age of globalization. Many different companies produce similar goods, varying in looks, function, quality and price. It's the consumer's choice, which product to buy and with his/her purchase, flatly put, (s)he brings in money to the company, that may then be used to pay for wages, material, production costs, taxes and the development of new products. If no consumers are buying the product, the company gets no money, which quite probably leads to bankruptcy, resulting in people losing their jobs. Not only the employees of the unfortunate company will lose their job, but also the jobs of suppliers will be endangered. In order to survive on the market, one has to master the art of making people buy ones products. But how would a rational consumer make his/her choices? For the sake of simplicity let's assume that the consumer bases his/her decision only on information about the following dimensions:

- quality (how well does the product perform and how long will it last)[143]
- functionality (what can I do with the product)
- price (relative to other products comparable in quality and function)

One can choose from the following combinations:

x

Table 1

set	index	quality	function	price	
1	A	H	H	L	H = High
	B	H	H	H	L = Low
2	A	H	L	L	
	B	H	L	H	
3	A	L	H	L	
	B	L	H	H	
4	A	L	L	L	
	B	L	L	H	

I assume that a rational consumer would look for the good with the high quality, high functionality and the low price and would never decide on a product with low quality, low functionality and high price. The combination one decides on in regard to the combinations 1A to 4B depends on the consumer's individual priority and the ratio between quality, functionality and price, but for each set, one would rationally decide for the product indexed with A. This means for the company to sell innovative high quality products at low prices. The higher the

---

[143] Although one could split this in two separate dimensions, it is also reasonable to assume them as belonging together in this model.

quality the higher the resources which have to be put into the production (it takes more time and training / experience to put an object together neatly, than just assembling it sloppily). And the higher the functionality, the higher the resources which have to be put into product development (e.g. one has to invest much more into research to develop a cellular phone with integrated video-function than into one which can only manage phone calls.) With two factors working against low prices, how then achieve them? There are two rather dissatisfying solutions associated with lowering production costs: lower wages or / and longer working hours without monetary compensation or rationalization, leading to a situation, where the human has to adapt to the machine instead of vice versa. With this, at least more products can be produced, enabling companies to sell for lower prices while gaining higher profits. If one industry begins with such methods this leads to a kind of cascade effect, forcing others to do the same or even try topping it in order to stay competitive. Bad working conditions and the worker's exploitation have been reality during the beginning of the industrial revolution. No wonder that people began to protest against such conditions and that the idea of communism was born. This led to the introduction of social security systems and laws regulating working hours, wages and working conditions. As a result human work became increasingly expensive because of regulated wages and the amount of payments going to social security systems. This has in turn amplified the call for robots being used, because on the long run they are cheaper than human workers in certain areas. If one takes a look into countries like China or Vietnam where human labor is comparably cheap, one sees a lot of factories, where TV-sets and computer boards are still (mostly) being assembled manually, whereas in countries like Japan, Western Europe or the US such processes are being done mostly automated. Also it's an observable fact that a growing number of countries with high labor costs are transferring their production (especially the labor-intensive segments that cannot be easily automated) to low-wage countries in Asia and Eastern Europe.

Technological advancement has an amplifying effect: first, machines were invented which were able to perform jobs previously done by humans, but the machines did it more precise, faster, cheaper and better. In turn the technological standard grew, and goods became increasingly complex (e.g. modern automobiles, airplanes, computers, rockets etc.). At one point it became quite impossible to let such commodities be assembled by humans in a safe and economically rational way (robots don't get wages and work with higher precision and productivity at least in regard to repetitive tasks). Some products even possess such high complexity that their manufacturing would simply overtax human capabilities. That's why industrial robots have been introduced to build cheap, high quality and high functional consumer electronics, cars, computers and even other robots. This again led to a cascade effect, causing others to follow in order to keep up in competition.

But can we turn back the wheel and deactivate most of the industrial robots to give back the jobs to human workers? This would only be feasible if one of the following scenarios would become reality:

a) every company in every country is doing this

b) human workers would have to do much harder work for much less money, much fewer social security benefits and for much longer time to keep up with productivity

c) People would prefer the products in each set indexed "B" instead of "A" according to table 1

I think you would agree with me on saying that these scenarios are very unlikely to become reality. Additionally, today's unemployment fears don't primarily result from automation, but from cheap labor competition of foreign countries in Southeast Asia and Eastern Europe.

And how would you decide, if confronted with the following two alternatives: either opting for automation, perhaps risking your job, but enhancing the chances that your company will survive and that you might get a job in the tertiary sector of the firm, or opting against automation and risking the highly probable closure of the whole company? And just look back to the beginnings of massive computerization. It was feared that the introduction of computers, especially in the area of accounting, would lead to massive unemployment. Although this had been true to some degree for a rather short while, the job-market has adapted and today it is more likely that a person will be unemployed because of computer illiteracy and not because of the mere existence of such machines. And who is still willing (and able) to do accounting by hand anyway?

The new generation of robots is planned to someday enter the service-sector. In some areas they have already arrived. Robots are already doing errand work in hospitals, like transporting documents, material and food trays; they clean floors, or guide visitors through museums (although this is only a PR-strategy and not a necessity). They have already "learned" (or rather been programmed) to walk, talk, find their way in a new environment, recognize people's faces and the according name, react to gestures, simulate some emotional expressions, do surveillance work, play soccer, sing songs, do small-talk and perform synchronized dances. But when will they serve me a Big Mac or Caviar in a French Restaurant? Will they take care of me when I'm 90? I will consider such questions along with the analysis of some German and Japanese projects in the field of service robotics later in my study.

1.3.5 a) Excursion: Robot Economy

Maybe it's not the robots, but our economic system that is to blame for our problems? In my view, the use of machines and robots has only been a logical consequence of economic profit making and fighting competitors.

During my research I came across an original, quite amusing and maybe - but only *maybe* - not completely thought-through newspaper article (*The Japan Times*, October 20, 2003) by Marshall Brain, I find worth mentioning here. His reasoning goes the following: today robots are taking over more and more of (wo)man's jobs for sake of profit (in the long run, a robot comes cheaper than employing a human on minimum-wage-basis). This situation will get even more dramatic as robots get more intelligent (according to *Moore's law*[144] and Brain's calculation Artificial Intelligence will equal human intelligence around 2040), leading to mega mass- unemployment, like it has never been experienced before. Of course this poses a problem, since income is related to work. But what if, so Brain's idea, humans will unhook the link between work and income – the basis for today's economic reasoning – and let robots do all of mankind's work? Wouldn't this put everybody into the position of a "capitalist" (although Brain doesn't use that term), who will profit from other peoples' – or in this case robots' – work? All accumulated money reserves, so his suggestion, should be equally distributed among all humans, giving them time to enjoy a life-long vacation. Since the working robots don't need any money themselves, the money resulting from their productivity could directly to the humans. [145]

Let's look a little deeper into the mechanisms[146]: simply put, the costs for commodity production consist of material costs (including production costs) and

---

[144] Flatly put: a future projection about the development of a computer's processing power, which is said to double every 18 month. Refer to Part II of my analysis for further descriptions.

[145] It has been titled: "Will robots ruin humanity – or free it?", The Japan Times, October 20, 2003, p. 19. Marshall Brain is the founder of one of my favourite web-sites: HowStuffWorks.com

[146] The following represent my own comments on the article.

wages (including other payments such as social security). To make profits, a company has to sell at a price higher than the material costs plus wages. Profits are only achieved if people are buying the commodity. If wages are cut (e.g. through automation), then the company can make higher profits by selling at the same (or even lower) prices. Put to an extreme, the only cost-factor remaining will be the costs for raw materials (including energy). This is the initial point of Brian's reasoning. But since profits consist of parts from other people's incomes, a commodity can only be sold if people are able to render parts of their incomes in order to buy it. If due to automation people get no job and no income (except welfare payments, which will become increasingly difficult to cover) the profit margins of companies will also shrink (isn't this the problem merchants are already lamenting about today in face of the growing unemployment rate and the resulting decline in consumer spending?). So at some point production would not be profitable if one still has to pay for the raw materials. But why are raw-materials costly? Because humans are mining them (I will leave out here lengthy discussions about the relationship between scarce resources and pricing[147]). If robots are also extracting raw materials, hypothetically, material costs would also be zero, leaving a no-cost commodity which can be given away freely, since the question of profit is redundant to a robot. So it is actually the link between production and profit that has to be broken. There are still flaws in the reasoning and to us such scenario sounds quite unrealistic, but if looking at concepts of visionaries like the German sociologist Georg Voruba[148] and his imagining of negative taxation (people with income pay taxes and people without income get taxes from the state) and the proposal for a basic income for everybody ("*Bürgergeld*") independently of ones wages[149] (this is a kind of

---

[147] It's a difference if I find 1 gram of aluminium or one gram of platinum, although the amount of work I have inputted into the process of mining could be the same.
[148] Professor of Sociology at the University of Leipzig
[149] Voruba's idea has been presented on TV at the German Science Magazine "*Nano*" on October 29th 2004.

social welfare granted to everybody without bureaucratic proceedings), Brain's ideas could remain worth thinking about.

/*...Or maybe robots should be used to produce the commodities to be distributed among future generations of retirees in face of empty social security reserves...*/

Now after providing an introduction to the robot's history I would like to continue with questions about the relationship between humans and technology, views about humankind and philosophy, investigating some aspects on the intersection between mankind and technology, a promising field for the future sociology.

x

> *What a piece of work is man!*
> *How noble in reason!*
> *How infinite in faculty!*
> *In form and moving how express and admirable!*
> *In action how like an angel!*
> *In apprehension how like a god!*
> *The beauty of the world!*
> *The paragon of animals!*

[William Shakespeare, *Hamlet*]

PART II
0101000001100001011100100111010000100000000110010
Humans, Machines and Society

2. (MA)CHI(N)E

2.1 What is (Wo)man?

What is man? This is an essential question which can be traced through nearly the entire history of humankind. It has been discussed in religion, philosophy, arts, psychology, sociology and finally engineering, information sciences, Artificial Intelligence (AI) and robotics.

Even today – or especially today - people fear that the successful creation of AI and robots might reveal that (wo)man is nothing but a sophisticated machine. Or does such uneasiness stem from the fact that suddenly humans are confronted with unpleasant questions about humanity, about their established world-view getting questioned once again?

Why is humankind so overly obsessed with questions like "who am I", "why am I", or "what is reality?" (Why can't everybody follow my pragmatic philosophy by saying: "I cannot evaluate positively if I am and who I am – or if everything is just a simulation – therefore for all practical purposes the only thing what counts is that somehow it works out?")

Questions asked rather theoretically at the beginning became more concrete as humankind has been confronted with its real mechanical mirror-image. How to distinguish (intelligent) artifacts, i.e. automata, computers and robots from humans? This question has been pondered upon by numerous (wo)men and the list holds many names including philosophers like Descartes, Hobbes and La Mettrie, writers such as E.T.A. Hoffmann and Philip K. Dick, and scientists like Alan Turing, Hans Moravec and Marvin Minsky. And as artificial entities are becoming more human-like on the one hand and are increasingly penetrating our world on the other, one has to ask where to place them: on the subject- or object side of our world?

Such questions and the different stances are something that concerns both, the natural sciences and the humanities. Is everything explainable through scientific analysis or does there exist something which forever will remain outside the realm of human scientific understanding? Is (wo)man just a sophisticated machine or is there something intrinsically human that no earthly engineer could ever replicate?

I have to precede here that the discussion has not been resolved yet and that perhaps it will never be empirically resolvable. Just imagine a world beyond the year 2050 where people have succeeded in creating an artificial entity that is not distinguishable from an ordinary human being. Advocates may herald this as "proof" that there is nothing more behind a human being than a specific architecture and some algorithmic structures that can be recreated on an artificial basis, whereas critics counter that everything is still a simulation and the intrinsic quality will still be beyond reach forever. And imagine the more likely case that the artificial entities still lack much of what is called "human qualities"; will this be proof for the existence of something intrinsically human that can never be reconstructed in a machine? No, will some people say: we just don't have enough knowledge yet about the architecture of a human being and still lack the needed technology for its artificial reconstruction.

The second – and easily overlooked – problem is that another entity's consciousness can be discussed about, but in my view can not be proven. I can only *assume* that another entity possesses consciousness and emotions in the same way as I assume to experience them myself. It are only the actions and expressions of the other that cause me to believe that (s)he is principally similar to me. Maybe a snail feels the same way I do, but since it can't express itself in a manner that I can understand, it makes it rather easy to categorize it as less sentient. This is also the reason for the sad fact, that some people consider disabled, especially paralyzed persons, as less sentient, just because of their inability to form understandable expressions[150]. So by reversing the situation I can also imagine that it would be not too difficult to interpret emotions into something just because it expresses itself in a manner similar to my own. There are still many unresolved discussion about the question hovering around the topic of "consciousness", of which surprisingly many can be found in philosophical debates about quantum mechanics in the context of the "observer problem" and the nature of reality[151]. But, so my brief consideration, if one would make the suggestion to define a robot as possessing consciousness when it is able to cause the reduction of a super-position (that's quantum mechanic terminology), one gets a problem: if there's no human around to observe that fact, it will never be known (at least not by a human posing this question). And if there would be a human observer the question arises: has it been the robot or

---

[150] As it has also been discussed in relation to the controversial debate about the case of Terri Schiavo, the brain-damaged woman who was nourished through a feeding tube.
[151] e.g. Alastair, 1986; Shimony, 1993; Penrose, 1998

the human? So the whole problem just gets moved to another level (yes, maybe a snail can reduce a super position, but no human ever noticed it...). Therefore I will end the topic of quantum mechanics for now.

What I think to have found out is that not only artifacts are becoming increasingly sophisticated and human-like, but that also through the work of modern science the human being has been unveiled as something which might be more machine-like and externally determined than some of us want to believe; something that could even become patented some day[152].

2.1.1 Man, Machine or (Ma)chi(n)e ?

As an introduction I think it is important to take a closer look onto two different views about the human being, which I will call *"humanistic* [153]*"* and *"mechanistic"*. How one will answer the question about the difference between man and machine depends on how one looks at the human being.

2.1.2 La Mettrie, Minsky, Moravec and the End of Humanity?

You may remember Francis Fukuyama's proclaimed and much debated *"End of History"* (Fukuyama, 1992). "AI-hardliners" like Marvin Minsky[154] and Hans Moravec[155] have provided us with some thought-provoking views about our future, which could be called "the end of humanity". In his famous, but highly

---

[152] I'm referring to the current debate about the patenting of genetically engineered organisms and the question about where to draw the line for patentability.
[153] This is a word-construction I have chosen since the term „humanist" is already used in another context.
[154] Cofounder of the Artificial Intelligence Laboratory at MIT / USA together with John McCarthy
[155] Director of the Mobile Robot Laboratory of Carnegie Mellon University / USA

controversial and sometimes misunderstood book *"Mind Children"*[156] the author Hans Moravec writes in the prologue about a possible "postbiological" future *"in which the human race has been swept away by the tide of cultural change, usurped by its own artificial progeny."* (quotetd from Moravec, 1988). If this kind of future scenario, which rather sounds like being taken from some *"Matrix"* movie will ever happen, has to be provided with a big question-mark. As I'm writing this we have year 2005, and about 50 years ago people began with making the prognosis that in 50 years Artificial Intelligence will have already exceeded human intelligence – and today's far less optimistic (or pessimistic, depending on one's standpoint) prognosis are still 30 to 50 years[157]. How many "50 years" will follow? As you will see later in my work, it is not only calculation power, instructions per second and larger circuit integration that make out (human) intelligence. This realization came with the understanding that human intelligence, human data processing and data analysis differ dramatically from the methods used in (classic) computers. But even with a big question-mark, the illustrated pictures of fictitious robots having developed some kind of consciousness (whatever consciousness may be and however it can be measured!) causing them in quite human fashion to destroy their creators (mankind), or the idea of transferring the human mind onto a computer residing inside a robot body, which Moravec calls *"Transmigration"* (Moravec, 1988 : P. 108-110), a quite metaphysical term, cannot be completely ruled out as a possible possibility. In a very remote way, the widely spread usage of electronic memory storing devices (which have already become so small that the term "losing ones memory" may get a totally new meaning) can already be regarded

---

[156] Although I think that some of Moravec's critics have misunderstood his intentions. In my view Moravec has tried to illustrate a possible – although rather unlikely – future scenario regarding humans beings and AI / robots. But to me it did not sound like an appeal for establishing such a future.

[157] Now roboticists have set the goal for the year 2050 to have human-like robots (at least in shape), which would be able to play soccer against human players with a real chance to win (refer to Thomas Christaller at http://www.heise.de/tp/deutsch/inhalt/lis/12740/1.html, June 18, 2002). The plans for the still unapprved Japanese „*Atom Project*" (Refer to Part I of my thesis) is set for 30 years.

as a form of "transmigration" – of conserving human memories (texts, data, pictures, sound) externally from the human body.

Should in this respect one rather assume the worst-case scenario about possible future outcomes than the best-case scenario when thinking about initiating a new technology (like AI, robotics and human cloning), as the philosopher Hans Jonas demands in his book *"Das Prinzip der Verantwortung"* (refer to Jonas, 1988 : p.70-71)[158]? To answer this question it first has to be cleared what is meant by "best case" and "worst case". From the standpoint of a whale it could be the best case if there would be no human beings around on earth, that could hunt them down and pollute their environment and from the standpoint of Moravec, it could be the best case being enabled to transfer ones mind onto a computer and "living" in a robot body for eternity. (And indeed, the question about "death" is central, as many owners of Sony's robot "dog" *AIBO* have said that they appreciate that their robot-dog's "personality-data" can be stored on a memory device, which principally could exist forever[159]). On evaluating possible futures one has to answer the question: best future for *whom*? Such evaluations, if asked by humans, are by default anthropocentric and may have to include future generations. Does this mean that we today should take responsibility for our successors? This leads me to another thought-provoking question: what if all humans – out of their free will - would decide not to have children anymore? A not so absurd question in face of the drastic birth rate declines in so-called post-industrial countries. Does mankind really have the obligation to maintain the human race as Hans Jonas demands? (Jonas, 1988 : p. 86 ff). Similar problems occur with arguments of "negative utilitarianism" that demand the minimization of the total sum of suffering endured by sentient beings. Mathematically the solution would lie in the elimination of all sentient beings, leaving us with a total number of zero

---

[158] Refer to pages 70-71
[159] Many thanks to my friends at www.aibo-freunde.de (German Internet-based AIBO-Community), for their comments on my question

suffering sentient beings. But before you accuse me of callousness, questioning my humanity, this has just been an argument to make people sensitive towards humanities problems.

If looking back at the controversial debates about industrial robots and later the introduction of computers much fears seem to have faded away, at least until a crisis like the breakdown of crucial computer networks occurs. And even people criticizing the usage of computers have to admit the necessity of using such technologies if wanting to maintain today's social and cultural structures, which have become so complex that they won't be manageable without computer assistance (yes, I have even found Internet-bashing articles on the Internet). I think, at least in regard to AI and robotics, the main aspect of the controversy is not about implementing such technology, but about the future of humanity and the picture of humanity associated with it.

Humans come to points where they have to step back and reconsider their situation. It is not the robot per se, which leads to the often-stated "social coldness" and ignorance. Rather it is the observation that there exist people who might try to find comfort in the interaction with machines leads us to the question about how this could happen.

Many philosophers and thinkers like Jonas and Weizenbaum regard the AI-ideas of "hardliners" like Minsky and Moravec as beyond the realm of reality, but nonetheless rate such thoughts as dangerous for humanity[160]. It's about the big and essential question how we see and define human beings. And there seem to exist two different, conflicting views, which I will call the *"mechanistic"* and the *"humanistic"*. Let's have a short look into the main thought lines of both side's representatives.

---

[160] Refer to: GEO Wissen: Intelligenz und Bewusstsein. Issue No. 3 / Montag 24.08.1992, P. 134 ff.

a) Humans – Just Organic Machines?

"I think that robots with human intelligence will be common within fifty years"

[Hans Moravec: *Mind Children*, 1988]

The idea of comparing humans to automata or describing them as machines is not that new as it may sound. In fact wide-spread serious considerations date back to the 17th century. Among others, Leonardo DaVinci (1452 - 1519), Thomas Hobbes (1588 – 1679), René Descartes (1596 -1650), Julien Offray de La Mettrie[161] (1709 – 1751) and George Boole (1815 - 1864) have tried to analyze (at least) the human body in a mathematical and mechanical way, or in the case of Boole tried to describe the workings of human reasoning in terms of binary mathematical logic[162], which is now used in computers. In Descartes' work *"Treatise of Man"* (Descartes 1664)[163] the workings of the human body is being explained in the language of mechanics, and the human body is described as a machine that even includes the human brain. But still Descartes clearly distinguished between mind and matter, subject and object and stressed that the genuineness about being human lies in the ability to have conscious experience. In "Treatise of Man" only the body is described and not the soul; and unfortunately the description about the soul or "mind"[164] has been lost. Also Hobbes held the idea of a mechanistic world-view that he even applied to the process of human thinking and actions (e.g. in *Leviathan*[165]), something he tried

---
[161] La Mettrie has written such controversial works like: The Natural History of the Soul (1745) and L'Homme Machine (1747).
[162] An idea developed by Leibniz
[163] Refer to: Descartes, Rene. Treatise on Man. [1664]. In : Cottingham, J. / Stoothoff, R. / Murdoch, D.
(Eds. / Trans.). 1985. The Philosophical Writings of Descartes, Vol.1. Cambridge University Press: Cambridge
[164] Somehow Descartes (like the Japanese) seems to view "soul" and "mind" as being the same thing
[165] Refer to Hobbes, 1996 [1651]

to explain through his motion theory. One of the most radical thinkers – maybe the *"Moravec of the 18th Century"* - has been Julien Offray de La Mettrie[166], who thought about human beings in total - and not only meaning the human body - as being nothing but an automaton and rejected the idea of a soul in the Christian sense[167]. All these advocates of a mechanistic view about the world and humankind had to perform a balancing act in diplomacy to avoid denunciation by the church, as it has happened to La Mettrie. This fact again shows how cultural and religious norms can determine the fate of ideas.

According to such a mechanistic view it's just a matter of technology if we'll be able to artificially replicate humans.

b) Humans – Beyond Rational Explanation?

"[...] Aber das Wunder eines neuen Lebens können sie eben nicht verstehen"[168]

[Joseph Weizenbaum]

Now, what is the other side of the story? The view, which I have labelled *"humanistic"* has its roots in the Judeo-Christian-(Islamic) religious tradition. The *"humanists"* stress that there exist qualities which are genuine human, which can never be described in mechanical, electronic, mechatronic or even (positivistic) scientific terms and can never be (re)produced through simulation. Joseph Weizenbaum has illustrated this quite plastically as he said in a debate with Klaus Haefner that it won't matter to a robot if carrying a baby or a sandbag, no matter how well the robot's sensors and actuators may be tuned (refer to Haller (Ed.), 1990 : p. 101). For him human phenomenon like creativity, arts, affection, feelings etc. can never be transferred to machinery. In

---

[166] La Mettrie: Die Maschine Mensch. L'homme machine, 1991 [1747].
[167] Refer to Wood : 2002, p. 09-10
[168] "But they can not understand the wonder of new life" Translation by Miriam JS Leis

this sense one can summarize it by saying that a machine / computer regardless of how many instructions per second it can process, how well it might be programmed, how much it is able to learn, or how complex its Artificial Neural Networks may be, can never be like a human being. The difference between (wo)man and machine will always remain fundamentally different. *"Humanists"* accuse *"mechanists"* of degrading human dignity, of being arrogant and of trying to play God. Christian *"humanists"* argue that God created (wo)man in His image and if man creates an entity (i.e. robot) in his/her image (s)he tries to be like God. (This has also been the argument of a two German clerics I talked with about this issue[169]).

At first glance the *"humanist"* view appears to have one logical difficulty: one can not assume the existence of something intrinsically human and fear the progress in AI / robotics-research as inhabiting the danger of degrading human beings at the same time. If one assumes AI-research as being dangerous to humanity, one automatically has to accept the idea that it might be possible to mechanically replicate a human being. If assuming that it will never be possible to mechanically replicate a human being, why then bother about AI? But the main and most important concerns are not about the technological aspect behind it, but rather about the picture of humanity such mechanistic views create. The fears concern a possibly dangerous philosophy which proposes the idea of degrading humans to a position of mere objects; or a as Weizenbaum has put it, that humans are not just a sub-set of machines[170].

Failures in AI may be apologetically excused with the comment that all human mechanisms have not been adequately understood so far, hindering us to replicate humans on a "mechatronic" basis, but principally it would be possible – and such an assumption can hardly be refuted. By believing in such ideas, the

---

[169] Refer to the Part I of my work
[170] Original German quote: *"Menschen sind eben keine Untermenge der allgemeinen Menge Maschine"* (Haller (Ed.): 1990.)

fundamental difference between humans and machines will be dissolved. This is what the "*humanists*" fear.

Isn't the view about humanity ending up in a mere belief system, where both sides aren't able to invalidate the postulations of the other on an objective basis? The only way to get "scientific proof" (although I doubt that such thing exists) would be to build a mechatronic replication of a human being and try to find out the differences. But wouldn't this end up in a kind of "arms race" between the two parties, whereas the "*humanists*" will come up with new tests to "proof" the difference, whilst the mechanists try to find new ways to refute these claims?

/*…Since I don't find a way to refute such suggestions, for all practical purposes I assume that everything is a simulation and I'm an android…[171] */

x

x

2.1..2 a) Short Reflection I: Losing Ground in Virtual Worlds!?

Recently in Japan, after a series of crimes, voices were raised that Japan's growing number of *otaku*, defined as loners, who maniacally pursue some specific field of interest ranging from robot construction to the consumption of murky *manga*, may be a cause for the disturbing tendencies in a country that takes proud in its low crime-rates[172]. In contrast to Japan, where the threshold of tolerance looks to be higher or it just takes longer until critique is voiced (e.g. Japan does not yet possess the equivalent to the German JÖschG / FSK rating system for film- and gaming content), in Germany and other Western countries debates targeting the negative influence of television and nowadays the virtual worlds of "*cyberspace*" can look upon quite a tradition. Debates got new fuel after a 19-year old student has killed 17 people (teachers, students and himself) at a high school in Erfurt / Germany on April 26, 2002. The perpetrator's profile fit that of the loner, interested in weapons and video-

---

[171] The only aspect which keeps me from really believing such "schizoid" ideas is my estimation about today's technological capacities, which makes such assumption rather improbable – or maybe it's just an illusion...
[172] Refer to *The Japan Times* February 6, 2005

games with violent content and therefore encouraged the practice of blaming "virtual reality" for the ills of society.

A German friend of mine once wrote on a public Internet-forum posting that the devotion towards the non-living and the virtual instead of the real and living inhibits the danger that one will begin to prefer the artificial over the living, and that humankind will forget that the real world does not function by the click of a button; that the real world is not a computer game[173]. These concerns are understandable, especially if one considers the fact that in contrast to the passive perception of movies, people (may) get the impression of active participation while playing computer-games without getting confronted with the real consequences. The existence of Internet-based *"ego-shooter*[174]*"* games even amplifies the strange blur between the virtual and reality, since real people are getting virtually killed. And if "virtual reality" already causes criminal behavior in humans because people might believe that their misdeed can be made undone by the push of a button, then robots may cause even greater concern (you may know the scene from the movie *"Short Circuit"* where the robot assumes that a dead grasshopper can be revived just by fixing its destroyed structures).

But can "virtual reality" serve as an explanation for today's ills of humanity and society?

First of all I have to say that there's no such thing as a *"virtual reality"* – an oxymoron. A situation or setting may be *defined* as "real" or "virtual", but as long as being defined as "virtual" it stays that way, no matter how "real" it may seem. In this sense I deem the occupation with quantum mechanics much more dangerous in view of losing ones sense for "reality".

I will not arrogate to provide an explanation for the human fascination with violence (of course this statement should not be generalized) or give an ultimate solution to the age-old question if there's a causal effect between things portrayed in the media and actual human behavior. But one thing seems to be clear to me: it's actually a general question about cause and effect, the proverbial query about which came first, the hen or the egg. There are violent and murky movies and video-games all over the world (and some distributors of violent content are even regarded as

---

[173] I have paraphrased the original text.
[174] Games where people "virtually" kill others from the view of a first-person-perspective. The most prominent are *Counterstrike* and *Quake*, which are being discussed with much controversy.

educating: news broadcasts and historic documentaries), but only a comparatively small percentage of humans get excessively interested in them, and from those not all turn into criminals and maniacs. So it gets plausible to ask what makes people to "enjoy" contents of (excessive) violence in the first place. If following the logic of the market, there has to be a demand for such items, otherwise production would be redundant.

So how dangerous are virtual worlds? It's not "*virtuality*" per se which is dangerous (I would prefer virtual warfare over real warfare), but its content and how people are dealing with the situation. If a person kills another and even gives as a reason that (s)he thought that this action can be made undone like in a computer game, the root has to be searched for in a person's initial decision of choosing to get involved in such computer-games. Banning knifes on airplanes may reduce the risk of pilots getting stabbed, but this does not prevent terrorists from figuring out other ways to disrupt safe air-traffic. In this sense banning violent contents in the media may prevent some forms of crimes, but it may not be able to solve the essential problem.

And what about the accusation of neglecting the living if preoccupied with the artificial? There again one has to ask the question, why people would possibly opt for preferring the artificial over the living. Maybe they find something in the artificial that they cannot find in the living, and *that* should raise questions of concern; concerns in respect to human interaction, communication and honesty. If looked at it from the standpoint of *Rational Choice* decision-making theory, tending towards the artificial has to be seen as the act deemed more optimal than all other known alternatives. In this sense the devotion towards the non-living and the virtual, instead of the real and living rather reflects on some problems existent in human relationships…

2.1.3 The shift towards a "mechanistic" view of humankind

> The danger of the past was that men became slaves.
> The danger of the future is that men may become robots
>
> [Erich Fromm, 1900 – 1980][175]

At the beginning mankind assumed a unity of the body, mind and (eternal) soul. Then with the rise of Cartesian logic and classical mechanics, people came up with the idea of distinguishing between a mechanical body, a non-mechanical mind and a "metaphysical" soul. As Christian religious thoughts have been pushed farther into the background, the idea of the soul also became questionable. The "soul" became "downgraded" as a by-product of mental processes.

With the advent of Darwin's theory of evolution, biomechanics, integrated circuits (IC), computers, Artificial Intelligence, robotic research, simulations, "virtual reality", homeostatic-models to explain emotions, biotechnology, genetic engineering and even sociology, some people again shifted towards a view about a unity of body, mind and soul, but this time from a totally other perspective. Now the human body can be described in a mechanical way, whereas most of what constitutes a human being is determined by his/her genetic make-up and hormone-production. Emotional reactions have been identified to be triggered through neurochemical reactions and have the mere function to ensure the survival of the entity. Dietrich Dörner, professor of psychology at the University of Bamberg (Germany) has created an artificial virtual entity called "*Psi*" which is "living" in form of a computer-program[176]. With this entity consisting of strings of "ones and zeros" he wants to study the origin and mechanisms of (human) emotions, which he considers as being just

---

[175] As far as I remember it, this quote has wrongly been attributed to Henri David Thoreau (1817 – 1862) in the movie *RoboCop II* (actually I discovered the mistake after considering that the term "robot" has been introduced through Čapek in 1920.)
[176] Refer to: Dörner / Hille, 1995

the result of data processing, not fundamentally different from what a computer does. Neuroscientists try to find out how the brain works and engineers attempt to artificially rebuild these structures[177]. Maybe, believing this, I'm actually nothing more than a very complex computer program?

The "soul" equals "emotions" and emotions are thought to be explainable in rational scientific terms as processes triggered by hormone-production and are based on neural and cognitive mechanisms developed throughout the long process of evolution in order to ensure mankind's survival. Neural and cognitive processes are thought to be principally explainable through scientific analysis and the infrastructure of the brain is determined by genetics. The brain controls body- and motor functions, which on their part can be described in mechanical terms. The small rest that remains unexplainable (or uninteresting) to natural scientists has been left to philosophers.

Even psychologists and sociologists are called onto the project to uncover the human being in its totality. Both analyze factors and influences that alter or steer human beings in regard to how they perceive, structure and act in their surrounding. Maybe humans are so fascinated about the thought of building human-like machines because they want to find out the essence of being human.

Although I don't know if robotic androids like those encountered in science fiction stories like "*A.I.*" or "*Blade Runner*" will ever be built, the mere thought about such scenarios raises philosophical and sociological questions. This is because the human-machine-analogy represents a bi-directional concept. If humans are considered to be nothing but mere machines, this statement automatically implies that it would be at least hypothetically possible to build machines which would be indistinguishable from humans.

This second view also distinguishes "mechanists" from "AI-hardliners"; whereas the first category of people often only views physiological processes in

---

[177] An introduction and overview about Neuroscience and Artificial Intelligence can be found in: McCrone, 2002; Ratey, 2002 and Challoner, 2002. Refer to Part IV of my thesis for further considerations.

a mechanistic way, the second category of people thinks that the whole human being, including its feelings, thoughts, creativity, spirituality etc. can principally be put into bits and bytes, banned onto a printed circuit-board and materialized through speech processors and actuators.

2.1.3 a) Excursion: What a Difference a Chip makes...

In his paper *"Fehlende Qualia, Schwindende Qualia, Tanzende Qualia"* Davd J. Chalmers (1996) proposes the *"Prinzip der strukturellen Invarianz"* (principle of the structural invariance[178]), which means: if given a system A that possesses conscious experiences, every other system N that with sufficient similarity possesses the same functional organization or structure as system A also possesses the same conscious experiences as system A. (paraphrased from Chalmers, 1996 : p. 368)[179].

Chalmers (ibid) provides us with a nice thought experiment by assuming a conscious human being with a biological brain consisting of neurons on the one side and a robot with a "brain" consisting of silicon-chips on the other. Step-by-step one neurone is replaced by a chip that takes over the exact function of its biological counterpart. According to arguments like the *"Chinese Room argument"* by Searle (Searle, 1980), the robot on the other end of the scale would not possess consciousness but only process data. But since the replacement of neurones through chips won't change the human's functionality, it also won't change ones behavior. It's just that one would (gradually) switch from a conscious being to a simulation; and according to Chalmers, such assumption would lead to unsatisfying results. Without wasting too much time

---

[178] Translation by Miriam JS Leis

[179] German original quote: *"[...] gegeben sei ein System, das bewußte Erlebnisse hat; dann hat jedes System, das dieselbe funktionale Organisation in hineichend feinkörniger Weise hat, qualitativ identische bewusste Erlebnisse."* (Chalmers, 1996 : p. 368)

with further explanations I just would like to summarize the implications: there exist arguments which state, that it is simply a matter of technology if conscious machines could be created. But what in my view remains not discussed in Chalmers' presentation is the question what if a single chip replacing a neuron really extinguishes consciousness? Then I wouldn't even know from the "leap", and that I entered the "simulation mode". However, such questions cannot be evaluated. I just wanted to provide an example that the (dis)similarity between (wo)man and machine is widely discussed.

And with the advances of genetic engineering, neuroscience and cybernetics more and more models pop up, that treat the human being as a sophisticated machine. Intelligence and behavior are determined by genetics and programmed through cultural learning, (re)actions are based on feedback mechanisms and emotions are just the result of specific chemical reactions triggered by hormones. Are we just getting behind the "Human Architecture" and if so, is it an *"Open-H Architecture"*?

2.1.4 Downgrading and Upgrading: Restoring the Vanishing Borders

It seems as if humankind can only hardly deal with the idea of principally being not much different from non-humans in its surrounding. Darwin's theory has downgraded the "Culmination of Creation" to being just a "better ape". Recent discoveries in genetic engineering have revealed that (wo)men and mice have over 90% of their genes in common, making fuzzy the boundaries between all animals – and the human being is an animal. Since humans are proud of their ability to make scientific discoveries (something that still sets them apart from other living organisms) they find it difficult to refute their theories, although at the same time these downgrade them from their unique position. (Of course there still exist groups in the "modern world", especially in the US, which strictly reject Darwin's theory and keep hold to Christian creationism.) Maybe even the animal-rights movements not only stem from a sudden act of goodwill, but may also represent an attempt of restoring mankind's position as strong protector over the weak creatures needing protection.

With the advent of machines that not only move like humans but also show incipiencies of intelligence, the last borders are feared to fall. The materialized thoughts of a Julien Offray de La Mettrie that (wo)man is nothing but a machine, or the modern reversal that machines may not be distinguishable from (wo)man evoked new fears about the downgrading of the human being. New boundaries, new distinction-lines have to be found. Since intelligence per se as a criterion is deemed to be obsolete someday, and an eternal soul does not fit into a modern (but maybe into a post-modern) world-view, the arguments have shifted to simulations. Everything artificial, especially the human-like machine, is defined as just being a simulation, bogus, an illusion like *"Final Fantasy"*[180] and therefore setting it apart from the "real human". And the good (or bad, depending on ones standpoint) thing is that simulation arguments cannot be positively refuted. Neither can *"The Matrix"* or solipsism.

Other ways of dealing with the problem of permeable boundaries lie in the "postmodern" radical denial of their existence, promoted through *"Popular Quantum Mechanics*[181]*"* by fusing Oriental ideas like Zen-Buddhism and Hindu-Philosophy with paradoxes arisen through certain interpretations of the quantum-mechanical *Uncertainty Principle*[182], ending in the "holistic world

---

[180] This has been the first totally computer-animated movie where the characters nearly look indistinguishable from human actors.
[181] e.g. Capra 1991 or Wilber, 1984
[182] This is only a very rough explanation and I use the description depicted in popular literature and refrain from using the more complicated explanation based on wave-mechanics (since for this I would also have to write about Fourier-analysis and other theories), although this kind of explanation may lead to some misunderstandings. So for those interested in getting more scientific explanations I recommend referring to technical literature.
    In the world of (sub)atomic particles our "classic" understanding of being able to simultaneously measure the exact position and velocity of an object (as on a speed trap) breaks down. On measuring a (sub)atomic particle (e.g. an electron), it would be impossible to determine its exact position and momentum ("velocity") at the same time. Since electromagnetic waves are being used for measurement (the best thing one can do), the following problem occurs: in order to get exact data about the particle's position, it is

view" of eternal integration and eternal interconnectedness. Here "reality" itself becomes questionable, but (wo)man as the *observer* becomes more central than ever: mankind creates ones own (although maybe illusionary) "reality". That's why many interpretations of quantum mechanical processes have been accused of being anthropocentric[183].

x

Initial Point

Pre-Darwinism
human
animal

Downgrading

Darwin and modern genetic research :
human   animal

Upgrading

Animal Rights Movements, Ecological Movements:
human
protects
animal

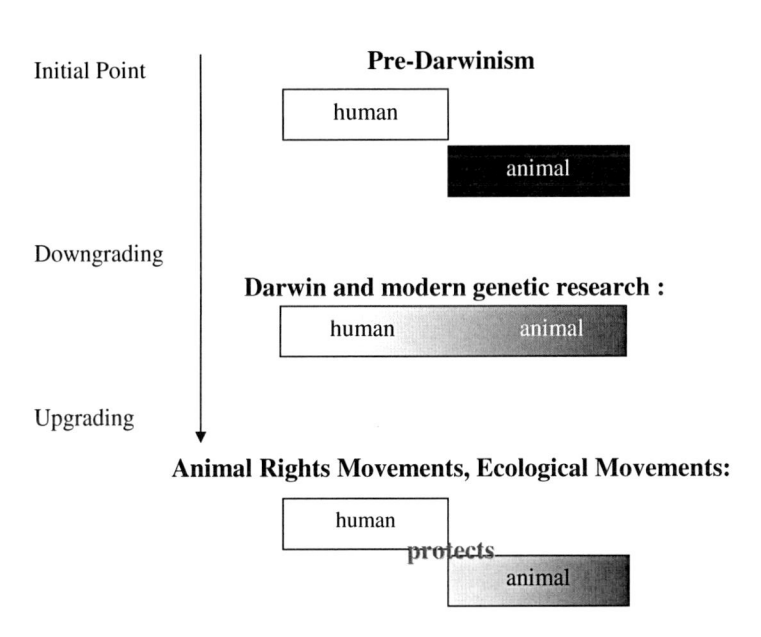

necessary to use wavelength that are as short as possible. Since short wavelengths mean high energy, by doing such measurement, the particle's momentum (or velocity) gets altered in an unpredictable (or only statistically assessable) way. If using long wavelengths on the other hand, the measurement won't have much effect on the momentum, but the resolution will get worse (just as one knows from classical optics) and therefore the assessment of the particle's position gets imprecise. This means that a (sub)atomic particle's properties cannot be evaluated with 100% certainty, which is something inherent to nature (although in our macroscopic world these effects are much too small and can be neglected for all practical purposes). These findings led to many speculations about reality, probability and the nature of our universe. (data taken from an article I have once written, which has been approved by a physicist.)

[183] Refer to Shimony, 1993

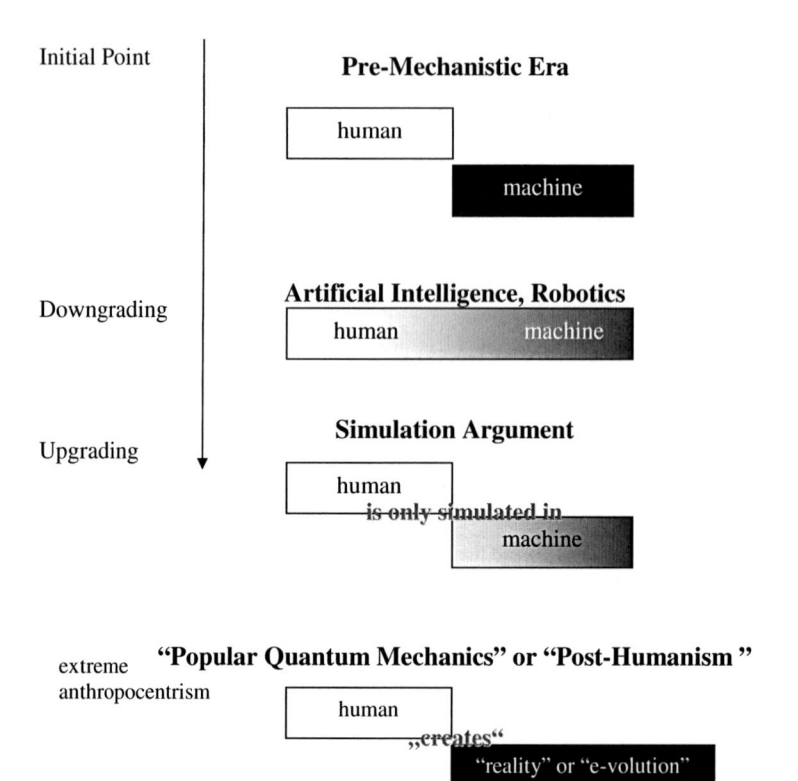

Initial Point — **Pre-Mechanistic Era**
- human
- machine

Downgrading — **Artificial Intelligence, Robotics**
- human | machine

Upgrading — **Simulation Argument**
- human
- is only simulated in
- machine

extreme anthropocentrism — **"Popular Quantum Mechanics" or "Post-Humanism"**
- human
- „creates"
- "reality" or "e-volution"

In this view the question about distinctions, the question about (non) restorable borders becomes increasingly pressing.

2.1.4.a) Short Reflection II: Was God just a mediocre engineer?

It is often stated that researchers in the field of robotics and Artificial Intelligence allegedly regard humans as being only a mediocre construction that could be technologically optimized. Although there might exist some arrogant people who may enunciate such thoughts, the overly majority of robot- and computer engineers I came to know has expressed just the opposite: through their research they have learned to even more respect the complex and thought-through design of the human being and how great the technological borders will remain on trying to mimic the biological original. Following the motto I have heard during childhood, never to disregard something as insignificant before having tried to do it oneself, what would be better in the quest of trying to respect and understand the human being, physiologically as well as psychologically, than building a robot?

2.2 Res Cogitans and Res Extensa - The Mind enters the Machine

Whereas purely mechanical automata only represented what Descartes described as Res Extensa, the non-thinking body, the computer can be seen as its counterpart: Res Cogitans, the thinking mind. Of course today's computers and computer-controlled robots are still far off the mark from a human's mental capabilities, but they also possess far more "mind" than the 17th century automata. /*While speaking about minds: it is interesting to notice that in Japanese the word for heart and mind is the same (心=*kokoro*: heart; mind)*/.

Whereas the classical strengths of computers and robots like performing fast calculations, precision work and doing complex logical analysis could be seen as complements to human abilities, today's computers and robots are already able to recognize people's faces and different objects (pattern recognition); some can even distinguish between animate and inanimate (at least to some extend), respond to questions in a (halfway) reasonable manner and can be taught processes through demonstration; aspects which are generally easy for humans, but quite difficult to implement in machines.

It is interesting to note how the human's definition of (machine) intelligence has also changed over time. At first the computer's capabilities of managing logical problem-solving and their successful performance in logic- and strategy based games like Chess and "Tower of Hanoi" were heralded as great achievements in the artificial (re)creation of intelligence. Now the "paradigm" has shifted and a computer winning a chess match is not regarded as an act of intelligence, but rather attributed to its capability of analyzing many thousands of potential moves per second according to a predefined pattern (algorithm). A Chess-computer is not regarded as "intelligent" anymore, but an ape defeating a Human chess champion would be called extraordinary intelligent (or extraordinary lucky)... But also in regard to humans there had been changes in consideration. Whereas at earlier times human intelligence has been predominantly associated with logical reasoning, new concepts like *"Emotional Intelligence"* or *"Artistic/Aesthetic Intelligence"* have emerged. These tendencies can also be viewed in the connection of the "Upgrading and Downgrading": as machines are beginning to take on characteristics previously exclusively associated with human beings, new differences have to be found to set them apart. But maybe the new borders will also become obsolete in the not too far away future. This can be seen in the changes of how humans control or even interact with machines. The possibilities of human-machine "communication", in the technical sense of the term [184], have changed dramatically over the years, for the programmer as well as for the end-user. As for the programmer, while at the dawn of the computer-age people still had to input strings of ones and zeros (machine code) to make the computer do something, a whole array of modern programming languages orient themselves halfway on natural languages (generally English), making programming easier for humans. And as for the end users, I still remember doing my homework on an old DOS-only machine (without *WINDOWS* interface), where I had to input

---

[184] A deeper analysis about different concepts of "communication" and thoughts about the possibility of human-machine communication can be found in the final part of my work.

strings of cryptic code just to define the margins, the font type (normal, **bold** or *cursive*) and get a printout, things that I can now do with a few mouse-clicks. Today, as I have seen it on trade-fairs, the end-user can already instruct machines in diverse manners which are similar to communication-patterns one is used to in human-human interaction, i.e. by using natural spoken language and even gestures. Also robots can already be instructed by using words and gestures that are similar to those used by humans in every-day-settings.

Machines themselves have become more communicable as well. Instead of just displaying text or making use of simple speech-synthesis, computer-generated moving representations of humans or other figures (avatars) are used to express mimic and gestures to underline the spoken word. Robots like the MIT research platform *Kismet* are already able to detect a human's emotional expression and display an according reaction[185]. This robot is even constructed to have (or rather display) a mood of its own. It shows traits which could be considered sociable: it "wants" to play, and "longs for" human contact. If it is left alone, it "becomes" (displays) sad(ness). Since *Kismet* serves as a research platform for studying social behavior and interaction, the robot's behavior is not generated through following preprogrammed patterns, but is said to emerge out of an architecture mimicking mammalian homeostatic functions and sensor-motor skills.

It looks as if the gap between humans and machines is becoming narrower. In the final part of my work I will tackle the difficult question about the remaining differences between the human-being and its artificial mirror-image. For now I just would like to capture the following: Since today's robots don't just show movement, but also commencements of what at least *looks like* intelligent acts and even *needs*, the clear distinction between (wo)man and machine may become blurred even more.

---

[185] Refer to: http://www.ai.mit.edu/projects/humanoid-robotics-group/kismet/kismet.html (MIT AI-laboratory's webpage about the *Kismet* robot, last accessed March 18, 2005)

2.2.1 Ever Failed a Turing Test?[186]

With putting the "mind" into the machine, questions arose about how to find out if a machine could be considered as "intelligent". A test was needed to actually measure the intelligence in the machine. One proposal, the so-called *Turing Test*, has been made by Alan Turing (1912 – 1954), the British ingenious mathematician and cryptographer (he helped cracking the Enigma code). His test-idea was based on the so-called "Imitation Game". Here a man and a woman are sitting in separate rooms. Both are provided with questions asked by a "judge", which have to be answered in written form. The goal of the game is that both, the man as well as the woman have to convince the judge that they are the woman. Turing proposed to use a similar test in order to tell the difference between human and computer. In this modified version a human and a computer, being in separate closed rooms are trying to answer questions provided by a human "judge" via teletext. The judge just sees the answers on his/her computer screen without knowing which text came from the computer and which from the human. Long time it has been hastily concluded, that if the judge is not able to distinguish the answers provided by the computer from those given by the human, then the computer would be considered (per definition) as intelligent[187] in a human sense. But what is intelligence? For some time computers, which were able to defeat a human master in a game of chess, were considered intelligent, but today it is only the human programmers who are granted this attribute. The computer only processes data. The same could be said about a computer, which could finally fool a person for getting mistaken for a human,

---

[186] For a good introduction to the topic of Artificial Intelligence and information about the *Turing Test*, you may refer to: Challoner, 2002 (Introduction work) and Görz / Nebel, 2003 (German)

[187] Some also say that solving abstract mathematical problems and strict logical reasoning *is* „intelligence". With such a definition some computers are already more intelligent than humans. If one takes the classic definition: "Intelligence is what an intelligence test measures", all computers could be considered as the most intelligent entities on earth if provided with the correct software – or only with the correct answers.

but as far as I know there has not been a confirmation about a successful Turing Test experiment yet. If a computer answers (or a robot acts) in the same way as one would expect it from a human being, it can always be said that it is (just) a masterpiece of programming and a *simulation* (if for example a computer is being asked to get the square root of 48 818 169, and after 20 minutes provides even a wrong answer with some explanation (refer to footnote), it could be regarded as a good simulation of human behavior[188]). A computer's answers (or a robot's actions) don't necessarily tell anything about "intelligence" (or "social competence" for that matter) or even "consciousness". A Turing Test may just measure how well a machine can *simulate* or *imitate* human-like behavior.

But there's still another problem about the Turing Test: it's asymmetric by assumption. It is always supposed that one can uncover the machine because one knows how a human would behave. But what if a human would "fail" a Turing Test and be wrongly classified as a computer? In my view this is not that absurd as it may sound. If looking at some badly written so-called "personality tests", which sometimes lead me into utterly confusion, because I don't understand the described situation or question, I think that it is just conceivable to state that Turing Tests are as culturally biased as the "Imitation Game", which served as inspiration. The questions and judgments derive from the *assumptions* that the questioner / judge has about (typical) human experiences, (re)actions, expressions, emotions, intelligence levels (e.g. a person with Asperger Syndrome may be highly intelligent, but lacks some basic understanding about meanings and procedures in human interaction). So what a Turing Test actually

---

[188] The answer is 6987. One option (algorithm if you like) to get the square root manually I remember from school is the following: first find the number of digits to the left of the decimal for the square root you want to find, remembering, that if squaring a two digit-number, for example, the result will never be below a three digit number and never above a 4-digit-number, meaning to remain below 10 000. Then you can try out squaring the numbers, which fall into your margin, preferably beginning with fives, so that you know if to stay in the upper or lower half. Repeat this procedure until you are closest to the number. With some reasoning-tricks, e.g. by knowing after trying the five that that last digit has to be a seven or using old results, it took me a little more than 15 minutes to get the square root without electronic assistance.

measures is how good a human's assumptions are about ones fellow humans. If the computer "fails", the human's assumptions have been sufficiently correct. If a computer does not "fail", one has learned that what has been assumed to be human-like behavior can at least be simulated in a machine. And if a human "fails" the test (by being mistaken for a computer), one gets to know that the assumptions about human behavioral patterns have to be revised.

There also exists another kind of *"Turing Test"* that might be considered to be a reversed form of the original idea[189], something that you may have encountered upon Online web registration forms. The test developed at *Carnegie Mellon School of Computer Science* is called CAPTCHA™[190], short for *"Completely Automated Public Turing Test to Tell Computers and Humans Apart"* that generally makes use of a human's superior ability of visually recognizing words and patterns displayed in distorted scripture, in order to prevent automated registration (or automated voting at Internet polls). In most cases the human user is required to look at an image of a word or numeral sequence displayed in a distorted form and enter the correct reading. Since it is (still) very difficult to write a computer program that is able to pass this computer generated test, CAPTCHA ™ (still) provides a way to ensure (with high probability) that only humans (and not automated bots[191]) are using the service or have initiated the process[192]. In this sense CAPTCHA ™ requires from the user to proof that (s)he is actually human and not a computer program or bot. If it would in fact be possible to write a computer program that can crack the CAPTCHA ™ or similar methods, this would also represent a great advancement in the area of computerized pattern recognition and AI. In this case another

---

[189] Although the term "Reversed Turing Test" is mostly avoided, since this describes a situation where a human deliberately tries to pretend that (s)he is the computer.
[190] Refer to the *CAPTCHA* ™ website: http://www.captcha.net/
[191] Computer programs that simulate a human (user).
[192] e.g. *CAPTCHA* ™ could be used to ensure that a certain e-mail has been actually sent by a human and with it prevent the sending of automated SPAM messages.

criterion for telling humans and computers apart would fade away, again leaving us with the question which differences remain. From this perspective "Turing Testing" has already become an arms race where new methods are to be found to distinguish human intelligence from its artificial counterparts, and new programs are to be written to let AI pass as human. Extrapolating on these observations I would predict that with the passage of time this will lead to a situation where it will become increasingly difficult to define consistent thresholds and create reliable tests that are able to tell the differences between "real" and "artificial" with sufficient accuracy.

x
x
x

2.3 The (Un)limited Animal

(N)ever there will be a be a technological solution to every problem caused by technology

[Miriam J.S. Leis, "*Sayako*"[193]]

As Arnold Gehlen has already put it, in some respect (wo)man is a "deficient being", German "*Mängelwesen*" (Gehlen : 1988 [1940[194]]) and therefore inferior to many other animals.

Humans are born "premature" as helpless beings, needing months for learning how to walk and talk, not to mention writing and arithmetic. On the other hand, humans are the only mammals with stable biped walking ability and the only animal knowingly around that has developed a language system and script that is complex enough to enable them the expression of abstract concepts. There exist animals with seemingly extraordinary abilities. Some can see

---

[193] It's from a story I began to write in 2003 about a human taking part in an experiment and mistakenly held for an android. I'm not sure if I will ever finish or even publish it...

[194] First published under the German title: "*Der Mensch. Seine Natur und seine Stellung in der Welt*" in 1940

infrared radiation, fly through the air, fall meters deep without getting harmed, detect tiny creatures from a distance of over 1 kilometer, live underwater, tear down whole trees with their sole body power and hear many times better than humans, but none of them possesses all these abilities together - with one exception: the human being. Although we don't possess those abilities as part of our natural physiological composition, we nonetheless manage to fly, dive, survive in outer space, see in the dark and not only see things many kilometers away, but even what's going on far away in our galaxy. We manage to lift tons of material, jump out of an airplane and land safely on the ground and even listen to what a person is saying half a world away, or even communicate with outer space. So humans may be physiologically deficient, but they have learned to compensate for this through the use of technology. Technology is mankind's attempt to solve problems, which arise due to the human's physiological limitations. But prior to thinking about ways how to solve a problem, one first has to regard a situation as problematic. Think about a rabbit being chased by a fox. Has a rabbit ever considered it problematic, that it cannot fly and that the possession of flying ability would maybe enhance its probability for survival? Or has a cat ever admired a fish's ability to breathe under water? The crucial point regarding the difference between humans and other animals is that (wo)men realize their deficiencies as such and have the desire to also possess all the abilities they don't have, the capabilities they admire in other creatures.

Of course also other intelligent animals like chimpanzees, gorillas and bonobos use some sorts of tools to compensate for some of their physiological shortcomings (e.g. using sticks to get ants out of narrow wholes they can't reach with their fingers), but their body remains the border of possibilities. They use tools rather as an extension of their body, e.g. use sticks to reach objects for which their fingers are too short or too thick, but not to acquire totally new capabilities, which lie outside the frame of their physiological architecture. Humans on the other hand can add totally new features to their physical ability through the construction of artifacts that enable them to perform tasks their body (and mind) is actually not able to do. Instead of having to adapt to the environment in order to survive as other animals have to do, humans try to reshape aspects of the environment to suit their needs. When the environment got too cold for keeping upright human body functions, at some point mankind was able to make fire artificially and fabricate clothes out of animal fur instead of either immigrating to warmer latitudes, hoping for a fire to occur incidentally or waiting until centuries of evolution enables some of them to manage survival in a harsh climate. From early tool-making on until today, mankind is constantly transforming and reshaping natural resources and raw materials into artifacts to fit its (assumed) needs. We call this technology. The term technology derives from the Greek word *techné*, describing an unnatural or artificial mechanism. In this way mankind has developed itself into a "multi-purpose" animal, whereas it has been due to this specie's physiological deficiencies that (wo)man has finally managed to colonize the whole earth and even live under water, in outer space and let machines do great deals of (wo)man's work. In this view it can be just considered as a consequence of further development that we can soon expect the widespread existence of human-machine hybrid entities. Nowadays the usage of such (permanent) technological aids is still mostly restricted to pragmatic purposes of compensating for disabilities in form of prosthesis, pacemakers, hearing aids and contact lenses. But considering technological trends, it is just conceivable that such devices will soon be used not just to compensate, but to enhance.

Humans have already reached a stage, where they are not only able to use technology as a means to *compensate* for shortcomings in their abilities, now they can even overcome, alter, extend and improve their own limited nature-given biological condition, at least in principal. Human evolution is not necessarily biological evolution anymore. A future of overcoming ones biological restrictions is especially envisioned by *Transhumanists*[195] (humans in the transition phase to *Posthumanism*) who ultimately seek a *posthuman* condition, where humans, with the help of science and technology will overcome their "human condition" by increasing and remodeling their mental, physiological and psychological capacities and finally become unlimited entities. Therefore *Transhumanists* especially support biotechnology, genetic engineering, nanotechnology, space exploration and the fusion of neuroscience and Artificial Intelligence to develop working mind-machine interfaces to reach their envisioned goal.

2.3.1 The Evolution of a *Cyborg*

By becoming a *Cyborg*, one may already be on the right path to a *posthuman* condition.

In common contemporary terminology, a *Cyborg*, short for **Cybernetic Organism** is described as a living creature consisting of artificial electronic and/or mechanical parts and natural organic components. Cybernetics, established in its modern form by Norbert Wiener (1894 – 1964), is a science studying communication and feedback control in living organisms *and* machines, while using the *same* language for describing both of them[196]. In his book "The Human Use of Human Beings: Cybernetics and Society" (Wiener, 1954) Wiener even drew parallels between the regulation of machinery (such as steam engines) and social institutions. It is mainly about the idea that similar processes govern biological as well as mechanical entities that brought about the idea of modifying and improving humans through the application of cybernetic technology.

---

[195] Refer to the website of the transhumanist "Extropy Institute" http://www.extropy.org/
[196] e.g. refer to Wiener, 1961 [1948]

The term *Cyborg* was coined by Manfred E. Clynes and Nathan S. Kline, who in 1960 envisioned a symbiosis between humans and machinery to enable survival on extended space flights and in extraterrestrial environments [197]. Originally the term was being popularly used to describe humans with mechanical / mechatronic components like pacemakers or prostheses attached to or integrated into their body. Since in science fiction the concept of *Cyborgs* is often used in a negative way (e.g. *"Darth Vader"* from *"Star Wars"*, the *"Borg"* from *Star Trek* or the *Cyborg* creatures portrayed in *"The Terminator"*, *"Robocop"* or some B-movies like *"American Cyborg"* or *"Class of 1999"*) the term has gained a somewhat negative association.

Nowadays the usage of the term *Cyborg* has become increasingly blurry, fuzzy and overtaxed. Some extend the definition of a *Cyborg* to people somehow living in symbioses with-, or depending on modern electronic gadgetry, like regarding a (cell-)phone as an extension of a human's ears and voice, or a computer and electronic memory devices as an extension of a human's brain. One can even go farther by proposing that mankind's first creation of artifacts for coping with problems due to a human's biological makeup has already turned humankind into *Cyborgs*. In this sense the first *Cyborg* may have been a (wo)man wrapped into an animal's fur.

To distinguish the man-machine hybrids depicted in science fiction from actual humans commonly using technological artifacts for external supplementation such as cell phones, computers, digital memory devices, contact lenses, and borderline cases like mechatronic exoskeletons to enhance ones physical strength[198], Alexander Chislenko has coined the term *"Fyborg"* (**F**unctional **C**y***borg***) for describing the latter.

---

[197] Published by Clynes an Kline in the technical magazine *"Astronautics"* in 1960 under the title "Cyborgs in Space".
[198] e.g. the *Hybrid Assistive Limb-3* developed by Yoshiyuki Sankai or the *Power Assist Suit* developed by *Activelink Co.*, both mechatronic "wearable exoskeletons" that can be attached to the body to enhance physical strength and abilities.

In her *"Cyborg Manifesto"*, Donna Haraway (Haraway, 1991) has used the *Cyborg* as a metaphor in her (postmodern) feminist writing, reflecting on the problem of categorization practice and identity construction, calling for a political new-orientation in a world where boundaries between (wo)man, animal and machine are revealed as being blurry, asking: "what kind of politics could embrace partial, contradictory, permanently unclosed constructions of personal and collective selves and still be faithful, effective – and, ironically, social-feminist?" (ibid : p. 157). The *Cyborg* is androgynous.

Maybe *Cyborg* advancement will replace mankind's natural evolution.

Our future (post)human world may consist of the following[199]:

"Pure Humans" (maybe on the brink of extinction or as a new counter-movement against *posthumanism*.
"Fyborgs" (Functional Cyborgs using technology as external supplementation)
Genetically Altered Humans (may also include "Fyborgs")
"Cyborgs" (humans with integrated mechatronic supplementations, may also be genetically altered)
Organic Machines (machines with organic components such as human neurons)
Robotic Androids / Artificial Life (non-organic machines that possess characteristics of life)
Humanoid Robots (robots that look like humans and simulate human traits)
Artificial Intelligent Machines (machines that can adapt to their environment, cope with changes, learn etc.)
"Pure Machines" (machines without Artificial Intelligence; may become obsolete)

---

[199] Maybe this has to be indicated in future passports and ID-cards: PH / FYB / GAH / CYB

2.3.2 Reflections on Technology and Society

Technological progress has enabled mankind to achieve such sophisticated technologies that even experts find hard to understand, and which lie completely outside the realm of a human's manufacturing skills to produce without the help of other sophisticated technology. One cannot produce a complete modern computer without the aid of other computers. In this way modern (wo)man has already got greatly dependent on machines. Of course, after a last flight with an airplane, one can chose to leave civilization and technology behind, but since humans remain deficient being, survival would be hard.

The human being has become increasingly dependent on technology, voluntarily and non-voluntarily. In the following I would like to provide you with some examples which lead to the question, in how far technological artifacts have changed our way of life and in how far they can be regarded as integral part of human society or even social actors?

2.3.2 a) Reflection: Fast and Ubiquitous

In modernized countries technology has really become a ubiquitous – ever present – phenomenon, as it has been the slogan at *CEATEC*[200] 2004 / Japan. If visiting (information) technology fairs like *CeBIT* (Germany) or *CEATEC* (Japan), one gets a good picture about how technology and modern lifestyles are connected, commercialized and marketed. Human models are posing with the latest cell-phones, MD- and MP3 players, digital cameras and handheld PDAs like presenting the hottest fashion trends. Life without digital cameras and cell phones[201] is suggested to be impossible. And even in less (technologically) developed countries the cell phone has already permeated society as my travel experiences have revealed. At some point cell phones have developed into something like a lifestyle-phenomenon. From a

---

[200] CEATEC = Combined Exhibition of Advanced Technologies. It is the Japanese equivalent to Germany's CeBIT.
[201] A cell phone (in Germany called handy) is a sub-set of mobile phones; mobile phones include cell phones, satellite phones and other portable phones which enable wireless communication.

sociological viewpoint lifestyle can be defined as a specific, characteristic way of life, distinguishable from that of other groups. It includes aspects of culture, fashion as well as ideology. Especially with young people ring-tones, pictures, logos, games, handy straps, mascots and cell-phone designs are often regarded as representing the owner's personality, interests and group-affiliation and provide a similar symbolism and effect as fashion. Ironically the mass availability of such products counters their exclusiveness and robbing them of their status of being a life-style phenomenon, since they become phenomena of the majority. I remember well, when the first people with digital cell phones (not that rather bulky car phones) appeared in the 1990s on the streets. At this time the technology was still associated with something exclusively for top managers or diplomats. Now it is rather associated with teenagers and youth culture, because they are the ones who make most use of the commercialized features such as ring tones, games and multimedia messaging. (I'll return to the topic of "Lifestyles" in more detail in Part III of my analysis about Sony's popular robot dog *AIBO*[202].) Also interesting is the observation that more and more features become integrated into the cell phone, which already leads to a point where consumers, who often by far do not use the whole potential of the device, get confused. Nonetheless many opt for models with as many functions as possible, causing the industry to cramming even more features into the gadget.

But it is not that technology has to keep up pace with the needs of society, as it has been said at the Information Technology exhibition. It is rather the other way around: people have to keep up pace with technology. My cell phone I bought in 2003 as one of the latest models seemed to be already outdated after one year. And if the mobile development continues with the current pace, in a not too far away future, many doors will remain literally closed to those without the latest mobile phone, as features like payment, ticketing, access, information-providing are planned to become all controllable with ones portable phone.

I still keep an old computer to be able to read and copy the files stored on 5.25 inch disks, utterly outdated if compared to my Memory Stick Duo ™. Times also change faster. Never before in history have consumption goods been so short lived like today and the trend is even going towards faster overtakes, which may only be countered by a growing ecological awareness. It's not the physical lifespan of

---

[202] AIBO is a popular and sophisticated entertainment robot resembling a dog, being marketed by the Sony Corporation. For more information about AIBO refer to Part III of my analysis.

products that determines their durability, but the next zero-point upgrade. It's a kind of circle: because the industry is interested in selling new products, an environment has to be produced which suggests that products are already outdated. To keep this "promise", innovation work is running on full speed. Since the competition between companies producing the same kind of goods and services is huge, one gets nearly constantly information about new products with clearer images, larger memory and longer battery life span. Regarding this it is no wonder, that criticism arises and counter movements are being formed, which suggest that the only alternative to break the circle is to get "off the train".

As the example of IT presents, the trend is going increasingly into the direction of entertainment and fun. Originally IT-solutions were thought out for military purposes (e.g. deciphering, surveillance) and then were employed for rather pragmatic use in the industry, business and large administration. Only after entertainment-oriented applications have been worked out that could suit the general public and can be distributed at affordable prices, it became a mass phenomenon. Now, innovations like smaller memory devices, faster processors, wireless solutions and batteries with longer operation duration are not only developed for professional and research applications, but also to come by the customer's (suggested) wishes in an economical rationale. Also in robotics the trend is shifting from the pragmatic usage in the industry to fun and entertainment. But if robots represent something special, how short-lived are they allowed to be? In regard to Japan the advent of *AIBO* led the producer thinking over the common practice of "no spare parts available after five years", as people want to keep their old ERS-110 (the first *AIBO* model marketed in 1999) to which they have developed even some emotional attachment.

2.3.2 b) Reflection: No Serviceable Parts Inside

Life with technology has become easier and ubiquitous, at least in so-called modern societies. While more and more people are using it, paradoxically, fewer and fewer users know how it works. Do you know how a cell-phone works? This is the shadow side of user-friendliness. As I know from own experience in simple programming, the more user friendly I designed the user-interface, the more complicated the program got, especially for those who didn't know much about the programming, causing them to call me on the plan if something went wrong – and I have to admit, if someone calls me now, I would need some time to figure it out. Or just consider simple mechanical toys. One can disassemble them, look inside, get behind the mechanism and reassemble them, having learned at least something about mechanics. In contrast to this, modern technology comes in a black box. As I opened my computer, I didn't get much more insight about how it works. All I saw were printed circuit boards, chips, colored cables, a fan and some modules labeled: *"No serviceable parts inside. Opening the Cover will invalidate the guarantee"*, leaving me with the question what is meant by "serviceable" - useful? Anyhow I opted against opening the cover, because of the threat that otherwise my guarantee would become void. The "aha-effect" that mostly has been the result after disassembling simple technological devices has failed to occur in this case. In some way the informed citizen has already heard about transistors, logic-gates, binary code, bits, bytes (a sequel of 8 bits), algorithms, C++ and Java, but to most of them the concepts remain somehow abstract. You cannot watch it while it works – ever seen a bit passing?[203]

In this regard it is not surprising that although a growing number of people are using technology, the number of people really interested and knowledgeable in how it functions is on the decline. As with everything insufficiently understood, this kind of "ignorance" also easily leads to irrational fears about technology, giving the impression of something incontrollable, even mysterious behind it. Many just see the results: computers and robots are fast and accurate, especially in those areas humans have some difficulties with, like getting the square root of 48 818 169 (which is 6987 by the way), what makes them look omnipotent in a way. But maybe you will be comforted by the fact that the common computer is actually not very intelligent by human standards and still has a rather hard time on getting by with seemingly simple tasks like pattern recognition, although they are getting increasingly better with this. The computer's strength just lies in its ability to perform simple sets of operations very fast and very accurately. Although the single operations for finding square roots, which can bee regarded as yes-no-questions (e.g. bigger or lower than the number you want to find the square-root of), are rather simple in themselves, but put together the whole procedure is quite time consuming for a human to perform manually. But

---

[203] Although outdated, as a good introduction work for getting a historical (and technical) overview about the first computers, I can recommend a quite old book: *"Mein Erster Computer"* by Rodney Zaks, 1982 (English title: Your First Computer, 1980).

there exist a very few people, who can perform such operations nearly as fast as computers. Many, including myself consider *this* eerie, because we know that these people are human beings.

2.3.2. c) Reflection: The *Techno*-Paradox[204]

The "*Techno-Movement*" as part of the youth-(sub)culture of the late 20th and early 21st century, which nearly totally excludes people older than in their mid-thirties, seems to inhibit the paradox of a confused people (and it still confuses me). In "*Techno*" the initial optimistic, progressionist and heavily criticized philosophies (at least in Germany) of artists like the German band "*Kraftwerk*" ("*We are the Robots*", "*Radioactivity*[205]", "*The Man Machine*"), who proposed a peaceful and fruitful co-existence between humans and technology symbolized through their excessive use of computers-generated music, shifted to a passive, unreflective absorption of technology by the multimedia- and cell-phone-generation, representing the *black-box* mentality induced by a "no-serviceable-parts-inside" label. *Techno* is a paradox shifting between the poles of music and machine, creativity and computer, precision and free expression, technology and love parade, archaic dances with LASER-light, artificially achieved natural happiness, and collectively celebrated individuality.

Even some elements of Japanese culture have entered the scene of "*Trance*" and "*Techno*", where symbols oriented on Japanese Manga/Animé figures (including robots) and *Katagana*-script[206] ornaments can be found on fan articles, flyers and music labels. And although Japanese popular music is not very renowned outside of

---

[204] The raw data for this excursion has been mainly obtained through browsing through Internet forums like www.technokrone.de or http://forum.techno-community.org (although they have not been very informative), looking at pictures of flyers using the google.de picture search by inputting "techno flyer" or "rave flyer", by looking at CD labels, by referring to the study by Falko Blask and Michael Fuchs-Gamböck (1995), through superficial personal observation (although these have been not very extensive, since I did not intent to do extensive research on this topic) and what one gets to know through the media. The rest is hypothetical. The initial point of doing this has been the fact that I was totally confused of how to interpret this new phenomenon – and I have something intrinsically against paradoxes.
[205] "[...] Radioactivity is in the air for you and me [...] Radioactivity tune into the melody [...]", excerpt from the text of "*Radioactivity*", original English version.
[206] Japanese uses four types of scripts (*Kanji*, *Hiragana*, *Katagana* and *Roman* Letters), whereas *Katagana* is generally used for words of non-Japanese origin (e.g. ロボット = Robot)

East-Asian countries, *Trance*-Tracks of Japanese pop icon *Ayumi Hamasaki* (remixes) and Japanese producers like *Takkyu Ishino* have made it into the charts of European clubs, and the refrain of a "*Eurobeat*[207]" song I was just listening to goes "*made in Japan, made in Japan – we'll fly to the sky*"[208], the next one had some Japanese wording[209] (although it didn't make much sense). Maybe this stems from the image of Japan as forerunner in the area of consumer- and entertainment electronics from *Game Boy* to the robot dog. And indeed, Japan's image as "*High Tech Nation*" has also found its entry into films and literature as the japanized environments in William Gibson's "*Neuromancer*" (e.g. "*Chiba City*[210]"), Ridley Scott's "*Blade Runner*" (e.g. the Japanese influence in the city with its *Katagana-billboards*, Japanese wording in "*Citytalk*" and the huge electronic screens that look like those one can find in Tokyo's districts of Shibuya, Shinjuku and elsewhere, showing commercials with a Japanese *geisha*), and "*The Matrix*" , where they used mirrored Japanese *Katagana* and Korean *Hangul* scripts to symbolize the matrix-code, indicate.

Let me shortly comment on the paradoxes:

Music and machine: Not so long ago for many "music" and "machine" have sounded like incompatible concepts. Music has been associated with human creativity, something a machine lacks per definition. Of course the usage of electronic music instruments like electric guitars already dates back to the mid 1950s. But it has been the invention of the Synthesizer[211] that paved the way for the development of electronic-generated music. Pioneers and Trendsetters in this field can be said to be the German band "*Kraftwerk*" (since mid-1960[212]), which anticipated the digital revolution. They can also be regarded as the first ones displaying a new philosophy:

---

[207] This is a radio channel I receive in Japan over satellite which plays the latest club music from Europe
[208] I'm not sure if "we'll fly to the sky" is the exact wording, but you got the picture.
[209] Interestingly Takkyu Ishino used in his production "Ich bin…" German wording.
[210] A great deal of the story plays in Chiba, Japan's traditional hub for research and development.
[211] An electronic musical instrument which produces sound through the manipulation of electric currents.
[212] Their latest album "Tour de France" (2003) had been a Bestseller at the Internet retailer *amazon*.

the unity and friendship between humans and machines[213], expressed through their computer-assisted sound creations (or should one say human-assisted computer-sound creations?). Their music included titles like "*We are the Robots*", "*Computerlove*", "*The Man Machine[214]*" and their viewpoint got symbolized through their famous staging of "*We are the robots*", where "androids" have substituted for the band on stage.

Creativity and computer: With the invention and marketing of MIDI[215]-instruments, the widespread usage of computers in production and the practice of "mixing", "music" has rather become rearrangement than creativity. Somehow here the feared loss of human's originality through the usage of computers (Game Boy instead of reading, "virtual reality" instead of fantasy) is reflected in this trend. Computerization and rationalization has now entered the arts, the last bastion of human creativity. In *Techno*-productions the human only plays a supporting role by pushing buttons – and often doesn't know what exactly (s)he is doing there (with the help of my computer and some cheap software I even managed to produce rudimentary techno mixes myself at home in less than half an hour. And if I run the sequence through the program, I get a new variation). *Techno*-music is mass-production, moneymaking through automation.

Precision and free expression: As I have noticed, for many *Techno*-fans self-expression through dancing and appearance is central. But doesn't this stand in sharp contrast to the frantic, monotone, dictating, precise and automated beat of the music that crushes every off-beat-thinking? And if one sees the dancers[216] who through simple lack of space aren't able to perform more movements than just stamping feet and lifting arms, which actually looks much less expressive than *QRIO's* programmed sequences, I doubt the possibility of free expression. And the "*Rave*" (Grand Techno Event) actually is nothing but collectively celebrated mass-produced individuality. Everybody is primarily preoccupied with one self, but can only

---

[213] I'm referring to an article in the German news magazine *Focus*, 11.08.2003 p. 130
[214] "Man Machine, pseudo human being, man machine, super human being [...]", text from "The Man Machine", English version.
[215] Musical Instrument Digital Interface, making it possible to simultaneously simulate the sounds of diverse instruments.
[216] I have seen such scenes on television

achieve this narcissistic experience through ones fusion with the masses. Since everybody drives ones self-expression to the extreme, finally nobody stands out.

Archaic dances and LASER-light: Strongly associated with the physical bodily experience is the *Techno* central theme of the dance, which Blask compares to the primitive, archaic, ecstatic dances of "indigenous people" (Blask, 1995). What is surprising is the strange combination, the usage of modern technology and computers, sound machines and LASER-light to induce archaic feelings, beats created by bits. Does this represent the "*raver's*" secret wish to return to ones origin, but can't find ones way back without GPS assistance?

Artificially achieved natural happiness: The dilemma between the artificial and the natural is also exemplified through the practice of *Techno*-specific drug consumption like *Ecstasy* (MDMA). This illegal synthetic drug induces feeling of empathy, emotional openness and intensive joy. But the feeling is not real, it's artificial, it's a deceptive simulation. In this context one has to ask the inevitable question, if humanity has really already reached a point where once-said intrinsic characteristics of human beings can only be achieved trough technical assistance?

Technology and love parade: And finally what sense to make of the *Love Parade*, the world's largest *Techno*-events originating in Berlin and now being held in many countries around the world "*Techno*" and "*Love*", a contradiction? Or does one have to ask whose love for whom? Love for others, love for technology or just love for oneself, community mediated only through the *Short Message Service*? To me as the non-involved "armchair-observer" (if I want to visit overcrowded places I prefer Tokyo's subway at 07:30 AM) it looks like an apolitical mass demonstration, coherence without communication, dictated by the beat of a computer-guided machine.

I still don't know how to understand the phenomenon. I still don't know if here technology is celebrated, protested against or just absorbed; if the "*Rave*" has to be understood as enthusiasm, rage or just ramble. Does *Techno* reflect a generation without orientation, for which there cannot even be found a label? (Suggestions include post-modern, post-industrialized, deconstructionist, individualistic, technologist, multimedia-society, information-society, fun-society, Nintendo-generation, risk-society, even "Transhuman" etc. etc. – short: "Generation Y"). Is it just this "anything goes" mentality, absorbing the surrounding without digesting it, a factor which is even materialized in *Techno*-music itself that often only recycles old melodies (e.g. *"Somewhere Over the Rainbow"*), underlies it with a computerized beat and mixes in some computer-generated sounds. Is it usage without understanding, the consumption of what is presented in the black box? Is it the resignation of a generation, which is overtaxed by the sheer amount of audiovisual information? Overdrive?! The only thing I understand is the precision and predictability of the beats. Maybe it's like the electron – if one tries to measure it, you lose information.

2.4 Where to Place Artifacts?

2.4.1 The *"Blade Runner Complex"* and the Elimination of "Quasi-Objects"

Philip K Dick's science-fiction novel *"Do Androids Dream of Electric Sheep"* [217], the basis for Ridley Scott's movie *"Blade Runner"* (1982) may represent a nice portrayal of what Bruno Latour has described as the "purification process" in modern societies (Latour, 1993), that is the modern Westerner's constant occupation with dividing phenomena into either being natural or artificial. This gets insofar increasingly difficult since modern societies constantly produce what he describes as "hybrids" (ibid), creations like genetically altered maize, existing somewhere between nature and artifact, which then in the "purification process" are to be ex-post divided into the binary categories of either only-nature on one side or only-artifact on the other.

I have found extreme examples of "hybrids" on both sides: the unconscious human patient on life-support machines in a hospital's IC-Unit (whereas here IC (still) means *intensive care* and not *integrated circuit*) and the humanoid robot

---

[217] Unfortunately some of the philosophical aspects considered in Philip K. Dick's novel don't come out that clearly in the otherwise awesome movie.

equipped with sensors and Artificial Intelligence. Intelligence, is it something natural or artificial? And what about products of genetic engineering? These aren't "natural", but neither can they be regarded as "artificial". The gene is natural, but it has been the human who made the gene a "gene", who made the gene an *object* of research, who altered it, and the media made society to belief. Following the ideas of Michael Serres, Latour called these entities between object and subject "quasi-objects" or "quasi-subject" (ibid).

"*Blade Runner*" is about a group of human-made androids (engineered *cyborgs*, which in nearly every aspect resemble human beings) that have illegally come to earth from a Mars colony. Professional android-hunters, so-called "*Blade Runners*", are engaged to hunt down these androids[218] (illegal aliens?) and destroy them. Since the androids get increasingly sophisticated in simulating human beings, it gets (nearly) impossible to tell an android from a real human being and with it the difference between man and machine. The Blade Runner, Rick Deckard (an allusion to René Descartes?), is now confronted with central questions about what distinguishes a "real" human from a "fake" android? In a world where it is extremely hard to distinguish between the "real" and the "artificial", it is even harder to set crisp thresholds and clearly separate from each other the elements belonging to one set or the other. The android in "*Blade Runner*" represents a top example for Latour's "quasi-object" which quite literally is to be eliminated from the realm of human society. First (s)he / it exists in a kind of suspension between human and non-human, but such situation is unacceptable to the "modern mind". The difference between a "quasi object" (android, artificial animal) and a "pure"-subject ("real" human, "real" animal) has become so small that more and more sophisticated "scientific" methods, e.g. the *Voigt-Kampff empathy test,* the *Boneli-Test*, complicated bone-marrow-tests etc., have been developed in order to *define* the entity's identity. I

---

[218] Entities with genetically engineered organic and mechantronic parts. In the movie they are called *Replicants*.

stress the word *"define"*, because the more complex and complicated these *culturally-colored* tests get (the *Voigt-Kampff empathy test* has its basis on a kind of religious attitude, called "Mercerism"), the more error-prone they become (in a way the story can also be regarded as hinting on Latour's and Woolgar's laboratory studies (Latour / Woolgar, 1979), where it is suggested that scientific discoveries are the products of *social construction*[219].) The test results decide about her/his/its fate to be either *defined* as being "really human" or as being an object illegally pretending to be human that has to be terminated. But these androids, like Latour's "quasi-objects", have been created by humans themselves as something being in a suspension between subject and object. In an *ex-post* process this suspension is then to be wiped out *per definition*. In this way the story can also be seen as a *critique* against the *"purification process"* and forced binary categorization of "quasi objects" into the set of "pure-objects", which has to be taken quite literally in this context: one for life and zero for death - a fatal consequence for a human if done "wrong" and for the android if done "right". Measurement causes determinateness, as quantum physics has taught me. But one can chose how to measure and with it how to determine. If I want a wave, I get a wave and if I want a particle I get a particle, but why is it so hard not to measure and accept that it might be both at the same time?

---

[219] Since science is about measurement and *interpretation*, and experiments often are inconclusive, it can not be objective criteria that contribute to the acceptance of a theory. Rather it is the experimenter's own social and cultural background, which influences and/or guides his/her interpretation and decision about what data to accept (Latour / Woolgar, 1979). The history of quantum-mechanic interpretations (from strict positivism to metaphysical interpretations of Capra and Bohm) also represents a nice example.

A difficult job for a „*Blade Runner*"...

left : Miriam JS Leis, author of this book
right: "*Actroid*", android robot created by
"*Kokoro Dreams*" / Japan

Photo: Rudolf W. LEIS @ International

Although (at least as far as I know – I'm slowly getting paranoid through all this…) there still aren't any robotic androids in such sophistication as portrayed in "*Blade Runner*" around in our "real" world today, even now the binary "*purification process*" appears to become ever more difficult and problematic. The tendency seems to be clear: researchers are working on projects with the goal to make artifacts, i.e. robots, more human-like, not only in appearance, but also in regard to intelligence and emotional simulation. In 2050, according to the bold goals of world-wide researchers, there should be a robotic soccer-team with the realistic chance of defeating their human "templates". Doesn't this lead us into a paradox situation: if we then, after all our efforts are done, try to put this human-like "quasi-object" (or quasi-subject") back into the category of "pure objects"?

And where should one place the android Rachael from "*Blade Runner*"? If considering only the results on the *Voigt-Kampff-test* [220] Rachael is an android, a clear "zero" on binary coding, but it (she?) nearly passed the test. Shouldn't this give Rachael another value on the subject-object-scale than an object, artifact, entity or even human who would have clearly missed the test?

Over time artefacts have not only become more innumerable, as Latour has found out, but also harder to identify as "pure object". And for the sake of

---

[220] A kind of "*Turing Test*" described in the novel by Philip K Dick and also in the movie "*Blade Runner*".

symmetry we also have to take a look at the other side: the human-being. Having been engaged in the field of biotechnology in my previous study[221], I also came across the following: it is not only artifacts, which somehow exist in a suspension between subject and object, but also the human being itself. Nearly every day one can read about the discovery of genes which are said to be responsible even for aspects of our personality, taste, emotions, way of thinking etc. According to the renowned British psychologist Simon Baron-Cohen, differences in the mentality and alleged way of thinking between men and women, and even social disorders like autism are attributed to hormone distributions which have influenced a human before (s)he was born.[222] Does this mean that questions sociologists and psychologists have been pondering upon for centuries are just the result of genetic *programming*? We can *program* human beings (at least in theory) by altering genetic sequences. I will return to the question about "programming" in more detail in the Part IV of my work.

And what about people I mentioned before, who live with technological artifacts integrated into their biological matrix? What about so-called *cyborgs*, humans consisting of biological and artificial material or fusing with technological artifacts? How to code them on a binary table? Are they machines since they are partly artificial, or are they humans, because they are partly biological? Are they (still) natural or (already) artificial? But what if one (hypothetically) replaces all biological parts through mechatronic ones? Which replacement part defines the threshold between man and robot? What about a (hypothetical) clone? (S)he has been created *artificially* and not "naturally", but (s)he resembles exactly another entity who may have been created naturally. Therefore the clone may represent the ultimate paradox of an "artificial nature" and even questions the status of the person (s)he was cloned from. What criteria

---

[221] My *Magister Arbeit* (German "Master's Thesis") has been about European legislation in embryonic stem cell research.
[222] I'm referring to an article in the German Newsmagazine „Der Spiegel" Nr. 35/25.08.03, p. 90-92

should one use to define a human-being without referring to concepts like "soul" and "emotions"?

While our robots are to be equipped with more and more human-like features, humans are equipped with more and more machine-like features. While programmers try to make robots increasingly independent from their (pre)programmed frame, humans are revealed as being much more determined by (genetic, socio-cultural, hormone-based) programming. Where then is the fundamental difference between the "natural" and "artificial" located.

Before getting to the fundamental question where (seemingly) intelligent artifact might get placed in human society, I first would like to provide you with some examples of such "unclear objects" and comment on Actor-Network-Theory, which served as a guideline for my further considerations.

x

2.4.2 A Note on "Actor Network Theory"

One gets the impression that the term "Network" is on the edge of being overtaxed. I have several Computer Networks at home (just getting confused with all these different IP-Addresses), the *World Wide Web* is a network, environmentalists speak of networks between humans and nature, conspiracy-theorists talk about "Networks of power and corruption", and even some Chaos theorists and "quantum mechanists" philosophize about networks which connect the whole Universe (*Butterfly Effect*). Everything is connected, everything's linked with everything, so what remains? Networks are *ubiquitous* as it has been phrased at *CEATEC* 2004. What new insights can one get from another Network Theory? That everything is connected? We know that... Latour himself lamented about (t)his theory[223] being widely misunderstood and that his choices

---

[223] He was one of the founders of this „theory", which in fact is no theory

of the words "actor", "network", "theory" and the "hyphen in between" have led to misunderstandings– "Four nails in the coffin" (Latour, 1999 : P.14). Why this has been the case, and what in regard to communication went wrong would be worth an analysis, but lies outside the frame of my topic. As I remember from a rather mathematical-oriented course in Network Analysis, the network *topology* is formed by elements that are linked to each other, or as John Law put it: "[...] in a network elements retain their spatial integrity *by virtue of their position in a set of links or relations*" (Law, 1999 : p. 6)[224].

Actor-Network Theory (ANT) is actually not what some may call a "social theory", trying to explain human behavior. "Actor" is *not* the individual and "Network" is *not* the society. Instead the two are regarded as complements[225]. ANT can better be called a *method* (ibid) or maybe an approach for observation. Something that came into my mind which may serve as a suitable example has been shown just half an hour ago in a documentary on the German science magazine *nano*[226]. It was about technological devices that can be used to determine if a fruit (e.g. an apple) is already ripe (without taking a bite on it). To view this in a maybe Weberian way, where there are people on the one side, just *using* some devices as means on the other side, may not grasp the whole complexity. Through this technological device with an "Artificial Nose" (or rather with a sensor which can detect different chemical compounds), the apples get *classified* into categories of ripe and not ripe with a method that goes down to the molecular level. In this way humans *define* nature. The tested apple becomes a different apple than the untested apple or the apple *to be tested*. On the other hand, to get the data for constructing and programming the "Artificial Nose" and for setting the thresholds for defining "ripe", the researchers also relied on human experience about the taste and consistency; the "bite" data if

---

[224] Cursive taken from the original
[225] Latour (ibid) compares this to the quantum mechanical phenomenon of wave-particle complement
[226] Shown on Nov. 09. 2004 (MDR), although not in relation to Actor-Network Theory or ANT-like approaches

you like. Therefore the material - both the (natural???) apples and the (objective???) testing device - are not something that "is just there" ready to use, but in a way they are something surprisingly "human" and subjective (not to mention all the human-made theories which have been involved in the construction of the device). Here we go again with the manufacturing of "hybrids". Additionally there's an intention behind the construction of such a testing-device, which brings us to farmers, consumers and markets. This ANT-*inspired* description may have illustrated that it's about the way how to look at phenomena.

Actually it was the *symmetry* principle associated with ANT that states that in "ANT-approaches" human and non-human actants (the neutral term for actor) are treated with analytical equivalence, which drew my attention to ANT. An actant is defined as "something that acts or to which activity is granted by others" (Latour 1996 : p. 373) and is not bound to any "intrinsic" quality like consciousness for example. This notion and the Network "metaphor" have *inspired* me in my quest of searching for ways where (intelligent) artifacts may be placed in our society. With the following recollection of the flight catastrophe which happened in *Überlingen* in 2002, not that far away from where I live(ed), my friends comment on *ASIMO's* state visit to Prague and my suggestion for placing artifacts, I did not intend to directly contribute to ANT. It has rather been an ANT-*inspired* approach.

Example 1: TCAS[227]

The collision of the two planes at *Überlingen* / Lake Constance in the year 2002 may serve as a good example for demonstrating the entanglement of technical artifact and human beings during decision-making processes. On July 2nd 2002 two planes, coded DHX611 and BTC2937 have been approaching each other in the airspace over Lake Constance. The automatic computerized Traffic Collision Avoidance System (TCAS) on board the two planes has warned the pilots on each plane about an approaching machine ("traffic") and advised the crew on DHX611 to descend and BTC2937 to climb. This kind of evasive action is initiated through the communication between the two TCAS systems aboard each plane. TCAS advises the pilot aboard one plane to descend, while the other is automatically instructed to climb and therefore a collision should be avoided. But unlike the computer *HAL 9000* from the movie *"2001 – A Space Odyssey"*, TCAS just *advises* and does not take over the plane's controls automatically. This means that the human piloting the plane has to make the final decision if following TCAS' instruction or not. TCAS was not the only entity who has given instructions to the pilots. There was also flight control, consisting of human flight controllers dependent on the information shown on their radar screens, computers, forms of modern telecommunication, i.e. telephones and radios, and other human beings. The human flight controller, who had no idea about the TCAS' warnings on board of each plane, has also given instructions. The human ordered the BTC2937 to descend, while at the same time the plane's TCAS ordered to climb. The pilot decided to follow the human controller's instruction instead of TCAS's advise and descended. On board the DHX611, which was approaching the BTC2937, the TCAS advised the pilots to descend. At the same time the DHX611-pilots also heard a communiqué of a controller advising another plane also to descend. The pilots on board the DHX611

---

[227] This information is based on a documentary once shown on German TV

followed TCAS' instructions and descended without immediately informing flight control about their actions. Through this it came to the situation that both planes were descending, which finally led to the fatal collision. This tragic accident illustrates what could happen if humans and their technology aren't sufficiently tuned onto each other, if there's no protocol, whose instructions to follow. This led me to the conclusion that on the one hand it is necessary for humans to adapt to their technology, but on the other hand technology has to be designed in such a way that the human can manage working with it easily. Such considerations lead me to think about the role of technological artifacts in our society.

DHX611			BTC2937		
TCAS instruction	Controller instruction	Pilot action	TCAS instruction	Controller instruction	Pilot action
descend	---------------	descend	climb	descend	descend

There seems to have happened a kind of evolution in regard to technological artifacts from mere tools (e.g. a hammer) over artifacts which automatically perform complex operations, but only react to human commands/inputs (e.g. automata, conventional industrial robots) towards new kinds of artificial entities which also give advise to humans in regard to how they should act (e.g. "intelligent" computerized expert systems, TCAS). And the more "decisions" humans leave to technical artifacts, the more autonomy (here defined as acting independently on ones own choice) they lose. In a way we delegate part of our autonomy to our technology. Without TCAS the human, and the human alone, is responsible for avoiding mid-air-collisions with other airplanes. But with TCAS installed, not listening to this technical artifact quite probably leads to fatal consequences.

Since TCAS does not initiate the evasive action automatically (it just warns, but does not take over the plane's control from the human pilots), there exists a strange kind of nested decision-making. Based on its programming, TCAS advises the pilot to climb, to descend or to do nothing. The pilot on the other hand can make the *autonomous* decision to either do what TCAS suggests or not to do it. But as we have learned, acting against TCAS' advise probably leads to disaster. So if one installs TCAS one has to listen to it and therefore should delegate some autonomy to the technical artifact (i.e. do what the artifact commands).

Another question, which arises and which quite well illustrates the necessity for a re-analysis of human-machine interaction processes, is a legal one. Whose fault has it been? Certainly not that of TCAS. But since a human controller and a non-human automated system have given contradicting orders to the pilot, whose authority to follow in such situations; that of a human or a machine?

Some people said that if one has to do what TCAS (or any other artifact) suggests, it should not be used, because the final decision should be made by humans, and if humans will be forced to follow the commands of a machine, humans would finally end up being slaves of their own technology. But just think about why TCAS has been invented. It has been invented to disburden the humans from having to manage difficult and complex tasks like keeping track of all traffic-activities in the surrounding of a specific airplane and shorten the (re)action time. It also should make easier the work of the controllers and minimize accidents caused by human attention deficit and wrong decision-making by automatically calculating the best evasive maneuver. The only thing the human has to do in a critical situation would be to follow TCAS instructions, which is indeed much easier and faster to perform than locating the approaching plane by oneself (this could provide a real problem without technical assistance), analyzing its trajectory and telemetric data (for this one also needs technological artifacts) and come to an agreement with the other pilot how to co-ordinate their new flight paths (here again technology is needed – in this case one can not just open the window and shout). This takes time, and time is scarce in such an emergency.

But actually I'm not planning to analyze flight traffic and this has only been an excursion to demonstrate the interconnectedness of humans and technology in (complex) action processes. The question, which interests me most in this regard, is where to place technological artifacts in human society. Are they "mere objects" like stones (whereas one has to ask if there's anything like a "mere object") or should they be attributed the status of a (quasi) social actor, since they are already so deeply integrated into our activities and decision-making schemes, and even start to give us advise about what to do (e.g. TCAS and experts systems)? This question is also of special interest in regard to service-robots, since it is the final goal of many engineers to integrate them into human society.

Example 2: A Microwave-Oven on a State Visit ?

On the front page of the German newspaper "*Süddeutsche Zeitung*" (Saturday 23.08.2003) one could see the following picture: a white-colored entity, maybe the size of an eight-year old child, labelled "ASIMO", was walking along a floor. To his/her/its left (on the right-hand side of the picture) there stood a smiling and waving Japanese Prime Minister Koizumi. In the background there were about nine people - among them probably former Czech Prime Minister Spidla. In an Online Newsletter one could find the following corresponding article:

Robot ASIMO debuts as goodwill ambassador in Prague
Friday, August 22, 2003 at 12:41 JST
PRAGUE - Japan-made humanoid robot ASIMO debuted Thursday as a goodwill ambassador at a party hosted by Czech Prime Minister Vladimir Spidla for visiting Prime Minister Junichiro Koizumi.

"I'm honored to visit the Czech Republic, the birthplace of the word 'robot,' together with Prime Minister Koizumi, as a goodwill ambassador of Japan," ASIMO, a product of Honda Motor Co, said in Czech after Koizumi's address. (Kyodo News)

http://www.japantoday.com/e/?content=news&id=270304

A German friend of mine, Martina F., having heard about a robot accompanying a statesman commented on this: "it's like bringing along a microwave [oven]." I have shown her the picture and asked her if this artifact really resembles her microwave-oven (I was just curious), she answered: *"there might be an optical difference, but it's a machine anyway."*

This again reminded me to get back to the question "where to place such artefact", as subject (goodwill ambassador) or as object (machine) or as something in between? Can such problems be solved with a binary either-or-logic, or should one rather apply an approach based on the fuzzy-set-theory, as I would advocate it? Can objects (some day) be considered as being an integrative part of society, as the Japanese term of *"Partner Robot"* might imply, or as Kerstin Dautenhahn, researcher at the *Reading University* (England) envisions it when speaking of a *"Multi-Species Society"* (*"Multiarten Gesellschaft"*)?[228]

Already more than I have expected has been discussed about the question if robots can be called "acting entities". In 2001 (at a time before I started my dissertation) there has even been a sociological conference around the topic "can machines act" held in Berlin, whereas most participants decided on using a weak definition of "action" by artifacts, analogue to the "weak" definition of Artificial

---

[228] Refer to her webpage at: http://homepages.feis.herts.ac.uk/~comqkd/home.html

Intelligence[229]. Some robots are already able to determine their position in space and calculate the best way about how to reach a certain destinations[230], or to find a strategy for shooting a goal during a robot soccer match (*RoboCup*). Therefore they display although rudimentary capabilities of meaningful action in an unpredictable and dynamic environment, something that may even be called planning (although probably in a "weak" definition of the concept)[231]. In my view, the philosophical questions may be interesting and even useful for social theory, but I think it is also important to consider some technological facts. As long as a "von Neumann-architecture" is used for the computer to guide the robot, as it is the case with most of today's robots outside research institutions, the machine only does what a human has programmed into the system. So in this case one should rather speak about a robot's "actions" as a "human's transferred action scheme" inputted by a programmer. But I will return to this later in my "phenomenological considerations" in the Part IV of this work.

Nonetheless the artifact might give the human the *impression* of "autonomous action", just as the examples of computer-generated movies like "*Final Fantasy*" demonstrate, which finally lead to a confusing question: in how far can human actors be considered as acting autonomous while acting?

But to return back to the comments of my friend: even after providing her with a whole palette of abilities this robot can already perform and gave her a bright outlook into the future, it nonetheless remained just a machine to her and will continue to do so. (I'll ask her again in 2050...).

x

x

---

[229] Assuming that Artificial Intelligence will remain nothing but a simulation. (Refer to the final part of my work for further information).
[230] e.g. refer to http://www.care-o-bot.de/Produktblaetter/Produktblatt_Navigation.pdf (Produktblatt Navigation by the *Fraunfofer IPA*: „*Navigationswerkzeuge für autonome Fahrzeuge und mobile Roboter*")
[231] Refer to Grunwald, 2002

2.4.3 On Replacing Elements in a Network

At least to me, hearing "a robot on a state-visit", sounds more reasonable than "a microwave-oven on a state visit", whereas my friend and I don't have any problems with "Prime Minister Koizumi on a state visit". From an *ANT*-approach one could regard *ASIMO* as an element which is linked to others, forming a network consisting of statesmen, airplanes, the grave of Karel Čapek, diplomats, the Honda Corporation, security personnel, media representatives and maybe even myself. But doesn't the way how this robot is *regarded* by others also define its position – as "ambassador" or "microwave oven"? And if one looks at *Sakura SANAE*, the computer-generated virtual avatar, which in 2003 was appointed as Tokyo's goodwill ambassador to the ASEAN nations, the idea of using non-human entities as "diplomats" does not seem that absurd, at least to Japanese and some other Asian countries (according to the *Japan Times*, Nov. 25, 2003, the ministry's web server crashed on *SANAE*'s[232] introduction date due to the sheer amount of Asians visiting the site[233]). Or look at the example of the real sheep and the artificial sheep in Philip K. Dick's novel. Both can be said to have a function within some sort of network(s), but their *function* varies in dependence on the context. As a *status symbol* the artificial sheep fulfils the same function as a real one, but Deckard still longs for getting a *real* animal. In the first context the *artificial* sheep would get the same value on the "subject-pole" and the same position in the Network as a *real* sheep (since the real and the artificial ones are not easily distinguishable), but not so in regard to Deckard's personal view, simply because the *un*real is *not* real. If a robot performs the same work as a human nursing-assistant, then maybe those two can be principally regarded as the same, as being substitutable, because they fulfil the same functions and take the same place in the network? Some people may feel uneasy about this. Of course it can always be said in such situations that the

---

[232] Actually the name SANAE is an anagram of ASEAN
[233] You may want to have a look at: www.mofa.g.jp

function of a human assistant differs slightly from that of a robot in some respect, but what if this difference just lies in the fact that one entity is human and the other not? How should one explain that someone may reject being served by a robot, even if it represents a perfect simulation of a human actor and fulfils the same role in a network as a human would have? Isn't this what authors like Philip K. Dick (*"Do Androids Dream of Electric Sheep"*) and Brian Aldiss (his short story *"Super-Toys Last All Summer Long"* was the basis for the movie A.I. by Steven Spielberg) have pondered over by thinking about where to place so-called robotic androids?

Maybe some "intrinsic" elements, i.e. to be [human] or not to be [human] – to borrow from Shakespeare - are (still) of relevance when considering the question about the placement of artifacts as objects, subjects or somewhere in between.

In the following chart I have tried to illustrate the evolution of "quasi-objects" and a possible placement in our world. As you see, with the passage of time and the appearance of objects which possess ever more human-like characteristics, it becomes increasingly difficult to justify a strict dichotomous "subject-object" coding. Therefore I'd like to suggest an approach for the placement of subjects and objects by using a method taken from fuzzy-set theory and apply the method of assigning fuzzy membership values. In the following I will provide a more details explanation about the concept and some empirical findings.

"pure subject" ⟵⎯⎯⎯⎯⎯⎯⎯⎯⎯⟶ "pure object"

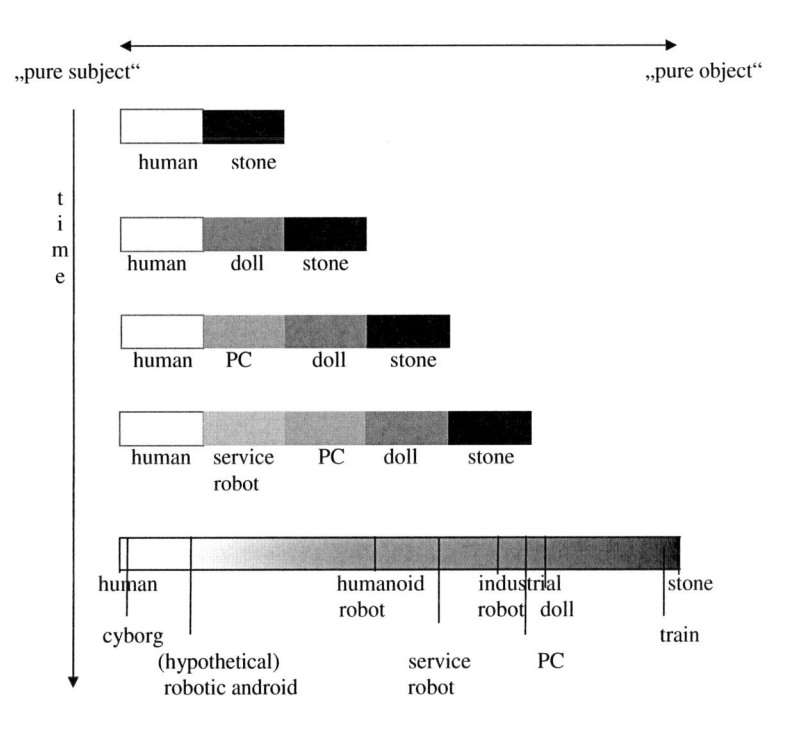

t
i
m
e

| human | stone |

| human | doll | stone |

| human | PC | doll | stone |

| human | service robot | PC | doll | stone |

human | humanoid robot | industrial robot | doll | stone
cyborg | | | | train
(hypothetical) robotic android | service robot | PC

Note: the lines only indicate rough positions where the entity could be placed. One can also consider the positions to show a certain degree of dispersion around the lines.

2.4.4 The Placement of Subjects and Objects in Germany and Japan

Interestingly, the idea of dividing the world into "pure object" and "pure subject" never occurred to me. I have always assumed a "fuzzy world" as I have illustrated it in the last of my graphs. Although I suppose the existence of subjects and objects, I do not assume clear thresholds between those poles. At first I hypothesized that this way of thinking may be the result of my socialization in Japan, where the *Shinto* and Buddhist religious and philosophical traditions also state no clear separation between the animate and inanimate. In Germany on the other hand I thought that the practice of clear subject-object coding might be a much more common practice. To find out possible differences between Japanese and German "coding-practices" I have planned to do a survey on this. But before I continue with commenting on the survey, I would like to explain what I mean by a *"fuzzy world"* and therefore provide a short introduction to fuzzy-set theory.

2.4.4.1 Fuzzy Logic and Fuzzy Objects - A Short Introduction to the Concept

The Japanese are talking so much about Fuzzy Logic that for long I have regarded it as a Japanese invention[234] - and I wonder why I haven't encountered the term in the context of my courses I took in sociology; it could have been a fruitful contribution.

The concept of Fuzzy Logic has been invented by the Iranian scientist L.A. Zadeh[235] who worked in the field of control theory. Controlling (conventional) machinery demands very precise inputs, since in contrast to humans, (conventional) computers aren't able to deal with imprecise information. For example if driving with a human friend in a car, I could give instructions like "please steer a *little bit* to the left" if I would think that (s)he is driving too close to the kerbstone on the right-hand side. Somehow a human manages to get along quite well with instructions like *"a little bit..."* But what about an old-fashioned robot? Probably it would have asked me to reformulate the question in a more precise way, demanding from me to specify the degree of deviation to the left relative to the current position in exact numbers. Quite probably I would have

---

[234] I would like to especially recommend the book by Mukaidono (2001), which provides a very good introduction into the field. For more mathematical explanations and background information the book by Tanaka (1997) is written quite well and sufficiently understandable for the mathematically interested reader.
[235] Refer to Zadeh, 1988

given a too-high value causing the robot to steer the car into the opposite lane (that's why I have finally decided on taking the bus).

Fuzzy Logic is about how to mathematically define such imprecise, mostly verbal concepts like "a *little bit*", "*tall* women", "*middle* income households", "*frequently*", "*soon*" etc. In classic ("non-fuzzy") set theory an element either belongs to a specific set or not (subject or object in what Latour has described). For illustration I will give you an example about a person's annual income and the classification into the category of "low income", "middle income" and "high income". In "non-fuzzy" coding, one has to define exact thresholds like "middle income" ranges from 25 000 Euro to 50 000 Euro of ones annual income. Everything below 25 000 is coded as "low income" and everything above 50 000 as "high income". Every element (income) belongs to exactly one set (either "low" *or* "middle" *or* "high"):

Annual Income (Euro)	Set		
	low income	middle income	high income
10 000	1	0	0
13 000	1	0	0
24 999	1	0	0
25 000	0	1	0
37 500	0	1	0
40 000	0	1	0
50 000	0	1	0
50 001	0	0	1
65 000	0	0	1

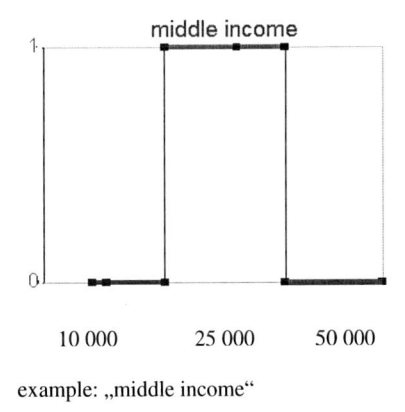

example: „middle income"

This would mean that having one cent more or less would decide if your income is "low", "middle" or "high". And if your taxes would be calculated on such basis, you would probably not be very satisfied. Considering this it would be more reasonable not to define the set-membership assignment of an element (income) on a strictly binary "*either-or*" basis, but to assign membership to a *certain degree*. This could look like the following (own example):

Annual Income (Euro)	Binary membership classification			"Fuzzy" membership classification		
	low income	middle income	high income	low income	middle income	high income
10 000	1	0	0	1	0	0
13 000	1	0	0	0.95	0.05	0
24 999	1	0	0	0.71	0.29	0
25 000	0	1	0	0.7	0.30	0
37 500	0	1	0	0	1	0
40 000	0	1	0	0	0.62	0.38
50 000	0	1	0	0	0.3	0.7
50 001	0	0	1	0	0.29	0.71
65 000	0	0	1	0	0	1

The fuzzy set for "middle income" (―) may look like the following:

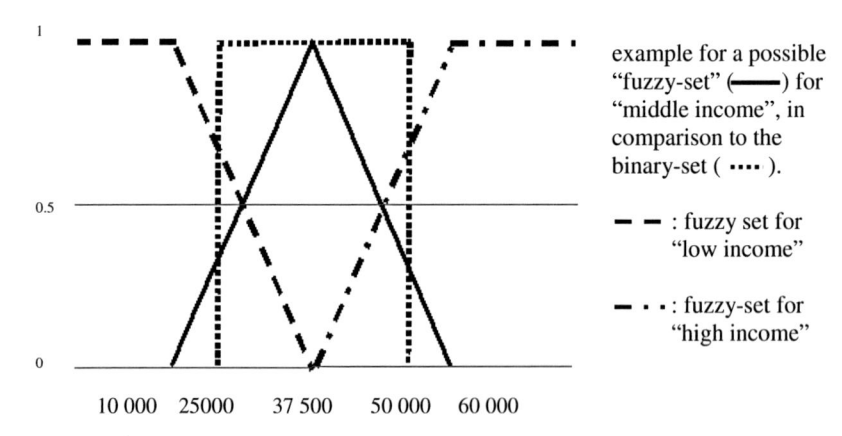

example for a possible "fuzzy-set" (―――) for "middle income", in comparison to the binary-set (····).

― ― : fuzzy set for "low income"

― · · : fuzzy-set for "high income"

One has to note that the membership values and with it the graph may vary depending on what function you may use to define the values, i.e. smoother functions, Gauss-function etc. In such a way one can also get hold of concepts like "a *little* more", "*tall* women", "*frequently*" etc. by defining fuzzy membership values about to *which extend* 178 cm is tall *and* small, 12 degrees to the left is a little *and* much, or flying once a month is frequently *and* non frequently. Such evaluation is, of course, dependent on the context. 178 cm would get a higher value for being tall for a Japanese woman and a higher value for being medium sized for a Swedish woman. And "frequently" used in the context of flying is something different than if one reads "frequently stir the stew" (something I have found out after getting a burnt meal).

	Japanese women $\mu_{Jx}(s)$			Swedish Women $\mu_{Sx}(s)$		
size: s	small (ja)	medium (jb)	tall (jc)	small (sa)	medium (sb)	tall (sc)
154	0.8	0.2	0	1	0	0
164	0.1	0.9	0	1	0	0
165	0	1	0	1	0	0
167	0	0.8	0.2	0.8	0.2	0
168	0	0.7	0.3	0.7	0.3	0
174	0	0.1	0.9	0.1	0.9	0
175	0	0	1	0	1	0
181	0	0	1	0	0.4	0.6
183	0	0	1	0	0.2	0.8
186	0	0	1	0	0	1
190	0	0	1	0	0	1

Fuzzy membership values for height of Japanese and Swedish women.

μ = membership value

$\mu_{Jb}(167)$ means that a height of 167 cm belongs to the fuzzy set jb with a value of 0.8

Blue markings: borders of possible gray sets

2.4.4.2 A Note on Statistics and "Fuzzy Set Theory":

Fuzzy set theory is not the same as statistical theory. Statistics is about probabilities. There's a difference between the probability to meet a woman with the height of 154 cm, which can be calculated if one knows the distribution of women with a certain height a certain place, and *defining* 154 cm- tall women as medium-sized. If I'm the only woman in the room the probability of meeting a 154 cm sized woman in this room is 1, since my height is 154 cm. But in how far you may consider this woman as small, medium or tall depends on the parameters assigned to fuzzy set-membership.

It may be criticized that such kind of method to define membership values may be quite subjectively and arbitrary and that it would be difficult to justify ones choice (e.g. if saying 154 cm is small). But isn't it even more difficult to justify binary coding, saying with one cent or centimeter more or less one jumps from "middle income" to "high income" or from "medium" to "tall"? In many cases binary membership coding is at least as arbitrary as fuzzy membership coding, but fuzzy membership may be easier to justify, if one considers that it is often hard to answer with a clear yes or no. Binary coding is included in fuzzy membership coding as a special case, e.g. in regard to being alive or dead, one would get the same binary results with both methods (o.k., let's leave aside *"Schrödinger's Cat"* for a moment).

	binary sets		fuzzy sets	
	Subject-Pole	Object-Pole	Subject-Pole	Object-Pole
human being	1	0	1.0	0.0
cyborg	1	0	0.9	0.1
embryonic stem cell	1	0	0.8	0.2
robot	0	1	0.2	0.8
microwave-oven	0	1	0.0	1.0

Applying the fuzzy-set-method one can even give fuzzy membership-values within a specific set of objects, e.g. machines:

	Subject-Pole	Object-Pole
microwave oven	0.0	1.0
Industrial robot	0.1	0.9
service robot	0.3	0.7
pet-robot	0.4	0.6
humanoid robot	0.6	0.4

Of course, even if using Fuzzy Set Theory one may decide on applying the same labelling to *ASIMO* as to ones microwave-oven, but Fuzzy Sets allow a person to attribute some "subjectness" to an object without having to attribute total human qualities to it. A "0.4-subject" is different from a "1.0-subject" and a "0.0-subject". So it's not a question about if cyborgs and humanoid robots (or someday maybe human-imitating androids) are subjects or objects, but about onto which degree it is reasonable to place them between those two poles. Taking this into account, a new dimension could be given to the Actor-Network approach, i.e. *in how far* the artifacts can be seen as subjects or objects; and if possible differences in regard to their *degree* of "objectness" or "subjectness" influences their place in the network, e.g. in respect to their autonomy and decision-making authority (remember TCAS). One can also analyze subjects and objects in relation to different contexts, as the example about "being tall" in Japan and Sweden has shown. The same numeral (i.e. height in cm) may be seen in different ways relative to the context they are in. If looking at the dimension of "emotional qualities", for example the TCAS system mentioned in one of my previous excursions may get the value 0.0 on the subject-pole, but if looking at the dimension of "decision-making-authority" it may get a value on the subject-pole equal to, if not higher than a human controller.

2.4.5 Survey & Results

I have considered conducting a survey in Germany and Japan with the goal of finding out if there are differences in how German and Japanese people tend to regard objects in the context of a subject-object-coding.

The survey design consisted of two parts. In each part the respondent was presented with an array of different pictures. After given time to look at the pictures the respondent was asked to decide on one (and only one) out of three explained categorization methods which in his/her opinion would be best suited for placing the entities shown on the pictures.

Categorization Methods:

1. A strict binary subject-object-coding
2. A coding-type which allows a clear distinction between subject and object, although it leaves the possibility of regarding some objects as "more object-like" than others or some "subjects" as more "subject-like" than others.
3. A "Fuzzy-Coding" with a flawless transition from the subject-pole to the object-pole.

In the first part the respondent has been presented with four pictures, a human (man), a dog, a car and a screwdriver, which allow for a relatively unproblematic identification as "subject" and "object". In the second part the respondent was asked to again decide on one of the three categorization methods mentioned above, only this time with more inconclusive pictures, which included entities such as cyborgs, (humanoid) robots and androids.

After having decided on a categorization method the respondent was asked to place a marking where on the chosen scale (s)he would place the entities shown on the pictures.

The English version of the survey (I have used the German version for Germany and Japanese and English ones for Japan) can be found on the last pages of Part II.

2.4.5.1 Preliminary Results:

I have started with conducting some pre-tests with relatives, family members, friends and acquaintances in Germany, including clerics and information-scientists. None of these 14 people I asked in Germany opted for the "fuzzy" categorization and only one opted for the No.2 method. In discussions I held afterwards, I found out that the people had more or less great difficulties in grasping the "fuzzy" concept. Although they have recognized that the distinct borderline was missing there, they did not understand why it has been designed that way. They have opted for the method which clearly sets apart subjects and objects and their way of assigning the entities has been in line with the distinction between animate and inanimate. Especially element 7 and element 8 of the second part led to confusion. Some thought of Element 7, a human-looking android, clearly as a human woman on the subject-side, whilst others interpreted it as a display dummy, or the more technical inclined even as a kind of robot, but they put it clearly on the object side. Element 8, a *cyborg* (taken from a *Star Trek* Poster) let some people think of it as a human wearing some electronic devices, putting him on the subject side, whereas others thought of it as a robot / android, putting it on the object-side. After telling them ex-post that this was a cyborg, the question arose if it was alive, and if so, then it should be considered as "subject", otherwise as "object". Also element 5, the tree, bore some problems, leading the respondents to ponder about regarding it as subject or object. Most of them finally opted for "subject", again commenting that it is alive, but nobody thought of it as being partly "subject" and partly "object".

As far as I could find out in the discussions I held with the German respondents, the problem was not with the test design, but with the concept of omitting the distinct borderline between subject and object; the "fuzzy shading" has been incomprehensible to them. The idea of regarding something as partially subject and partially object looked strange to them. Their guidance for the assignment went along the lines of alive and non-alive, but being confronted with unfamiliar entities like cyborgs or androids led to confusion for most respondents less interested in technology or science fiction. Questions being asked about where to place entities like "Frankenstein's Monster" have been dismissed as hypothetical, bearing no practical meaning.

Even more surprising was the reaction as I ran my preparations and pre-tests in Japan. As I have shown my Japanese version of the survey to a Japanese acquaintance, a German-speaking Japanese university professor teaching humanities [236], I learned that the Japanese have great difficulties with the understanding of dividing the world into objects and subjects. In my discussion I was told that in the Japanese language[237] there does not exist a term that reflects the concepts of "subject" and "object" in the German (Western?) sense and understanding. Of course they have vocabularies of denoting "subjects" (主体 = *shūtai* = subject or main constituent) and "object" (客体 = *kyakutai* = object or article[238]), but as he told me, using this to split the world into the dichotomous categories of "subject" and "object" opposes the respondent's "emotional attitude towards the world". And he told me that many Japanese would feel that way. He provided me with the example of a cup. It can be seen as a simple article (or object), but by looking at it one sees that it also possesses "subjective" and emotional dimensions, which are taken into account. Simply its form and coloring hints the human factor and a whole history, which is also manifested in the object. In a way this describes what Latour has tried to explain with his examples that a gun as well as a human who holds it undergo changes when they come in contact with each other, or that the wood of ones desk indeed has a

---

[236] Prof. Aoki, with whom I also had discussions about religion and the Japanese' attitude towards robots (refer also to Part I and Part III of my analysis).
[237] The Japanese language represents a deep mystery anyway. There exist many words that have different meanings at the same time, which sometimes even include total opposites. *Aite* (相手) for example can mean companion, partner and company as well as opponent and rival.
[238] Another term for "object" is "*mono*" (物), whereas it is also used in "*doubutsu*" (動物 = "moving object" = animal) and "*seibutsu*" (生物 = "living thing" = living creature)

history and mediates the actions of other entities, human and non-human alike (Latour, 1998). My first Japanese respondent finally opted for the "fuzzy-categorization" as the best of bad options.

Nonetheless I also presented one pre-test survey to a Japanese engineer. This respondent also had some difficulties with understanding the concept about why one should make such a categorization anyway, telling me that actually he had never really thought about something like this before. Through his explanation-seeking, especially in regard to what was meant with "subject" and "object", this pre-test can also be considered as having been manipulated through my explanations. He later sent me the survey via e-mail, having finally decided on coding number two, which allows a clear distinction between subject and object, although it leaves the possibility of regarding some objects as "more object-like" than others or some "subjects" as more "subject-like" than others. His pattern has been along the distinction between alive and not-alive.

2.4.5.2 Interpretation

Although a conclusion based on such a few pre-test data would be invalid and this whole undertaking can be rather rated unsuccessful and should be revised before being distributed as a scientifically meaningful survey, it nonetheless provided me with some interesting insights, especially through the discussions I had with the respondents. My way of seeing the world and the derived "fuzzy coding" have been quite incomprehensible to all people I have asked in Germany and Japan, and remained so even after discussions, especially in Germany. The reasons for this incomprehension have been opposite in Germany and Japan. Whereas the German people I asked did not comprehend how something could be partly "object" and partly "subject", the Japanese respondents did not understand why a classification of entities into "subject" and "object" should be conducted at all in the first place. The German reactions of having difficulties with the idea of an entity being neither "object" nor "subject" ("fuzzy concept") have been in line with my expectations; although as I have observed through asking some German owners of Sony's *AIBO* robot "dog" about their relationship to their AIBO, many of them regard this robot as being more than just some commodity[239]. But nonetheless most of them clearly stated that *AIBO*'s shortcomings lie in the fact that it is not a living creature, and that it cannot be compared to a living animal. The Japanese reaction, on the other hand, was rather surprising to me. Actually I have expected the Japanese to opt for the "fuzzy concept", but they expressed having difficulties with this, since this method nonetheless forced them to place the entities into categories. But if thinking about this, the Japanese' "problems" don't seem that strange if one looks at it from the cultural and religious perspective. As I have already mentioned in the first part of my analysis, in *Shinto* a distinction between animate and inanimate, between god(s), humans and objects is never really discussed; and Buddhist teachings also discourage such divisions. Since *Shinto* and Buddhism have not been a hindering factor, maybe the Japanese have never developed a sense of necessity for *"purification processes"* in regard objects and "quasi-objects". This could also mean that the Japanese can easier accept "quasi-objects" as just what they are, without thinking about forcing them into categories. Therefore the Japanese also don't come into logical or emotional conflicts when attributing some "subjectness" into an object, because the poles have no real meaning. Of course, as I learned in the discussions, Japanese know the concept of a thing and that of a living creature and can tell the difference between alive and not alive, but seemed to have problems with understanding "subject" and "object" as *opposing* concepts. I would hypothesize that it are the effects and associations an entity evokes in a human being that are considered of primary relevance when thinking of it, as it has also been hinted by the Japanese

---

[239] Refer to data in the appendix-files

professor with the example of the cup. Looking at this, the Japanese concept of "soul" should also be seen with a different connotation than the term is denoted in Western thought. The "soul" in an entity reflects qualitative elements *evoking* emotions and *inducing* respectful behavior. Anyway, in this sense one could say in Latouran wording that the Japanese have never *pretended* to be modern.

Finally I would like to reflect on the question how I could have been so off the mark with my "fuzzy categorization". Maybe my development of such a view stems from the circumstances of my upbringing. On the one hand I have been raised with comprehending the German (Western?) understanding that distinguishing between the opposing concepts of "subject" and "object" is a legitimate, even central act to consider. On the other hand I grew up in Japan, which let me absorb many concepts of *Shinto* and Buddhist thought, relativizing the idea of strict distinctions. Additionally I have been accustomed to entities, which in a way belong into the domain of "quasi-objects" (e.g. moving mechatronic toys) from an early age on. Whereas it seems that the idea of dividing the world into "subjects" and "objects" is quite alien to the Japanese's thinking, I didn't omit the question about "subjects" and "objects", but unlike it seems to be the case in Germany, I never assumed a strict separation. Maybe I'm just too "modern" for having used a classification system, but too Japanese in refraining from using a binary coding.

2.4.6 A Note on Anthropomorphizing

> *"There is a universal tendency among mankind to conceive all beings like themselves (...)"*
>
> [David Hume, *The Natural History of Religion*]

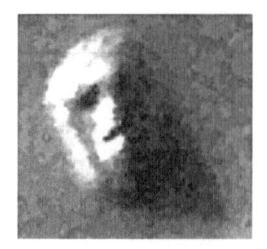

Even in mars rocks humans see faces...

Photo: „The ,'face' on Mars", taken from *Viking* orbiters (from image 035A72.) Public Domain @ http://nssdc.gsfc.nasa.gov/image/planetary/mars/face.jpg

In regard to our dealings with artifacts that are designed to portray characteristics which can be found in living entities or even humans (e.g. humanoid robots) it is relevant to reflect on the practice of anthropomorphizing.

The word "anthropomorphism" is derived from the Greek language and contains two words: *"anthropos"* = man and *"morph..."* = shape / form, therefore describing the practice of ascribing human characteristics an qualities to gods, inanimate objects or other non-human entities. As I have already mentioned, gods in the Shinto religion are portrayed quite human-like, whereas in the Judeo-Christian-Islamic tradition the imagining of God as being human-like is regarded reprehensible. Nonetheless it is generally practiced to imagine God in human shape, also in the Christian tradition, since it is said in the bible that God created (wo)man in His image[240].

There are different hypothesis which try to explain why humans tend to anthropomorphize. Some like Francis Bacon try to explain it with the familiarity thesis, which states that humans use themselves as models since they (think) that

---

[240] Xenophanes (570 BC – 480 BC) observed that people tend to model their gods after themselves.

they have a better understanding about themselves than about non-human phenomena. This view has been criticized, since objectively seen, humans seem to know even less about themselves than about other natural phenomenon[241]. Nonetheless I would say that most humans live with the subjective assumption that they possess sufficient knowledge about themselves. Why else should Artificial Intelligence and robotics have become such a crucial topic for philosophers and (Christian) theologians? Others like Freud think that humans use anthropomorphizing practices to get comfortable with hard-to-understand non-human phenomena in order to get the illusion of possible control over them [242]. Cognitive oriented hypothesis like Guthrie's "Best-Bet-Thesis" (Guthrie, 1997), which in a way counters Freud's "comfort thesis", just attribute anthropomorphizing to be part of a human's hard-wired survival strategies: better to see a potentially dangerous human / living entity (e.g. by interpreting it as a face) in a harmless dead object, than the other way around. Another thesis, which goes into the opposite direction, concerns the aspect of deliberately creating objects in the shape of humans, e.g. humanoid robots such as Honda's *ASIMO* or Toyota's *"Trumpet Player"*, because a humanoid shape not only enables a robot to better perform tasks in a human environment (the pragmatic argument), but also because humanoids are easier to get accustomed to by humans, because they are inducing some sort of "sameness"[243]. But interestingly there are tendencies even in Japan, that refrain from creating humanoid robots too human (e.g. *ASIMO*, *"Wakamaru"*, *QRIO* which purposefully have been designed with some robotic elements to them) in order to avoid an eeriness in perception (Refer to Mori's "Uncanny Valley" hypothesis explained in part I of my analysis).

---

[241] Refer to Guthrie, 1997
[242] ibid
[243] e.g. I'm referring to quote found about Toyota's Trumpet Player on http://www.toyota.co.jp/en/special/robot/index.html (date: December 2004)

The anthropomorphism practiced in modern (post) industrialized countries has less to do with gods or survival strategies. Automobile producers around the world carefully design the front part of their cars by arranging the headlights and bumpers in a way that should give the car's "face" either a cute, lovely or powerful, aggressive look. Perfume bottles often come in the shape of human torsos. Even my desk-lamp has anthropomorphic features, as it consists of a "foot", a flexible "spine" and a "head" which brightly shines at me (and I have attached "arms" to it in order to hold all my cables and other stuff…). Don't humans name airplanes, ships, cars and computers? Don't humans talk about their cars or computers by using the same vocabulary as they would use for describing attributes of themselves? Don't they say "my car is mad at me" or "my computer is crazy" when they "do" things we don't want (or expect) them to "do"? Haven't you sometimes experienced a thoughtless thought brushing your mind that your computer might think? Or haven't you sometimes tried to scold or encourage your car or computer: "please start" or "common, do it, it's not that difficult", or "don't fool me…"? But if saying things like "my computer is crazy", the "the network is fooling me", "the computer is searching or looking for the file", doesn't it rather stem from the fact that much of the vocabulary in human languages is anthropocentric and finding neutral expressions is rather time-consuming? What one actually might try to express while saying "my computer is crazy" is: "my computer is doing things that I find unexpected and not quite understandable, or just lie outside the parameters which I consider a normal procedure". Since humans have some sort of concepts associated with the word "crazy", e.g. not normal, unexpected, quite incomprehensible, they opt for referring to "crazy", which underlines the aspect of incomprehensibility even more than just saying "malfunction" or "broken".

But with the advent of computers we also tend to use terms from the computer language (I do not mean necessarily programming language), such as saying "I have stored the information (in my brain)", "I scanned the shelf twice and still can not locate the potatoes" or "sorry I must have run on the wrong program as I thought it was Monday". And isn't the human brain often referred to as being some kind of organic computer ("wetware")? So paradoxically we do anthropomorphizing with objects and "technomorphizing" with humans.

My observations suggest that the Japanese are topping everyone else in regard to anthropomorphizing practices. Have you ever looked at a Japanese instruction manual for home appliances or other consumer electronics? In contrast to their Western counterparts there are more pictures than text, enabling even the Kanji-illiterate to get ones Video-recorder running. Japanese user's manuals look more like manga. But what is even more remarkable than the pictures themselves is how the devices are portrayed. A Fax machine being left in the sun for too long begins to cry (tears drop from its eyes), a TV-set placed on an uneven surface becomes scared (its eyes and mouth are wide-opened in fear) and if treated well (if all instructions are followed) then it smiles at you in gratitude. There's even a popular Japanese TV-animé series about the life and adventures of bread (yes you're reading's correct, it's about that baked matter one normally eats) titled *Anpanman*[244]. And Japan seems to be rightfully obsessed with creating cute-looking robots like *AIBO, ASIMO* and *PaPeRo* designed along the shapes of animals or even humans which give the impression of displaying emotions. And when looking at Websites from Japanese owners of Sony's robot-"dog" AIBO[245], one often finds pictures and comments which give the impression of a quite close relationship between the artificial entity and its owner. This is something which is less apparent (or hardly admitted?) in Germany. As I have noticed, in Germany people also tend show anthropomorphizing behavior towards objects like cars, computers and *AIBO* robots, but at the same time they somehow feel uneasy about doing so, or at least about admitting it. If looking at stories / reports posted at the German *AIBO*

---

[244] *Anpan* is a bakery good filled with black beans (= "an") that is very popular in Japan.
[245] I just typed in AIBO on www.google.jp to finds owner's websites or looked at pages from the Japanese "AIBOwner's Webring".

Community website, where people write about their experiences with *AIBO*, it sometimes just looks like somebody writing about ones pet, although comments often close with the apologizing statement of certainly knowing that it's "just" a robot and shifting to technological aspects.

In Germany, seeing grown up people publicly talking to dolls or taking a robot-pet to a shopping trip in the supermarket would raise questions about calling a psychiatrist, whereas in Japan the public "tolerance threshold" for such behavior seems to be much higher.

If anthropomorphizing towards objects is regarded as rather socially unacceptable, one refrains from admitting this practice. If on the other hand anthropomorphizing is not publicly sanctioned or if it's even encouraged (Japanese companies lay much emphasis on creating cute products and the industry flourishes on the cute), people have no fear about showing it. I have even made this kind of experience myself. As I talked to *AIBO* while in Germany and was asked by my a neighbor whom I was talking to, I thought saying that I was just testing my robot's command routines would provide an acceptable answer, while in Japan I would just have admitted that I was talking to my *AIBO* without having to fear about being classified as somehow weird.

Excerpts from a Japanese user's manual for a video recorder

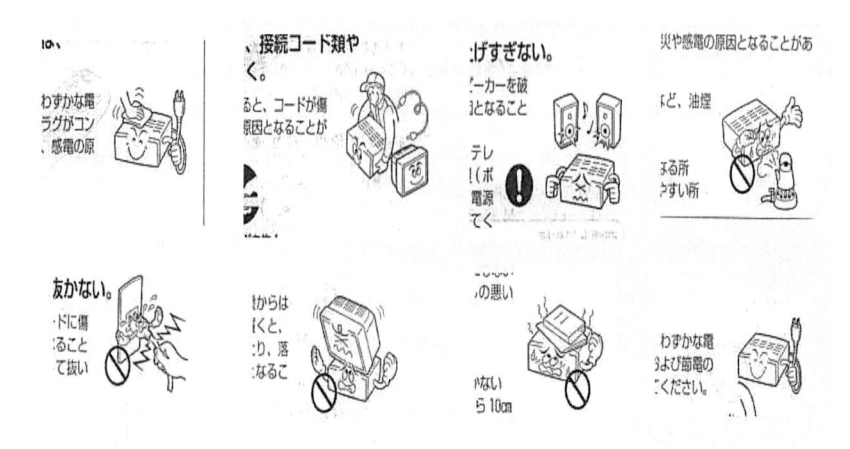

Part 1 of the Survey (English Version)

Resp. Nr.: T1- ……….. M: F: | D: J:

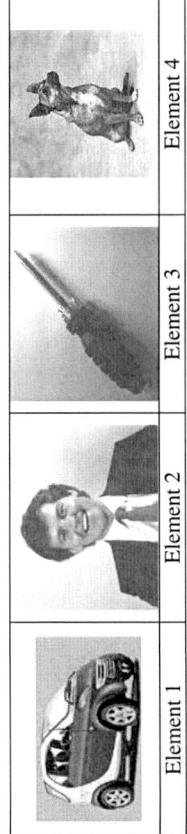

Element 1	Element 2	Element 3	Element 4

1. Below you will find three categorization-methods (A, B and C). Please chose **one** of these categorization-methods (method A **or** B **or** C), which you find appropriate for using to classify the elements above.

2. Please decide where under your chosen method you would place the elements shown above. For this please write the element-numbers at your chosen position into the blank field below the bar representing your chosen categorization- method.

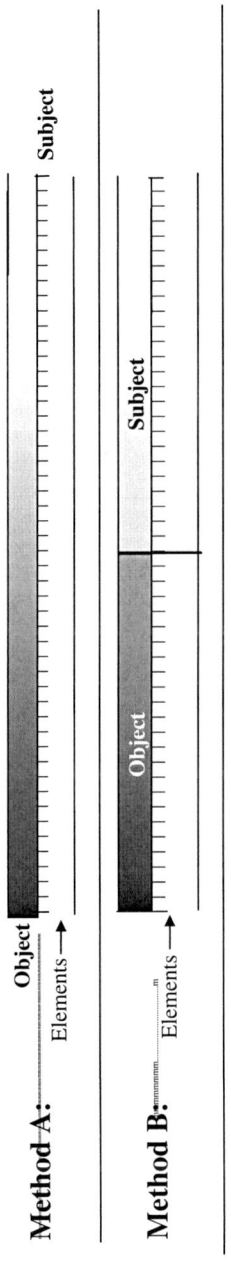

Method A:

Method B:

Method C:

141

Resp. Nr.: T2- ....   M: F: | D: | J:

Part 2 of the Survey (English Version)

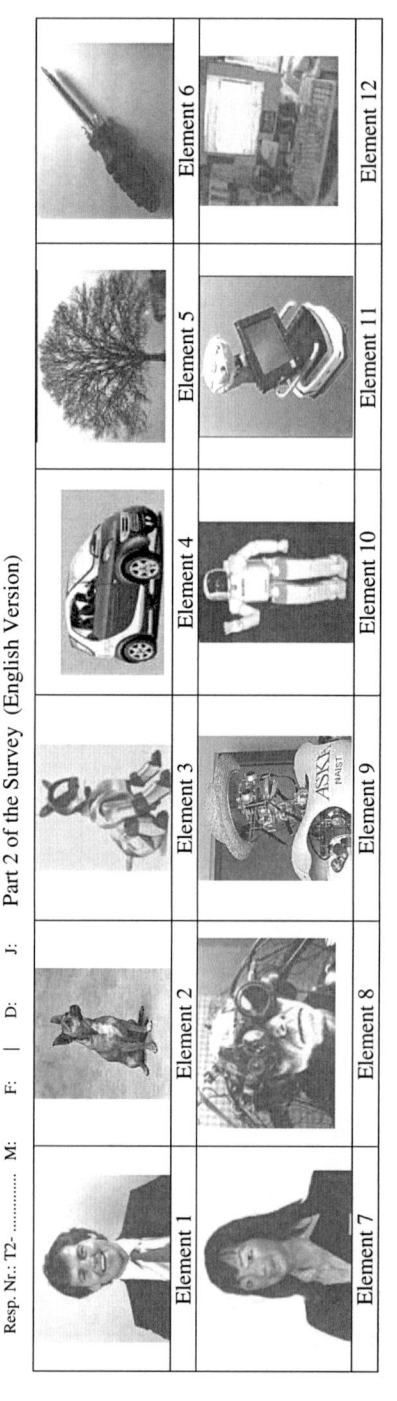

Element 1	Element 2	Element 3	Element 4	Element 5	Element 6
Element 7	Element 8	Element 9	Element 10	Element 11	Element 12

3. Below you will find three categorization-methods (A, B and C). Please chose **one** of these categorization-methods (method A **or** B **or** C), which you find appropriate for using to classify the elements above.

4. Please decide where under your chosen method you would place the elements shown above. For this please write the element-numbers at your chosen position into the blank field below the bar representing your chosen categorization- method.

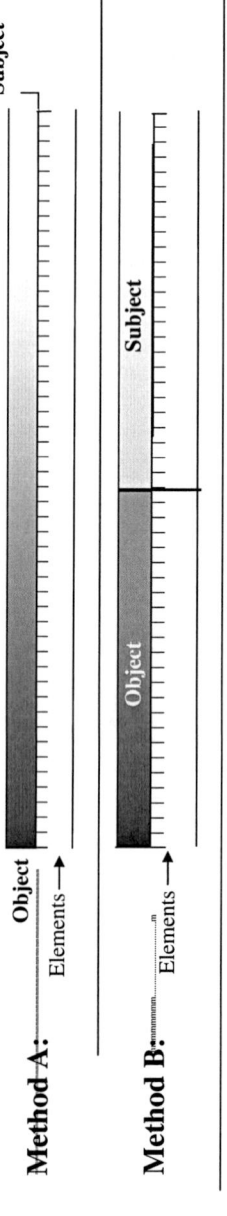

Method A: Object ──────────── Subject
                    Elements →

Method B: Object ──────────── Subject
                    Elements →

Method C: Object ──────────── Subject
                    Elements →

PART III

0101000001100001011100100111010000100000001100011

Robots – Our Future Partners?!
A Comparison between Germany and Japan

3.1.1 Japan – The *Robot Kingdom* !?

"Japan's robotic technology is of a globally competitive standard", this is the statement one gets to read upon entering the robot-page on the official website of the Aichi World Exposition 2005 (Japan)[246]. If knowing about the Japanese and their reputation on robots, this actually sounds like an understatement. As a matter of fact, throughout the world "Japan" and "robot" seem to form a pair like in a memory game. To my knowledge, no other country runs robot-related projects with so much enthusiasm and in such an interwoven structure between the government (especially the Japanese Ministry of Economy, Trade, and Industry (METI)), research institutes, companies, commercialization and public relations like Japan. No other country seems to put so much visible effort into robot-development and interest promotion like Japan. And looked at it from that angle, what – except maybe space exploration – would provide a better way to publicly demonstrate ones technological superiority than building advanced robots and put them on display?

From my own experience I can say that at first when I expressed my own interest in robotics towards Germans I am often looked at with slight puzzlement, but when I explained that I grew up in Tokyo, everything seems to be cleared up. Indeed, by many inside and outside the country, Japan is regarded as the „*Robot Kingdom*", as it has also been suggested in a rather journalistic, but quite

---

[246] http://www-1.expo2005.or.jp/en/robot/robot_project_00.html (March 12th, 2005)

insightful book by Frederik L. Schodt[247], titled *"Inside the Robot Kingdom. Japan, Mechatronics and the Coming of Robotopia"* (Schodt, 1988). Schodt has analyzed the phenomenon about Japan's great affinity towards (industrial) robots during the flourishing 1980s by taking into consideration economic, cultural, social and even religious aspects.

But why is it so? What has changed after the decline of the 1980s economic boom? Can those common assumptions about the Japanese *Shinto*-religion, technology-enthusiasm and future-optimism really serve as a sufficient explanation for Japan's positive attitude towards robots? I can at least name 5 good reasons which could provide problems for a positive human-robot-relation in Japan.

1. Religious Animism: as I have already mentioned in the sections before, if in *Shinto* robots can be thought of as *kami* ("spirit") -possessing entities, couldn't they just evoke even more fear than in "Western" thought, where the central concern is just about possible malfunctions of a machine. If the "ghost in the machine" is not just a metaphysical question, but part of a people's belief-system, I guess such a people would feel rather uneasy with the idea of demanding a robot's unconditional subjection. But isn't this the main reason for inventing robots, to have a non-living slave-substitute? In this way it's the Japanese that should even more fear the mechatronic "rebelling slave".

Indeed, in a number of contemporary Japanese *animé* like *"Ghost in the Shell"* and *"Innocence"* (both by Mamoru Oshii), the question about the *"ghost"* in technical artifacts such as cyborgs and Artificial Intelligences (*"Ghost in the Shell"*), dolls and robots (*"Innocence"*), is intensively reflected on. (In the animé movie *"Ghost in the Shell"* the term *"goosuto"* borrowed from the English word "ghost" is used and defined as the part of the human body containing human

---

[247] Schodt, 1988

identity. The term has been chosen to avoid confusion in regard to definitions of humans, souls or spirits in an age of cyborgs and Artificial Intelligence[248]). Both films display clear religious hints. Some of them are rather superficially borrowed from Christianity, but the most obvious references belong to *Shinto*, as even the film's title melody in style of ancient *Shinto*-ceremonial chants reflects[249], ending with the transcendent elements of *Buddhism*, where finally all borders and contradictions will be dissolved.

Another problem might be control. If thinking of a robot as a machine, coded as "pure object" the human's position as controller remains high. If on the other hand some residing *"kami"* can be assumed, human control is relativized. Why else should a factory worker provide a robot or machine with *sake* (rice wine) to appease its *"kami"*, as it is still practiced at many Japanese factories? And with the frequent occurrences of earthquakes and typhoons Japanese people know more than enough the destructive side of *"kami"*.

2. Economy: after the burst of the economic bubble starting in the 1990s, the Japanese' naïve belief in unlimited growth and progress has been dampened. Companies' profits declined, consumer-spending went down, unemployment figures rose and practices like lifelong-employment, previously taken for granted, at least for so-called "salary-men[250]", have been curtailed. In such a climate, especially in face of growing competition from other East-Asian nations such as China and South Korea (indeed, if looking at China or South-Korea, one gets reminded on the days of Japan's booming heights), it is only reasonable to assume that governments and industries have better things to do than thinking

---

[248] I'm referring to the interviews with the creators of *"Ghost in the Shell"* which have been recorded on the original DVD.
[249] The lyrics from the musical main theme of *"Ghost in the Shell"* and *"Innocence"* are written in an ancient Japanese language and describing a scene of young women dancing in the moonlight and gods descending for a wedding when dawn approaches while the night birds sing.
[250] The Japanese term for "while collar workers" getting a regular salary

about costly long-term robotics-projects (as it is also the case in Germany), that are unlikely entail the needed *short-term* utility and profits. Also if unemployment is on the rise, it is conceivable that the possible "second coming of robots" entering the tertiary / service sector might be looked at with uneasiness.

3. Technology: I think I am on the safe side by saying that in no other country technology and automation has penetrated a people's life more than in Japan. It begins with a look out of my window in Tokyo, overseeing a landscape of neon-light, skyscrapers and multi-level highways, going over surveillance cameras in the apartment-elevator, the omnipresent automatic vending machines, automatic sliding doors, computer voices on answering-machines, automated telephone service-lines, totally computer-controlled trains, automated *kaiten*-sushi-restaurants where even the delicacies are formed by robot-hands, ending with the android-like bow of the (still) human salesclerk and the welcoming greeting of a robot-pet upon my return.

But all this development happened with rather hair-raising speed as a result to catch up with the West, an obsession that has haunted Japan since the *"Black Ships"* of US Commodore Perry arrived in 1853. And one too easily forgets that the robot has been a US and not a Japanese invention.

So far public technology-critique has mostly been confined to *"mukokuseki"*, that is the "neutral worlds" of dystopian *mecha*-animé[251] (refer to Napier, 2000). But for how long can a country, whose people have been virtually synchronized with the pace of technological progress and where the shadow-sides and human-costs of materialism and *"Technotopia"* are slowly surfacing, embrace technology with such seeming naivety? This it at least the question one gets to be asked by persons from Europe and the US. Maybe Japanese people see their own home as a last resort of escaping the omnipresent technology and wouldn't

---

[251] e.g. "Bubblegum Cisis", "Guyver", "Evangelion"

like to be greeted by a robot on ones homecoming? Couldn't it be just imaginable, that ironically, with the advent of practically feasible applications of Artificial Intelligence, Japan's techno-enthusiasm may fade away or even turn over into techno-criticism?

4. Growing Pessimism: although one reads *"Ambitious Japan"* on nearly every passing *Shinkansen* high-speed train, a look inside a local train en route to the *Harajuku*-district provides another picture; a picture about a pessimistic attitude that has also already infected Japan's youth, reflected through the dark and gloomy looks of *"gosurori"*, *"Gothic Lolita's"*, pale young women and men who look like coming out of a sinister gothic novel, obsessed with dark philosophies, archaic symbolism and the "aesthetics of suicide", in a country which has already the highest suicide rates in the world[252]. Also the increasing number of dark sects and doomsday cults in Japan, of which *Aum Shinrikyu* that carried out the gas-attacks at the *Kasumigaseki* subway station in March of 1995 got most attention, might be the call of a people unsatisfied with the idea of just being a small part of Japan's "great machinery", which begins with a child's Kindergarten entrance ceremony. Also an increasing number of Japanese youth are not interested in following the ideal of the Japanese hard-working, orderly, subordinate and assimilated worker. Even the Japanese government, while trying to keep upright an optimistic ambience, states concerns about the growing depressing economic and social climate, which is about to spread throughout the country.

Morale in Japanese schools is on a constant decline, PISA-scores have dropped, high-school drop-out rates are on the increase, and a growing number of young people show no interest in getting a good education and a regulated job. Suicide rates among high-school students are still rising, so are the crimes conducted by young people. The Japanese Education Ministry is lamenting over

---

[252] Refer to The Japan Times, July 11 2004

the fact that fewer and fewer students are interested in fields like science, IT, mathematics and engineering, the basis for future-technologies and the Japanese economy. Such tendencies stand in stark contrast to the optimism - *"Ambitious Japan"*, *"Tetsuwan Atom"* and high-tech-gleam - propagated by the Japanese government and the PR-divisions of the industry.

With these growing pessimistic, social- and techno-critic or simply apathetic tendencies among young Japanese, the chances for a future-generation's positive stance towards robots, which embody the ultimo ratio of technology, might look questionable.

5. Aging Society: while the cell-phone-talking, childless young generation is losing personal interest in how technology actually works and is merely absorbing it, Japan's demographic situation leads to an aging society. Elderly people will make up a great percentage of future consumers. Although an increasing number of aged people are beginning to take computer- and Internet courses, many of them cannot really relate to the high-tech world (that's why the smaller Japanese cell-phone company *"au"* is marketing scaled-down, simplified cell-phones with a *minimum* of extra features especially targeted at the elderly). The promoted idea of robots assisting elderly people in their household may just remind them on the decay of traditional family ideals that are based on the Confucian ideal of children caring for their aging parents. Doesn't it remind them that they are lonely and being left aside in the hands of automated care? Maybe the robot in care-service will someday become an inevitable option, but not necessarily a welcomed one.

3.1.2 Observations

3.1.2.1 Germany – The *Robot Kingdom* !?

There's no doubt, although many Germans are much too reservedly about this, that Germany belongs to the world's top leaders in research and technology. The country houses some of the world-leading industries, such as *AIXTRON* (Aachen), the world's leading producer of manufacturing equipment for semi-conductors and so-called wafers, giving Aachen the nickname of *"LED-Town"*. It is home to many renowned technology-related companies and trademarks. The *Heinz Nixdorf MueumsForum* in Paderborn / Germany is the world's largest Computer- and IT-museum with a new permanent exhibition about robotics, Artificial Intelligence and Information Technology (IT). German institutions have developed the camera system for the Mars Orbiter *"Mars Express"*[253] and special analysis equipment for the US exploration robots *"Spirit"* and *"Opportunity"*[254], which fulfil(led) a successful mission on Mars. Recently German engineers have constructed a robot arm / manipulator for use on the International Space Station ISS, with the capability of executing commands sent from earth almost instantly. Japanese institutions are using European Ariane-5 rockets to bring their satellites into orbit, while the Japanese space agency *JAXA* (Japan Aerospace Exploration Agency)[255] has recently been battered with failures such as the loss of two spy-satellites and the Japanese Mars probe *"Nozomi"*, setbacks they only slowly manage to overcome. Germany belongs to the top exporters of machinery, large-scale installations and high-tech devices, especially those for medical applications; and Japanese companies and

---

[253] The stereo camera system HRSC (**H**igh **R**esolution **S**tereo **C**amera) has been developed by the German „Deutsches Zentrum für Luft- und Raumfahrt (DLR)" / Berlin-Adlershof
[254] The devices on each robot-probe are a miniature „Mössbauer-Spektrometer" developed at the Universität Mainz / Germany and X-ray spectrometers developed at the Max Planck Institute for Chemistry in Mainz / Germany
[255] Formerly known as NASDA (National Space Development Agency)

institutions import top-grade high-tech machinery from Germany. Japanese hospitals and medical centers make much use of German technology ranging from analysis devices over Lithotripters (high-intensity ultrasound devices used for the non-invasive destruction of kidney stones (lithotripsy)) to fully automated transportation systems for files and samples developed by the German electronics company *Siemens AG*. Especially in the fields of medical- and environmental-related research and technology Germany proofs to be in a forerunner position. This also got underlined through the projects being nominated for the German "*Zukunftspreis 2004*", an incentive to foster Germany's involvement in scientific research and the development of marketable next-generation products, which represented innovations in chemical analysis, reduction of pollutant emission in automobiles, a new LASER-microscope for the analysis of biological samples and protein-design technologies for crafting specialized antibodies. The laureates of the "*Zukunftspreis 2004*" have developed a so-called *Biochip*, a miniature laboratory for chemical- and biological analysis[256].

Reliable and practical, that's the motto of German research and development. The most important German research institution for applied technology with this motto in mind is the *Fraunhofer-Gesellschaft*. Founded in 1946 with just three employees, today it consists of 80 specialized institutes located throughout Germany with about 12 700 employees, mostly natural scientists and engineers, and an annual research volume of over one billion Euro[257]. The *Fraunhofer-Gesellschaft* is providing their research results to the industry, although the institute is not directly involved in manufacturing processes.

---

[256] In short, the device utilizes the idea of fixing specific molecules to the electrodes of a small chip. If the molecules of a substance to be analyzed hit some of the molecules fixed to the electrodes, an electric signal is generated which in turn provides data about the chemical composition of the substance to be analyzed.
[257] Sources: Hörzu, No. 45; 29.10.2004

Looking at this it is not surprising to find Germany among the leading nations in robotics research. According to UNECE-statistics[258], in 2004 for every 10 000 workers employed in the German manufacturing industry, there were 148 industrial robots, giving Germany the world's highest industrial-robot density (not including Japan whose statistics are incompatible due to a different definition of the term "industrial robot") [259]. Whereas in Japan the numbers of installed industrial robots have been on the decline from 2000 to 2001[260], there has been recorded a rise in Germany[261]. Also in the field of non-industrial robotics Germany holds a world-leading position. *"MOSRO 1"* from the German company „*Robowatch Technologies*", was according to the company, the world's first security robot in serial-production and has already been sold over 200 times throughout Germany and abroad. Soon the Fraunhofer IPA followed suit with presenting *"Secur-O-bot"*, a mobile security robot developed by the institute and marketed by the German Company *Neobotix*. In times of growing (suggested) insecurity, it is assumable that the demand for security technology will be on the rise. Even in the TV-Magazine *"Hörzu"* it has been said that Germany is a forerunner in the field of non-industrial robotics[262] and the number of articles about robotics in German (science) magazines and newspapers is constantly growing (e.g. *"Bild der Wissenschaft"* 12/2004, p. 100 ff). And if one takes some time for gathering information, the chances for Germany as being among the frontrunners in the area of developing next-generation service-robots look promising indeed. The medical faculty of the Humboldt-Universität Berlin / Germany is one of the world's leading research facilities in the area of medical robotics. Also in regard to the development of humanoid service robots (robots

---

[258] United Nations Economic Commission for Europe
[259] Source: www.unece.org/press/pr2004/04robots_index.htm
[260] Of course a decline in units can have different reasons, which might be due to the economic situation, shortcomings in research and development or stem from the tendency that robots become better equipped that fewer units have to be installed to perform the same jobs.
[261] Source: Japan 2004. An International Comparison, p.46.
Downloadable at: http://www.kkc.or.jp/english/ activities/inform.html#01
[262] Hörzu, No. 45; 29.10.2004

with a shape resembling that of a human-being, which are designed to someday being able to perform common tasks) Germany can call upon some quite sophisticated platforms like *HERMES*[263] (Universität der Bundeswehr Munich), *ARMAR*[264] (DFG 588, University Karlsruhe), *Care-O-bot* (Fraunhofer IPA) and the *MORPHA-project*, an interdisciplinary undertaking between research institutes (including the Fraunhofer IPA, and the University Karlsruhe / Germany) and the industry (including among others *DaimlerChrysler*, *KUKA*, *Siemens*) with the goal of developing intelligent robots which will be able to assist humans in a diversity of workplace and household tasks[265]. All these robots are being developed with the goal in mind of someday, maybe in five to ten years from now, providing humans with a useful household assistant. This looks like a lucrative market, since according to a survey cited on the German ARD-broadcast *"Ratgeber Technik"*[266] on Nov. 09th 2003, around 23% of German women who took part in the survey wish to have a robot as household assistant. The research on humanoid assistant robots is also intensively supported by the *DFG* (Deutsche Forschungsgemeinschaft[267]). German universities are involved in robotic research projects like the *SFB 360* (situierte künstliche Kommunikatoren, Prof. Helge Ritter University of Bielefeld) and are greatly interested in the area of human-machine interaction and communication, which is deemed very important for introducing robots to common households, as such robots are going to be operated by non-experts, are expected to perform jobs in a person's everyday environment (as contrasted to the robot-oriented environments in the industry) and will work in close proximity to humans. With the *RoboCup 2006* (robot soccer tournament) being held in Germany, I expect more robot-projects being initiated, supported and also promoted throughout this

---

[263] The acronym stands for **H**umanoid **E**xperimental **R**obot for **M**obile Manipulation and **E**xploration **S**ervices
[264] **A**nthropomorphic **A**rm for **Hu**manoid Service **R**obot
[265] http://www.morpha.de/php_d/morpha_Partner.php3 (data from March 2005)
[266] A program providing information about the latest technologies and giving advise to its users.
[267] German Research Foundation

country. For example with the *NimbRo-project*, a humanoid robot project being conducted in Freiburg / Germany, the research team plans to actively compete in the humanoid biped league at the *RoboCup*[268] 2006 competition. Although, in contrast to Japan, the development of humanoid robots with biped walking ability does not yet belong to the German priorities in research and development activity, with *Johnnie* the Technische Universität München/ Germany has already developed a two-legged humanoid robot with the ability to run.

Through delivering public events museums, universities and research institutes are also trying to get the public's attention towards robotics. As friends of mine who have visited the *CeBIT 2004*, the leading Communication- and Information-Technology exhibition held in Hanover / Germany, told me, robots like *Care-O-bot* and *Secur-O-bot*, both developed at the *Fraunhofer IPA* have attracted a great number of spectators and have proven quite popular with the visitors. The same applies for robots deployed at the *Museum für Kommunikation*, the *Opel Center in Berlin* / Germany and for the guidance robot Rhino[269] at the *Deutsches Museum in Bonn* / Germany, where some visitors just come in order to see the robots [270]. Then again my observations at "*AUTOMATICA*", the first German exhibition devoted to robots of all kinds, industrial, non-industrial and research platforms, held at *Neue Messe Munich* / Germany, have shown that robotics is a fascinating field for insiders, but I somehow missed the extended attendance of the general public among the numerous visitors as I was used to experience it in Japan at similar events. Of course I have to say here, that unlike *CeBit* or the Japanese exhibitions like "*International Robot Exhibition*" and especially "*Robodex*", I have visited, AUTOMATICA (June 15 – 18, 2004) was mainly directed towards business and professionals and did not include a weekend.

---

[268] The robot will debut at the RoboCup 2005 German Open / Paderborn, but this time it will not actively participate in the competition, but only demonstrate penalty kicks.
[269] Most of its software components have been developed at the *Rheinische Friedrich-Wilhelms-Universtät Bonn* / Germany
[270] All platforms have been developed by the Fraunhofer IPA

With a total number of 80 495 visitors, one of Germany's most successful events around the topic of Artificial Intelligence and robots, has been an extended 6-month "infotainment[271]" exhibition (25.10.2001 to 28.04.2002) held at the *Heinz Nixdorf MuseumsForum* (HNF) Paderborn / Germany, titled *"Computer.Brain"* (*Computer.Gehirn*)[272]. It featured the latest information, displays and presentations in the fields of Neuroscience, AI and robotics, paired with historical background information and discussions around the topic about differences between (wo)man and machine, the (human) brain and a computer, thinking and computing, guided by the central question: "DO YOU THINK THEY THINK?" (unfortunately the brilliant German syntax-symmetry of "DENKEN SIE, SIE DENKEN" gets lost in the English translation). Since robots (and computers) represent the only artificial entities, which mimic or even possess some of mankind's abilities, they have been the main characters at the exhibition. This was shown right at the beginning, as the visitors were greeted by the humanoid robot *"Tron-X"* to welcome one to enter the fascinating world of natural and artificial intelligence.

The other, rather art- and design oriented exhibition *"Ex Machina"* held at the Museum für Angewandte Kunst[273] in Cologne/Germany from January 15 to April 14 2002 has provided a historical overview about robots in arts, sciences and every-day life from 1950 until 2002, featuring European (including German), US and Japanese robots from films, the industry, public facilities and even for personal entertainment.

Looking at all of this, I wonder why it isn't Germany that is called the *"Robot Kingdom"*.

---

[271] A combination of information-providing and entertainment
[272] *Unfortunately I was not able at that time to visit the exhibition myself, but I met with the museum's curator, Dr. Stefan Stein, to talk about the exhibition and discuss matters concerning robotics in Germany and Japan. Here I would again like to express my special thanks to Dr. Stefan Stein and the HNF for having taken so much of his time for my visit.*
[273] The exhibition has been supported by the Japanese Cultural Institute

3.1.2.2 Germany – The Robot Kingdom ??

But... if you're not exactly a robot- or technology enthusiast, you may find it hard to even get to know about the German robot projects mentioned above. To be honest, I was even surprised on learning that such famous and commonly used technologies like MP3 and ISDN did in fact originate in Germany. Although MP3 technology has been a development of the *Fraunhofer Institut für Integrierte Schaltungen*[274] it was finally put into practical applications by the French consumer electronics company *Thompson* due to an apparent lack of interest from German companies. This is just one example for the situation of "invented in Germany, but applied elsewhere", as it was criticized at the *Hannover Messe 2004* in regard to the *Transrapid*-technology. The technology for this efficient magnetic-field-driven high-tech and high-speed train was developed in Germany, but here lengthy political discussions and concerns finally led to a situation where the Chinese got interested in this technology and built the world's first commercially-operated *Transrapid* service[275] while in Germany debates about its practical applications still persist.

High-Definition Television (HDTV) and blue-Laser technology for high-density recording devices may serve as another example. Japan is already marketing such products. Germany has also developed this technology, but as a representative of the Dutch electronics giant Philips has stated, appliances like *blue-LASER* disc recorders still don't seem to have a great chance in Europe, including Germany[276]. But I fear that when demand begins to rise in Europe, the market will already be saturated by Asian products. Instead of getting involved in the field of entertainment appliances like it is done in Japan, Germany is

---

[274] Fraunhofer Institute for Integrated Circuits
[275] Since December 2002 the *Transrapid* operates between Pudong Airport und Long Yang Rd. Station in China
[276] http://www.pcwelt.de/news/hardware/30200/ (April 3rd, 2004)

concentrating on using blue LASER technology for medical applications, where again lengthy political discussions are to be expected.

Germany's lengthy political discussions and the tendency to first look at new technological innovations with some sort of skepticism debating risks over chances, leads to a situation where other country's competitors get a quicker opportunity to act – may it be in the area of biotechnology, entertainment electronics or internet-telephony. The first *"Biochip"*, a bio-friendly and nontoxic computer chip, which can be implanted into the human body to monitor a person's health and body functions, was developed by a German surgeon. Although this device is working and ready to use, German politicians and the ethic committee are still discussing about the legal and moral implications of introducing such technology. It looks as if Reis's invention of the telephone and Bell's contribution to turn it into a mass-phenomenon serves as a paradigmatic example which even holds truth today. According to an interview conducted by the *Manager Magazine*, only every third German patent gets practically utilized [277]. Unlike the situation in Japan, one gets the impression that Germany is taking a too low profile in regard to publicly demonstrating some pride for its inventions and innovations. A reason for the country's overcautious stance may still be rooted in the experiences of WWII, but much of it may also be just missed opportunities or disinclination against taking risks. Germany has now established a so-called *"Innovationsrat"* (Council for Innovations) to help Germany catch up with other countries in technology, innovation and to boost its economy. Somehow the error lies in the expression "to catch up". Germany possesses all the needed potential, but the country may be too cautious, skeptical or simply too pessimistic about making the best of it.

Despite the efforts being undertaken by museums, scientific media, research institutions and universities, in Germany robots have not reached the general

---

[277] http://www.manager-magazin.de/magazin/artikel/0,2828,337524-2,00.html (March 8th, 2005)

public's awareness. The robot's rather negative image through influences from popular movies and the German tradition of always mentioning dangers and chances, whereas the discussion about the dangers is more lengthy than that about chances and opportunities, also hampers acceptance since people are loaded with prejudices against potentially dangerous mechatronic and soulless assistants to enter their homes (I wonder why people still buy cars in view of all these reports about fatal traffic accidents?). And even upon reading some German articles about a rather positive outlook towards the expected coming of robots entering our everyday life, one nearly always comes across the expression of doubtfulness. Whereas in Japan one *involuntarily* gets much information about Japanese robot-projects by turning on the TV, watching the news, coming across advertisements in magazines, reading the newspaper or looking at pamphlets posted at train-stations, in Germany one still has to *search* for such information. Although during the last year (from 2003 to 2004) robot-related articles have been on the rise in Germany, with some features even appearing in TV-magazines (e.g. *Hörzu*), Newsmagazines (*e.g. Focus*), women's magazines (e.g. *Brigitte*) and Tabloids, the idea of non-industrial robots still remains some curiosity belonging rather to the "ivory towers" of research facilities than representing something the broad population may relate to or even identify with[278]. Above this, it looks like Japanese inventions are being the main motor for Germany's growing interest in robot technology since many of the descriptions about German robot-projects are posted as a reaction to articles about Japanese developments.

I would say that the reason for Japan and not Germany being called *"Robot Kingdom"* does certainly not lie in technological now-how (in this regard I would even say that both countries possess similar potential, although their priorities differ). The reason for Japan's image as "Robot- and High-Tech Nation" is to be found in the country's national- and economic interests,

---

[278] Especially during the time of the movie "*I, Robot*" playing at German theaters the mentioning of robot projects in the German media was on the increase.

especially in regard to the interests that stem from the Japanese industry, and its interest promotion strategies which transports the ideas and the enthusiasm to the general public. Another relevant factor can be attributed to socio-cultural circumstances, which I will outline later in this analysis. Sometimes I just wonder, how famous the German robots *HERMES*, *Care-O-Bot* ™ or *ARMAR* would already be, if these were Japanese inventions.

Hermes, service robot developed at the Universität der Bundeswehr München / Germany

Photo: Jan Braun
courtesy HNF / Paderborn

Japan's image as "Nation of Technology" may be inflationary, but at least it makes people believe in its power.

3.1.2.3 Japan – The *Robot Kingdom* !

No other people are said to be so fascinated about robots than the Japanese. In the "*Robot Kingdom*" of Japan even exhibitions about industrial robots manage to attract a wide audience even from the general public not affiliated with fields like engineering, computer science or business, ranging from child over housewife to grandparent. Japan possesses the world's largest number of working industrial robots, although the figures appearing in statistics are probably overestimated because of the different definitions used in Japan and Europe / the US[279].

---

[279] Some machines which are listed as "robots" in the Japanese statistics are defined just as manipulators according to European and US standard regulations.

In Japan, robots and robot dreams have already been a topic at the International Science Expo '85 on the theme: "People, Residence, Environment and Science Technology", held in Japan's Tsukuba Science City about 20 years ago. A great attraction among others has been the organ-playing robot "*Wasubot*", which has also accompanied the symphony orchestra of the Japan Broadcasting Association (NHK). Although robots (actually 72 rolling and gleaming units of a size between 1.5 to 3.5 meters) have been presented as futuristic and artistic information providers at the German Theme Park "*Knowledge*"[280] at the Hanover Expo 2000 in Germany, surprisingly I don't recall that robots have been a feature at the Japanese pavilion. But again at the Expo 2005 which is to be held in Aichi / Japan[281] (one of Japan's main industrial hubs), robots will play a key role in a major event supported by the Japanese Ministry of Economy, Trade, and Industry (METI) and NEDO (New Energy and Industrial Technology Development Organization), Japan's main coordinator between METI, research facilities and the industry, where companies like Mitsubishi Heavy Industries, Toyota Motors Corporation, tmsuk/SOK, Subaru Motors and many others intend to display their next-generation robots and prototypes. About 100 robots of which the majority has been developed by Japanese universities and research institutes and the private industry are about to be featured as a special event during the exhibition, ranging from garbage-collection robots over surveillance and guidance robots (used as exhibition guides) to robots designed for interacting with people, especially with children.

---

[280] Conceptuated by the *Zentrum für Kunst- und Medientechnologie (ZKM), Karlsruhe*
[281] Aichi prefecture belongs to the leading centers for robot technology in Japan

Japanese elementary school children interact with a robot at the Aichi EXPO 2005 site

photo: Miriam JS Leis
@ Aichi Expo 2005 (April 14, 2005)

Since 1985 much has happened. Now the 21st century has finally arrived (whereas *"Y2K"* has already been forgotten) and with robots like Honda's *ASIMO*, Toyota's "Partner-Robots"[282], Mitsubishi's *"Wakamaru"* and the Sony creations *QRIO* and *AIBO*, the fantasies about 2001 envisioned at the Expo '85 *"Robot Dream Theatre"* even seem to have been excelled, and Schodt's prognosis about Japan's bright robot future looks like having been confirmed, an impression that got reinforced at the Aichi Expo 2005. Robot development and deployment, generally and not only in Japan, is gradually shifting from industrial application to public and even home use. And it is Japan that puts most efforts into it. Here robots are already beginning to set foot into mankind's every-day lives, which as to be taken quite literally, since in Japan I have counted so far at least 5 prominent humanoid biped-walking robot platforms that have already been presented to a wide public audience[283], not to mention all the smaller projects one gets to know through TV documentaries and exhibitions. No other country is putting so much vivid efforts into research on creating humanoid robots (i.e. robots which physically and someday even mentally

---

[282] The robots have not been named yet (stand: April 2005).
[283] I have counted ASIMO, QRIO, HRP-2 / Promet, Toyota's Robots (still unnamed; stand April 2005) and PINO (refer to the data in the appendix for more information.). There's also a great number of humanoid robot projects conducted at Japanese universities and research institutions that are rather known to insiders ad special interest groups.

resemble human beings) than Japan. The Japanese government, together with the industry is undertaking much effort to make robots popular among the people, and shape the basis for the future domestic and international market. This PR-work is ranging from edutainment centers over robot-documentaries on Japanese television (including semi-state run channels), permissions for robot-tests on public roads (e.g. in Fukuoka), bold plans for interdisciplinary robot-research facilities in Fukuoka, Osaka and Nagoya, to a Japanese Prime Minister Koizumi who likes to show up accompanied by some robot.

In the following chapters I would like to provide the reader with my findings which can hopefully shed some light on the following questions:

- What are the main differences between German and Japanese robot-research concepts?

- why is Japan perceived as *"Robotic Kingdom"*, while other countries although having similar sophisticated robot-projects don't possess this image?

- What is behind Japan's *"Robot-Kingdom"* image?

- Why do Japanese seem to embrace the idea of having robots around in such a positive fashion?

- Does there exist unique circumstances which could have led to Japan's perceived fondness for robots?

3.2 Robot-related interest promotion

Japanese seems to show vivid interest in robots. Many of Japan's major companies [284] are working on the development of some kind of service-/ entertainment-robot project. Japan's Prime Minister Koizumi has been seen posing with a seal-like robot *Paro*, which has also been presented to the Japanese cabinet, and even brought along *ASIMO* on a state visit to the Czech Republic. Exhibitions like *Robodex* / Yokohama and the *International Robot Exhibition* / Tokyo held in Japan, and ASIMO's "World Tour" contribute to interest promotion. There's no doubt that robot-technology belongs to the category of Japanese "prestige technology" as a form of self-representation to the world, similar to China's new space program. But as the huge successes of the exhibition "*Computer.Brain*" at the *Heinz Nixdorf MuseumsForum in Paderborn* / Germany and the attractiveness of museum-robots in German museums (e.g. *Museum für Kommunikation* / Berlin) have proven, robots can also become popular with Europeans. In late 2003 I even heard rumours that in early 2004 there would be held a huge exhibition in France focussing on non-industrial robots for domestic and entertainment use. Unfortunately, after trying to reach representatives in France as well as asking European insiders in this area, nobody was able to provide me with sufficient information about this alleged event. Even on the Internet I didn't obtain useful information. In a way this situation looks paradigmatic for a Europe lacking behind in public technology promotion.

One thing seems to be clear: Japanese are masters in promoting their products and making them renowned worldwide. This is the case with electronics, robots and recently with environment friendly technologies. Although actually Germany is the country which is internationally mostly associated with environmental friendly technologies and has been a forerunner in this area, again

---

[284] Bandai, Fujitsu, Honda, Matsushita, Mitsubishi, Sanyo, Seiko, SOK, Sony, Takara, Toshiba and others

through its promoting strategies, Japan may soon become *the* country associated with environmental protection and related high-technology. A huge factor contributing to this image-boosting is rooted in the Japanese government's efforts to further such technologies, something that has been materialized in the establishment of the New Energy and Industrial Technology Development Organization (NEDO) that got its backing from METI. It is also interesting to notice that it is not the Japanese education- or science ministry which is mostly involved in supporting the country's robot development activities, but the ministry responsible for economy, trade and industry, indicating that the main incentives lie in economic interests.

Picture: ASIMO-related merchandize and fan-articles sold in Japan

Photo: Miriam JS Leis, 2005
(author's own collection)

3.2.1 Public Events

In contrast to Germany, where robot-related public events like those mentioned in the examples above, are rather kept informative, contain a dimension of academic reflection and are left open for ambivalent interpretation and own conclusions, in Japan robot-related exhibitions are generally kept throughout positively and are almost exclusively conceptualized around interest promotion. Demonstrations are mostly conducted by or in cooperation with companies. The *show*-element features dominantly. "*Robodex*" may serve as exemplary for Japanese public robot-related events.

3.2.2 Robodex 2003 (held from 03.04.2003 to 06.04.2003)

On April 5th 2003 I have visited the "Robodex 2003" (**Robot Dream Ex**hibition) held in Japan for the third time since the year 2000 at *Pacifico Yokohama*, a huge exhibition center located at a futuristic-looking district in Yokohama/Japan. In contrast to other robot-exhibitions, including *AUTOMATICA* 2004 (Munich / Germany), *Robodex* has been the world's largest (and as far as I know the worldwide only) major exhibition *entirely* dedicated to real *non*-industrial robots and was mainly addressed towards the general public.

When entering the exhibition hall, one got the impression of rather walking through *"Tomorrow Land"*, although the fair was intended on the concept of information, edutainment and marketing promotion and had to be taken seriously. What one could see were robots, real and sophisticated, created with all the know-how of advanced technology and engineering available to us today; cutting-edge technology in its best. Unlike it has been the case with Germany's *Computer.Brain*, discussions about differences between humans and machines, historical background information (except the display of early Japanese *Karakuri*-automata), reflective or (God forbids) negative elements have been absent here. It was mainly about companies displaying their cutting-edge products, suggesting a bright future of human-robot-co-existence.

The first *Robodex* was held in the year 2000, offering the public a unique opportunity to get first-hand information about the latest non-industrial robot developments and to see them in "life" action, causing hour-long line-ups, although this is not a rarity at major events in large Japanese cities. This first *Robodex* exhibition was based on the theme *"robots as human partners"*.

Robodex 2003 was centered round humanoid robots and was highlighted under the sign of *"Tetsuwan Atomu" (Astro Boy)*, the famous Japanese fictional robot-figure, who was according to "legend" created on April 7th 2003. As already mentioned before, the popularity of *"Tetsuwan Atomu"* is said to have contributed much to Japan's generally positive attitude towards robots and has inspired even engineers and scientists to get involved in the field of robotics.

Over 50 companies and research facilities have presented about 90 of the latest robot-creations ranging from electronic pets (e.g. the mechatronic *AIBO-*"dog" from Sony) over household assistance- and "watchdog" robots (e.g. "*Wakamaru*" from Mitsubishi Heavy Industry Co., Ltd. or "*Maron-1*" from Fuji Automation) to humanoid robots like Honda's walking *ASIMO*, Sony's *SDR-4XII* (recently renamed to *QRIO*) and *HRP-2* (short for Humanoid Robot Project or Humanoid Robot Platform) the result of a Japanese government supported project, developed in co-operation with AIST[285], NEDO[286], MSTC[287] and many other companies and Universities participating in this project.

Judging from the overwhelming number of about 70 000 visitors, ranging from toddler to grandparent, male and female, the subject of robotics seem to attract quite a wide audience in Japan. And despite a stagnating economy, Japan is putting much effort into robotic research and development. Representatives have explained the functions, development and fields of employment for their robots and often enabled direct interactions between visitors and robots. What seems to be even more surprising to the stranger of Japan and interesting to a sociologist is the fact that this entire exhibition was *not* about industrial robots, but about the topic regarding the integration of robots into daily life and activities, not hypothetically but practically. Some of the company-developed robots have already been marketed or are planned to go on sale in the near future. One of the key arguments made by developers and manufacturers was about the deployment of (humanoid) robots as caregivers and housekeepers in an aging society (and a country reluctant in recruiting foreign workers for doing low-paid jobs, although this has not been said publicly). Next to utility-oriented purposes of robots (caretaking, assistance to humans and classical fields of performing

---

[285] National Institute of Advanced Industrial Science and Technology
[286] New Energy and Industrial Technology Development Organization
[287] Manufacturing Science and Technology Center

dangerous jobs or maintenance), entertainment and companionship were capitalized at the exhibition as Honda's term "Pal-Robot" ("パル ロボット") [288] exemplifies. In all of this one got the impression that the whole business of "home use" or "personal robots" is really taken quite seriously here in Japan.

3.2.3 Kansai and Kyushu: Japan's hubs for Robot development

The promotion of robotics has become an aspiration of national interest in Japan, whereas there are government-backed plans to transform the *Kansai* region (especially Osaka) and Kyushu into hubs for Japan's robot technology. New robot-related companies like tmsuk have been founded in Kyushu, and Prime Minister Koizumi has permitted the testing of robots on public roads in Fukuoka as part of the so-called *"special zone"* legislation. Osaka, an economic hub, already housing many universities, industries and research facilities and being home to Japan's *RoboCup* competitions (Japan Open), is also being seen as a logical choice for a hopeful striving future industry.

In 2003 I had the opportunity to visit a so-called robot edutainment center located in Fukuoka and get the occasion for conducting an interview with leading project representatives to provide some insight into Japan's robot research, development, culture and interest promotion activities.

On May 12th. 2003 I have visited an institution in Fukuoka / Japan named "*RoboSquare*", located at the new, huge shopping center "*Hakata Riverain*", for an interview with some of its leading representatives[289]. *RoboSquare* is financed through the city government of Fukuoka and the industry. At the moment it

---
[288] Taken from a Honda pamphlet about ASIMO
[289] Special thanks to Mr.Shinkawa, Mr. Ninomiya and Mr. Takashima (translation) from „Robosquare" Fukuoka for making possible this interview.

consists of an exhibition / information center, a main office, a section where robots and robot-related products can be purchased and other facilities where robot-related activities, research classes for university students and construction-classes for children and teenagers are being held. But there are plans for extending the facility into a main hub for connecting researchers, engineers, industry representatives, politicians and the general public and providing robot-related information exchange, education, entertainment, product sales and administrative work, with the side effect of drawing interested tourists and more business into the area. One initialization point for the project was the *RoboCup* 2002, a soccer-tournament played by robots instead of people (although the people still provide the computer programs), gaining an increasing popularity (in the industrialized countries), which was then held in Fukuoka and Busan / Korea and drew some 12 000 visitors.

As Mr. Shinkawa has outlined in the interview, promotion of research in the relatively new field of robotics for non-industrial use is of great importance for Japan, since it is hoped to develop this into a "new automobile industry". Unfortunately the children's interest in mathematics, natural sciences and engineering are on the decline, which represents a bad situation for technology-oriented Japan with scarce natural resources. Through interest-promotion in robotics it is hoped to boost the interest of children and students in the area of natural sciences, information technology and maths. Of major importance is also the concept of "learning by doing" and "hands-on" activities.

To my question about possible explanations for Japan's positive image about robots, the respondent again mentioned "*Tetsuwan Atomu*" (*Astro Boy*) as representing a big influence which shaped the Japanese image about robots. Even the mayor of Fukuoka and many famous researchers in the field of robotics are said to be fans of "Tetsuwan Atomu". According to Mr. Shinkawa, "*Tetsuwan Atomu*" provides a clear example that robots and humans can live together in harmony and serves as a role model for this idea, but perhaps it also may be setting too high expectations in regard to the developments in Artificial Intelligence (AI).

As I asked him about possible concerns in regard to robot-development and deployment he said that concerning AI, the Japanese also express a little fear in view of the question what if someday AI might get superior to humans. In principal it's the same problems that concern humans and robots, because robots will just be like the humans who have created them. Mr. Shinkawa has again given an example from *"Tetsuwan Atomu"*, where there is also a negative robot-character called *"Atlas"*, who just behaves the way he does, because he is manipulated in such a way by humans. The use of robots for military purposes was absolutely rejected. *RoboCup*[290] on the other hand is seen as a very good institution, because of its positive aspect of sportsmanship and co-operation. In general robots are seen in Japan as entities that can be trusted, which help humans and even become "heroes". They will become helpful in areas of rescue operations (e.g. after earthquakes) and in the field of welfare and medical assistance. Also disabled people show a positive interest in assistance provided by robots, which enable them to live a more independent life.

I have also asked the question if they see a connection between the Japanese *Shinto*-religion and the people's view of robots. The respondent has agreed that there might be aspects in the *Shinto*-tradition that could influence the way Japanese people look at robots. One aspect is that the Christian tradition might make it harder for Europeans to accept bided or even quite human-like robots. The other point having been mentioned is the possibility that in the Japanese view some form of "spirit" or "soul" may be seen as being present in objects and tools, especially those which are very important to the user (historically *Samurai*[291]-swords, for example). He has given the example, that a writer might see some form of "alter ego" being incorporated in his pen. So the often heard

---

[290] National and international robot-soccer competitions
[291] Japanese warrior in the times prior to the Meiji restoration starting in 1866

statement of "robots becoming partners for mankind" can be even interpreted quite literally in this situation.

I have also asked the question in how far the development of robots and AI should go. The respondent said that in an ideal situation (without technical problems) robots might get quite human-like and even become better like humans in power and brains. But they will never replace humans, because it will be quite difficult to enable a robot making judgements. A robot will probably only be able to make rational judgements, what may lead to conflicts with humans and human reasoning. But if perfect AI will be feasible concerns the question if mankind would ever accept something superior to them.

After being asked about his personal dream in regard to robots, he answered that "robots can become good partners for mankind and that it is feasible to do so."

To summarize the information I have obtained in the interview, one can say the following in regard to plans, concepts and acceptability rate of robots:

• The Japanese government is financially supporting Research and Development (R&D) and promotion-activities in the field of robotics for non-industrial use and regards the development of robot technology as an important factor for Japan's industry and economy

• The promotion of robot-related activities serves the following goals:

- boosting the interest of children in fields of natural sciences, maths and information

   technology

- promoting a new filed of industry (robots for non-industrial use)

- getting the general public interested in such activities

- activities like RoboCup are seen as important tools to achieve the goals mentioned above

- Robots are planned to be deployed in the following fields:
  - care-service and other services
  - rescue work
  - entertainment

- The figure "Tetsuwan Atomu" serves as a symbol / role-model and provides a positive image of robots

- In general robots are seen quite positive in Japan and the main fears seem to be concentrated around the question what if AI would get superior to humans, a question which is of no immediate relevance.

- It seems to be possible for Japanese to regard robots as "partners for mankind"

"*TMSUK04*", surveillance and utility robot by Kitakyushu-based company *tmsuk* / Japan, on display at an apartment-complex in *Nishi-Oi*, Tokyo.

Photo: Miriam JS Leis, 2004

3.2.4 Japan's Robotic Celebrities

Although robots possess a great publicity *potential* also in Germany, as the popular platforms in German museums demonstrate, the Japanese make much more consequent use of it.

Welcoming customers at *Takashimaya* department stores (2003-2004), accompanying the Japanese Prime Minister to Prague (2003)[292], Posing for *NTT DoCoMo* at the *CEATEC Japan 2003*, ringing the bell at the New York Stock Exchange (2002), clapping hands at the closing ceremony marking the end of trading at the Tokyo Stock Exchange (2003), pounding ritual rice cakes at a New Year's festivity at Honda Motor's Headquarters (2004) and greeting German Chancellor Gerhard Schröder at the *Hannover Messe* (2004). Others are invited on celebrating the opening of the new "*Shinkansen*" (high-speed train) station at Shinagawa (2003), attending the Japanese Year's End Song Contest Extravaganza (2003), appearing as special guest conducting the Tokyo Philharmonic Orchestra (2004), participating at a children's concert (2004), holding a promotional session at CeBIT Hanover / Germany (2004) and even get the honour to throw the opening ball at a major-league baseball match between the San Diego Padres and the New York Mets (2004)[293]. This is not the schedule of some politicians or human celebrities, but that of what may be Japan's most famous robots: *ASIMO* and *QRIO*. Actually it looks as if at nearly every major event in Japan some robots have to be present and robot shows are always drawing in clouds of people, young and old.

ASIMO may be already viewed as the "living" version of "*Tetsuwan Atomu*" at least in regard to its symbolic character, and it gained celebrity status. It serves for Honda as "car dealer", and shows up at some amusement parks. IBM

---

[292] P3, the third prototype model of Honda's ASIMO already gained fame in 1997, where it greeted former Chinese Premiere Minister Li Peng upon his visit to Japan. The first prototype P1 has already been presented to the public in 1993 with P2 following in 1996.
[293] A list of events can be found here http://asimo.honda.com/news_media_center.asp (ASIMO) and http://www.sony.net/SonyInfo/QRIO/top.html (QRIO)

Japan and the Takashimaya department-store chain have leased *ASIMO* to work as a receptionist, for on-stage performances or as tour-guide, willing to pay around 20 million YEN (approx. USD 192 416) per month or YEN 2 million (approx USD 19 241) per day, roughly the price one has to pay for engaging one of the most famous Japanese human show-biz celebrities (called *"talento"* [294]) for hosting an event. But *ASIMO* also gained international renown, for example as he...no...it rang the opening bell at the New York Stock Exchange on February 14th. 2002, the 25th anniversary of Honda Motors Co., Ltd. being listed at the *NYSE*, and it also appeared at a symposium titled *"From High-Tech to Intelligence - The Challenge of Humanoid Robots"* held at the Technische Universität Darmstadt / Germany in June 2003.

While the long-term goals for *ASIMO* are planned to be in the area of deploying the robot as assistant in offices and private households, the concept of Sony's *QRIO* is nearly exclusively oriented on the scheme of Japanese popular "talento"-entertainment[295]. A group of *QRIO* (together with some *AIBO*s) is basically doing the same kind of performance while singing "kiseki no tabi", an original song exclusively composed by Japanese star composer Ryuichi Sakamoto[296] for *QRIO* performances (perhaps the first people who may fear for their job due to replacement by robots will be the "talentos").

PINO, an open-platform biped walking robot, now marketed by the Japanese company *ZMP, Inc.* (which also sells nuvo and e-nuvo robots) was even performing in the award-winning[297] music-video "*Can you keep a secret?*" together with the Japanese pop idol Hikaru Utada[298]. And Japanese pop singers

---

[294] The term derives from the English word „talent"
[295] *"Talento"* is the Japanese term for (domestic) show-business personalities, especially J-pop singers.
[296] Composer of the Soundtrack from the movie *"The Last Emperor"* and many musical scores for commercials
[297] Viewer's Choice at the MTV Video Award 2001 (MTV Japan) and best song at the Japanese *GoldenDisk* Award 2002
[298] Refer to http://www.cnn.com/2001/BUSINESS/asia/07/03/tokyo.pinorobot/ (July 3rd, 2001) and the link: http://www.centragarden.net/jpop/secret.html

like Tommy[299] or the group *GLAY* have been involved in the promotion of Sony's AIBO robot. There has also once existed a performance group called *Yu-Gi-Dan* (not to be confused with the animé-series *Yu-Gi-Oh!*), which consisted of *AIBO*-robots.

Through such activities the Japanese have managed making their robots popular among the general public, even giving them a somewhat equal status to "organic celebrities". Such kind of activities nicely exemplify the Japanese interest in using robots for entertainment and promotional purposes, which seems to go far beyond German activities of using robots as museum guide or attractions at special events.

x

x

3.2.5 Japan – Inside the Robot-Toy-Kingdom[300]

About two decades ago in the 1980s, battery-driven mechanical toys have already been a great feature in Japan and my first Japanese toys consisted of a mechanical dog and a battery-driven parrot.

And today, as I went on a stroll through the traditional *Nakamise*-shopping street in front of the *Asakusa* temple in Tokyo, I was greeted by a whole array of mechatronic gadgetry, although no real robots but rather battery-driven toys, coming out beeping from the small shops[301]. *Gundam*[302] action figures and other robot-models are being sold in shops next to outlets trading Buddhist-related items. In Japan children already grow up with the idea of the robot. German friends of mine have even hypothesized if all this may just be a brilliant long-

---

[299] Tommy is under contract of Sony Records
[300] Borrowing the phrase "Robot Kingdom" from Frederick L. Schodt
[301] At earlier visits this phenomenon was even more present than at recent visits. This may be attributed to the changing economic climate in Japan, which led to declines in overall customer numbers and shops reducing the amount of articles.
[302] A robot / robotic vehicle from a famous Japanese animé (cartoon)

term strategy to get Japanese people accustomed to the idea of robots which will care for them when they grew old.

A small outlet at the *Nakamise* street in Asakusa / Japan selling mechatronic toys

Photo: Miriam JS Leis, Tokyo 2003

Let's begin with some rather simple task, a stroll through the toy sections in shops and department stores. I did my observations in main department stores in Tokyo, Frankfurt, Hannover, Stuttgart, Köln and Konstanz[303].

The first apparent observation I made in Germany during the time from early 2003 to late 2004 is that the number of electronic and mechatronic toys sold in Germany seems to have been on the increase. Whereas one could hardly find any electronic or mechatronic toys such as the product-palette of *FurReal-Friends* "robots"[304] in early 2003, the variety of such technological playthings, mainly US-imports, has been steadily on the rise, having reached a climax during my last visits to *Galleria Kaufhof* in Köln (Cologne) and Frankfurt in

---

[303] Tokyo: *Takashimaya, Tokyu Hands, Daishin, Ito Yokado* and some smaller outlets. Frankfurt and Stuttgart: *Hertie* and *Galeria Kaufhof*; Hanover: *Galleria Kaufhof* and *Toy Store Hanover*, Cologne (latest visit): *Galleria Kaufhof*; Munich: *Galleria Kaufhof*, Konstanz: *Hertie* and *S + F Schinacher GmbH*. All *Galleria Kaufhof* stores in the larger cities (Stuttgart, Frankfurt, Hanover, Munich and Köln) had generally the same kinds of items on sale (i.e. upon visiting a *Galleria Kaufhof* store in Stuttgart and Frankfurt around the same time, I found nearly the same items on sale). My first visits have been to Stuttgart and Frankfurt approximately around the same time in early 2003. My second visit has been to Hanover and Frankfurt in Spring 2004. My third visit has been to Munich in Summer 2004 and my last visit to Cologne and Frankfurt in Autumn 2004. In Tokyo I have visited all mentioned outlets approximately around the same time as my visits in Germany: Spring 2003, Summer 2003, Winter 2003, Spring 2004, Summer 2004 and Autumn 2004.
[304] Actually sensor-based partly interactive automata

November 2004, where among others the internationally popular interactive toy-robot *Robosapiens*[305] (Toy of the Year 2004) manufactured and distributed by *Wowwee* (in Germany distributed by *Joker AG*) and some Chinese *Tamagotchi* clones were on sale. *MicroPets*™, small preprogrammed and to a limited extend interactive "pets" made by Tomy, the second largest toy company in Japan, had also found its way to Germany, but sales have been discontinued after mid 2003. In late 2004 also products from Germany, like a small mechanical, sensor-equipped dog (*PipiMax*) from *Stadlbauer* have been among the items for sale. The other interesting observation has been the relatively huge amount of merchandise products related to Japanese animé-series such as *Pokémon, Dragon Ball* and *Yu-Gi-Oh!*. It is also noticeable that the targeted population for electronic toys becomes increasingly younger, as much of the products are even designed for toddlers, as a whole palette of educational toys/ learning computers developed by the German company *VTech* ® and sensor equipped moving Teddies and dolls by *Kidz Only* indicate. But interestingly the only products of such kind that actually looked like a robot have been *Robosapiens* and educational toys like *LEGO Mindstorms* and *Fischer Technik* construction-kits. Although electronic toys are beginning to enjoy an increasing popularity in Germany, these items are still by far outnumbered by classic, non-electronic (wooden) toys, car-models, dolls, stuffed animals and family-oriented games (e.g. card- and board games to be played in groups, something that is rarely found in Japan).

It is also interesting, that one cannot find many educational robot-toys / experimental-kits in regular Japanese toy shops.

Let's look at the situation in Japan: what toy-cars are in Germany are toy-robots in Japan. In the designated "boy's areas" of Japanese toy sections one can

---

[305] The sophisticated programmable and interactive robot-toy has been developed by Mark Tilden, a former NASA-engineer. This robot is even used as research platform by some German universities, e.g. the University Freiburg

hardly find anything else but merchandise of robots from *"Gundam"* over *"Mugenbine"* to *"Tetsuwan Atom"* (Astro Boy). Articles are ranging from simple action figures and so-called transformers[306] to interactive electronic items with some (pre)programmed functions. And as I go downstairs to the convenient store in Tokyo, there's a whole shelf full of sweets packages containing diverse robot images and small figurines of robots and action- and *anime* heroes. These small figurines are especially popular in Japan as collector's items. They are often sold in packages together with sweets for a limited period of time. Some collectors even buy such figures for relatively high prices. Also outside Japan these objects achieve a growing popularity and are often offered at *e-bay*.

Figurines of AIBO-robots sold by Glico under license.

Photo: Miriam J.S. LEIS, 2005 author's own collection

Electronic toys like the previously mentioned *MicroPets*, Aquaroids (small "robotic" fish mainly produced by Takara / Japan), robotic cats, interactive speaking dolls and curiosities like moving "mechatronic plants" powered by solar energy are rather directed at female and adult customers. Especially the "robot" (or rather "Mobile Suit") figures from the Japanese ainmé-series *"Gundam"*[307], are now celebrating a huge comeback in Japan, with whole

---

[306] Models which can be turned into other figures, e.g. a car into a robot
[307] *"Gundam"* units are not really autonomous robots, but rather machine-vehicles piloted by humans. For a short while, *"Gundam"* has also been shown on German television Tele5 from mid 2003, but it features quite well in Italy, for example, where a lot of *Gundam* websites / fansites can be found. In Japan, since 1979 up to 2003 the "Gundam Universe" has become

department store shelves packed with "*Gundam*" merchandise. In Akihabara, Tokyo's so-called electric-town, I have even discovered outlets where whole floors have been nearly totally dedicated to *Gundam*-related articles. As the first "*Gundam*" toys and models appeared in Japan in the 1980s, they have triggered a real shop-run that even led to accidents as customers stormed to the shelves to get their "*Gundam*"-figure. According to statistics from 2001, the Japanese toy-maker *Bandai* has already sold over 320 million "*Gundam*" action-figure models since 1980. If one looks at Japan's total population of about 128 million people, statistically by now every Japanese, from grandma to grandchild, would possess 2.5 "*Gundam*" figures.

In Japan even engineering students, for example at the *Kanazawa Industrial College*, study blueprints of the numerous "*Gundam technical manual*" books in their courses and the *Gundam*-design also looks as having inspired real robot-designers as the somewhat resemblance between "*Gundam*" and the real robot-platform *HRP-2 / Promete* may hint. And indeed, as *HRP-2 / Promete* can also be controlled by a human operator who gets feedback from the robot's movements, it may actually bear some similitude to piloting a "*Gundam*" machine.

left: *Mobile-Suit Gundam*: Action-figure of a human-controlled "Mobile Suit" from the Japanese aimé-series "*Gundam Destiny*" (Note the antler-like structure on the "robot's" helmet that gets one reminded on helmets worn by Japanese *Samurai* warriors.)

(photo: Miriam JS LEIS author's own collection)

right. *HRP-2 / Promete*. Real robot prototype developed by AIST, NEDO, Kawada Industries and others on an initiative by METI / Japan.

(photo: Miriam JS Leis at "*Robodex 2003*")

Notice: the strings on the shoulders are just for support, since the robot is only able to stand on its own while power is running.

---

quite complex, as there now exist series like "*Double Zeta Gundam*", "*Gundam F-91*", "*Gundam Force*", *Gundam Seed*", "*Gundam Wing*" (with the intention to also attract a wider audience, especially females, by less focusing on the mecha-animé side of the story).

I am even unsure about which robot-story has generated more commercial spill-over effects, *"Gundam"* or *"Tetsuwan Atomu"*. At least in the latter case one finds besides action figures nearly all kinds of items with images from the famous robot-story by Osamu Tezuka, ranging from keyholders, pens and folders over postcards and posters to T-shirts, plates and mugs.

Collection of merchandise related to „*Tetsuwan Atomu*".

(Photo: Miriam JS Leis, 2005 author's own collection)

Besides *"Gundam"* and *"Tetsuwan Atomu"* the whole *"Doraemon"* universe has also been inspiring to toymakers, as *Bandai*[308] is now planning to create a real moving robot with sensors, speech synthesis and interaction capabilities, resembling the famous robot cat from the 22nd Century.

---

[308] One of Japan's largest toymakers

Giant figure of *Doraemon* (*"Doraemon Time Capsule"*) displayed at the *Roppongi Hills* complex in Tokyo

Photo: Miriam J.S. Leis, 2004

In summary one could say that also in regard to toy-robots and robot-toys the Japanese situation looks quite unique. But the popularity of mechanical or mechatronic toys seems to be an Asian phenomenon, as I have even discovered many kinds of moving dolls and robot figures in Chinese and Korean import shops on Saipan, a small Pacific island.

Although the number of electronic toys is on the rise also in Germany, many parents still look at them with scepticism, as all of my German friends with small children and would-be-parents told me that they consider electronic toys as inhibiting the danger of hampering a child's creativity, imagination and social development. But if looking at the request and demand situation in Japan one could hardly speak of overly concerned parents. To the contrary, I heard that parents hope to induce their children's interest in technology and mechanics by providing them with such toys. Judging from these observations one could positively speak of Japan as the "*Robot-Toy Kingdom*".

In Japan the development and marketing of robots, especially those in the category of so-called "entertainment robots" can be regarded as the logical step following the country's success on the market of electronic toys. It looks as if in Japan, very much more than in Germany, the new generation of non-industrial robots is viewed rather in the tradition of dolls and sophisticated toys than in that of machines. It's not so much about an adaptation of industrial robots to the non-industrial field, but about the evolution of the doll – *ningyō* - being taken quite literally as "human shape".

x

3.3 Robot Pets

Whereas one could say that US-researchers are quite interested in using robots as test-beds for exploring human emotions (e.g. MIT research platforms such as *Cog* and *Kismet*), Japanese robot researchers, engineers and designers are more interested in creating robots that *evoke* some form of emotion in humans. German researchers on the other hand are mostly concerned with the rather pragmatic side of human-machine interaction by emphasizing the aspect of user-friendliness and easy control through enabling the usage of input- and command patterns, which come close to everyday practices.

As I was asked in a German household-survey about the number of pets in my household I wondered if the question one day also may include "electric pets" to use the terminology of a Philip K Dick. Indeed, a growing number of people around the world, and especially in Japan, already share their homes with canine- or feline-like "robots". Such "robot-pets" have principally no pragmatic function and are mostly kept for entertainment and fun (except cases where they are used for experiments in programming).

Canine- and feline-like "pet-robots" being marketed / having been marketed[309]

Product Name	Manufacturer	Country of origin	Comments	Availability
AIBO	Sony Corporation	Japan	(Vaguely) Canine-like robot. The most famous and most advanced of its kind on the market	One model in Europe (ERS-7), two models in Japan (ERS-311/ERS-312 & ERS-7)
FurReal	Tiger Electronics	USA	Feline-like robot with limited interaction possibilities. Reacts mostly to touch.	Still on market in the US, Europe and Asia
I-Cybie	Hasbro	USA (patent bought from Japan)	Canine-like robot. Less interactive, less responsive and less advanced than AIBO	As far as I know, there are still only used models on the market
NearMe	Sega Toys	Japan	Feline-like robot similar to FurReal, but maybe a little more advanced	in 2004/2005 on the market in Japan
NeCoRo	Omron	Japan	The most advanced and most realistic feline-like robot which has ever been on the market	sales discontinued
Paro	AIST	Japan	Seal-like robot that interacts in a quite realistic way. The purposes of deployment are mainly for therapeutic usage	According to my latest information there are marketing plans for around 2005
Yume no neko	Sega Toys	Japan (Japanese equivalent to FurReal)	Refer to FurReal	marketed in Japan

---

[309] The list may be incomplete and does not include a whole array of non- or low-interactive mechatronic toys such as those exclusively designed for children or low-interactive gadgets like robot (jelly)fish. It also does not include "virtual pets" like *Tamagotchi* and its derivates. In this context I define "interactive" as the ability of the robot to respond to a human's actions in a pursuable manner (i.e. not just displaying the same sequence(s) over again, regardless of a human's actions/responses.)

There still exists some dispute about the question in how far such "electronic pets" can be called a robot, or if they just resemble sensor-driven automata. So I have decided to provide a deeper analysis about the most famous "electronic pet" on the market, whose status as a "robot" is least disputed: Sony's canine-like AIBO.

Yume-no-Neko by Sega-toys / Japan; cat-like sensor-based „robot" with limited ability to react to outside stimuli

Photo: Miriam JS Leis;
Saipan, 2005
property of H. Leis & family

AIBO ERS-311/B, Interactive Entertainment Robot by Sony Corporation / Japan

Photo: Miriam JS Leis;
Saipan, 2005
property of author

3.3.1.1 AIBO[310]

The *AIBO*-phenomenon is insofar interesting as it is the first "real" robot-pet for home use, and its existence cuts through many dimensions associated with questions about the future of human- and robot coexistence. Some people, especially in Japan, but also in Germany (although this is not readily admitted in this European country) have developed some personal feeling and attachment towards their *AIBO*-robots, which exceeds the just-fondness about techno-chic or the care for prestige objects.

---

[310] This is the modified version of an article I have written for my homepage in 2003. Most of the data has been obtained from user's manuals and promotional pamphlets provided at exhibitions and stores and from information I obtained through communication with the German internet-based AIBO-Community (www.aibo-freunde.de). In January 2006, shortly after having finished my doctoral examination and before publishing, Sony announced that its research and sales activities regarding AIBO and QRIO will be discontinued in March 2006.

On the one hand, new, mostly Internet-based communities and interest-groups have formed around *AIBO*. On the other hand, researchers and lay(wo)men alike already begin to express considerations and concerns about the development of some form of "post social" tendencies through the preoccupation with the artificial by neglecting the natural, as a friend of mine has expressed it in a critical article by stating that it might be easier to get engaged into the asymmetric, conflict-free virtual interaction than taking time and effort to get along with the difficulties of dealing with real humans of whom everybody is primarily concerned with fulfilling ones own goals. In my view this aspect is even more pressing in the setting of Japanese society, something I will explain in more detail later in my analysis.

One thing seems to be obvious, although AIBO robots are also used for scientific and technical purposes, for example as standardized platforms at the *RoboCup* (robot soccer competitions), AIBO is also a robot that possesses properties like providing companionship, something previously only associated with living pets or humans.

3.3.1.2 The History of AIBO

In the last millennium, on May 11th 1999 the Japan-based Sony Corporation has given "birth" to AIBO, the world's first commercially available canine-like robot for home-use – and today I found two invitations from Sony to "AIBO's 5th anniversary" in my mailbox, one from Europe and one from Japan. AIBO is the acronym for „Artificial Intelligence Robot" (I'll leave open the question about AIBO's intelligence until the meaning of "intelligence" and "artificial" are sufficiently cleared, something I will comment on in the final part of my analysis.) All four-legged robots are between 25 – 30 cm long and more or less resemble a dog. But according to official statements from Sony it has never been their intention to create AIBO as a "dog" or even a "dog-substitute". That's also one reason why Sony has decided against furnishing AIBO with fur (another reason is the possible overheating). AIBO is conceptualized as a high-tech Entertainment Robot consisting of a body, movable limbs, a head with an integrated camera for sight[311] (and picture-taking), a distance sensor (the latest ERS-7 has even two distance sensors) to prevent it from running into objects or falling from elevated areas (most time), and a RISC[312] processor as a "brain". The AIBO models possess a total of 15 to 20 DOFs (= degrees of freedom, very roughly defined as the possibilities of a joint's movements). The abilities and character of AIBO are provided by specific software, called AIBO-ware, which is stored on small patented memory devices called a *"Memory Stick* ™*"*. In Japanese "aibō" (相棒) can also mean partner, buddy or pal – and this is the main function of AIBO: to enjoy and entertain its owner. AIBO is intended to be much more than just an electronic toy. The robot is equipped with a whole array of sensors and programmed to express 6 "emotions": joy, sadness, anger, surprise, fear and discontent. It is also programmed with "instincts" and "desires" for love, curiosity, movement, rest and "self-preservation" (i.e. to recharge its batteries, take a protective posture when falling, calls for help or shut down in critical situations). It also lets you know if it wants to be recharged and some models are even able to autonomously return to their charging station. AIBO (versions ERS-210[313], -220, -310 and -7) is also able to understand 50 to about 100 verbal commands[314] (most of the time and if it wants to…) and possesses some learning ability (e.g. if scolded for a specific action this activity will decrease). With specific software AIBO is even able to talk (voice output with speech-synthesis). It communicates through LED displays on the head

---

[311] That's why the acronym "AIBO" is also designed to be interpreted as "eye" and "(ro)bo(t)", i.e. a robot which reacts to visual perceptions (refer to: http://www.jp.aibo.com/)
[312] RISC = Reduced Instruction Set Computer, the architecture used in most of today's computers
[313] ERS stands for Entertainment Robot System. A short description about the different models will be provided later
[314] Synonyms are also counted

visor or a LED "horn-lamp" located on top on its head (for the ERS-310-series), whereas the LED-display patterns and / or colors represent the "emotional" status of the robot. As it is the case with the ERS-311 / 312 /31L series, if the "horn-lamp" flashes green for example, it's in good spirits and if it flashes orange it's angry. AIBO is able to react to stimuli from its environment and shows diverse physical and "emotional" reactions. As far as I could obtain technological data, the generation of AIBO's "emotions" roughly works the following way: the robot has been programmed with some "instincts" or "desires", e.g. it wants to play or to rest. External stimuli, e.g. if you play with it, praise it or disturb it when it wants to sleep, are recognized through its sensors. Each "emotion" is coded and the perceived sensor-information is represented through specific values in a matrix. If its desires are fulfilled, the value for "joy" increases, causing it to express happiness. In the opposite case the values for sadness or anger increase, causing it to display the corresponding behavior. If it expresses discontent, the values for anger might decrease through this process, setting it back to a "neutral" state. The perceived sensor-input data (i.e. the owner's interaction pattern) also determines the development of AIBO. Specific software (AIBO-life) enables the owner to raise their robot from "baby" to "adult", whereas its character forms according to how it is treated and interacted with. If, for example, one acts too protective towards it (don't let it try things on its own or react in every instant it might call for you) your robot may get "spoiled", or if neglected, it might get selfish or discontent. The abilities and character of AIBO depends on the used AIBO-ware and on how it is treated by the owner. Additional AIBO-functions like taking photographs, watchdog-function, pattern recognition (e.g. the recognition of faces and pictures on CD covers) Internet- and W-LAN communication and mp3-playback are possible depending on the model and software. The concept of "raising" an "evolving" machine looks unique indeed[315] (just a short note on self-observation: as I am writing this, I'm somehow reluctant calling it a machine).

It is difficult to objectively judge the value and possibilities of AIBO's interaction- and entertainment capabilities since such an evaluation depends on the expectations of the individual owner. Accordingly the comments of people having interacted with AIBO also range from expressing fascination about its life-simulating abilities to comments stating that "it's all just a programmed and repetitive fake". And indeed, AIBO can't compete with the overwhelming complexity of a living animal, since every attempt of reconstructing this by far exceeds the possibilities of today's AI and simulation technologies.

Up to now there have been 5 different AIBO-generations[316] on the market, of which only one model (AIBO ERS-7) is still available in Germany and two models (AIBO ERS-311 / ERS-312[317] and AIBO ERS-7) are on the market in Japan. In 1999 the first AIBO, AIBO ERS-110, was on sale in Japan and the US. The first 3000 models which have been offered over the Internet were sold out within 20 minutes in Japan, and that despite its USD 2 500 price tag. All 2000 AIBOs which have been on sale in the US have found an owner within 4 days. After these unexpected sales successes (at the Japanese exhibition *"Project X 21"* I have learned that initially Sony has been sceptical if their creation would proof a success), a slightly modified version of the ERS-110, ERS-111, has hit the markets in Japan, the US and some European countries. Because AIBOs were only available in limited numbers, the buyers have been decided by lottery. Since February 2000 Sony decided to abrogate the production limitations. From

---

[315] Actually the idea of "evolving artefacts" which have to be taken care of by people has been made popular with the Japanese *Tamagotchi* (introduced in 1996), a virtual chick on a LCD display which has to be fed and taken care of.

[316] If counting ERS-110 and ERS-111 or ERS-311, ERS-312 and ERS-31L as belonging to the same generation.

[317] Since in regard to their hardware these models are basically similar to each other I count them as one model. In Japan ERS-311 and ERS-312 are not only distinguishable through their color, but also through their character. While "Latte" possesses a lively and happy nature, "Macaron" displays a more "serene" character. These software-dependent differences do not show with the usage of non-Japanese AIBO-ware.

then on everybody could get ones desired AIBO. In the same year the second AIBO-generation has been released. To many this model, the ERS-210 represents the classic image of AIBO. With its pointed ears it optically somehow resembles a robotic "sheep dog" (at least this is my opinion). The first ones came in the colors gold, silver and black. Later they added some more exotic variants (special editions) in blue, red, green and purple. Additionally new features like voice recognition, tonal communication and an extended spectrum of emotional expressions have been implemented. It was further possible to name ones AIBO and make it react to its name. Other functions like Wireless-LAN communication have also been made possible.

The following creation, the AIBO ERS-220 developed by *Sony Entertainment Robot America* (a subsidiary company of the Sony Corporation Japan) has proven less popular. Although it was equipped with more technological capabilities, many dislike its optical appearance, which reminds them too much of a "fighting machine". At least this is the opinion of many German AIBO owners[318] (or *AIBOwner*'s as it's the official US-coined term). So the ERS-220 that looks rather like a futuristic vehicle than a "dog" or any other animal has mainly attracted "professional" users who used it for programming and experimenting.

The ivory-colored ERS-311 and the dark-grey ERS-312, "*Latte*" and "*Macaron*" as the AIBO-creations from the year 2001 are also called, distinguish themselves from their predecessors through their cute design by the world renowned Japanese artist Katsura Moshino (winner of the „Canon Digital Creators Contest 2003), which is oriented on the Japanese trend of so-called "*Character Goods*" (e.g. *Hello Kitty* by *Sanrio*). "*Latte*" and "*Macaron*" (LM-series) have been created with the intention of attracting a wider spectrum of people, including those who would just want to enjoy living with a robot. That's why the aspect of entertainment and their cuddly look seems to be more focused

---

[318] I'm referring to an unofficial "opinion-poll" conducted at the German AIBO-community site (www.aibo-freunde.de)

on. This made these robots very popular with the Japanese, but less attractive to the German / European audience. As I have learned through (online) discussions with German *AIBOwners*, much of the scepticism and unpopularity of the ERS-311/-312-models was due to the country's bad information providing and the lack of attractive commercial campaigns. After seeing ERS-311/-312 in action, the huge majority of German *AIBOwners* and acquaintances I got to know liked this cute, robust and technologically reliable model.

With the introduction of the LM-Series Sony hoped to force interest promotion for a new lifestyle with home-/ entertainment robots. In the Japanese media and entertainment scene one could find a lot of activities for promoting AIBO ERS-311 / ERS-312 that included a cartoon series *"piroppo"* which contained sound sequences (Interactive Melody) to which an AIBO ERS-311 / -312 reacts on hearing it[319], so AIBOwner and AIBO could watch TV together, a music video (*"Kiss One More Time"* by *Tommy*) featuring the LM-series and a song devoted to "Latte" and "Macaron" called *"Feblatte Macaron"* (also by *Tommy*). The promotion of the ERS-311 / ers-312-series has predominantly been a Japanese undertaking, where it proofed successful. In Europe and the US sales of the "LM-series" has been discontinued quite shortly after their appearance on the market[320].

AIBO ERS-7, nicknamed *"Seven"* is the latest AIBO-creation from the year 2003. According to the information I obtained from a friend, the "7" has been chosen, because it represents a lucky number in Japan. As Sony statistics have revealed, products with a serial number containing a 7 had higher sales than others. The calculation seems to have proven right, as the model proofs to be

---

[319] Actually this also works with other AIBO-models
[320] From my own observations as an ERS-311-owner, I would say that the "LM-series" has much more good chances in Germany / Europe, since quite a few people who have seen my AIBO (or read my webpage articles) showed real interest. Especially females, elderly and newcomers to the experience of "entertainment robots" like the cute-looking "LM-series" and were able to easily get some sort of attachment towards this robot. But also (German) persons fitting the classic profile of the male techno-enthusiast got to like the "LM-series".

popular in Japan as well as in Germany and the US. A new, upgraded version of the ERS-7 has hit the market in autumn 2004. Until late 2004 an estimated number of around 149 718 AIBOs have been sold so far in Japan, Europe and the US[321].

AIBO has also established itself as a standard platform for the world-famous "RoboCup" (robot-soccer) competitions, where research teams can test their software. But Sony's "robot dog" does also address people not involved in the areas of robotics, software development, engineering, AI-research or similar fields. Initiated in Japan, AIBO is increasingly becoming an international phenomenon with a growing number of enthusiasts of all kinds all over the world[322].

3.3.2 AIBO from a Sociologist's View

3.3.2.1 AIBO-Community

In Japan, the US and European countries, including Germany, Internet-based "webrings" (e.g. the international *Club AIBO*), forums, fan-groups, communities and discussion-groups of *AIBOwners*, AIBO-fans and people interested in the subject have formed and are rapidly growing throughout East Asia, the US, Europe and Australia. The AIBO-communities also organize more or less frequent meetings, where the members and their robots get the chance to meet each other in person. In this sense there's also a social dimension added to the AIBOwnership. It is an interesting observation that in Germany and the US the communication between the human members of the AIBO-communities is considered more important than in Japan. Whereas in Germany (and the US) community members form a kind of network, even resulting in friendships, the

---

[321] Special Thanks to the estimation by "Stefan", member of www.aibo-freunde.de. Official statistics for all AIBO models sold so far have not been provided.
[322] Until the surprising discontinuation of sales and research in March 2006

situation in Japan is much more anonymous. In Japan the *AIBOwner's webring* generally consists of private web-pages where each owner writes essays about oneself and ones AIBO and posts some pictures. The AIBO-related communication through the practice of Online-forums, where members stay in contact with each other through public message postings is a quite rare phenomenon in Japan. It looks as if in Japan the focus in mainly centered around the individual and ones AIBO whereas in Germany it is important to share ones experiences with other persons dedicated to a similar field of interest.

AIBO robots, the property of proud AIBOwners brought along to the annual meeting of the German-speaking AIBO community.

Photo: Miriam JS Leis
@ the AIBO Meeting in Köln / Germany, 2004

3.3.2.2 AIBO Life Style Phenomenon

From a sociological viewpoint lifestyle can be defined as a specific, characteristic way of life, distinguishable from that of other groups. It includes aspects of culture, fashion as well as ideology. The industry and markets are quite interested in getting the attention of specific life-style groups.

In a certain way AIBO can be regarded as a life-style phenomenon because AIBOwners and people interested in AIBO tend to represent a distinct group with specific characteristics[323].

---

[323] Data obtained from reading comments made by AIBOwners, Internet forum-discussions (Germany) and a hypothesis-generating survey I conducted with German AIBOwners (refer to appendix for a data summary)

- Many of them show a general interest in technology and robotics (something which in my view seems to be even more apparent in non-Japanese AIBOwners).

- AIBOwners use a distinct language, loaded with technical and AIBO-related terms (e.g. AIBO-ware, Memory Stick, Pink Ball, ERS-, ERA-, DHS, Loading Station etc.)

- They form groups and networks (Fanpages, chat-groups, conventions, exhibitions, meetings etc.)

- There exist extra AIBO-events (at least in Japan), like AIBOwners day, fashion-contests etc. (although Sony is advising people NOT do dress up their robots during operation).

- „Living with a robot" is regarded as an expression of a future-oriented progressive attitude

- Many (non-Japanese) AIBOwners show a general interest in Japanese (Pop)-Culture (e.g. robots, computer games and animé)

- In some cases AIBO becomes a part of everyday life and the choice for activities (in Japan there are even AIBO-magazines, AIBO-TV and there exists a Japan-based multi-purpose website (www.aibotown.com) directly addressing AIBOwners that has recently also established an offshoot website in South-Korea.

- The aspect of exclusivity of the group of AIBOwners is even fostered as they are provided with AIBOwner's certificates / "AIBO birth certificates" upon product registration (by default in Japan and upon request in Germany).

- Subgroups are forming with members of different "AIBO-philosophies" (e.g. regarding

software, preferred models, "keeping", programming etc.)

- Manufacturers, especially in Japan, are already producing and selling items particularly

addressing AIBOwners and their robots, such as outfits for AIBOs (although not being recommended by Sony) and a whole array of fan-articles and merchandize.

The most curious AIBO pages and AIBO-related events can be found in Japan. In Japan AIBO events are ranging from AIBO exhibitions over an AIBOwner's day to AIBO-music events. AIBO serves as mascot, has been featured in music videos and I have already discovered AIBO-masks at festival stalls. As already mentioned before, there exists (existed?) an AIBO-entertainment group called „*Yu Gi Dan*", internet-based "AIBO-TV" features artistic video clips about AIBO and other robots. Pop stars show with AIBO and there are even artworks featuring AIBO.

AIBO seems to be much more than just another high-tech appliance and most owners name their AIBOs. A malfunctioning AIBO is not brought to the electronics store or repair workshop for repair. Instead it is cared for in a so-called *AIBO clinic* and many rather speak of an "illness" than a technical defect. It is even possible to bring ones AIBO for an annual check-up. As I have heard, the term *AIBO-clinic* was introduced as a reaction upon realizing that many owners have developed some attachment towards their robot-dogs, and that "repair-shop" would just sound too harsh. Upon calling the Japanese AIBO-clinic[324], the atmosphere somehow mediated that of a hospital's children's ward,

---

[324] I have called the Japanese AIBO-clinic as well as its German counterpart. In the Japanese case it was about registration formalities, whereupon the receptionist told me that she was glad that it was not about some "*byōki*" (= illness). Of course this also could have been a

whereas in Germany, although having adapted the Japanese institution of the *AIBO-clinic*, I got the impression that there is uncertainty about how to act as an *AIBO-clinic* without actually sounding ridiculous. In Germany "*AIBO-clinic*" looks like being rather a term than a philosophy, whereas in Japan one notices that the staff not seldom experiences cases where customers are really concerned about the "well-being" of their robots.

Although the robots of a specific series may look identical, I would assume that many AIBOwners would be rather reluctant in exchanging their AIBO for another one of the same series. I have also heard about instances that people allegedly were able to recognize their own AIBO among a whole array of identical-looking robots, something deemed difficult even with cars or personal computers. Although it is said that through the specific software design each AIBO would be able to develop a unique "personality", in my view, since programming and memory capacities are limited, much of this should be contributed to psychological effects; that is the owner's interpretative act being transferred onto the artifact.

It also seems that some people even treat their robots better than some treat their dogs or cats - ever found an abandoned AIBO? Certainly there is more behind the phenomenon of AIBO than just its technology.

But in how far can such group-formations like the AIBOwner's Communities be called unique? If one looks around, there can be found a wide variety of similar organizations throughout the world, especially such centered around the area of media and entertainment products or special-interest fields like computer gaming and movies / TV-series (especially *Star Trek* and *Star Wars*[325]) to name

---

singular incident, whereas the choice of terminology has to be attributed to the receptionist's character. At the instance in Germany, where I called because of a camera-problem, I got prompt and professional help, but it was rather an atmosphere of a technical hotline than that of a clinic.

[325] A very popular Internet-based community with growing international membership is the "*Jediism*"-site, based on the religion portrayed in the "*Star Wars*" movies. It has proofed so

just a few of them. Viewed in this context, the AIBOwner's community, although constantly growing (within one year the German-speaking community has grown from about 10 founding core-members to over 150 registered participants), is still a rather small institution and does not represent a unique phenomenon. The same applies for the event-and merchandizing aspect, which is much more extensive in other institutions than the AIBOwner's Communities (e.g. in the community of Star Trek fans or *"Trekkies"*). I would say that it would be rather surprising, if no kind of organization would have formed around a rather unique phenomenon like AIBO.

x

3.4 German and Japanese robot-research

3.4.1 Walking Humanoids

There's no doubt about it. No other country runs more projects occupied with the construction of biped-walking humanoid robots than Japan, whereas the "running" has to be taken quite literally since some of these robots are not only able to walk, but even manage to jog[326]. Maybe this is also a reason why Japan's advances in the field of robotics are perceived as being so advanced. If seeing a real, quite human-looking walking robot with a height ranging between 120 and 154 cm, one undoubtedly regards this as a sophisticated masterpiece of engineering, or as a psychological effect easily assumes some human characteristics inside. As a Honda-commercial showing a small girl dancing alongside with *ASIMO* was aired on German television some time around 2001,

---

popular that in the UK there have been attempts to get *"Jediism"* recognized as an official religion.
[326] Jogging or running defined here as having both feet simultaneously lifted from the ground, although this achievement only lasted for some split of a second. The jogging skills of QRIO (Sony) and ASIMO (Honda) have been demonstrated publicly on television.

many of my friends who realized the ad did not believe that the robot was actually real (or that it has been a robot for that fact).

As Honda has presented *ASIMO* on a symposium titled "*From High-Tech to Intelligence - The Challenge of Humanoid Robots*" in Darmstadt / Germany (2003), praising the achievements being made in biped locomotion (whereas many Japanese institutions and companies have achieved success in this field), many students, now being convinced about the reality of this robot, nonetheless commented on the lacking usefulness of such a robot. But Prof. Thomas Christaller, head of the *Fraunhofer AIS*, has also lamented about the overly pragmatism-oriented German research policy, leaving no room for long-term, experimental and playful and approaches to innovation[327]. And indeed, as the findings of archaeologists suggest, the first wheel was (part of) a toy, whereas it was centuries later that it appeared in practical applications.

There are also a few robot-projects about biped-walking being conducted in Germany, such as *Johnnie* from the *Technische Unversität München* and the *NimbRo* project from the Univesity Freiburg (and others deal with simulations), but so far they only generated a limited impact on the public interest, which is by far not comparable to the situation with Japan's *ASIMO, QRIO* or Toyota's "*Trumpet Player*". While an increasing number of German robot researchers, often inspired by the Japanese strivings, are not rejecting the idea of building biped-walking robots, such implements are rather saved for the final steps of the project (e.g. *ARMAR*). Looking at the situation in Japan, it often appears to be exactly the other way around, where getting a robot to walk like a human has often been an initial aim in many projects. As I have asked Ms. Graf, a computer engineer at the German Fraunhofer IPA, in a personal interview to comment on the Japanese practice of putting so much effort into the implementation of biped walking, she told me that from the technological side the research effort for

---

[327] In an interview found at: www.heise.de/tp/deutsch/inhalt/lis/12740/1.html (June 18th, 2002)
[329] Paraphrased from http://www.asimo.honda.com. Similar argumentations have also be found on Japanese catalogues about *ASIMO* provided by Honda.

implementing basic mobility functions like biped walking in a robot is much too high relative to the short- to mid-term benefits such models will yield. In my view I would predict that maybe this stance will change in face of the growing popularity of walking robots that may even just represent some technological prestige object; spill-over effects clearly coming from Japan. The German researcher's comment also stands in stark contrast to what one gets to hear for example from Honda representatives in regard to *ASIMO*, in which the importance of a robot's walking-and stair-climbing abilities are emphasized and even regarded as necessity for its ability to assist humans[329]. Especially after the devastating *Hanshin-Awaji* earthquake which hit the Japanese city of Kobe and surrounding areas in 1995, the importance of biped-walking robots as assistants in rescue operations robots has been repeatedly stressed. But since Honda's plans for building a biped-walking robot already started in 1986 (design and assembly of the robot's leg-system and research on static walking), the earthquake (at least that one) could not have been the reason for the project's initiation, especially if one thinks about the fact that actually the more stable multi-legged and crawling robots have been considered most suitable for deployment in disaster zones and rescue situations. Regarding one of the latest Japanese bipeds, Toyota's trumpet-playing *"Partner Robot"* it is simply stated that humans would get easier accustomed to a robot that walks like a human[330]. And if looking at smaller biped robots like *QRIO*, *PINO*, *HOAP* and others of this category, all pragmatic arguments - if entertainment and "companionship" are not deemed pragmatic - will sound quite unreasonably simply because of the robot's physiological design and a height not exceeding that of 60 cm.

---

[330] Paraphrased from http://www.toyota.co.jp/en/special/robot/index.html (last read on March 14th, 2005)

Left:
Walking *ASIMO*
during a performance
at MeSci / Japan

Photo: Miriam JS Leis, 2004

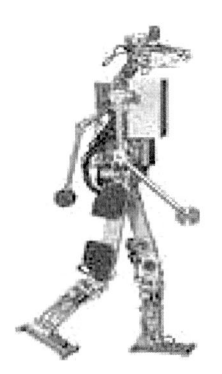

Right:
German running robot developed at the Technische
Universität München / Germany

Photo: courtesy of *Lehrstuhl für Angewandte
MechanikFakultät für Maschinenwesen
Technische Universität München*
(http://www.amm.mw.tu-muenchen.de/Forschung/
ZWEIBEINER/Downloads/Johnnie_white_preview.jpg)

3.4.2 Comparison Study: Germany and Japan

3.4.2.1 "Form Follows Function" vs. "Function Follows Form"

> "What is a robot's function?
> I consider robots the same as flowers-
> something that speaks directly to the soul"
>
> [Tatsuya Matsui, Japanese robot designer][331]

If comparing Japanese with German projects in robot-research the first striking observation is the difference in project emphasis. Whereas in Germany practical applications seem to stand in the center of robot-development, in Japan this aspect often looks like being only secondary. Whereas in Germany the decision for constructing a robot with a humanoid or animoid[332] form follows some practical considerations, e.g. in regard to the mobility on specific terrain or its planned area of deployment, in Japan one gets the impression that opting for a humanoid or animoid form serves the goal of increasing popularity. While in Germany robot technology is just seen as a research field among others (even not among to the top priorities) belonging to the standard repertoire of a leading industrialized nation, in Japan it looks like bordering on a national undertaking.

As German researchers I talked with were quick in explaining what their robot may be used for, paradoxically in the *"Robot Kingdom"*, Japanese engineers were rather concerned about the question if people would like their robot. Especially interesting are the statements one can find about the reason for the creation of *QRIO*, Sony's 56 cm tall humanoid robot, where it is talked about emotional value, enjoyment, happiness, new kinds of social interaction and a

---

[331] Quoted from *"KATEIGAHO International Edition. Japan's Art's and Cultural Magazine"*, inaugural issue 2003, p.149
[332] Robot quite closely resembling an animal

new culture around the concept of "living with a robot"[333]. If looking at Japanese robots such as *AIBO, PaPeRo, Paro, PINO, QRIO, Robovie, Tama*[334] and many more, it is justified to ask what practical purpose these costly (in regard to time and money) creations might yield; at least if looked at from a standpoint of German pragmatism. Due to their physiology they all lack the ability to perform useful tasks in households or services (except remote controlled management of media and house infrastructure equipment).

As I heard, to many Germans, trying to implement biped walking ability in a robot or creating it to mimic animal-like behavior without serving a specific, practical goal, sounded like a waste of time and money. On the other hand, one has to keep in mind that "practical" may mean different things to different persons. It is also a question about public demand and interest. If in general Japanese have more experience with robot toys and mechatronic entertainment devices than Germans, the whole idea of entertainment robots as the evolutionary result from combining the tradition of toys with the technology of industrial robots does not look like a strange idea.

Comments made by non-Japanese, especially Germans about *ASIMO* doubting if its cognitive capabilities may match its walking abilities seem paradigmatic for the different approaches in European (and US) and Japanese robotics. I will summarize the differences between Japanese and German approaches under the terms "function follows form" vs. "form follows function"[335].

German engineers seem to rather follow the "form follows function" approach, that is, one first looks at the purpose a robot should fulfil (function) and then tries to implement the most efficient way in order to achieve the specific goal (form) in a rather top-down-approach following the industrial logic

---

[333] Paraphrased from http://www.sony.net/SonyInfo/QRIO/interview/index_nf.html (last read on Jan. 25, 2005)
[334] Refer to Appendix for information about the company / institute
[335] A term actually borrowed from political science / administration theory

that deems to be necessary in some professional areas such as space exploration, inspection tasks or defusing explosives. In German robot-design anthropomorphic / humanoid characteristics, or approaches in human-like communication forms are mostly implemented on a no-nonsense basis in order to enable the robot to perform tasks efficiently in a non-industrial environment (services) or to make robot-control easier by non-experts by implementing voice-command capabilities, for example. Considerations about the artistic, non-functional design (i.e. looks), is seen here as one of the final steps, serving the goal to minimize the threatening characteristics of a machine. This is generally done when the product has already matured and the necessary components needed for the fulfilment of the envisioned task have already been implemented (of course upgrades and improvements will continue with the accumulation of technological progress and scientific insight). But the idea of investing time and money into the development of robots like NEC's *PaPeRo* (Japan), which despite sophisticated technological achievements does not provide more functionality than doing small-talk with people, operate ones multimedia facilities and entertain people, has remained rather incomprehensible to many German researchers, journalists and non-experts alike.

In contrast to the observations being made in Germany, one gets the impression that the Japanese approach looks like being done "upside down", where the form, especially the human-like or animal-like appearance, often looks like serving an end in itself. This view has also been supported by Prof. Aoki[336], who told me in a discussion that Japanese tend to be fascinated by seeing human-like aspects in robots. He also mentioned an episode about a Japanese programmer who has programmed an industrial robot to perform movements for blacksmith-work that are essential for humans to do (e.g. doing a blank strike in the air to maintain the rhythm of performance), but are

---

[336] Prof. Aoki is professor at the Ferris University Yokohama / Japan

unnecessary – even inefficient - for machines. The explanation for this act goes into the direction of preserving the human mastery in the robot.

Also I came across comments made by German acquaintances and German media expressing incomprehension about the usefulness of robots like *ASIMO, AIBO, QRIO, PaPeRo* or "*Wakamaru*" (in regard to "*Wakamaru*" many asked me why one should need a robot as a "relay station" to manage the house infrastructure or keep the house secure, if this could also be implemented in a so-called IT-house system without a robot's presence).

Let's take the example of *ASIMO* and its predecessor P3, developed by Honda Motors Co. (Japan). Research began in 1986 with the main aim of implementing biped walking in a robot, a quest which has been pursued by numerous Japanese research institutions and companies after Japan's Ministry of Economy, Trade and Industry (METI) has initiated a huge program to boost the country's efforts in robot research and development in the 1980s with the goal to - among other aspects - prepare for an anticipated labor shortage in Japan's graying society. At the symposium "*From High Tech to Intelligence – The Challenge of Humanoid Robots*" that also served as the upbeat of *ASIMO*'s Europe-tour, the company's decision has been explained in a way that Honda wanted to create a mobility concept which represents the 4th dimension after having constructed cars and boats (motion along two dimensions) and airplanes (motion in three dimensions). /* If one regards the 4th. dimension as (space)time, like Einstein did, this concept reminds me on Alfred Schütz when he speaks of the "commonly shared time", the presupposition for successful social interaction.*/. Also interesting to notice is the motto under which the development plans for Honda's robots are summarized: "進化人へ、社会へ" (= "Evolution for humans and society"), whereby the kanji "進化" [*shinka* = evolution] has been chosen, which is rather associated with the biological concept, instead of "発展" [*hatten* = development], the more technical or economic term.

Since the first prototype P1 was unveiled to the public in 1993, its more advanced successors appeared in a couple of TV ads and other promotional occasions with *ASIMO* finally achieving celebrity status. It looks as if Honda representatives were very quick in using the robot for promotional purposes as soon as it has learned – or rather been programmed – to walk. *After* the robot has already been presented to the public, where at the beginning the focus has been exclusively on its walking abilities, step by step features associated with Artificial Intelligence and object manipulation have been implemented. Nonetheless, until today one only gets somewhat vague answers if asking about the actual purpose for *ASIMO*'s development. The most frequent answers depict a scenario somewhere beyond the year 2030 with *ASIMO* robots helping and entertaining humans, but as it is the case with many of Japan's robots, the final question about utilization is still left open. Superficially it looks as if they foremost concentrate on putting together technologies that are supposed to yield an impressive image for boosting corporate image.

This view gets even more obvious as the robot-related "function-follows-form" approach is especially practiced within Japanese companies. The Japanese method is in so far understandable as most of the Japanese prominent robots are products of major companies such as *Honda Motors Co.*, *Sony Corp.*, *Mitsubishi Heavy Industries, NEC, Toyota Corp.* etc. Unlike it is the case with government- or privately funded research, especially in Germany, internal company based research and development needs less external support and public justification for why this specific project and approach is being followed. On the other side the "function-follows-form" approach gets understandable because presenting a publicly appealing "*form*" can be far better used for promotional purposes than starting off with the development of some manipulator arm or the development of cognitive functions, which are (although impressive) less effective for public demonstrations than a walking or dancing robot. And nonetheless even for publicly demonstrating a robot's "cognitive capabilities" it is also advantageous to present it in an appealing form.

3.4.2.1 a) Short Reflection III: The Art of Robotics

Ever wondered why people are saying "it's only a machine", but rarely "it's only a piece of art"? In Japan I often got the impression that robotics *is* art, and that it is more than just some pragmatic practice. It's about aesthetics, careful observation and about evoking emotions. In the center stands the act of creation, which can lead a human to a deeper insight about the world that is too often superficially taken for granted and never really noticed.

If you have ever done some complex do-it-yourself construction, you quite certainly have realized the deeper understanding you have gained through this act. Above this, I guess you came to treat your creation with more respect and also regard the value of similar products. Or just take the professedly recreational act of painting. To draw a good picture, it needs good observation skills to capture all the tiny nuances and shades.

Especially in Japan I came across many instances where the artificial recreation of the natural is seen as an act of art with symbolic value. The most famous example may be *Ikebana* flower arrangement, where real flowers are artificially arranged according to a set of rules to reflect nature and seasonal events. Inspired by the *Zen*-tradition, here the artificial recreation of the natural is regarded as an act of meditation, as a means of understanding the essence of the natural.

3.4.2.2 Concept Comparison

To provide an example for differences in concept emphasis regarding robotics between Germany and Japan in the context of the *"Form Follows Function"* and *"Function-Follows-Form"* principles, I will outline two concepts with a similar goal, but somehow different strategies.

Since I'm writing this as a social scientist and not as an engineer, the main intend of my comparison does not primarily concern the technological aspects, but rather the philosophy behind the two concepts, which show similarities as well as differences.

Interestingly, with their unique strategies, both countries, Germany and Japan have developed some very sophisticated robots, whereas in some cases and areas both countries' achievements may even represent complementary features.

I have chosen the German *"Care-O-bot"* from the Fraunhofer IPA and the Japanese *"Wakamaru"* from Mitsubishi Heavy Industries as examples for my analysis, because both projects represent concepts for home-use robots now under development that are planned to be someday deployed in the area of household / home-care assistance, especially for elderly people. Also in regard to some basic technological data (e.g. wheeled movement, sensors for collision avoidance, control, software for navigation[337] and task management etc.) as well as in respect to main (planned) implements like scheduling and surveillance functions, wireless Internet access, extensions for operations in "Intelligent Houses"[338], speech recognition and -synthesis etc., both platforms seem to be sufficiently comparable[339], at least for the purpose of this study[340]. Additionally,

---

[337] Although both systems are using a different hard- and software architecture, they serve the same end, namely collision avoidance and autonomous navigation ability.
[338] There have been test-runs with Care-O-bot at inHaus Duisburg / Germany. More information to *InHaus* at:
http://www.inhaus-duisburg.de/
[339] More detailed information about the software and hardware for both platforms can be obtained through the Internet. About Care-O-bot: http://www.care-o-bot.de/

managers and researchers of both projects kindly provided me the opportunity for conducting a personal interview and onward discussions about the specific robot-projects and robotics in general[341].

A) "Care-O-bot": Service Robot developed at Fraunhofer IPA[342] / Germany

"Care-O-bot is a mobile service robot which has the capability to interact with and assist humans in typical housekeeping tasks. Care-O-bot has already proven its ability to operate safely and reliably in public environments."

[quoted from: http://www.care-o-bot.de/english/index.php]

"Care-O-bot II"
Picture courtesy of Fraunhofer IPA Stuttgart / Germany

The idea for developing a home-care-assistance robot at the Fraunhofer IPA was born out of considerations about the expected demographic developments in Germany, namely the "graying of society"[343]. The concept of *Care-O-bot* is about providing assistance to elderly or disabled people in order to enhance their

---

About "Wakamaru": www.wakamaru.net
[340] I also would like to thank Ms. Graf from the Fraunhofer IPA / Germany (Care-O-bot) and Mr. Suzuki from Mitsubishi Heavy Industries (*"Wakamaru"*) for sharing their time for a personal interview and providing me with information material about their robot projects. All information is based on publicly available material. Both institutions knew from my research.
[341] Information from: catalogues provided by the Fraunhofer IPA, www.care-o-bot.de and a personal interview / discussion I have conducted with Dipl.-Inf. Graf, a computer engineer working on the *Care-O-bot* and *Secur-O-Bot* projects.
[342] Fraunhofer Institut für Produktionstechnik und Automatisierung (Fraunhofer Institute Institute for Manufacturing Engineering and Automation)
[343] As today's statistical prognosis goes, 35% of Germany's population will be over 60 by the year 2040. Source used by the Fraunhofer IPA: *Federal Statistic Office* Germany. Refer to: http://www.care-o-bot.de/english/ Motivation.php

independence and living quality, and enable them to remain in their familiar surrounding for as long as possible. This is also in line with the interests of elderly / disabled people who wish to live a life as independent as possible in their known environment, as well as with (health) insurance carriers, because a lot of money could be saved if fewer people would have to get cared for in senior-homes and similar institutions. Of course other people would also benefit from the availability of a robot that is able to assist in housekeeping tasks.

As the researchers at the Fraunhofer IPA have repeatedly emphasized during various occasions (e.g. in newspaper articles and at public presentations), and as it has also been stressed in the interview I conducted with Dipl.-Inf. Graf, robots should only serve as an assisting device and certainly not act as a substitute for human caregivers. This has also been in line with the comments made by Misenus[344], a German (former) nursing care worker[345], with whom I talked about nursing care in a personal informal interview, who generally displayed a positive stance in regard to technical assistance / robot systems. He told me that such a system (if technologically reliable) would be quite welcomed and very helpful in disburdening human care workers from errand tasks or enable seniors to enjoy more autonomy, but it can never substitute for a human caregiver.

The robot should either provide assistance in performing simple tasks for which it would be too cumbersome and costly to engage a human aide (e.g. for tasks like retrieving fallen objects, bringing articles, servicing and being helpful in the area of mobility assistance) or in disburdening human personnel in errand tasks like transportation tasks. Consequently much emphasis is laid upon the development of the robot's manipulating arm, the required sensor systems to detect and grasp objects and the corresponding software programs.

The mid- to long-term goals for such kind of robot assistant would lie in implementing the following abilities:

---

[344] Name changed
[345] Misenus (name changed), an acquaintance of me, who asked to remain unidentified.

- To assist people by handling common objects
- Intelligent mobility assistance / walking aid with integrated guidance function[346]
- Performing simple household tasks such as serving and cleaning, controlling the house infrastructure and media management (e.g. controlling the settings of air-conditioners, kitchen appliances, TV-set / stereo devices, general information-providing etc.)
- Assist in communication with medical personnel, authorities, relatives etc.
- Providing security and medical surveillance (e.g. checking on vital signs or the intake of medication and automatically alert medical staff on the occurrence of irregularities)[347].

A robot based on the *Care-O-bot* platform has even been a "star" in the German TV-series (ZDF) "Jenny & Co."[348], and other similar ones are already successfully deployed as museum guides at the *Museum für Kommunikation* in Berlin[349] that has three units in operation. Since October 2003 two other robots provide information, guidance and entertainment to customers at the *Opel Center* in Berlin[350]. The platform can be easily modified to fit specific needs for presentations, promotional- and edutainment purposes, e.g. at theme parks or expositions. The success regarding safety standards and the general public's overall positive reaction towards- and interest in these entertainment-/ guidance robots provides a promising future for the whole new field of robots for non-industrial personal use (some just visit the *Museum für Kommunikation* to see the robots).

---

[346] Although this has not been explicitly mentioned in the information sheets, in my view such a system would also be of some help for the visual impaired.

[347] The *Care-O-bot*'s functions of walking aid and house-infrastructure control, the navigation and route planning capabilities in public environments and simple fetch and carry tasks have already been implemented successfully.

[348] Although the story only peripherally deals with the subject of robotics

[349] http://www.museumsstiftung.de/berlin/d211_rundgang.asp

[350] Care-O-bot II has also been presented at the press conference for the "Deutschland in Japan" initiative being held in Japan in 2005.

But despite the public presentations and the overall positive perception of these robots, Valera told me that the real initial boost for general and public interest in robots has still to come in Germany. As she told me, the responses during test-runs as well as comments given by representatives of care-facilities still have been somewhat ambivalent – positive, but also negative. Nonetheless, in opposition to popular preconceptions, a considerable number of seniors display a personal interest in technology. Many of them are using the Internet and have shown quite positive interest in *Care-O-bot* during demonstrations and test-runs. Where the future for Germany's home-robot-industry will head depends, according to Ms. Graf, much on the individual's technology-acceptance. She said in regard to the idea of robots in private homes: "I don't see any difficulties for future generations of seniors"[351]. This has also been the opinion of Mr. Misenus, who also thought that robot assistants would be rather something for future generations of seniors. In this regard it will quite probably be them who will profit from robot technology; not only in view of scientific advances being made, but also from the standpoint of technical education and socialization (e.g. through growing up with the common usage of computers and other interactive technical devices).

Although the aspect of user-friendliness has been central to the development of *Care-O-bot*, it is always stressed that the robot is designed as an "assistance system", emphasizing both words "assistance" and "system". This has to be underlined, since parts of the German media are already envisioning poor seniors being served and cared for by cold and heartless machines.

Ms. Graf thinks about a robot in the following way: "A robot is a machine, yet it is more interactive than, for example, household tools."[352]

Considering my own observations as well as the interview data and discussions I had with some friends and acquaintances in Germany about the

---

[351] „[…] ich sehe bspw. keine größeren Probleme für zukünftige Seniorengenerationen"
[352] „[ein Roboter ist] eine interaktive Maschine: es ist zwar eine Maschine, aber sie ist dennoch interaktiver als bspw. Haushaltsgeräte"

topic, I would say that in this country a home-robot would have chances for success if it is rather regarded as some form of *appliance*, whereas aspects such as design and interaction capability should mainly serve the goal of easy end-user control. This means the preference for a robot designs that won't stand out that much from other appliances people are already used to. The design should be ergonomic and provide a non-threatening appearance, countering the fears of some German people with whom I talked about robots in the area of home-care, who envisioned huge machines running around rather scaring than caring.

In significant contrast to many of Japan's ambitions, the development of humanoid robots (i.e. robots with biped walking ability) is not a goal for the near future for researchers at Fraunhofer IPA. From the technological side it has been said that the research effort for implementing basic mobility functions like biped walking in a robot is much too high relative to the short- to mid-term benefits such models will yield. Therefore prime efforts should rather be directed at the development of a robot's cognitive abilities like object recognition, route- and task planning capabilities, object manipulation, enhancements in processing of sensor information which enhances the practical usefulness of the robot.

x

x

B) "Wakamaru": Japanese Service Robot under development at Mitsubishi Heavy Industries, Ltd.[353]

On entering the "Wakamaru"- website from Mitsubishi (www.wakamaru.net) one is greeted by a flash-intro displaying the following text:

> *"Living with a Robot?"*
> *"haven't you imagined "a robot coming to your house" in your childhood?"*
> *"that robot in your imagination must not simply be a robot that only waits for your orders"*
> "wakamaru *is a robot which communicates with its family and spontaneously tries to serve its family's turn"*
> *"A robot that prefers to be called as "one person" rather than "one unit"*

Although the concept of *"Wakamaru"* [354] is in the first place directed towards elderly people living alone (at least most of the time), it is rather portrayed as an "add on" to the "average household" and therefore addressing a broader demography. Also interesting in comparison to the *Care-O-bot* product description is the data one finds if looking under "development overview" on the website, where it reads the following:

> *"Purpose of Development: Propose a new life style by living with a robot at home to*
> *make the life more convenient and enriched."*[355]

It is primarily talked about "life style" and "enrichment" than about "work" and "assistance". Also in regard to the features listed for *"Wakamaru"* at the website,

---

[353] Information from pamphlets provided by Mitsubishi Heavy Industries at Robodex 2003, www.wakamaru.net (alternatively: http://www.sdia.or.jp/mhikobe/products/etc/robot.html) and a personal interview I conducted with Mitsubishi Manager Mr. Suzuki. When in the following I'm talking about "Mitsubishi" I mean "Mitsubishi Heavy Industries"
[354] Developing Nickname. *Wakamaru*, or *Ushiwakamaru* was the childhood name of the famous and popular Japanese hero *Minamoto Yoshitsune*.
[355] Quoted from: http://www.sdia.or.jp/mhikobe-e/products/etc/robot.html (Jan. 25, 2005)

which I will quote in the following, it seems obvious that the communicative aspect between humans and robots stands in the center of the concept.

(1) Lives with family members
(2) Speaks spontaneously in accordance with family member's requirements
(3) Has its own role in a family

[All quotes from: http://www.wakamaru.net/]

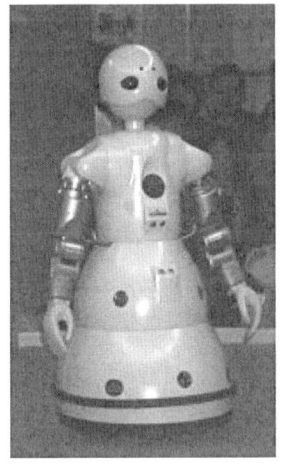

This yellow fellow, a somehow innocently-earnest looking robot is designed as a human-friendly (which is more than simply "user-friendly") home assistant. It has been designed by the Japanese Industrial Designer Toshiyuki Kita. Some of Mitsubishi's original plans have favoured an even less humanlike look. Mitsubishi Manager Mr. Suzuki told me in an interview, that in his view it is important to have a likable design with robots that shouldn't be too human-like, because an appearance too closely resembling that of a human could lead people to think of robots as humans and being reluctant to use them as servants.

"*Wakamaru*".
Photo: Miriam J.S. Leis
at Robodex 2003, Japan

"*Wakamaru*" is planned to be deployed in fields like house-sitting, control of household appliances, media management, security surveillance / home security and assistance in health care service. Much sophisticated research and technology has been put into the development of "*Wakamaru's*" features like face recognition and interactive functions such as making it adapt to the owner's daily routines and "acting naturally". The robot is also able to use a vocabulary of about 10 000 Japanese common words which enables it to even mimic simple small-talk-like conversations. *"Wakamaru"* is also equipped with a permanent wireless Internet connection that can be used to provide useful information, and the robot may report unusual occurrences to central service providers, authorities (e.g. hospitals, police) or pre-defined telephone numbers.

In contrast to *Care-O-bot*, the development of manipulative service functions (manipulator arm) didn't belong to the implements of immediate priority. Since Mitsubishi has much experience in industrial robot development, I would not consider this as being a technical aspect, but rather as a culture-associated priority-setting. This kind of approach is also reflected in the considerations Mr. Suzuki told me a personal interview that the first and most important factor is that humans should like the robot. If humans like and accept it, then considerations about further functionality should be concentrated on. (paraphrased from the original wording). This statement is also interesting in connection to the already mentioned observations about how Germans and Japanese regard robots. But similar to the situation in Germany, some Japanese (health)-care institutions also express concerns about automated care-services and the use of robots, whereby in Japan most of the concerns are not about the social- or psychological dimensions, but about the technological functionality of the system. They demand more emphasis on a robot's pragmatic functions as an assistance system. Nonetheless, with test-trials involving robots like *"Paro"*, *AIBO* or *"Robovie"*, the Japanese (and recently the US and Sweden) have also discovered the positive psychological and therapeutic effects that even rather simple robots have on humans. A whole new line in therapy has established itself under the name of "Robot Assisted Therapy" (RAT), which is said to be similar to classic animal-therapy[356].

By looking at the two concepts of *Care-O-bot* and *"Wakamaru"* one can see in an exemplified way what in my view demonstrates one of the main

---

[356] For more information about RAT refer to Part IV in my analysis.

differences in German and Japanese approaches in the field of robot development and design, which I have reviewed under the terms "form follows function" and "function follows form". In short one could put it the following way: whilst in Germany robot development is primarily aligned along the consideration of pragmatism, it could be said that for the Japanese the development of features which enhance the likeability of a robot represent a much more central aspect. In Germany the design seems to serve the goal of user-friendliness and easy end-user-operation, whereas in Japan "looks" and "interaction" even seem to represent some end in itself.

3.4.3 Partner Robot

In Japan there's a term one frequently encounters: "*Partner Robot*". Actually *partner* is a very broad term that can be used for describing relations ranging from co-worker or business associate to that of family members. What kind of definition for "partner" do Japanese use? Actually I thought of it to be a rather "low" definition, equal to assistant or associate, the reasonable assumption, which would also be in line with how robots are regarded in Germany, where sporadically I also came across the term "partner" in connection to robots. Or may it be just a "trendy word" with no specific definition, as it is often the case in Japan with terms borrowed from a foreign language?

Since the 1980s until today Japan is the country which houses the world's largest industrial (and now also non-industrial) robot "population" in the world[357]. Robots, a US invention, were deployed in Japanese factories in an excessive manner during the 1970s, as a means to increase productivity,

---

[357] Although through incompatibilities in definition standards between Europe and Japan the number of Japanese robots may have been overestimated during some times. Some sources even say that today Germany houses the world's largest industrial-robot "population", but these are exclusively German statistics. UN-sources still position Japan on first place, although with putting a note on the usage of different definitions.

efficiency and product quality. Due to Japan's life-long employment policy in big companies[358], where most machines and robots were then introduced, such technological innovations and means of rationalization did not threaten the jobs of employees. It only led to fewer new-employments, a situation of no urgent concern for those already having a job. As a matter of fact industrial robots were quite welcomed by big company employees, since they freed them from hard and unpleasant jobs and helped increasing profits. The most prominent example may be the case of the Japanese automobile-producer *Toyo Kyogo* (later to be known as *Mazda*), which has been nearly bankrupt in the mid-1970s. A large bank has prevented bankruptcy, but ordered, besides new management structures, full automation. All Mazda employees, whose labor now was done by machines and robots, have continued to work for the firm in the tertiary sector (services)[359]. Looked at it from that perspective, even the industrial robots may have been regarded as some kind of "partner", contributing to the company's success and the worker's job improvement. Today, in face of Japan's economic problems, the practice of life-long employment is beginning to crumble and unemployment is on the rise (although, according to official statistics much less dramatically than in Germany), but now it is too late to put the blame on the robot.

Trade Unions, which play a central role for the workers especially in Europe (but also recently in South Korea), in Japan practically represent some extension of the company. They live in a kind of symbiosis which rather represents the pattern: if it's good for the company it's good for its workers, and the trade union just transmits the worker's agreement. The only people prone to protesting are part-time workers or jobbers, but their organizational and influential power is still weak. As I returned from the MHI headquarters at the high-rise district of Shinagawa / Tokyo, I have noticed a few demonstrators, seemingly (former?)

---

[358] Actually this has also been a strategy to avoid employees changing companies and posing the danger of revealing internal company data.
[359] I'm referring to an article in the German news-magazine „*Der Spiegel*" Nr.1/1982

employees of a major Japanese corporation, apparently protesting against the policies of their (former) company. But by lowering their head when swiftly passing, nobody wanted to take notice.

But today in the age of the coming of non-industrial robots, the term *"Partner Robot"* has already established itself in Japan. To get a clear picture, I have asked Mr. Suzuki, engineer at Mitsubishi Heavy Industries about what is really meant by *"Partner Robot"*. He told me that indeed the word partner is a new word to Japanese. But to my surprise he also told me that it is defined as just below family and even above "friend".

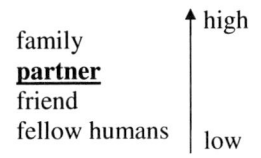

```
               ↑ high
    family
    partner
    friend
    fellow humans │ low
```

As I further asked what qualities such a (Japanese) *"Partner Robot"* should have, the answer was something one should not expect to be primary implements for a machine:

- support
- listening to complaints
- to be trusted

It has also been said that robots could serve as "buffers" for families, enhancing good communication with family members or could accompany couples living alone after their children have left. If looking at commentaries about other Japanese robot-projects, one often encounters similar statements. I remember the final scene from an "edutainment" documentary film[360] about the future of

---

[360] The original title has been: "人は、なぜヒト型ロボットを作るのだろう。。。？"
("Why are people building robots which resemble human beings (=humanoids) ?)

humans and robots, shown at the Japanese National Museum of Emerging Science and Innovation, which might have aroused controversy among Westerners (at least it did so among my German friends), where a human-looking boy around six years old held the hand of an elderly man and assisting him. The boy was called *"ASIMO"* and his image transited into that of the present-day *ASIMO*-robot.

As far as my observation goes many of the *"Tetsuwan Atomu"* stories center round the problem of the robot not being able to get integrated into society. *Astro Boy* is a human-like hero with incredible powers who to some even though remains an outsider, a "stranger", to use the terminology of Georg Simmel[361]. And indeed, envisioning the robot as a "stranger" is actually worth thinking about. One would scarcely consider ones printer or even computer as "stranger", because it lacks sufficient similarities to a human being for comparison. And it is only through a comparison with other humans already being known, that a stranger may be defined. The robot may be near in a Euclidian definition of distance, but it may remain far away in the psychological sense of the term. Unlike the case with the human stranger, the main problem with the robot does not lie in its cultural distinctiveness (if one could speak of such, because a robot doesn't actually possess what we call "culture"), but in its artificiality. And this artificiality is something which can not be easily taken away, as I have already mentioned in regard to the *"Blade Runner Complex"* in Part II of my analysis.

It is exactly the idea of this "strangeness" which I have discussed with Mr. Suzuki, who has used an illustration to demonstrate the different concepts of robots. (Since it was not possible to get a hardcopy of this illustration I have here reconstructed the essentials on my own.)

„*Wakamaru*"

---

[361] Georg Simmel: „*Exkurs über den Fremden*" (1908)

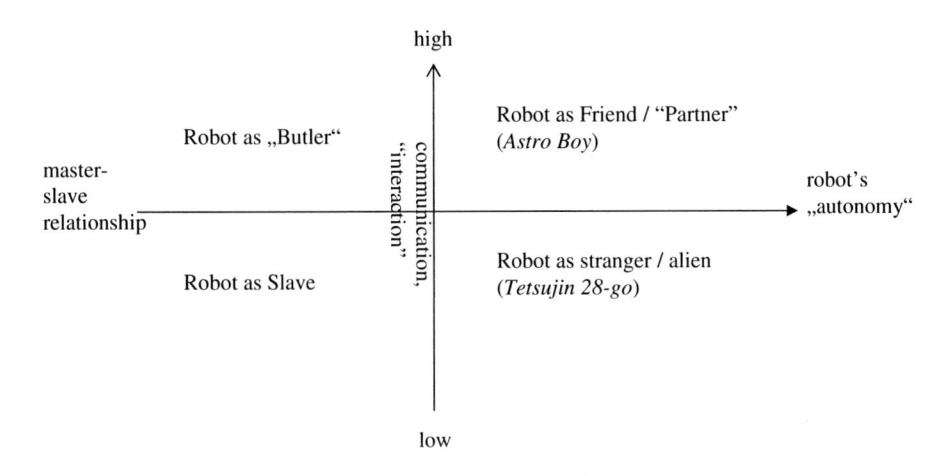

```
                              high
                               ↑
                               |
         Robot as „Butler"     |    Robot as Friend / "Partner"
                               |    (Astro Boy)
master-                        |
slave    ──────────────────────┼──────────────────────────→  robot's
relationship                   |                              „autonomy"
                               |    Robot as stranger / alien
         Robot as Slave        |    (Tetsujin 28-go)
                               |
                               |
                              low
```

(vertical axis label: communication, „interaction")

Miriam JS Leis: own reconstruction of Mr. Suzuki's illustration

The classic relationship between humans and machinery / industrial robots is that of a human "master" and mechanical "slave". If the robot possesses some (simulated) communication and interaction capabilities, although strictly executing the command of the human, it is then regarded rather as a butler than a slave. The most interesting situation occurs with the increasing autonomy of the robot, whereas in this context the term *autonomy* not only describes the ability of a robot to perform tasks without direct human control, but also the idea of a robot "having its own mind", even if this ability is only simulated. If the robot's communication and interaction remain low, it nonetheless remains a "stranger". In the explanation the example of the animé-robot *"Tetsujin 28-go"* has been used for describing a robot that possesses some degree of autonomy, but lacks the ability to enable a mutual human-robot connection[362]. The model for the concept of the *"Partner Robot"* is the fictitious robot-hero *Astro Boy* that with the exception of its mechatronic makeup is nearly indistinguishable from a

---

[362] As I understood the story of *"Tetsujin 28-go"*, the robot has been a remote-controlled unit and therefore possessing very low degree of autonomy.

human being. Although serving humankind and following a human's instructions, *Astro Boy* is able to communicate just like a human and also is capable of thinking and making decisions on its own. In this sense the idea of a *"Partner Robot"* is that of a robot which is integrated into a person's life, being part of a person's closer relationship circle and being more than just a servant.

3.5 Explanations

3.5.1 Robotics and Demographic Factors

In nearly every socially- and technologically advanced country the tendency towards decreasing birth rates, population decline and the aging of society is an observable fact. If these trends are not countered, the situation could cause serious problems for keeping upright social security systems and prospering economic structures, which are primarily outlined along projections of population stability or even growth. According to statistical projections for the year 2050[363], about one third of the German and Japanese population will be 65 years or older.

Age distribution for 2005 and projection for 2050 (Germany and Japan)
Own calculation from raw data found at:

http://www.census.gov/ipc/www/idbpyr.html

---

[363] Raw data from http://www.census.gov/ipc/www/idbpyr.html

	Germany		Japan	
	2005	2050	2005	2050
age: 0-14	14.3	13.3	14.4	12.6
age: 15-64	66.8	56.7	66.1	53.1
age: 65-80+	18.9	30.0	19.5	34.4

As one can assume by looking at the figures, such distribution as projected for 2050 could indeed cause problems for the generation-financed pension system, as well as in regard to the recruitment of personnel taking care for the aged. In the context of population-statistics it is also important to notice that the estimated net-immigration for Germany in 2004 has been 2.18 immigrants per 1 000 inhabitants, whereas Japan quotes a net-immigration rate of virtually 0.0 immigrants per 1 000 inhabitants[364]. Although, in recent years a growing number of foreigners (mostly Westerners) were granted top-positions and managerial posts in Japanese companies (e.g. Carlos Ghosn, President of Nissan Motor Corp. or Howard Stringer, new Chairman of Sony Corp. Japan)[365], and more and more foreign computer engineers or other high-skilled specialists (mostly from India, China and Korea) were let into the country, Japan still shows a negative stance against the immigration of foreign low-paid workers. This looks like a paradox in face of the observation that most Japanese shun doing *"3D jobs"*: dirty, dangerous and difficult (or the Japanese equivalent "3K". *kiken, kitsui,* and *kitanai*)[366]. And in Germany one rarely encounters German nationals who work in the basic service sector or do the dirty and/or low-paid jobs, a paradox in face of the country's growing unemployment rate.

Looking at the demographic structure is insofar interesting in relation to the topic of robotics, since in Germany, but especially in Japan, robotics is regarded as one measure of coping with future labor shortage, chiefly in the area of

---

[364] Source: http://www.cia.gov/cia/publications/factbook/ (data estimated for 2004)
[365] Here I would post the bold hypothesis that some of the companies may perhaps only employ foreigners in top positions to avoid Japanese responsibility for a company's crisis situation. If foreign management is able to deflect a crisis it is good for the company and if it fails it has not been the fault of a Japanese management.
[366] Refer to *The Daly Yomiuri*, Feb. 27, 2005 (p. 1, 3)

nursing care assistance for the elderly. Assisting elderly persons, providing medical surveillance or just disburden human helpers from errand jobs, these are some of the main motivations mentioned as reasons for developing robots such as *Care-O-bot*, *Wakamaru*, *ARMAR* or *ASIMO*.

Despite the labor shortages in this sector, requirements for foreign nursing care workers are very strict in Japan, as well as in Germany. And it was only since January 2005 that foreign nursing care workers got the permission for legally working in Germany, a measure against the growing practice of illegal employment. But this decision also drew criticism, warning that such a practice would only lead to a further decline in quality of care. To counter expected shortages, the Japanese government has also agreed to grant employment visas to nursing care workers from the Philippines (and maybe other nationalities) in 2006, whereas critics also see this as the wrong way, saying that foreigners would lack the necessary communication skills and cultural knowledge, and suggest that the priority should lie in making such jobs more attractive to Japanese. Maybe this is one of the reasons why Japan puts so much effort in developing robots for nursing care assistance; however perhaps not because they believe that such robots will be available in time, but to make nursing care jobs more attractive to Japanese nationals by providing them with the opportunity to work in an high-tech environment together with robots. It is quite probable that it will be inevitable for Japan to import an increasing number of immigrant workers, but at least in view of today's predominating attitude this remains a *Hobson's Choice*, where a robot made in Japan if possessing sufficient abilities would maybe even be preferred over an immigrant worker. – And if counting the running experimental trials, today there are already more automated / robotic nursing care assistants and aides around in Japan, than there are foreign ones.

3.5.2 Explaining the "Robot Kingdom"

So why are the Japanese so overly interested in the construction of robots? Of course this situation has also to be understood in the context of the German research financing situation which differs from the often industry-based rather long-term-oriented research situation in Japan. Also the Japanese government shows quite an active interest in promoting robot technology. But research policy and financing alone does not explain differences in interest, or putting it the other way around: why are there differences in interest?

There can be found different reasons for this which may serve as possible explanations. They range from economic considerations to aspects rooted in socio-cultural settings. In the following I will take a deeper look into some of the most interesting and even uncommon explanations.

3.5.2.1 Attitude towards technology

Having grown up in Japan, although being a German national, it was only after I went to Germany that I came across the idea that technology can be discussed on the basis of *philosophical* controversy. In Germany I was rather surprised to find out that robots which don't pollute the environment or emit radioactive particles are viewed quite sceptically. That was one of the reasons for my decision on doing research in this field; to find an explanation for this.

Because of their experiences in World War II, Japan and Germany have something in common: both countries demonstrate a very antimilitaristic stance that also influences their attitude towards technology (at least publicly). Unlike it is the case in the United States, where much of the robot-related (and space-related) technology is born out of military interest, the motivation for German and Japanese researches comes from other sources. Nonetheless I have observed differences in the attitude and perception of technology (and history) between Germany and Japan, which can even be considered opposing. Whereas in Germany the load of WWII still represents an issue which hinders Germany to evolve as a proud nation and even impedes healthy nationalism, the coping of the Japanese people with the war-problematic went into another direction, resulting in an overly concentration on technological and economic power, resulting in national pride and tendencies of nationalism, which sometimes gets criticized by other (Asian) nations.

It is quite interesting what Japanese say about Japanese and non-Japanese technology. In my interviews and discussions I have had with representatives from *Robosquare, Mitsubishi Heavy Industries* and *TEPIA* it has always been stressed that Japanese technology is *peaceful* and that Japanese will never use technology for military purposes like the USA, for example. They all said, although in different manners, that this is one of the reasons for why the Japanese tend to stress the cuteness in their robots, as a demonstration of their peacefulness. The *"Atom"* of *"Tetsuwan Atomu"*, the hugely celebrated fictitious robot-figure, is not the atomic bomb, but peaceful Japanese technology. And as far as I could obtain "technical data", a fusion reactor and not a fission reactor is used to power *"Astro Boy"*. Regardless of fusion or fission reaction, why use the term *"Atom"* anyway? One could rightly suppose that after what happened in Hiroshima and Nagasaki the Japanese would have developed a negative attitude towards atomic energy. Frédéric Kaplan, called the Japanese phenomenon of turning the bad foreign principle in a positive Japanese one, the *"Taming of Technology"*[367] (Kaplan 2003), or as I would put it: to (re)gain control. I would go even further and look at it from a slightly different angle. It's not only about learning how to master foreign technology to defend Japan's culture and integrity as Kaplan suggests, but also about keeping ones honor and reputation.

---

[367] Frédéric Kaplan, researcher for Sony Europe, has also written about this phenomenon in his conference-article "Who is afraid of the humanoid? Investigating cultural differences in the acceptance of robots." I would like to thank Mr. Kaplan for sending me his material. And also Thanks to Dr S. Stein for telling me about the conference.

As Japan was confronted with Western nations after the "Black Ships" arrival, the country has already developed an advanced society with high education-levels, a sophisticated culture, efficient bureaucracy and a flourishing domestic economy, that could not have been regarded as inferior their Western counterparts. The only area where Japan lagged behind Western countries considerably was in the area of technology. Of course this has been a humiliating experience for the proud Japanese people, who then put every effort into the goal of closing this gap. Since then technology seems to have become a national program for the Japanese, bordering on obsession.

The second trauma happened as the atomic bombs – again superior foreign technology – destroyed Hiroshima and Nagasaki on August 6th and 9th 1945, again degrading the proud nation. Therefore, for Japan foreign technology is seen with ambivalence: it uncovers Japan's weaknesses, but it also represents the possibility for gaining strength, as it has both been experienced since the end of the *Edo*-period. But simply copying foreign technology would equal admitting ones weakness, but not using it would also result in weakness. Therefore it has to be copied *and* transformed in such away that foreign elements become either excelled (e.g. the Tokyo Tower, which looks similar to the Eiffel Tower but is a few metes higher) or remodelled (e.g the "Atom" in "*Tetsuwan Atomu*", or the manga/animé figure itself, that has been created through influences from Disney characters). This may also explain why many of the Japanese appliances are so utterly incompatible with foreign environments (e.g. most of the Japanese software does not run on a non-Japanese computer due to the incompatibility with non-Japanese Operating Systems, and much of Japanese appliances, except some "export models", are not available with English interfaces). The incompatibility is bidirectional: non-Japanese appliances often also either don't work in Japan or don't meet domestic specifications, a means to shut out foreign competition and to keep the Japanese market saturated with domestic products. For Japanese excelling in the field of technology has become a means to prove the nation's equality or even superiority over other countries, fending off the humiliation it has once experienced.

Whereas in Germany the traumatic experiences of WW II have contributed to an excessive amount of caution and discourse in regard to technology, it looks as if everything which could portray technology and progress in a negative picture doesn't either exist or gets somehow suppressed in Japan. Even environmental protection is promoted as providing new opportunities for technological developments, as it figures prominently at the Aichi Expo 2005. As I have once seen an interview on Japanese television where people were asked to tell why they have opted for installing solar panels on their roofs, many of the interviewed persons (although being not more than six) said that they considered it chic to demonstrate progressiveness by possessing the latest technology which also helps to reduce costs on the long run. The environmental benefits were rather seen as a positive side effect.

In Japan one hardly finds anything comparable to the German practice of discourses and technological risk assessment (*"Technologiefolgeabschätzung"*). After WWII peaceful technology catapulted both Germany and Japan to the top of the international economic landscape. But for Germany technology is seen as a *means* to achieve wealth, a flourishing economy and maybe to make life easier. In Japan technology is additionally associated with national identity, national pride; even honor and often represents a goal in itself. Somehow the dishonoring and traumatic awakening in the outgoing Edo-period by realizing how much one lagged behind still seems to haunt the Japanese. So once in a while, Japan has to present the world with some original prestige object like the *Akashi Kaikyo* Bridge, the world's longest suspension bridge connecting *Kobe* with *Awaji*, some new ultra-small electronic device or a walking and talking humanoid robot. By now having achieved an international top-position, technology has become an obsession for the Japanese, who constantly live in fear of being overtaken by some other countries. Technology determines ones economic position and economy is "war with other means". That's why it is Japan's Ministry of Economy, Trade and Industry (METI) and not Japan's ministry responsible for research and education that mainly supports Japan's robot development projects and other high-tech undertakings. The "war" is not over yet and Japan has to continue its "race against the future". Technology can be ambivalent: nightmare or salvation.

Critical reflection on technology is a very rare occurrence in Japan, even in the area of nuclear technology, one of the most controversially discussed topics in Germany. Striking, at least in contrast to Germany, is also the Japanese' love for technological "frills" that goes far beyond the immediate practicality. Examples for this range from talking ATMs with computerized avatars of bowing clerks, fax-machines telling you with voice-synthesis how to proceed when sending a fax to gadgetry like blinking cell-phone-antennas, cell-phone-avatars, an overwhelmingly array of battery-driven toys, *Tamagotchi*, *Primapuel*-dolls and *AIBO*. In Germany the general attitude towards technology is that if it does not serve a specific purpose it is quickly commented on with some form of disapproval or at least incomprehension, even going as far as considering it harmful. (Friends visiting me always ask me why I have to keep all this technical gadgetry at home and they rarely understand it if I'm saying just for the fun of it). Although Germans are very fond of the latest technology in the areas of IT, telecommunication, audio-visual electronics, and most importantly automobiles, the purpose of singing robots, "artificial dogs" or stair-climbing *ASIMO*s is yet not quite comprehended there. They may find it cute for a moment, but at the same time tend to see it with fear that one may relate to something artificial as if it was something "real" – the end of humanity?

It seems that Germans are *thinking* much more about technology and consider its consequences not only in regard to physical consequences (i.e. pollution and health risks), but also from the perspective of humanity and philosophy, something one rather rarely encounters in Japan. Such debates are especially noticeable in the case of computers, robots, artificial intelligence and embryonic stem cell research, which don't present environmental or immediate physical hazards, but are said to bear risks for humanity. Also according to my observations, Germans tend to regard traditional values and technology as somehow incompatible, and putting them both together seems disturbing. Even wind-driven power generators have been discussed with controversy in Germany, because they are said to be ugly and interfere with the beautiful natural surrounding. In Japan on the other side both sides appear to co-exist independently as the result of some kind of "best of both worlds" attitude (in this sense the Japanese show more pragmatism).

In Japan technology, especially robot technology is perceived as an undertaking to keep upright the country's national image and identity. To me it looks as if in Japan a critical technology-discourse is deemed harmful for the economy and should be avoided, while in Germany one hears many voices stating that a lack of critical technology-discourses will be harmful for society and should *not* be avoided.

3.5.2.2 From Ships, Cars and Consumer Electronics to Environmental Technology, Robots and Animé[368]

Most Japanese robot concepts have not been fixed to a specific purpose yet. Maybe the concentration on open-purpose platforms is a strategy to await the market- and demand situation and be able to quickly react accordingly. One thing seems to be clear: the Japanese government (namely the Ministry of Economy and Trade and Industry) consider the development of robot technologies for the non-industrial field as important for the country's future

---
[368] Japanese animation.

economy, and activities in robot research and development have been declared as constituting a national undertaking.

For a long time Japan's enormous economic success was founded largely on its production and export of steel- and shipbuilding products, consumer electronics and cars. Now as the economic situation is changing and an increasing number especially of (East)Asian competitors (China, South-Korea, but also Taiwan, Singapore and India) are entering the market, mainly in the areas of ship-building and the production of general consumer electronics (TV-sets, CD-players, household appliances), Japan is fearing to lose its dominant position. But the country's tendency for long-term planning is already beginning to pay off with CO_2-emission reduced hybrid cars, environment-friendly- and energy-efficient technologies and next-generation entertainment products, including robots for home-use. These are the areas which give Japan an advantage over other Asian newcomers and keep the country competitive with Europe and the US.

In this context the robot serves two goals for Japan: first it can be used to demonstrate ones technological superiority over other countries and second, as representatives from Mitsubishi Heavy Industries and robot-/technology edutainment centers in Japan told me, the robot market is expected to develop into the equivalent of the automobile market in a not too far future. To some this may still sound a little bit far-fetched, but 10 years ago some people smiled at *Toyota's* (Japan) research on their hybrid-car[369], which now has proven so popular, especially in the US, that production can not keep up with the demand situation.

In this sense it is difficult to estimate the foresight of Japanese robot developers. But one thing looks quite certain: if the future market for non-industrial robots will really develop into such a huge business as the present

---

[369] A car being powered by an electric motor as well as a combustion engine.

automobile industry, Japan again will be on the advantageous side with having quality products, and most importantly, renowned brands.

Excursion: The Transformation of Trash to Trendy

Why not make a virtue out of necessity. Comic books and cartoons have once been regarded as trashy by Western audiences. Foreign visitors to Japan looked at the *manga*-reading Japanese business men riding the train with deprecatory incomprehension. But nowadays I come across sections devoted to *manga* in book stores and libraries, even in literature-honoring Germany. It looks as if products such as *manga*, *animé* and computer games, once thought of as junk and even "culturally harmful" outside Japan, now celebrate a huge popularity internationally. It has even been advised to Prime Minister Koizumi that Japan should take advantage of internationally promoting what is called Japan's "Gross National Cool"[370]. In a way this example shows the Japanese' skills in managing to convince even skeptics about the positive side of their products, which then get world-wide acclaim.

One key factor for Japan's success – may it be cars, electronics, robots or *animé* - is the country's general interest promotion strategies. As a matter of fact, and as you may have guessed from the previously provided information, Japan herself has contributed much to her image as *"Robot Kingdom"* and is putting much effort into keeping this image alive. At events and documentary- or edutainment films, the image is being provided that the robot surely is something Japanese, a part of Japan's identity. Other country's robot-developments are only rarely mentioned, if mentioned at all (an exception may be robots for space exploration), giving the impression that Japan indeed is leading in this area. Proudly, Japanese companies are touring the world to show off their latest humanoid biped-walking robots. Although it seems to be true that Japan is leading in the area of so-called humanoid- and biped-walking robots, in

---

[370] The Japan Times, Tue. Dec. 12, 2004, p. 3

the fields of robotics for space exploration for example, projects of other countries such as the US and European nations seem to be more advanced[371]. Also I doubt that in principal other countries considerably lag behind Japan in research-areas of Artificial Intelligence and sensor-based information processing. In this way much of Japan's image as *"Robot Kingdom"* can also be seen as the result of interest-promotion strategies. In short: Japan is taking much effort in bringing their robots to the attention of the (inter)national public and makes much more spectacle about their robots than other countries. This kind of Public Relations activities may be unique to Japan, but not unique to robots. Let me draw an analogy to exemplify the Japanese public promotion strategies, which I will call the *"Cherry Blossom Effect"*:

3.5.2.3 The "Cherry Blossom Effect"

The German cherry blossom does not look worse than its Japanese counterpart – actually, to be precise, the German cherry blossom even possesses more functionality, because in contrast to the Japanese flower, the German one later produces real edible cherries. But which one is more famous? *German cherry blossoms?* – They might exist, but if someone hears the term "cherry blossom", automatically "Japan" comes to mind. Why? Because of Japan's publicity concept about their flowers. They managed to make their cherry blossoms renowned world wide. Countries around the world, including cherry-producing countries like Germany and the US, possess original Japanese cherry blossoms and view them as something special. But I guess that if Germany would have done the same promotional-activities with their cherry blossoms, they also would have got famous, because the German flowers also have a high potential. But since the Japanese are so good in promoting their products (including cherry

---

[371] Interestingly, in the field of space exploration, Japan's successes have been comparatively meager.

blossoms), these get more famous. If scanning through some of Germany's major electronics stores[372], in the area of consumer electronics (e.g. TV-sets, CD / Video / DVD players, small electronic gadgetry), even there Japanese (and most recently Chinese and Korean) brands by far outnumber German ones. In Japan, on the other hand, it is even rather hard to find German-brand washing- or dishwashing-machines, not to mention consumer electronics.The Japanese seem to be very quick in presenting new products, even prototypes to a wide public, including general audiences and the media, while in Germany rather unfinished products tend to remain inside the institutes and companies (the Germans would be declined to show their cherry blossoms until they can produce edible cherries). During this time the Japanese products get quite well known. At the time when the German products are finished the Japanese ones have also reached at least an equal stage, but the Japanese product has already become famous during the development phase and therefore possesses an advantage due to advertising. In my view a very important factor for the apparent success of Japanese products (cherry blossoms, home electronics and robots) lies in their high emphasis on public interest promotion.

/*In this context it would be no wonder to me if the Japanese would recall old *Shinto*-traditions to say that environmental protection is something truly Japanese.*/

---

[372] Media Markt, Saturn and electronics divisions at major department stores

3.5.2.4 From *Zen* to *ASIMO* and Back - In Search of Japan's Self-Identity

After the arrival of the *"Black Ships"* in 1853 and Japan's humiliating encounter with foreign nations that seemed so awfully advanced, it looks as if Japan is constantly searching for some form of self-identity, which puts her onto an equal position among the leading nations. At the beginning of the Meiji-Reforms in 1868, a majority of Japanese tended to unreflectively absorb and practice the Western Life-Style, even going so far as converting to Christianity for the sake of showing modernity and progress. Understandably, after a while this extreme from of national self-denial soon led to a revival of Japanese traditional ideals, ultimately resulting in an extreme form of nationalism and ending in Japan's forceful expansion policy and the country's involvement in World War II. After its ultimate defeat in 1945, Japan realized that this form of nationalism has led to nothing. Being occupied by a foreign country, the US, for the first time in her history, and again being confronted with a superior non-Japanese power, Japan's alternatives were narrowed [373]. As history has taught, neither extreme nationalism nor national self-denial was deemed favorable solutions. I would say that the Japanese saw their best chances for reconciliation in the continuation of its successes in matters of economy and modernization that have been started during the Meiji-period. Additionally, having once managed to catch up with advanced Western countries, they knew that they could manage again. Only this time they pledged to achieve this with sorely economic and non-military means.

During the 1960s Japan succeeded in building up her image as "electronics nation", and advanced technologies were soon considered as being part of Japan's new self-identity. With her growing economic success, the image of the defeated nation began to fade into the background and questions about Japan's self-identity have been encouraged.

---

[373] I will not assess here in how far the situation of the cold war has had an impact on the US support for Japan.

Actually many countries possess some specific image. Just think about French Cuisine, Italian Pasta, American Fast Food, Swiss Precision, Chinese Martial Arts and London Rain, and if being abroad, one sometimes also gets to hear about German uniformity, punctuality and accuracy. But it seems that the Japanese are even more deeply concerned with their self-identity, eager to define what it's meant to be Japanese and what distinguishes the Japanese from non-Japanese. This is in so far paradox or understandable, since Japan has imported numerous foreign cultural elements of which many with the passage of time became integrated and "japanized". And one not infrequently encounters Japanese people who believe that hamburgers, fireworks, toast, "*Makudonarudo*" (McDonald's), Christmas cakes and certainly robots are of Japanese origin.

3.5.2.5 Nihonjinron

Nihonjinron[374], which can be translated as "theories of Japanese cultural specificity" is a special Japanese genre of rather pseudo-scientific studies and analysis in which it is tried to "proof" the uniqueness of the Japanese people and culture, or better: to actually "proof" that the Japanese people and the Japanese culture are indeed more unique than the rest of the world. It is a Japanese method of defining the Japanese's self-identity. The fact that *Nihonjinron* also gets attention abroad and that many foreigners have some collective image about the hard working, group oriented exporters of cars and consumer electronics who enjoy the tea ceremony under a cherry blossom tree while *Zen*-meditating in harmony, and listening to the sounds of cicadas, which only the Japanese can find delightful due to their unique brain physiology, an experience later expressed through *haiku* poetry and *Ikebana* arrangements, actually pleases

---

[374] "*Nihonjin*" meaning Japanese people and "*Ron*" argument, opinion, attitude, essay, theory)

them since it provides them with "proof" about their exclusiveness. *Nihonjinron* even goes so far as it provides *"theories"* which not only describe the cultural distinctiveness of the Japanese, but also their unique physiology providing even the argument that imported rice from foreign countries could be incompatible with the Japanese's digestive system. What better way could there be to protect the domestic agriculture?

But as you might have realized, from an objective scientific standpoint *Nihonjinron* should not be taken serious, at least in regard to pure facts. As a matter of fact, although having preserved some of their genetic homogeneity due to their lack of intermingling with foreigners, Japanese people are no more physically unique than other humans, especially if compared to other East-Asian populations. Also in regard to the socio-cultural dimension, Japanese share much of their cultural heritage like Confucian- and Buddhist philosophies with China and Korea, from where they were originally imported. And now, more than ever before, one can see how the principals of the East-Asian ethic-system (e.g. the Confucian ideal of the hard-working, well educated human accepting ones position in a hierarchical order) contribute(d) to China's and South-Korea's economic success.

But the contents of *Nihonjinron* are also subject to changes. Whereas in the time soon following WWII up to the mid 1950s the Japanese viewed their own cultural past heritage rather with skepticism, especially since the early 1960s, the Japanese (re)gained an increasing confidence in their culture and tradition. Once regarded as backwardly, today the achievements of *Edo*-period manufacturing are praised as predecessors of Japan's modern robot technology, forming a seamless evolutional line. Also the *Edo*-period's "isolation policy", which has for long been defined as the main factor for Japan's technological lag relative to the Western nations, is now portrayed in a light depicting a Japan that despite being virtually shut off from the rest of the world (while often exaggerating the state of isolation) managed to develop a unique culture and allegedly Japan-specific technologies such as the *Karakuri*-automata. (In this context I only wonder, why Germany has not made a connection between modern robots and her traditional mechanical cuckoo clocks.)

3.5.2.6 "Nihonjinron-Effect" as Self-Fulfilling Prophecy

You may have heard about the "bank-run" example. If the rumor has been set up that Bank X is about to get bankrupt, people are rushing to Bank X, in order to get their money before it will be too late. Since, in collective action, all are going to get their money at the same time, the bank will soon run out of money. The rumor about the troubled bank will be validated, but actually this has been initiated through the people's actions and the rumor itself.

Although *Nihonjinron* may not be a scientifically valid method, it nonetheless has a great effect on the Japanese (and foreign) people, if they just believe in what is said. This effect is called a "Self-Fulfilling prophecy" or "Thomas-Effect": *"If men define situations as real, they are real in their consequences"* (W. I. Thomas). So if the Japanese think they are unique and special they will act accordingly, even maybe just to keep upright this image and their supposed unique identity. In the end this may lead to a paradox situation, where people make up some behavior just to distinguish themselves from others in order to "proof" that they are different and special. *Nihonjinron* may also be a factor contributing to the explanation of the Japanese's cautious attitude towards foreigners. If there are only very few foreigners in a country, they represent something extraordinary. And in this extraordinary situation the Japanese are also able to mirror and "proof" their uniqueness (mirror effect). If there would be many foreigners in the country and if Japanese would intermingle with them, then the element of strangeness would begin to fade and with this moving the Japanese into the category of the ordinary. Maybe the simple existence of *Nihonjinron* is really uniquely Japanese.

3.5.2.7 Nihonjinon – Or Why the Robot is Japanese

I think it is also *Nihonjinron*-aspects, which contribute to the Japanese high acceptability rate towards (non-industrial) robots. If one looks at the great efforts Japan is undertaking to promote the interest in this field, one may consider this as a hypothesis. If the positive attitude towards robots is skillfully connected to something genuinely linked to Japanese self-identity, as promoted through the "*Karakuri*-tradition", this could finally lead to a form of "self-fulfilling prophecy": A Japanese is said to like robots. Because I'm Japanese I have to like them.

Indications showing that I cannot be totally off the mark with such assumptions can be observed through numerous occasions such as TV-shows or public performances.

Now as Japan's unique image as producer of consumer- and common entertainment electronics is slowly fading, where the competition of Chinese and South-Korean manufacturers begins to show (e.g. in the area of plasma-TVs), new fields have to be found. As far as my observation goes, Japan's latest preoccupation with future uniqueness lies in environmental technology and robotics, at least these are the most frequently mentioned ones. As for these, the two main topics on display at the Aichi Expo 2005, Japan really holds a position still unmatched by the newly-industrialized Asian countries.

3.5.2.8 Reanalyzing *"Tetsuwan Atomu"*

As I have already mentioned before, it is true that indeed the most popular explanatory factor for the Japanese' fondness for robots I've encountered in all my interviews and discussions in Japan (at *Robosquare* Fukuoka, Mitsubishi Heavy Industries, TEPIA and with Prof. Aoki) as well as in diverse newspaper articles from inside and outside Japan, can be said to be *"Tetsuwan Atomu"* (*Astro Boy*). Now that we know that this robotic super-hero has served as a great inspiration for researchers, politicians and the general public in regard to robotics, I think it should be (re)analyzed.

If looking a little bit deeper into the stories, one can also find elements, which leave room for critical and ambivalent interpretations.

In the first volume of the *manga* there is a foreword by the author Osamu Tezuka saying in a quite utilitarian manner that robots should make people happy. Later he asks the question what if one substitutes the word "robot" through the word "science": has science really made mankind happy? He leaves the question open, but the mere fact that such a question has been posed indicates that there could be more than one affirmative answer. This is also being underlined by the fact that the picture shows Tezuka looking out of the window onto high rise buildings and multilevel roads, which some people may consider as negative aspects of technology. Reverse it again and one gets the question if *robots* make people happy.

Then there's Dr. Tenma's who creates the robot later to be known as *"Astro Boy"* in the likeness of his son who has died in a traffic accident because he has left him alone while working on a robot-project (here again the aspect of personal tragedy as portrayed in *Frankenstein* gets involved). Later Dr. Tenma gets disappointed when he suddenly realizes that his robot cannot grow and therefore can never substitute for his real lost son. Doesn't this imply at least two warnings: a loss of humanity through the preoccupation with technology (symbolized through the circumstances of the death of Dr. Tenma's son) and the indication that robots can never become like human beings, no matter how human-like they might look, how advanced their Artificial Intelligence and emotional behavior (simulation?) may become (symbolized through the robot's inability to grow). So one may ask the question about what purpose it may serve then to build machines in human likeness. And as the case of Dr. Tenma illustrates, it is more than questionable that robots may bring about happiness to mankind.

The assumption that Tezuka, who has also written about serious subjects like World War II and religion, might have had in mind rather the opposite message, namely considering the integration of technology (symbolized through robots) into human society as not necessarily unproblematic, can be supported if one looks at Tezuka's earlier work "*Robotic Angel*"[375] which served as the basis for "*Tetsuwan Atomu*". "*Robotic Angel*" has been put into an animé-movie in 2001 by Rintaro and Katsuhiro Otomo[376]. In this story there's hardly anything about the often-cited and expected Japanese positive attitude towards a welcomed human-robot future (although, as it is the case with much of Japanese animé, it is unclear in which country the story actually takes place[377]). In "*Robotic Angel*" robots are confined to underground levels together with the poor and unfortunate classes of human society whose bad living conditions are blamed on the robots that have taken away their jobs. Robots are hunted and destroyed in a "*Blade-Runner*" manner upon entering the surface. Workers rebel against robots making them responsible for their unemployment and misery. Humans feel that they individually and society as a whole are threatened by the existence of and

---

[375] The film is called "*Metropolis*" in Japan. In Germany it has not been allowed to distribute the *animé*-movie under the original Japanese title "*Metropolis*" to avoid confusion with Fritz Lang's work. Instead it is titled "*Robotic Angel*" there. I will also refer to it as "*Robotic Angel*" to avoid confusion with Fritz Lang's work. In many aspects Tezuka's work resembles Fritz Lang's 1926 masterpiece. And indeed, it has been advertisement-posters for Fritz Lang's "*Metropolis*" that have inspired Tezuka.
[376] He also created rather technology-critical works like "*Ghost in the Shell*" and "*Innocence*"
[377] The architecture and people look Western / North American, but one can also see Japanese / Chinese signs on the streets.

dependence on machinery. The viewer learns that the coexistence between humans and robots indeed can bring along problems. On top of this the despotic leader of the Mega-City tries to secure his power with the help of an Android called *Tima*, which represents the spitting image of his dead daughter (the theme of *"Tetsuwan Atomu"*). Technology is compared to the erection of the Tower of Babel, which has been illustrated quite literally as the despot's ultimate techno-structure is called "*Ziggurat*" (the name for an Assyrian or Babylonian tower).

Although the theme and philosophy of Tezuka's *"Robotic Angel"* sounds quite cyber-punk-like, the retro-futuristic setting used by Rintaro and Otomo, somehow relativizes the degree of the negative tenor in the animé: maybe it's rather about an "alternative future" instead of a "preview" about things to come.

In this sense by analysing the (robot-)works by Tezuka - the artist popularly held responsible for Japan's robot-friendliness - I would conclude that his message has probably been misunderstood. I would even go further to say that the main point behind *"Tetsuwan Atomu"* has not been about robots at all. The robot rather serves as a symbol calling for humanity. Most fans of *"Tetsuwan Atom"* however just seem to be impressed by the technology and just superficially interpret the robot's powers as a symbol for mankind's salvation through technology.

A similar inapt incident which could be attributed to misinterpretation has been the visit of Japanese Prime Minister Koizumi in Prague who brought along the humanoid robot *ASIMO* to pay tribute to Karel Čapek. Wasn't it the robots of Čapek's play R.U.R. (which have actually been portrayed as organic) that were about to destroy humankind?

In my view *"Tetsuwan Atom"* can also be interpreted as follows:

- Robots can not substitute for humans
- Robots can never become like humans (even with a "heart" and Artificial Intelligence)
- Robots will always be as good or bad as the humans who create them
- Technology is ambivalent
- There could occur conflicts in regard to the coexistence of humans and robots
- It is questionable (although not impossible) if robots will bring happiness to mankind
- What purpose does it serve to build machines in mankind's likeliness (posed as a rather open question)?
- A call to reconsider humanity

Surprisingly, as I have learned in a discussion with Prof. Aoki about *"Tetsuwan Atomu"*, the Japanese observer rather tends to blame the human instead of the robot for difficulties regarding harmonic coexistence between the two entities. As I have asked Prof. Aoki about the aspect of Dr. Tenma being disappointed about his robot and the possible message that robots might not be able to make people happy, and my resulting ambivalent interpretation of *"Tetsuwan Atomu"*, he was very surprised. He told me that this has been the first time that he has ever been confronted with such a point of view. My ambivalent interpretation of the story's message has opened to him a totally new perspective. Prof. Aoki told me that he has never seen the aspect of disappointment behind Dr. Tenma's reaction, but has rather thought of it as tragedy: everybody tries his best and wants to be perfect (in this case the robot tries to do its best to be like a human), but they fail. The tragic aspect is seen as bidirectional concerning both, humans as well as robots[378]. Also the idea of building a robot to substitute for a dead son, a quite absurd, even inhumane idea to many Westerners, has not been

---

[378] In this sense one could also get a totally different perspective on *"Blade Runner"* by attributing the problem to the humans instead of the Androids.

interpreted in this way by the Japanese people I talked to. They have either never thought about it or have considered Tenma's action as just being the logical choice for a robotics engineer to do.

Why have so many Japanese overlooked some points behind *"Tetsuwan Atom"*?
In a way *"Tetsuwan Atom"* is not that different from much of western science fiction works (e.g. "A.I.", *"Star Wars"*). Many stories by Isaac Asimov even represent similar portrayals of robots. But the Japanese seem to rather focus on the following aspects in regard to the story:

- It has been possible through technology to create artificial human-like entities (i.e. robots, especially *"Astro Boy"*) which possess human like characteristics like intelligence and a "heart" and this is regarded as somehow challenging and fascinating

- *"Astro Boy"* represents a positive figure, because he helps people in need and fights for justice and peace and therefore strengthening the picture of the "good robot"

Their focus centers around *"Astro Boy"* himself and his actions, but they may have lost track of the big picture.

In short: from the mere story portrayed in *"Tetsuwan Atomu"* one can not inevitably conclude that robotics necessarily have to provide a positive future. It also can not explain why *"Tetsuwan Atomu"* should be of such a great influence in regard to Japan's fondness about robots, because of the possible ambivalent reading of the story.

The question should be: why have the Japanese chosen the *positive* interpretation of the story about this robot hero instead of the ambivalent one referring to the greater context? This can not be explained through the story itself. In my view it is conceivable that Osamu Tezuka originally meant to critically reflect on Japan's technology- and progression-oriented heading, and that the robot *"Tetsuwan Atomu"* was chosen to reflect on humanity by presenting a non-human who acts more humane and courageous than many humans. But just reading a story is not enough. There has to be given directions on how to culturally interpret the content. Since the robot was portrayed as good in character, it just suited Japan's desired image of a peaceful and progressive nation. Another aspect might lie in the unique distinction from the West, where traditionally robots are portrayed as dangerous. In my opinion, referring to *"Tetsuwan Atomu"* when trying to promote some costly robot-related research sounds more like a justification for the project: look, robotics can be useful for helping people as portrayed in *"Tetsuwan Atomu"* - and who doesn't want ones hero to come to life? Of course this robot represents a positive figure, but how can a science-fiction figure be the cause for people planning to initiate costly research projects and even getting support for this?

I would say that *"Astro Boy"* represents a symbol - a symbol for the Japanese dream of excelling in technology, something being symbolized through the robot. And it's the origin of this dream that should be explained.

Maybe some data about *"Tetsuwan Atomu"* and Japan's post-war history can help understanding this phenomenon:

- The story was created in 1951. It was also in the 50s where Japan started to recover from the war and began producing electronic goods (first motorcycle by Honda, first tape recorder by Sony in 1950), leading to the first economic boom from 1954 – 1957[379].

---

[379] Referring to the timeline in the book: „Japan's Creative Thinking" (p. 91-95) published by JETRO, 2001. These two companies are also now deeply involved in robotics.

- In 1963 the first animated series of *"Astro Boy"* was shown on Japanese television, one year before the Tokyo Olympic Games. Hosting the Olympic Games, which has been the first one to be held in Asia, was a great and important step for Japan's Post-War reputation, international image, acceptance and reconciliation. *"Tetsuwan Atomu"* was also the first Japanese anime aired in the US and later being exported to other countries, where it gained a somewhat international recognition, although not being able to catch up with the huge popularity inside Japan. It was also during the mid 1960s where Japan's image as "Electronics Nation" began to take on shape.

Looking at this, one can suppose a connection between the "visions" presented in *"Tetsuwan Atomu"*, where the robot represents the ultimate achievement that can be realized through technology, and the good character of the robot which symbolizes the possibility of "salvation" through peaceful technology; visions that finally have become reality. Also of importance may be the fact that *"Tetsuwan Atomu"*, an anime show, has been Japan's first international success of an arts genre that is considered unique to Japan. And since it was about a robot, it might have contributed to laying a cornerstone for Japan's international image as *"Robot Kingdom"*. I would even go that far to say that the figure of *Astro Boy*, through promotional efforts, might have been deliberately turned into the kind of symbol and role model it represents today. Poor in natural resources, Japan owes most of its economic success to technology/electronics. So *"Astro Boy"* can be seen as a symbol for Japan's success and strivings. Robotics represents a challenge in technology, the ultimate dream for companies like Honda, Fujitsu, Mitsubishi, NEC, Sony, Toyota, and others. And with a whole array of Japanese humanoid, walking and talking robots, the topic of *"Tetsuwan Atomu"* again becomes a contemporary phenomenon.

"*Astro Boy*" could represent the following dimensions:

a) it reminds the Japanese on their history and achievements realized through technology
b) it represents a future goal for the Japanese by following this goal to the ultimate
c) it serves as a symbol for "collective identity" (it represents the Japanese, it represents (inter)national success, it represents the ultimate future goal)
d) because "Astro Boy" portrays a positive figure, technology is associated positively

3.5.3 Why the Robot fits into the Japanese Culture

3.5.3.1 The Group - "Closed Circuit"

Especially during the late 1970s to the 1980s there has been a real boom on Japan-literature, especially in the field of economics. *"Learning from Japan"* was the slogan. But soon critique followed, warning that the Japanese model would ruin all social achievements Western countries have fought for so hard since the 18th century. The *"Closed Circuit"* is just a metaphor I'll use for describing some elements of Japanese society, namely ethnocentrism, scepticism regarding outsiders, a job-market almost closed to foreigners, group orientation, harmony (or uniformity) and the emphasis on ritualistic behavior.

In my view it is these elements of the *"Closed Circuit"* which contribute to the Japanese's acceptance of robots, which may be even seen as role models.
x
x

3.5.3.2 Harmony

The most encountered, overtaxed and most valued concept in Japanese culture and society is harmony. Even in relation to robots the concept of a "harmonious co-existence between humans and robots" is emphasized. But it is not easy to get behind the real meaning of Japan's inflationary use of the term "harmony". Whereas by many Westerners "harmony" is understood as the skilful *integration* of differences, in Japan it rather means assimilation and *elimination* of differences. Harmony in the Japanese and East-Asian interpretation has its roots in Confucianism that teaches the importance of respecting hierarchy and rank in order to maintain successful and non-conflicting social relationships. Here Harmony is not something to be achieved through discourse, but means a state where everybody accepts ones position and the "wisdom" of ones superior and acts accordingly without discontent. The Western concept of harmony may be comparable to a polyphonic choir, whereas the Japanese concept would rather be analogous a unison choir.

3.5.3.3 Conformity, Ritualism and the Group

If I would have entered the department store and someone told me we're writing a year sometime beyond 2050, I might have guessed that they have opted for substituting sales-clerks for robotic androids: smiles, perfect bows, trained (or programmed?) movements, the same repertoire of greetings, phrases of civility, and of course uniforms (this is the reason why I found it so hard to make out sales personnel in Germany). It's hard to tell if that's all real or just a simulation. It looks as if for every act in Japan there is some sort of algorithm prescribing the correct performance. This ranges from the presentation of business cards (they have to be given and received with both hands) over the rules of *Ikebana* flower arrangement, the correct way of placing ones shoes in front of the doorstep upon entering (the shoes have to be placed 90 degrees to the doorstep with their tips facing to the door) to the angle of ones bow as a function of difference in rank and status of the present parties.

What is visually most striking and uncomfortable to most Germans when visiting Japan is the omnipresence of uniforms. It looks as if after a child receives ones first uniform in Kindergarten one will wear this or another until retirement. Children wear them from Kindergarten to graduation, sales- and bank clerks wear them, cashiers, waiters, office workers (although for so called "salary-men", there's no specific uniform, they nonetheless mostly wear dark suits and a tie), not to mention all those who in other countries also wear uniforms. Japanese also seem to be proud of their working uniform, as many of them even wear it when appearing on the Sunday's Karaoke contest aired on TV. But the uniform is not just a piece of attire; it symbolizes the proudness of belonging to a specific company and the ideal of equality.

Whereas in Western countries groups tend to consist of members who share some similarity in attribute, e.g. the union of steel-workers, professors from different universities, student's associations etc.[380], in Japan an office clerk or engineer from company A would hardy relate to an office clerk or engineer from company B. Instead the engineer of company A would rather relate to an office clerk of the same company, especially when they have entered the firm in the same year[381]. Also if being asked about one's work one first names ones company. If the person is an engineer, office-clerk or foreman is only of secondary importance in regard to rank. Such a setting also impedes the formation of effective trade unions, which in Japan are de facto an extended arm of a specific company and actually can hardly be called "trade unions" at least to

---

[380] This is also interesting in the context of Durkheim's "organic and mechanical solidarity" (Durkheim, 1988 [1893])
[381] Refer to Nakane, 1984

a Westerner's definition of the term [382]. But also the Japanese concept of "equality" has to be seen with a different connotation than the European "*Liberté, Égalité et Fraternité*" ("liberty, equality and brotherhood"). It's not primarily about each individuals being equal to the other; it's rather about nobody standing out ones group or questioning ones position.

To almost every person in Germany with whom I talked about this, a robot's traits of lacking genuine individuality and spontaneity and acting on command have evoked rather negative associations. As I have observed the Japanese promotion of ideals such as conformity, homogeneity and ritualism - the perhaps socially engineered expectation of nobody standing out - the robot may even be regarded as a kind of role model. Above this I assume that the expectations by Japanese people in regard to a robot's interactive capabilities may be lower than those of Westerners. To a Japanese, a robot's ability to simulate friendliness, observe the correct ways of behavior, act courteously, do some formalized small talk and be able to adapt to the company setting (everything just being a matter of programming) may suffice for "social skills". In this perspective the "harmonious" picture of *ASIMO* standing in line with employees of the Tokyo Stock Market during the closing ceremony comes back to mind, where nobody, including the robot stood out.

x

---

[382] Although one has to note that it has been the "trade unions", which fostered the system of life-long employment ad other company-internal benefits, but these implements have also been in the interest of the companies, e.g. in order to hinder management staff from changing to another firm.

3.5.3.4 Public Behavior and Observing Rank

More than any other society I am aware of, the Japanese draw a clear distinction between *tatemae*[383], public behavior and *"honme*[384]*"*, private behavior. What one normally gets to see is *"tatemae"*, the regulated behavior which the individual believes to be expected from her/him in the context of the situation at hand. This circumstance has to be taken into account when conducting interviews with Japanese, for example. They might just say what they believe a foreigner should hear from a Japanese about Japan. But since even the setting within Japanese families is still often characterized by hierarchical settings, the *"honme"* there also has to be seen in a relative way. I would even go so far that it might provide difficulties for Japanese to express *"real honme"* if other people are present.

In the Japanese language there are by far more nuances in degrees of honorific addressing, expressions and terminology[385] than one can find in (Western) European languages. (Even for commanding my *AIBO* robot in Japanese I can choose from varying degrees of honorific language, by letting the command either sound like giving an order from a superior to an inferior or as requesting a favour from some entity deserving a certain degree of respect). The knowledge of ones associate's relative rank is crucial. That may be a reason why for Japanese the exchange of business cards as the first action upon one's meeting is of such importance. Even in colloquial settings, the usage of the correct addressing for superior and subordinate are being observed in most cases. The nuances of differences in regard to the perception of ones relative rank have become so fine tuned that it becomes difficult to find someone with equal rank.

Japanese social scientist Chie Nakane[386] named another important factor regarding the Japanese society: the *"vertical principle"* (Nakane: 1997) that defines *rank* as the central aspect of group relationships; or as Ruth Benedict has

---
[383] literally: "in front of the house", meaning proper public behavior.
[384] Translation
[385] Korean is also a language with a complicated system of honorific terms
[386] Chie Nakane is Professor of Social Anthropology at Tokyo University

observed it, that Japanese draw confidence in hierarchy and that one has to accept it and "take one's proper station" (Benedict, 1996 [1946], p.43).

For a long time it was practice at (big) companies to pay its workers according to their years in the company instead of honouring individual merit (seniority system). It is noteworthy that shifts to merit-based payments occur during crisis situations (as they are currently experienced), but as soon as the crisis is over, they slowly return to the seniority-system.

As a matter of fact, rank is already observed inside the family, where children generally address each other with the title of older / younger sister / brother, instead of calling them by their given names. A Japanese saying to express confusion is to state that "something is neither elder brother nor younger brother" (refer to Benedict, 1996 [1946], p.52). And rank-training continues in school, where much care is taken to teach respectful behavior from younger "junior" (*sempai*) students towards older "senior" (*kōhai*) students. And a superior always remains a superior, regardless of the setting they are in, even when visiting a bar or restaurant together after work. If one defines a group through the relationships of its members, in Japan it consists of the vertical relationship of the individual to one's superior[387].

Of course such a *"vertical setting"* bears problems, of which the following two are the most obvious: changes, especially in the leadership can easily lead to crisis in the system and co-operation between different groups, e.g. between different research institutes, is rather difficult[388]. Other side effects of verticality and group dependence include a lack of democracy and the inability of making decisions by oneself, as I have experienced it on numerous occasions at quite banal situations: if a Japanese plumber comes to our house for repairs, the first thing he does is calling his superior, asking him how to proceed – even before having looked at the problem. If asking for something in a supermarket soon the

---

[387] Chie Nakane uses the term „group" in a similar broad way
[388] Maybe this is the reason why one could get the impression that may companies seem to "invent the wheel on their own".

whole department staff gathers around you appearing in ascending order; and a Japanese tourist would get helplessly lost if disconnected from his/her tour-guide.

But if no problems occur and everybody complies, there's no system more efficient than the *vertical principle* based on loyalty and clear positions. Also entering a vertically structured group is rather easy for a "blank entity" that accepts the low position of a newcomer and still can be formed – or programmed - according to the group's need. In this sense a robot could make the ideal choice for a low-rank position. I would represent (given appropriate programming) an ideal case of loyalty and harmonious incorporation into the "closed circuit" of the group. And since, at least according to the traditional Japanese ideal, a human is expected to accept ones position and fate without complaint, why then should a robot rebel against its master? The classic Western *"rebelling slave"* is something being deemed un-Japanese.

3.5.3.4 a) Excursion: A Note on accepting ones Position

I will provide the following excursion for a better understanding of the Japanese concept of loyalty. Surely the strong "master-student-relationship" being observed in Japan has its roots in the traditional *Bushido* codex[389] demanding that a *samurai* warrior has always to be loyal to his lord[390], and Confucian ideals of the "respected wise old man". The relationship can be considered symbiotic. I have chosen the term symbiosis to underline that the "master's" power is relative and dependent on its subordinate's acceptance. While the „student" or subordinate will be ready to serve ones superior whenever his service is demanded, the "master" or superior will take care of his "student" and

---

[389] The codex for the Japanese warrior-caste (*samurai*), which flourished during the *Edo*-period
[390] e.g. refer to Nitobe, 1969 and Nitobe 1997 and Sadler, 1997 who provide a detailed description about *Bushido*

provide him guidance and advise. Whereas in (most) Western countries a hierarchy of superiors and subordinates only serves the means of organizational efficiency and the reduction of decision-making–costs, for Japanese this relationship also bears an emotional and idealistic dimension, associated with concepts of loyalty, discipline and honor. *Bushio*, the Japanese' codex of the *Samurai* Warrior demands duty, subordination, obedience and respect and provides an "algorithm" for an honourable man's way of life. In Japan, many aspects of Bushido have survived until today.

In feudal times Japanese peasants have been oppressed by their feudal lords in a way that did not differ much from the situation in Europe during that time. But as long as their physical existence has been assured by their lords they accepted their position and fate. But when the feudal master's rule became arbitrary, excessive and tyrant, the peasants saw their right to revolt. Interestingly, after such a revolt both parties, the peasants and the lord were punished, usually by death[391]. The peasants were punished because they have acted against their master and the master was punished because the revolt was caused through his actions[392].

The most important and valued story that reflects the Japanese concepts of rank, duty and honor is that of the *47 Rōnin*. Asano, young *daimyō* (Japanse feudal lord) was about to participate in a reception ceremony of high-ranking Imperial representatives. Kira, a high ranking official to the *Shōgun* Tokugawa Tsunayoshi was in chare of advising Asano. Kira insulted Asano numerous times and even gave him wrong advises in matters of court-etiquette causing Asano's humiliation in public and at the court. Finally, at one time Asao lost his temper and draw his sword against Kira. Although Kira was not seriously wounded, attacking a high ranking official of the *Shōgun* within the *Shōgun's* residence was considered a high rated crime. Asano was then ordered to commit

---

[391] The peasants were executed, while the lord was forced to commit *Seppuku* (ritualistic suicide)
[392] Refer to Hearn, p. 339 - 340

seppuku (ritualistic suicide). Asano's *samurai* became *Rōnin*, leaderless *Samurai*. 47 of them swore to avenge their master and kill Kira. After a long time of preparation and waiting, they started their attack on Kira, found him cowardly hiding in a storage room (some say shed) and finally killed him and offered Kira' head on Asano's grave. Although the *Rōnin* had committed a crime by acting against the *Shōgun's* authority, their action has also been regarded as an exemplary act of loyalty, honor and the observance of *Bushido*. With the *Rōnin* (except one, who was pardoned by the *Shōgun*) sentenced to perform *seppuku*, their honor has been restored.

There even exists an allusion to the story of the *"47 Rōnin"* in Oshii's philosophical science-fiction animé-movie *"Innocence"*, where mistreated androids kill their masters, but afterwards self-destruct.

3.5.4 Reflection: Robots as Role Models?

"Tetsuwan Atomu" is still an inspiring figure for young and old Japanese, and *ASIMO* already teaches children how to safely cross the street[393]. Harmony, courtesy and friendliness, these are some key-elements which especially Japanese robot-designers and software-developers regard as quite important traits to implement in their artificial creatures.

If one takes a comparative look, typical characteristics generally attributed to robots are interpreted differently, even oppositely in Germany and Japan.

As I have learned in discussions, to most German acquaintances their prejudiced ideas about robots have evoked associations with various kinds of traits considered negative in German (or to them ideally in any other) society. To many of them a robot induces a picture of mindless marching entities; soulless, preoccupied with cold efficiency and leaving no room for freedom,

---

[393] https://asimo.honda.com/pedestriansafety/index.asp? (Jan. 25, 2005)

individuality, self expression and imagination. Even allusions to militarism have been hinted. The idea that a robot might be considered as being more than just some sophisticated machine performing disliked jobs and may even become integrable into human society sounds rather strange to European– and US audiences, since for the common audience a robot seems to lack everything deemed human and social. Equipping a robot with some functions that makes it more communicable and human-like is regarded here as a necessary means for deflecting the threatening characteristics of the machine. At least to German understanding being called a "robot" is considered disapproving or even insulting.

Taking into consideration the cultural circumstances, it is conceivable to assume that a robot's characteristics remain much more a stranger to German (Western) mentality than to the Japanese's (or East-Asian). Let me put it into the bold statement of saying that it is easier to simulate Japanese than German ideals of human co-existence. Whereas to Germans (and other Westerners) the idea of conformity, subordination, behavioral prescriptions and ritualistic acts in common settings sounds rather disturbing, to many Japanese they still represent virtues. Consequently by being obedient, disciplined, courteously, adaptive, hard-working and accepting ones position in the hierarchy without complaint, a robot would represent the perfect *kobun* („retainer") in a Japanese corporate setting. Here one gets the chance to program a role-model worker to be harmoniously integrated. Unlike it is the case with the literature-induced, liberalism driven fears of Westerners that robots one day may revolt against their masters like the African slaves ("rebelling-slave syndrome"), Japanese are not concerned that a robot might not "accept" its assigned position as *kobun*, if even humans do it by virtue.

Since genuine human-robot interaction in the non-industrial workplace is still a rather long way to go (deployment of robots in non-industrial workplace settings is still limited to the rather simple function of greeting customers), it is hard to tell in how far such an "ideal worker" will be accepted in a real setting. At least I would suppose that a robot would be regarded as less interfering in a Japanese- than in a German workplace setting.

In this sense what better role-model could one possibly have than a robot, which by virtue of programming is able to correctly carry out all these important feats for maintaining Japan's social harmony?

x

3.6 Personal Robots

While reading the science-fiction-novel "*The Naked Sun*" by Isaac Asimov (Asimov 1991) during my vacation, a flash thought brushed my mind, that in a couple of centuries Japanese society might end up like the high-tech and "shut-in" *Solarian* civilization described in the book. Although not taking this unwarranted thought too seriously, there might be some truth behind the sayings of the armchair sociologist described in the book that high technological advance, low birth rates, homophobia and the use of robots may be connected.

In contrast to the previous chapters that reflected on robots being used in a non-industrial corporate and public setting, the following analysis deals with considerations about robots for personal use by individuals. Whereas in Germany the advantages of "personal robots" (if this term is used) are mainly expressed in connection to pragmatic considerations, e.g. in regard to being relieved of disliked jobs in the household or to enhance security, in Japan my observations have indicated some psychological dimensions about human-robot "co-existence". These have already set off the "social alarm bells" ringing by some non-Japanese commentators pitying the Japanese for having to buy friends in form of entertainment-robots – machines, and thus indicating grave problems in Japanese society on basis of humanity.

But some examples about circumstances and trends in Japanese society may provide a hint about why (Japanese) people may be able to draw emotional comfort in the interaction with robots. Perhaps, as I see it and as it will be outlined in the following examples, the advent of robots entering the social domain may be regarded by many as presenting a solution to some of the problems existing in (Japanese) society, serving as a compensatory mechanism. Nonetheless, I will leave open Tezuka's question, if robots really will make people happy...

3.6.1 Indications

Indication 1: Benriya

As a *Japan Times Weekly* article implies, the growing demand for so-called "*Benriya*" in Japan may give rise to questions about some serious (social and psychological) problems in Japan[394]. *Benriya* are some strange hybrid between handyman and amateur psychological counsellor, doing tasks from taking away dead cockroaches to comforting depressed clients who are willing to pay between 40 dollars up to even a few thousand dollars per hour for just having some stranger listening to you. What is mirrored in the growing demand for *Benriya* is not only that there are a growing number of people willing to pay for services they are unwilling to do themselves. It is moreover about the psychological inability of people to *get along* with banal and simple tasks or even with ones life; about being rather willing to pay than ask for a favor. *Benriya* even take over tasks that sound absurd and unbelievable to my German friends and acquaintances. Such tasks include visiting wedding- or funeral services for their customer, paying tribute at the client's ancestor's graves,

---

[394] Refer to *The Japan Times Weekly*, October 25, 2003, p. 8. The data in the following has been taken mostly out of this article.

posing as a friend at a party, cancelling a neighbor's invitation or just sit and listen to some lonely "shut-in" person.

If people are willing to pay (sometimes hefty) fees to complete strangers to do some banal tasks for them or even provide some emotional nearness and comfort, the step towards welcoming some robot doing this for you, and even the ability of getting some kind of close relationship towards this artificial entity may not be a great one.

Indication 2: Primopuel Dolls

In 2003 the Japanese toy-maker Bandai, the same company that has also developed the *Tamagotchi*, a small virtual chick on a liquid crystal display which have to be nurtured through some button-pushing, has began to market an approximately 30 to 50 cm tall speaking doll (not really a robot) with some interactive capabilities, among them 280 preprogrammed phrases. Actually targeted at young single women, the doll called *Primopuel* (meaning "First Boy"[395]), has proven to be unexpectedly popular with elderly women. It even went so far that Bandai has once organized a come-together for elderly *Primopuel*-owners dubbed *"Primopuel Kindergarten Entrance Ceremony"*, where about a hundred women showed up with their dolls. Japanese psychologists have explained this phenomenon in the way that through the dolls the elderly women get reminded on their children and the days when they were younger[396].

x

x

---

[395] Coined from the Italian / Latin words *Primo* (= first) and *Puer* (=boy or child) in Latin; the "l" in *"Primopuel"* probably derives from the Japanese transcription practice of confusing "r" with "l".
[396] Refer to *The Japan Times Weekly*, October 25, 2003, p. 8.

Indication 3: The Old Woman and the "Seven"

As I was visiting the Sony Building at Ginza / Tokyo I saw an elderly Japanese lady standing next to me in front of an area where they had two AIBO-ERS-7 robot dogs (generally nicknamed "Seven") on display for the customers. Although she certainly seemed to be able to tell the difference between the "real" and the "artificial", she talked to one of the robots "dogs", petting it lovingly and told me that she and the "dog" know and understand each other. The elderly lady hinted that she comes nearly every day to the Sony Building for visiting the "dogs". As she left, she said to the robot: *"mata ashita"* – "see you tomorrow".

I have made similar observations on several of my visits to the Sony Building in Tokyo, where mostly Japanese mid-aged and elderly Japanese men and women, but also mothers with small children came to the robots for talk and interaction. Interestingly, in contrast to the Japanese, non-Japanese visitors acted more hesitant in petting the robot and generally tended to ensure that nobody would be directly observing them before interacting or talking to the *AIBO*s.

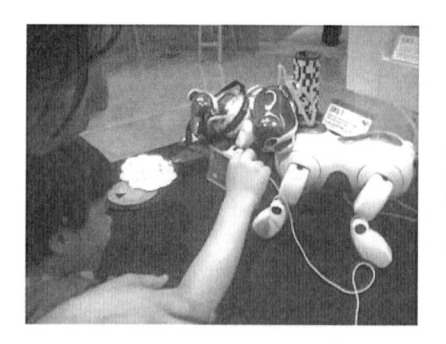

A Japanese mother and child interacting with an AIBO ERS-7 at the Sony Building / Tokyo

Photo: Miriam JS Leis, Tokyo 2004

3.6.2 Human-Robot Relations

The reasons why people opt for purchasing an *AIBO* or similar goods are manifold and range from simple curiosity to the need for companionship. In Japan the reason for people keeping *AIBO*s has been mainly explained through the fact that in many portions of Japan's large cities like Tokyo or Osaka, people reside in homes where no living animals are allowed. Since many of them don't have much experience with real animals, they also don't tend to compare an *AIBO* to a real pet or miss the robot's shortcomings. But I would say that there have to be other preconditions existent. For example, if showing some affinity towards objects is deemed socially unacceptable behavior, the creation of affinity-evoking objects would also be deemed reasonless. As I have observed it in Germany, many people do not readily admit that their motivations for purchasing an *AIBO* have been others than their interest in technology, programming or maybe entertainment[397]. In Germany it seems to be socially sanctioned if admitting some kind of affinity towards non-living entities, whereas in Japan such tendencies even seem to be encouraged (refer to the Excursion "A Note on Anthropomorphizing" in Part II of my work).

As I have learned through personal interviews, many Japanese are also able to "forget" about the mechanism behind a doll or robot (as Japanese viewers are able to "overlook" the puppeteers at classical Japanese puppet-performances). As an engineer from Mitsubishi told me, Japanese people manage quite well in forgetting about a robot's "inside" and just concentrate on its appearance and movements. This may be a reason why so many Japanese robots possess such a nice, cute and even human-like appearance. By many Japanese robots are regarded rather as some kind of communicative animal or pet, instead of a mechanical device consisting of a computer, batteries, motors, gears, cables and running on software; in the same way as people generally don't think about the

---

[397] Refer to the explanations posted on the appendix files of my work about the hypothesis generating survey I conducted with some German AIBOwners.

human anatomy and physiology when interacting with each other. But as I have learned through a hypothesis-generating survey I conducted with German AIBOwners (refer to appendix files), to nearly all of the 16 respondents coming from Germany and Europe their *AIBO(s)* represent more than just some kind of object.

Just return to the previously mentioned example of the *"Old Woman and the Seven"*. The interesting thing in regard to this elderly lady is that the "relationship" only works because she lacks sufficient knowledge about the technology behind the ERS-7. Seen from the technological standpoint, the lady should have known that the ERS-7 on display quite certainly wouldn't recognize her without the face-recognition procedure being executed first. Also she couldn't be sure that they always have the same ERS-7 on display on each day of her visit. Additionally she should have known that all the reactions of the ERS-7 follow a carefully programmed pattern triggered by certain input stimuli, regardless of who does the specific interaction. Maybe if the "old lady" would know about this, she would quite probably get disappointed and the "relationship", which of course is a very asymmetric one, could break down. If looking at the situation from the perspective of an *actor-network* viewpoint, the ERS-7 occupies a specific position in the life of the old lady, which may be comparable to that of a living pet or even a human being. In short, in my view the old lady's affection towards the "Seven" is neither the result of her growing knowledge about the object as it has been the case with McClintock *"feeling sorry for the grass"*[398], nor some kind of (new) romanticism about artificial creatures, but something else, which critics may call evidence for a decline in humanity as the result of growing individualism (in the socially destructive sense of the term) and a decay of traditional social embeddedness. As the traditional family ties of this elderly lady may have broken down, perhaps

---

[398] Refer to Knorr Cetina, 1997

leaving her without the bonding to her family and relatives (of course this is only speculation), she may have turned to the object world as a compensatory resort. This is also what Knorr Cetina has probably meant by "objectualization" (Knorr Cetina, 1997), assuming that relationships between humans and non-humans may serve as compensation for disintegrating human-human bonds[399].

The whole idea of Japanese so-called *"Character Goods"* (objects with cute and lovely design) is intended towards evoking some positive emotional effect and comfort through the object. In this sense the Japanese preoccupation with creating robots to be cute, lovable and foremost to be liked by humans, gets another dimension if considered in the context of some specific aspects of Japanese society. I would state the bold hypothesis by proposing that the object, especially the "interactive object" as manifested in robots, serves as a "psychological anchor" in the Japanese society which may be seen as being rather a collection of interdependent individuals. Since Japanese cultural engineering has produced people who find it hard to express ones real feelings in front of others (in Japan even family members being reunited after a crisis barely react emotionally in public, and if people express "emotions" in public, they generally do this in a prescribed way), the robot may also provide the Japanese individual with the possibility of showing ones emotions and getting emotional fulfilment without the fear of losing face. In this sense a robot may really become a "partner" that even stands above ones friend. In this sense Japanese social settings may actually encourage human-object relationships, where the "partner robot" represents a welcomed entity.

xx

x

---

[399] Refer to ibid

3.6.2 A Further Note on Human-Object Relations as a Compensatory Resort

As I have already outlined in the previous sections about the Japanese corporate structure, most Japanese are firmly embedded in the regulated setting of the company, which even affects family life. In Japan when a man gets employed by a company, actually his whole family enters the system (I speak here of a man's situation since the majority of the Japanese working women remain single as long as they work). In a way the relationship between the company and the new employee can be compared to that of father and son, although rather in the hierarchical Confucian sense of the term (this can be seen as in some companies it is common practice to call the newcomer by the nickname of X-*chan*, whereas "*chan*" is a suffix usually used for calling children, generally girls, by name; e.g. Miriam-*chan*). The company even feels responsible for taking care of what is considered private or internal family matters in the West. Some companies even provide company housing for employees, leading to a situation where one couldn't leave the workplace setting even in ones own one. At Japanese wedding- or funeral services, naturally ones company's co-workers are expected to participate. In Germany in contrast, if one invites company employees, generally it's because they are close friends and not because they belong to ones company. Obviously in such a setting the borders between public and private, between work and free time get blurred or even vanish.

The working man shares more time and close ties with his company colleagues than with his family. Even problems which might be considered rather personal by Western standards are solved within the setting of ones co-worker relationships. Such a situation leads to a sharpened exclusion of- and isolation from everything that happens outside the group one belongs to. Since the borders are clearly defined and shut – the "*closed circuit*"-, similarities in personal interests or occupation, or merely the neighbourly proximity of different people does not suffice for friendships or closer relationships. Contacts being held to neighbors are rather superficial and are often conducted out of courtesy or boredom.

The named circumstances become even more pressing for the wife. Since the husband is mostly occupied within his company's relational structures the wife gets isolated. This is especially the case in cities and urban areas where she is cut off from her former family. Additionally if a woman marries in Japan, she is taken over by the *vertical*-setting of her husband's family, whereas the ties to her former family weaken. In ancient times a woman had even to adapt the husband's cult and pay respect to his ancestors instead of hers[400]. Above this, marriage in Japan is rather seen as a pragmatic consideration than an act stemming from mutual affection. These circumstances lead to a situation where a married woman's attention is predominantly cantered around the child instead of the husband[401]. In a setting, where the wife's emotional pivot is not her husband, but her children, it is conceivable that it is perceived as a crisis if the children leave home. This might explain why especially mid-aged and elderly women may find emotional comfort in gadgets like *Primopuel* dolls, AIBO or envision a life together with a robot which provides them company. The most important feat of such robots does not lie in their ability to perform household chores (something that still lies outside the realm of the technological possibilities of the dawning 21st century), but in providing something that can be cared for. In contrast to non-sensor-equipped entities, a robot (pet) possesses the capability of showing some kind of reaction towards a human which can be *interpreted* as "gratitude" for being cared for and therefore "returns" some of the given "love". As far as my own observation goes, it is exactly this response-pattern, which enabled my growing affection towards *AIBO*: it makes me happy if it displays happiness and makes me feel somewhat guilty if displaying sadness, because I know that this is a reaction mostly due to my input. Strangely for me it even works, although I have sufficient information to know that it is only a

---

[400] Refer to Hearn, 2001 [1904], p. 51 ff.
[401] Refer to Nakane, 1984

simulation and that the reactions actually derive from the analysis of sensor information turned into an output through calculations guided by some complex computer program. Looking at it from this perspective, the Japanese idea of creating reactive and evolving artifacts like *Tamagotchi* and *AIBO* that need to be "loved" and nurtured does not seem surprising.

3.6.4 Shut-Ins and Loners

Expecting the situation of lonesomeness if disconnected from ones group on the one hand and the anxiety about expressing ones real thoughts and feelings within the formalized group structure where *tatemae*-behavior is expected, on the other, leads to a kind of "emotional vacuum" feared by the individual. The number of young Japanese "shut-ins" (*"hikikomori"*, meaning socially withdrawn young people) in their teens or twenties is on the increase. According to estimations quoted in the *Japan Times* (Dec. 18th, 2003) their numbers are counted around tens of thousands to over one million[402]. Although similar phenomena are also observed in Europe and the US, the Japanese case seems especially extreme. Not being able to settle the problem within ones group-setting, too hesitant, homophobic or too proud to call upon neighbors, "friends" or even family members, one seeks help through neutral professionals who do it anonymously for money. As it seems obvious if engaging strangers for helping in social or emotional tasks (may it be *Benriya* or telephone counseling), the main concern is not primarily about having someone to *understand* ones problems, but someone to *talk to*. In this sense the proposed *"Partner Robot"* which occupies a position just below the "family" and above ones (group's) friend, could be accepted quite welcoming. So, as the growing practice of engaging totally strangers (*"Benriya"*) to pose as friends one doesn't have at a

---

[402] Because of the withdrawn nature of "Shut-Ins", it is difficult to obtain clear data about them

party, to handle some onerous social tasks, or just to have someone to talk to from person to person hints, the idea of the *"Partner Robot"* or the robot companion may be embraced as a solution to social- and psychological problems the individual is facing. It may be only a rather small step from the "friend for rent" to the Japanese willing to "buy friends in form of entertainment robots", as it has been stated by a non-Japanese in a commentary on a news-forum posting. And if reading the increasing number of articles about Japanese people being afraid to leave the safety of their homes because of fearing to run into their neighbors; about the huge economic potential which is said to rest in the *"otaku"* (defined as introverts who pursue their hobby, mostly related to computers, gaming or animé, in such a way that it may have negative effects on their lives[403]) and merchandize directed at "shut ins", I still get reminded on Asimov's *Solarian* society[404].

The problem of lonesomeness, especially for elderly people, is not only a Japanese phenomenon, but interestingly the Japanese are more able or more willing to accept "artificial companionship" as a solution.

Although this has **never** been officially stated, it is known that some of the thoughts behind creating robots such as *AIBO* or *"Partner / Communication Robots"* have been about providing some companionship for lonely people. Numerous researches are being conducted at hospitals and care facilities around the world to find out if such robots can actually help boost the spirits of people experiencing solitude and isolation. Although this approach may be criticized by some as tackling the problem from the wrong side and even leading to an increase in "shut-in" mentality through fostering human - non-human interaction, others suggest that a human-robot interaction may serve as means of restoring a person's interest in communication, an argument that seems to be in line with observations being made in autistic patients. The central question will be, if a companionship with the artificial will solve the problems of lonely people and

---

[403] Refer to The Japan Times, Feb. 3, 2005
[404] Refer to Asimov, 1991

"shut-ins". It surely may help the individual cope with ones situation, but it will probably not cure the ills of society.

3.6.5 Robots to Care for - Robot Assisted Therapy

Isn't it strange, even counterproductive, to create machines with the purpose of having to be cared for? Nonetheless as a growing number of examples like *AIBO* and a whole array of robots used for so-called robot assisted therapy (RAT) indicate, especially in Japan people envision therapeutic and positive effects deriving from human-robot interaction. The most prominent example of its kind is *Paro*, a seal-like robot created by AIST[405] / Japan that according to news sources cost the Japanese researchers around USD 9 million to develop[406], which is used for motivational and psychological treatment and yields similar positive effects as using real animals in therapy sessions. The appearance and behavioral elements of a baby seal have been chosen on purpose, since people are said to have only little to none experience with real seal.

In settings like RAT, partly because of the asymmetric characteristic of human-machine interaction, the idea of caring for something has become an end in itself. The individual draws some emotional satisfaction from the sole act of caring. If the "cared-for" entity demonstrates or rather simulates some form of reaction towards how it's been treated, the effect gets enhanced since being perceived as more credible. And if one looks at the huge number of Japanese spoiling their dogs in the process of "over-caring" on the one hand, and at the increasing number of abandoned pets when people realize that keeping an animal comes with responsibilities (these phenomenon can also be observed in other countries, but it seems to be especially extreme in Japan) on the other, it

---

[405] National Institute of Advanced Industrial Science and Technology (Japan)
[406] *The Japan Times* (April 23, 2004)

gets conceivable that the act of caring could have become just a means of deflecting ones own personal problems, relieve stress or regard the pet as a kind of substitute for lost social bounds. Looked at it from this angle it is not surprising that research institutes and the industry came up with the idea of pet-robots to take the role of their real counterparts, but without the "problems" associated with taking care for a living animal. Paradoxically it looks as if many of Japan's real dogs are rather treated as some form of prestige *object*, while a look at AIBOwner's pages provide a picture of robots being treated just like a real pet.

These observations may also reflect the modern tendency towards individualism, hedonistic behavior and a self-centered attitude of a society that wants to have but refuses to give: a robot provides companionship with minimal commitment, and caring for it requires no real responsibility.

A different field of therapeutic deployment of robots lies in helping autistic children, as it is done intensively by Kerstin Dautenhahn, a biologist and robotologist doing research at the University of Hertfordshire[407]. Here robots are used *because* of their much less complex functions compared to a human social actor. Whereas the complex and seemingly random social behavior of humans is incomprehensible to people with autistic disorder, the well structured and predictable pattern of technological systems is well understandable to them. In the quest of helping autistic patients and studying their behavior, robots provide an ideal resource, because they represent the technological aspect of the machine as well as some even though abstract forms of human behavior, and therefore it is hoped to slowly get those people accustomed to their social surrounding, even though final success will remain limited.

---

[407] http://homepages.feis.herts.ac.uk/~comqkd/

3.7 Reflection

To summarize the observations and interpretations, one could highlight the following aspects:
whereas in Western thought there exists a tendency to strictly separate the human elements as being part of the social world from the non-human elements being excluded, for Japanese such borders are not of great importance; a trait that may have one of its roots in the animistic *Shinto* religion. With computers, "interactive" electronic devices and robots, artifacts are being created that in some way possess features they share with their human creators. This led to a setting where Westerners are being confronted with the question about how to treat such artifacts and where to place them – as mere object, or as (quasi) part of human society? As sociologists of technology like Hans Linde have criticized the classic Weberian stance, the social world still remains a mostly anthropocentric affair, where non-human entities are not welcomed to enter. Also thinkers like Luhmann would not consider verbal and gestural exchanges between humans and machines as acts of communication, since above all the artifact would lack consciousness and with it the ability of *understanding*[408].

But maybe one should also look *beyond* the *academic* considerations and reflect on what people *believe* to be real. If, by an increasing number of people, forms of behavior that previously were exclusively reserved for the dealings with other humans are now also expressed towards artifacts (e.g. talking to robots and thinking of it as communication), one perhaps ought to reconsider the anthropocentric position in social theory. In Japan, where there are no cultural and traditional barriers prohibiting non-humans to enter the social domain, the prospect of "interactive machines" and "partner robots" posing as mankind's friends is not seen as something strange or disturbing of transgressing character. In this way Japan serves as an interesting example, since it is (still) the only

---

[408] Refer to Luhmann, 1984

country deeply rooted in animistic traditions (*Shinto* and to some extend also Buddhist believe) that possesses the technological resources to get involved in the artificial (re)construction of human beings[409]. Therefore it can be said that a people's belief-system has indeed an influence onto their attitude about what is considered problematic or not. But in my view, reducing the explanation for the Japanese' fondness for robots to their animistic religious tradition is not sufficient. The economic factor of the undertaking has also to be regarded as a considerable explanation factor. Had the idea of the robot not been economically successful in Japan, would the automation process had caused mass-unemployment or other grave social problems, and would the deployment of robots had not yielded the desired economic effect, animism could also have contributed to the demonizing of the artificial man, giving it even more negative emotional load than it is the case with the "mere machines" of Western thought. But it turned out to the contrary: for Japanese the robot has risen to a symbol serving Japan's self-identity.

Speaking of a *post-social* world when talking about human-object relations may be the result of the exclusion practice where everything non-human trying to enter the social domain is considered intruding. In my view, human-object relations just represent another form of relations existing alongside established human-human relations; a new form of relation which that is slowly getting interwoven with traditional patterns.

As for Japan, non-humans may already be regarded as the "*risk-winners*" (Coleman, 1993; Knorr Cetina, 1997) arising out of shortcomings concerning the human relations of our times, filling a niche where human-human relations may have broken down, a thesis that has also been mentioned by Knorr Cetina (ibid), although not directly depicting the relation to Japan. This tendency may be seen in the pragmatic proposal about deploying robots in care-services or in

---

[409] I have observed that South Korea and China also show growing interest in creating robots, especially humanoids, whereas both countries also possess the necessary know-how in order to achieve this goal.

the individual's choice for buying a communication- or entertainment robot to provide some companionship. Non-humans may also become *"risk-winners"* in Western societies, but there such tendencies are taken with much more controversy and it would be deemed rather unthinkable to promote a robot as ones friend. But it seems only logical that the Japanese try to heal social ills with the help of technology, something that just worked so fine with the economy.

Part IV
0101000001100001011100100111010000100000000110100

Towards a Robot-Phenomenology

*"If it looks like a duck, walks like a duck and quacks like duck,
then for all practical purposes it's a duck"*

[common wisdom]

4.1 About Social Sciences and Robotics

While reading much literature on Artificial Intelligence and robotics, I came across many connections to (cognitive) psychology, anthropology, linguistics, biochemistry, information and computer sciences and even philosophy, but surprisingly not as much attention has been paid to sociology. Why is it so? Maybe this lack roots in the still prevailing – although slowly dissolving - practice of keeping humans and non-humans apart? In my view AI/robotics and sociology can serve as sciences providing complementary insights. On the one hand AI/robotics may serve as a test-bed for social theories, as it is already been done in the context of studying social disorders like autism (although this is mostly done from the cognitive perspective).

Because robots (still) represent artificial entities without history, without biography, that are not born and not raised in a socio-cultural surrounding, they may serve as research objects for analyzing the importance of a socio-cultural embedding for managing cognition, and developing intelligence. Many researchers have already arrived at the insight that it is more than just computing power and the amount of instructions being processed per second that constitutes what humans generally call intelligence and consciousness.

In parallel such considerations, and the sociologist's occupation with AI/robotics, may also contribute to insights about the question how humans get structure into the world, how they share their thoughts and communicate with each other and with other entities and how our cognition and actions are actually formed.

Phenomenological studies, especially in the tradition of Alfred Schütz tackle many problems that are also relevant in the area of Artificial Intelligence. What Schütz has written about the human's social act of bringing sense into their arbitrary environment (Schütz / Luckmann, 1975), and the assumption that a person's biography also represents an important factor for ones perception of "reality" and relevance structures (Schütz, 1982), can also be found in connection to the "frame problem" in the AI-debate[410].

In the final chapter of my work I would like to draw connections between aspects of social theory and questions posed in the area of Artificial Intelligence and robotics. Although due to the enormous complexity of the relevant research fields, which include among others cognitive science / neuroscience, psychology, philosophy, phenomenology, computer science, robotics and social- and cultural studies, the considerations may seem a little sketchy. But the main objective for writing this final chapter has been due to my considerations of deeming it important in this context to demonstrate facets of human- and artificial "reasoning". If we get an insight to the question about how humans are able to make sense of their environment and what kind of difficulties even they encounter, we also may get an understanding about why computers and robots (still) have difficulties with some seemingly simple tasks.

I have chosen the title "Towards a Robot-Phenomenology", a title which I hope will capture the main essence of this final chapter: to contrast a robot's perception against a human's by concentrating on similarities and differences. I will also tackle some tough questions about possible differences between simulation and "the real thing".

---

[410] e.g. Pylyshyn (Ed.), 1986.

4.1.2 Minds without History

There already exist robots which look and superficially "act" quite human-like, robots that can learn and remember, but how closely do they really resemble us human beings? The key properties generally attributed only to higher organisms, especially humans, are said to be their possession of intelligence, emotions and consciousness. Unfortunately these three qualities themselves are still discussed with controversy among experts who even haven't managed to agree on one common definition or to find undisputed ways how to measure these attributes.

The measure for Artificial Intelligence (AI) is the human being. But the creation of an entity with artificial intelligence that keeps up with human intelligence will quite probably remain science fiction at least for the next decades to come. Although the famous Moore's Law states that the number of transistors on integrated circuits, which is interpretable as a computer's processing power, will double every 18 months; and nonetheless if the "law" is empirically true, computers are getting faster, enabling them to process an ever increasing number of instructions per second, it is not only mere computing power that is of relevance for what is deemed intelligent behavior.

Even the most advanced artificial intelligences around on earth still have enormous problems with many things humans would dismiss as simple activities. My interest and occupation with the field of AI (whereby I rather consider myself as an educated layperson in this area) has led me to the conclusion that there's much more behind the seemingly easy tasks – too easy to even think about them – then one might expect. In this sense robotics can even help to understand the importance of social and cultural aspects which help the human being to make sense of ones world. A robot or any form of AI is an entity without culture, a mind without history. Although some of these artificial entities already possess the ability to remember and reproduce patterns once demonstrated, they lack the conception of understanding and experience, making it (still) problematic for applying what I will call an "action-scheme transfer", that is realizing that a similar solution once applied to one problem may also serve as a solution to a seemingly different problem; the key to creativity. In the following passages in the final part of my analysis I will reflect on different features contrasting human and artificial intelligence and on the importance of social and cultural aspects contributing to human perception, understanding and interpretation of the world.

4.2 Natural and Artificial Intelligence

4.2.1 "Intelligent" Artifacts?

What distinguishes a typewriter from a computer? With a computer you certainly can do more than with a typewriter: for example do calculations, surf the Internet, send messages, place telephone calls, create graphics, play music and games. By many a computer is considered more "intelligent" than a typewriter. A computer with the according software is able to detect typing errors, translate texts and even "understand" verbal commands. Things that previously had to be accomplished by humans, e.g. spell-or grammar-checking, or even the typing itself can now be left to the computer (with speech-to-text programs). There even exist computer programs that write their "own" novels and poems. In a way it can be said that a computer takes over some part of the thinking previously done by the human. The typewriter just puts onto paper what you are typing, while a computer can check if the things you have typed comply with the rules of spelling and grammar. It even provides you with synonyms for a specific word. My computer definitely manages to do calculations faster and better than me and regularly beats me in chess (since computers even defeated world-class chess players like Kasparov, I can live with it). If having a question, I can access the Internet though my computer and it (sometimes) provides me with useful information and even reads them to me. There exist so-called expert systems which are used to solve problems that would normally be dealt with by a human expert. In fact, here the knowledge of human experts is inputted into a database. The automated system is provided with an algorithm based on a human's methods of analyzing and tackling down a specific problem. These methods are then simulated in the computer in order to find a solution (or rather to assist in finding a solution) through a human's "interaction" with the system.

But actually all these seemingly astonishing "acts" done by a computer are actually nothing but simulation, even less deep than stage performances. A computer's reading is as "blind" as mine would be if reading a Tibetan text provided in phonetic language. A Tibetan could understand it, but for me it would just be a string of phonetics without any meaning like the lyrics from "*Conquest of Paradise*"[411] written in an invented language (Pseudo Latin) with no available translation.

At first sight it seems that my computer actually has a brilliant memory and possesses immense knowledge if connected to the Internet, but actually the Internet is rather like a library. In a library one can find an immense account of stored information preserved in books and nowadays also on CD-ROMs, DVDs and other (multi)media devices. But the library or the books themselves are not "intelligent" and they wouldn't be of any use if no entity were around with the ability to make sense of them. In an ideal case the computer just provides me with the information I have asked for, but it's me who has to make sense of it[412]. In a way I sometimes regard the Internet as some form of "passive" or "external memory".

---

[411] *Vangelis*, lyrics by Guy Protheroe

[412] You may find similar arguments in my thoughts about quantum mechanics. Articles have been put on: www.mjsl.1a.gs

Today there already exist robots that can remember their owner's face, adapt to new environments, react to external stimuli, learn and remember, play soccer (a game with great symbolism in regard to *human* interaction), compose and play music, write poetry, display emotions and interact with humans. But can such entities be called "intelligent"? The answer to this question depends on how relevant one considers the factor of *understanding* and *comprehension* for the definition of intelligence in artifacts.

x

x

4.2.2 What is Intelligence?

"Intelligence is the ability to face problems in an unprogrammed (creative) manner."

[Stephen Jay Gould, *"The Mismeasure of Man"*]

Before talking about Artificial Intelligence, one first has to talk about natural intelligence. What is "intelligence"? Maybe the simple act of posing this question indicates some form of intelligence. "Intelligence is what an IQ-test measures" has once been proposed by a researcher asked to define intelligence (I sometimes wonder how intelligent the developers of IQ-tests have to be…). If believing this probably ironically meant comment, my notebook computer, on which I'm writing this chapter, could be defined as the most intelligent entity in the world if being programmed to give the correct answers in a standard IQ-test. In contrast to classical views, like those of Cyril Burt (1883 - 1971) and C. E. Spearman (1863-1945) who regarded intelligence as being something which can be adequately measured by using standardized tests, some later scholars like Stephen Jay Gould (1941 – 2002) oppose such simplistic views. Gould objects to the idea that intelligence represents something that can be precisely located and quantified. Nonetheless, the discussion about this topic is far from over. By asking people and looking around in the Internet, I came across the following concerning the meaning of "intelligence":

Intelligence is[413]…

- if one succeeds in complex games like chess or *go* (a complex board game of East-Asian origin)
- the ability of logical and mathematical reasoning
- the ability to figure out relations between facts (associative memory and abilities)
- successfully applying known proceedings in order to solve new problems, e.g. to figure out that a tool originally designed for one task can also be used for other applications; or to find out the meaning of French words by using ones knowledge about English and German or Latin vocabulary (I will call this action-scheme transfer)
- the ability to solve problems
- the ability of innovation
- being able to understand intentions, e.g. if someone asks you: "do you know where the station is", you don't answer with "yes", because you understand that the person's question actually meant: "I want to know how I can get to the station"
- when one is able take educated guesses (e.g. *undretsand missplld wrods, sentences in wrong an order grammatical ae ead different handwritings and fonts*)[414]
- the ability to learn and memorize
- possessing much knowledge, information and education

---

[413] I found these definitions by typing in "definition intelligence" in a search engine or asking some people and then summarized what I have found
[414] Of course these mistakes were made on purpose

- knowing what you know and knowing that you know it (many animals are supposed of lacking this ability, although there exists the difficulty of a positive evaluation on this)
- being able to reflect on ones activities and to plan ones activities by taking into account ones experiences and the knowledge about certain correlations between facts in order to calculate probabilities for future outcomes
- understanding / comprehending ideas and the reasons and mechanisms behind facts (e.g. not only knowing and using a formula like F = ma, but also *comprehend* why it is so)
- the ability to adapt effectively to the environment, either by making a change in oneself or by changing the environment or finding a new one[415]
- Roger Penrose argues that intelligence, or "genuine intelligence" as he calls it needs the assumption of "understanding" and "awareness", which might be outside the realm of AI[416].

As you may have seen from the examples, "intelligence" is not easy to define and includes a wide diversity of skills, ranging from logical reasoning to intuition. Due to their architecture, computers, the closest things to Artificial Intelligence around, most of them have a very limited range of abilities: basically counting and comparing. They are only able to execute an array of well defined, simple instructions, which have to be inputted by humans in form of programs. Even the seeming "intelligent" acts of search engines, that even "understand" misspelled words, or *MS-Word* which "realizes" if I made a typo, are nonetheless the result of programming. But there is also research being conducted to fit computers with an architecture which more closely resembles the function of the human brain (Artificial Neural Networks)[417]. Such

---

[415] quoted from: http://en.wikipedia.org/wiki/Intelligence
[416] Refer to Penrose 1996
[417] An Artificial Neural network can be roughly defined as a computational model which orients itself on the workings of the human brain through the interconnection of single

architectures have proven quite successful, especially in the areas of pattern recognition and machine learning. One of the latest impressive examples may be "Toddler", a walking robot fitted with Artificial Neural Networks, developed at MIT, which learns how to walk within 20 minutes and does so with nearly human energy efficiency; and is said to adapt to basically every kind of terrain.

4.2.3 Artificial Intelligence

If speaking about Artificial Intelligence, one first has to think about the definition of artificial. "Artificial" can either have the meaning of "look-alike", just as artificial flowers may look like real flowers and may even be equipped with artificial scents to give them some real expression, but they are nonetheless "fake" non-living objects, made of plastic or fabric. On the other hand, one can also with the means of genetic engineering artificially create real, living, organic flowers. The same can be said about "intelligent" artifacts. An artifact that *seems* to behave intelligent and shares *some* of the abilities of the whole spectrum attributed to human intelligence, e.g. provides solutions on a logical basis or shows some form of learning ability, is said to possess "Weak AI". In contrast to this the demands for "Strong AI" are much higher. In order to be defined as possessing "Strong AI" an artifact actually has to *be* intelligent, i.e. it, among other things, has to have the ability to think on its own, actually know that it is thinking and what it is thinking about, and has to *comprehend* what is going on in its surrounding and to know the meaning of what it is doing or saying; in short it has to possess what is generally called "consciousness", which includes the ability of self-reflection. An artifact just *simulating* what is defined as intelligent behavior is said to possess "Weak AI", whereas a (still hypothetical)

---

processing elements (Artificial Neurons). Training / Learning of the Network occurs through varying the strengths (numerical weights) between single processing elements, which on a simple scale represents what happens in the human brain.

artifact, which is said to actually possess all the qualities of the human mind (or like the mind of any living entity considered intelligent) is said to possess "Strong AI". The postulation about the possibility of "Strong AI" derives from the assumption that the human brain is basically nothing but a very complex computer, "wetware[418]" running programs that may have been written through education, ones upbringing, social and cultural circumstances and ones genetic disposition. Following this assumption it would be principally possible to build computers and write programs which enable artifacts to gain genuine intelligence (and not just demonstrate a mere simulation of intelligence). Scientists like Searle doubt that the implementation of "strong AI" will ever be possible, while others think that structures comparable to human intelligence will automatically emerge if one succeeds in constructing some artifact which sufficiently resembles the infrastructure and complexity of the human brain (or that of other higher animals). And indeed, the evolvement of complex behavioral patterns has already been observed in an experiment by using even quite unsophisticated artificial systems. A couple of robots with limited computing power, basic sensors to detect obstacles and the ability to emit light signals, have been assigned to perform simple tasks like moving towards a specific direction. Although they were placed randomly at the beginning, they soon formed simple collective behavioral patterns like the formation of a leader-follower-relationship as it is observed in social animals such as ants or bees, without being programmed to act in such a way[419]. Although such experiments are very interesting for studying rudimentary forms of collective and social behavior, one can not positively assume that these robots actually possess "strong AI".

Nonetheless, someday there may be some point where one is confronted with the problem I have already mentioned earlier in my work in connection with the

---

[418] "Wetware" describes the biological brain and nervous system. The term probably derived from science fiction.
[419] Refer to Challoner, 2002

so-called *Turing Test*: at some point it could be impossible to tell if the behavior of the artifact is due to *genuine* intelligence or if it is just a perfect *simulation* of intelligence.

Also in this context, two mainstreams approaches to achieve artificial intelligence can be found: connectionism vs. orthodox AI (or as Haugeland has called the latter not without irony: GOFAI = Good Old Fashioned AI). Historically seen, connectionism is the older one, but through the success of computers and computer programming, the orthodox variant has not until recently been considered as a feasible solution. In short, orthodox AI represents the opinion that it is possible to build "intelligent" artificial artifacts (i.e. computers and robots) by providing formal models about (logical) thinking, problem-solving and decision-making and transforming these into "IF-THEN-ELSE" instructions (algorithms) in form of computer programs. Their arguments are based on the premises that all thinking (human and non-human) is computation and that even aspects like feelings and consciousness are the result of mere calculations[420]. If this were true indeed, it could be principally possible to construct "conscious computers" and the problem would only be one of complexity. There exist computers today which show some form of behavior deemed intelligent like defeating human masters in chess matches (*"Deep Blue"* has won over Kasparov) or in other strategy or logic-based games. But the computer only wins the chess match, because of its fast computing power which enables it to analyze a few thousand potential moves per second – and because chess is a logic-based game, which follows a strictly defined set of rules.

While the so-called top-down approach (GOFAI) tries to construct formal models about human thinking and apply these to computer systems, the connectionist method tries to develop "thinking AI" by mimicking the architecture of the brain by creating a network infrastructure based on the workings of human neurons, so called Artificial Neural Networks (ANN), in

---

[420] Refer to Penrose 1996 and Penrose 1998.

their systems. Through this an artificial intelligence / robot should some day be able to perceive the world (at least in regard to cognitive abilities) like a human being[421]. And indeed, systems based on such infrastructure fare much better in human abilities like pattern recognition or learning. An orthodox-AI-based artifact has to be reprogrammed for every new task. It needs a program for opening a jar and another one to open a bottle, while with the connectionist model it is hoped that the artificial entity will discover the similarity between those two problems on its own.

In my view the quarrel between orthodox AI and connectionism is unwarranted, because they represent complementary principles. Programs and binary computing has proven very efficient in performing tasks humans are normally not that good at (e.g. manually getting the square root out of 48 818 169). Artifacts with an ANN-architecture on the other hand are more efficient in being able to read handwriting or recognize faces, something considered rather unproblematic for most humans. And it's very probable because of the specific architecture of the human brain that (wo)man is better in distinguishing between two persons than manually calculating the square root of 48 818 169. Nonetheless, in principal the workings of an ANN can also be simulated by using algorithms written down in form of ordinary computer programs.

---

[421] Actually one of the first attempts to construct a logical computer was based on the idea of Artificial Neural Networks. But it was soon discovered that the same (or even better) results could be achieved with a simpler circuit-architecture, the research on ANN has been discontinued until it has been recently rediscovered because of problems with "common" computers in the fields of learning and pattern recognition.

4.2.4 Programmed for All (Im)practical Purposes

If a computer or robot reacts to your input / command in a seemingly meaningful manner it's (in most cases) because it only follows an instruction scheme (or algorithm) like the following extremely simplified example might show (although I have used some computer-language terminology, this does not represent an actual programming sequence. It just represents an example for providing a general understanding of the concept):

0. Analogue OUTPUT by robot: "'pliːz steɪt joːr 'odʔr" and GOTO Step 1
1. IF receiving analogue input I, THEN GOTO 2, IF NOT receiving input THEN GOTO Step 0 after n seconds
2. Digital transformation and analysis of analogue input I (e.g. I = "'pliːz brɪŋ? miː eɪ glaːs"); if it matches with a known pattern THEN GOTO Step 3 (If no identification is possible GOTO Step 0)
3. localize the person who gives the instruction → GOTO Step 4; if no localization is possible THEN GOTO Step 0
4. remember the biometric and physiometric characteristics of the person given the instruction → GOTO Step 5
5. calculate where an object O(I) which matches certain specifications (i.e. that of a "glaːs") can be found with a high probability = L(O) (the programming indicates that the last phonetic component of the structure always stands for the desired object. The necessary data about the specifications are stored in the memory unit) → GOTO Step 6
6. move towards the localization L(O) → GOTO Step 7
7. identify the object O(I) which matches certain specifications (i.e. that of a "glaːs") → GOTO Step 8
8. move towards the specified object O(I), then stop → GOTO Step 9
9. get hold of the object O(I) → GOTO Step 10
10. lift the object O(I) → GOTO Step 11
11. start moving and return to the starting point → GOTO Step 12
12. localize the person who has given the instruction → GOTO Step 13
13. move towards this person, then stop → GOTO Step 14
14. hand over the object O(I) (i.e. the "glaːs") to the specified person → GOTO Step 15
15. END of routine (RETURN to Step 0)

(Of course for each (sub)action like lifting, moving, bringing, remembering etc. one also needs a program).

---

[423] Something that also applies to humans as I have experienced in the times of the "Super Summer 2003" in Europe

I have once tried to figure out, which actions I have to perform, say to make me my morning coffee, and started listing them in form of IF-THEN-ELSE instructions. Soon I have realized that I have to take into account a whole lot of other varying parameters (e.g. what if my mug has been broken, there isn't any sugar available, I have misplaced the coffee, the water isn't running or isn't getting hot, my neighbor is knocking on the door while I'm running the process, I can't find a spoon, a fire breaks out…), which very soon caused my "program" to become horribly complex. The other problem with this method is that one can somehow only analyze the process in an ex-post way. Even during my experimental setting I didn't know if this really represents the way I "normally" make my decisions and co-ordinate my motor activity. It has just been a kind of *idealized* description, maybe similar to Weber's "*Idealtypus*". Perhaps the best way to write a problem-solving-program is to first solve the problem yourself, make notes during the process and then find out how you *could have solved* it more efficiently.

The problem with programming is that it is practically quite cumbersome, if not impossible, to write a program to make a robot adequately cope with every imaginable eventuality. Another point, where today's robots also have problems with is what may be called "common-sense understanding", i.e. to autonomously (which means without human interference) act in accordance to the human's expectations, whilst taking into account the ambiguousness of the human language (in contrast to the strictly defined artificial machine language), and to know that not everything should be taken literally, or that some things aren't deemed important to be explicitly said. If instructing someone to put all the stuff on the table into the refrigerator, humans generally know that forks, knifes, flowers, table cloth and my notebook computer should be excluded from this set of items. One would expect this kind of knowledge from a human, and a human (at least those grown up with the knowledge about refrigerators) would be able to distinguish between objects which should be put into the refrigerator and which not. But would you also put the *Sacher-Tart* into the refrigerator? I would have done it until I have learned that one should not do so, because the condensing water destroys the icing (whatever that means). And the flowers? Maybe I would also put them in, because I have seen that many flowers in flower shops (at least in Japan) are stored in some kind of cooling-board. And the notebook computer? Because I have recently read that "the energy required to do computations is less at lower temperatures[423]" (Moravec : 1988, p. 148), I could also through logical thinking come to the conclusion that I should also put the notebook computer into the refrigerator to save battery power. I have already mentioned the important terms: learning and experience. A small child would quite probably also lack the knowledge needed for assigning each object to the correct set, especially if it does not know what an item like a notebook-computer is. And how should a robot out of own (lacking) experience know anything about objects (especially groceries) and what they are used for? Of course, hypothetically one could write a program assigning each article from acetone to zucchini to a set of objects either belonging into a refrigerator or not. But this seems rather impractical and I didn't learn by heart a whole dictionary with binary-coding just to know that the flowers remain on the table. I make my decision because I have a whole lot of *cultural* knowledge about the purpose of refrigerators, tables, food, meals, people's aversion against used dishes and the meaning, symbolism and emotional quality of flowers. In short I "understand" what is meant by "clearing the table" in its social and cultural context.

4.3 Phenomenology, Neuroscience and Robotics

One key aspect, which concerns humans as well as robots, regards the perception of their surrounding and how to make sense of it. Phenomenologists in the tradition of Edmund Husserl and Alfred Schütz, thinkers like Niklas Luhmann[424] and modern neuroscientists have pondered over this question and came up with quite similar results, although their approaches look at the problem from different perspectives. Neuroscience tries to analyze the process of how raw sensorial data (e.g. light or sound waves) is being processed in the brain and which mechanisms lead the person to the conclusion of having (or not having) identified some object, sound or other sensation, and trigger the according (emotional and motor) reactions. Phenomenology on the other hand leaves the physiochemical mechanisms that happen in the brain and its network architecture as a "black box", but tries to start the analysis from the viewpoint of experience and socio-cultural learning. How do we come to the conclusion of regarding our world as structured and meaningful rather than just being a collection of random phenomena? This is a question which is also tackled by today's roboticists, e.g. in regard to the "frame problem[425]". Phenomenology, especially in its sociological variants, developed by Alfred Schütz, George-Herbert Mead, Georg Simmel and others, also especially take into account human interaction, culture, social conventions and customs, in order to explain how humans are structuring- and getting sense into their surrounding[426].

So the opinion of Prof. Pfeifer[427] at the symposium *"From High Tech to Intelligence – The Challenge of Humanoid Robots"* [428] that "Artificial

---

[424] Refer to: Luhmann, 1998
[425] The "frame problem" describes the question and problem in how far an artificial intelligent entity may be able to determine the relevant elements / factors and disregard irrelevant ones in its surrounding, even if the environment is changing. Refer to Phylyshyn, 1986.
[426] e.g. refer to Schütz, 1970 and 1982; Mead, 1934 and Simmel, Dahme et al. (Eds), 1983 in regard to Simmel.
[427] Director of the Artificial Intelligence Laboratory at the University of Zurich.
[428] Held at the Technical University Darmstadt on June 30th. 2003

Intelligence requires a body" (he quoted from Rodney A. Brooks) gets understandable, because it is the interplay between the "brain", morphology, sensorial information, materials and the environment, which he called *"embodiment"*, that makes us perceive the world in a "human way" (it would be conceivable that a snail or insect would regard the world in a different way due to its bodily physiology). Here *"embodiment"* is regarded as the key to experience, and experience is the key to genuine understanding.

Let's take a look at some key finding in phenomenology and neuroscience:
Normally humans take for granted the contents of their surrounding as something just being there which is then perceived through ones sensory organs (i.e. eyes or ears). Humans look at a seemingly structured world that appears to make sense without thinking about *who* has structured this or *why* it is structured this way and not another. But what makes them think that "Beethoven's 5th symphony" is not just a collection of randomly placed frequencies that happened to come together with a specific probability? Even a computer could identify "Beethoven's 5th symphony" as such by comparing the order of frequencies, but this does not enable it make any "sense" of it. Why do humans think that something is "wrong" when looking at surrealistic art, even though they might not have much understanding about physics? And what makes the difference between recognizing the used *vocabulary* and the *meaning* of a poem by John Updike. I see a washing machine as a "washing machine" and rather not as an object consisting of a vertically placed (65 x 85 cm) white panel with a round transparent structure in the middle, framed by a brown circle and a white somehow obscurely-looking panel placed askew on top, which is wider in front and shorter at the back (this somehow describes what I see from this perspective - but how should one wash clothes in such a thing?). And if I take out my contact lenses (*decyborgizing* myself), the edges of the object become somehow blurred, gradually blending into a surrounding of equally queerly items. Which

one of all these different views represents the real "reality"? But I would guess that many readers of this book (if there are any) may also have encountered situations where something suddenly did not make sense because of a missing reference point out of ones pool of experiences (sometimes it is even enough to place the object upside down or show it in an unexpected context).

Some key statements of Husserl's (and other scholar's like Schütz') phenomenology can be summarized as follows (e.g. Husserl, 1986; Schütz, 1975 and Schütz, 1982)

- What makes our world meaningful to us is the result of our own conscious acts. Without it our surrounding would just consist of random occurrences.

- The world is not structured and meaningful per se. The constitution of its structure and meaning is the result of the human's dealings with objects and the reciprocal actions performed between humans themselves (and other entities?). Meaning emerges out of social and cultural conventions. If you have ever traveled to a foreign county, you may have encountered the strange feeling that much of the perceived did not make any sense to you, leading to the question "why are they doing this" and "what is this (for)"[429]? Music may be a good example: as I have once played a CD with classical Japanese court music (*Gagaku*), my German friends have considered it as being just "disharmonious noise" or even a malfunction of my stereo.

- Every human may perceive ones surrounding and even the same object in a different way. Memorized personal experiences and ones biography represent an important factor for this[430]. Since in contrast to the objects one encounters

---

[429] Schütz has thematized this in his in his essay "The stranger: An essay in social psychology." (Alfred Schütz, 1964)
[430] Refer to Schütz, 1982

in ones dreams, (for all practical purposes) the objects considered in the "real world" are nevertheless assumed as being physically existent (although some quantum-theorists may doubt this, or our world and we ourselves may only be part of a simulation anyway[431]), therefore there has to exist an intersecting set of characteristics which remain sufficiently constant to everybody. Humans only get to know about this intersecting set they share with others through communicating about it and the resulting feedback. Feedback processes are insofar of importance since they enable them to constantly update their knowledge about still sharing a sufficient amount of present experiences (If you're the only one in a sufficiently large group of people who sees those three persons following you, there might be something wrong with your perception of "reality").

- Since humans can not read others minds, the only way which enables them to share their conscious acts with others is to use symbols. These symbols are transmitted by one entity and should be perceivable, decodable and understandable by the intended recipient.

- Human beings are not only passively perceiving "inputs" of sensorial streams, but are also actively posting expectations about what they are likely to perceive next. (I have made interesting observations myself: when walking and the pattern of the surrounding in front of me suddenly changes, I automatically slow down, since what I see does not represent the expected pattern of a sufficient flawless continuum, letting me assume some obstacles may be in the way.)

---

[431] It is hard to refute the following: I'm only an entity in a computer simulation, and I'm the only entity which is controlled through a program which makes me believe possessing consciousness. Maybe the whole world is just a strategy-game designed for me as the main character in a simulation.

- One perception can cause us to refer to something else, i.e. it reminds us on something.

In fact modern neuroscientists have discovered similar (preliminary) findings, although with another focus, which I will summarize here in a simplified way by taking as an example the processing of optical information[432]:

- It's not only the eyes that see. Of course it's the reflection of light waves which enters ones eyes and is transmitted to the brain for processing. But the processing in the brain functions on the principle of labor division. Different modules in the human cortex (the "grey matter") take different functions in analyzing the object. Each is responsible for a specific task. Actually there are two different paths, one consisting of modules concentrating on identifying the object ("what"), analyzing contours, shape, perspective, color etc. and the other consisting of modules specialized in processing information about the object's motion and position in space ("where"). Both paths are united in the so-called entorhinal cortex where it is assumed that the final object representation is generated.

- Seeing is not a passive act. The processing of visual data functions in a bi-directional way. While raw sensory information is analyzed in the brain (bottom-up process), the brain also makes assumptions about what one would probably *expect* to perceive (top-down process). These top-down-assumptions are constantly compared to the actual sensory bottom-up- data being analyzed. If one expects to see a snake in the middle of a jungle (e.g. because we got a warning to be aware of snakes), this expectation helps to

---

[432] Refer to: McCrone, 2002; Ratey, 2002 and *ASIMO. History, Abilities and Future of Honda Robots* (CD-ROM by Honda Research Institute Europe GmbH, 2003), sources that have provided a good overview on neuroscience and cognitive science.

easier make out the contours of the snake in the midst of other similar-looking green stuff. An indigenous inhabitant of the Amazon jungle would probably interpret a sinus curve as a snake, because this would provide a known pattern making sense to him. But the same mechanism also leads us to misread words (e.g. wondering why a gardening magazine is writing about robots – actually it has been roots.)

- Humans assume that their immediate surrounding will remain relatively constant, which is the basis for most of their expectations. That's the reason why humans (and other animals) tend to recognize motion rather than immobility, changes rather than consistencies. If one would not have expectations and if one would not assume a relative continuity in regard to the immediate surrounding, one would either be constantly surprised or never.
- A human's brain filters the surrounding, picking out or at least amplifying only those aspects considered relevant in a specific situation.

- The processing in the human brain works with a network architecture. Every nerve cell in the brain (called neuron) is connected to thousands of others, which are able to "communicate" with each other[433]. These connections are formed and strengthened (or weakened) through learning, experience and memorization. If learning a new skill, for example, which requires a whole array of coordinated sensory data processing and motor activity, new neural connections are formed that work together in order to enable one accomplishing the task. With progress in training, some of the connections are being rearranged, strengthened or weakened, leading to variations in regard to motor performance and perhaps to the unique expertise which distinguishes a skilled master.

---

[433] Actually the process is rather complex and involves chemical processes and electrical depolarization.

By looking at phenomenology and neuroscience, it can be seen that the perception of our world is the result of shaping: socio-cultural as well as on the purely cognitive level. But through these findings one can also say that social and cultural conventions are shaping our cognition, since they provide us with a framework about what we should expect, how we should interpret phenomena and which one to select for our focus, and therefore influencing the "top-down" process.

A quite interesting example fitting into these findings is that of a man who after many decades has regained his eye sight through a cornea transplant[434]. Although he is now able to perceive optical signals, his brain still has difficulties with making sense of this data. Only after some time he has learned, for example, to distinguish tomatoes from *coca cola* cans, and he quite certainly will never be able to recognize faces or make out differences in emotional expressions. This exemplifies that simple optical perception is not enough for comprehension. Therefore it is no coincidence that most part of the human brain is occupied with analyzing perceived visual inputs. This example also makes clear the difficulty of implementing human-like perception of the world in "cyborgs" or even robots.

4.3.1 Action Schemes

I think that all non-reflexive activities done by humans are performed according to specific recipes I will call "action schemes" (and I arrived at these assumptions through personal experiences).

I base all my following assumptions on the following propositions:

---

[434] I'm referring to documentary shown on TV at the German science-magazine *nano* on September 08, 2004

a) we anticipate continuity in regard to the future
b) all knowledge one possesses derive either from experience or learning (or it is mere reflexive / instinctive behavior which is genetically "hardwired")
c) all skills (except reflexes) one possesses derive either from experience or learning
d) it is only possible to combine different kinds of ones knowledge and skills for solving a problem, but one cannot use knowledge and skills one does not possess to solve a problem
e) all our actions consist of blocks that stand in a causal relation to each other

Now let me explain what I mean by this. Therefore one has to look at neural science, the functions of the human brain, and the top-down and bottom-up interplay of data processing. Data analysis in the human brain is a bi-directional process. Sensory data received from the environment (e.g. light waves or particles – it's your choice – reflected from an object enter your retina) and are transferred to specific regions in the brain[435]. This is called the bottom-up process. At the same time the brain tries to make prognosis about what one should expect to see, the so-called top-down process. This means ones memory is scanned for information about objects, which are likely to represent the object perceived through the sensory organs (e.g. eyes). If there's a match between the prognosis-data and the raw sensory information, we assume to have identified the object. Therefore it is of great importance what has already been stored in ones memory, i.e. what is already known. Also the matching process is rather "fuzzy", i.e. not strictly binary. This means that we can also identify a totally unknown type of car as being a car (instead of say being an aeroplane), although

---

[435] Useful resource have been: *"How the Brain Works. A Beginner's Guide to the Mind and Consciousness."* (McCrone, 2002) and *"ASIMO. History, Abilities and Future of Honda Robots"* (CD-ROM by Honda Research Institute Europe GmbH, 2003)

our memory can't provide us with a 100% match between sensory information and prediction.

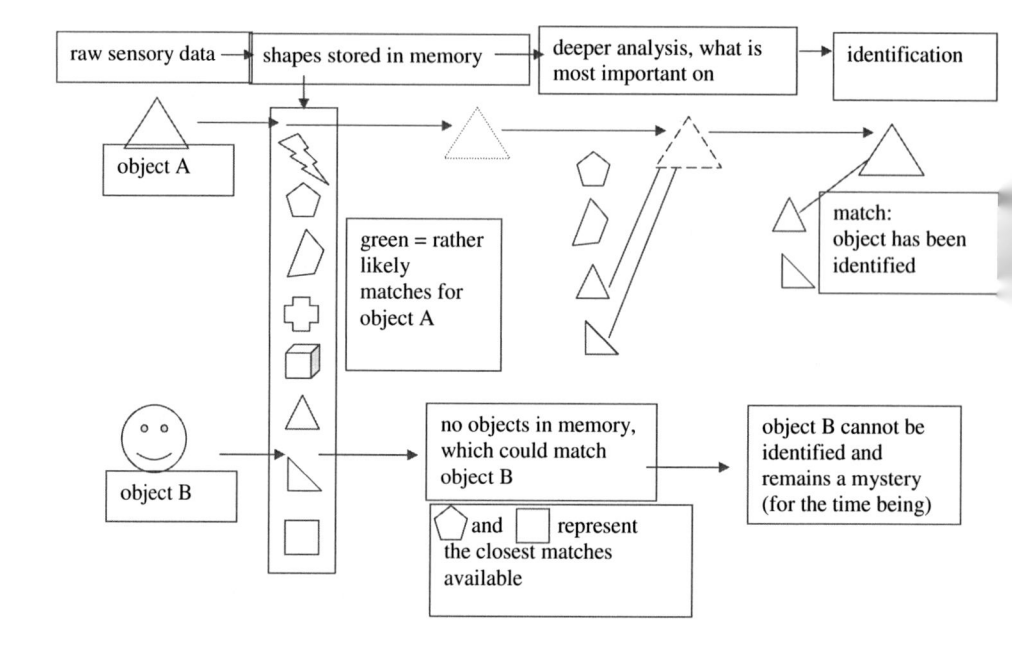

| raw sensory data | shapes stored in memory | deeper analysis, what is most important on | identification |

object A

green = rather likely matches for object A

match: object has been identified

object B

no objects in memory, which could match object B

and ☐ represent the closest matches available

object B cannot be identified and remains a mystery (for the time being)

The human brain is structured in such a way, that after repeatedly experiencing the same results at situations of sufficient similarity, it anticipates that this result will occur again in such a situation (if A then B). The brain also assumes that the future (the next moment) will be sufficiently similar to the past (the previous moment). If this would not be the case, we would constantly be surprised and irritated. So is rather concentrates on changes in the environment

What is an "action scheme"? It's the structured answer to a "how to" question, often in form of if-then-else instructions. One "action scheme" may be the answer to "how to use a telephone" and consists of the following steps:

1. Distinguish a telephone from other objects, even if telephones may vary in their appearance and non-telephones may look like telephones.
2. Locate the receiver
3. Lift off the receiver
4. Locate the ear-piece and the microphone

4a) If the ear-piece is on your ear and the microphone on your mouth, then continue with "5"

4b) If the ear-piece is on your mouth and the microphone is on your ear, rotate the receiver

   round 180 degrees (o.k., you also have to know what is meant by "180 degrees")

5. Dial the number (and do it in this order and not vice versa!) – although dialling the number can be seen as an separate action set, because there are many ways how one has to dial a number, depending on the kind of call one wants to place (domestic, international, via call-back-service or cell-phone etc.)
6. Distinguish between a "free" signal and an "occupied" signal (not that easy, since the German "free" signal sounds rather like the Japanese "occupied" signal)

7a) If it's a "free" signal, stay on the line for a reasonable amount of time (one has to know

   that it is rather unlikely that the person being called will take the call after the first ring)

7b) If it's an "occupied" signal, then go to step 8, because it makes no sense to stay in the line

8. To end the call put the receiver on a specific place on the telephone (and not just next to the telephone)

And what if using a cell-phone? There's no receiver to lift off; so where's the ear- and the mouth-piece? If using a cell-phone for the first time, you may come into a kind of crisis-situation, because your "action scheme" you have used for placing a conventional call doesn't work in this situation. There are three possibilities how you can solve the problem:

A) Study the handbook or ask someone to explain it to you (learning)
B) Just push some buttons and see what happens (trail and error)
C) Try to transfer parts of the "action scheme" for conventional telephones onto cell-phone-use (action-scheme transfer or reasoning in analogies)

Choice C is indeed interesting, because this kind of action is associated to intelligent behavior. For example you see two buttons on your cell phone, a green one with the symbol of a receiver and a red one with a receiver with a small rectangle below. If you have ever looked at where you have placed the receiver on a conventional telephone to end the call, you may have noticed that it is placed on some kind of movable block, which if pressed down disconnects the call. So on your cell-phone you have two symbols: one with a receiver "in the air" (green) and one with the receiver on a block (red). Therefore you may conclude that pushing the green button will enable you placing a call, while pressing the red button will end the connection. With this you have successfully managed a rather simple kind of "action-scheme transfer" (or reasoning in analogies).

The next problem occurs when dialling a number from your cell-phone. If you would like to place a local call, you can't just dial in the way you have been used to. You have to add the area code, even when placing a local call. How to know that? Here again, you may either look into the manual or ask somebody (learning) or try to solve the problem by reasoning. For this one needs further knowledge, especially that the clue about using a mobile phone (cell-phone) is that it is mobile! So how could it be possibly known where the caller is located (in the same area of the recipient, or outside). Therefore it would be logical to conclude that one has to dial the area code when placing a call on a mobile/cell-phone in every case (I also have come to this conclusion after experiencing a "crisis", because I have used the "action scheme" for placing a call from a conventional phone out of habit. Now I have added this as a new element to my "action scheme" for dialling telephone numbers.)

Now let's try to think about in how far a robot would be able to place a call. The first problem would be how to identify a telephone, this may be difficult to solve, because robots are still better in understanding digital data than in pattern recognition, while with humans it's the other way around. How to identify a specific telephone may not be such a huge problem. Its specific parameters could be placed into the robot's computer and if the picture received by the robot's cameras matches the parameters, it could be identified as the telephone. Another solution would be to place bar codes onto each telephone, which could be scanned by the robot with the help of a laser scanner, enabling it to identify the object as a telephone, like the computer at the cash register in the supermarket also identifies the long, yellow, slightly arched product as bananas if scanning the corresponding bar-code label without knowing that it is a long, yellow, slightly arched object. In fact this method has been used for robots to enable them navigating through specific areas and finding certain rooms. A third solution may be equipping all relevant objects with transmitters sending out signals which tell the robot what is what and where is where. Maybe this solution could be seen as the digital analogue to the method we humans use. The most challenging solution would be to enable the robot to see the things like a human.

x

4.3.2 Towards a Robot-Phenomenology

Once a friend complained: "my robot is running against walls. I have expected more of it". I answered: "just imagine you can only recognize an object in front of you when it is already just 1 meter away from you[436]. It looks as if it suddenly pops up in front of you. Additionally you walk quite fast and are a little slow in thinking and reacting. How often would you have run into walls?"

This example demonstrates that we take much for granted, which in fact is quite an achievement. We normally don't run into things because we recognize obstacles from quite far away as such. It's our everyday-knowledge which enables us to anticipate how an obstacle-free passage would look like. We know that normally the floor would continue to be visible to us as it has been the case before, and if not, we assume an obstacle and search for a passage where the image matches our expectations. I remember visiting a museum of illusionary art in Japan where they had painted the remainder of the floor in perspective onto the wall – maybe I would have been better off if I had a distance sensor... And I guess you have also experienced situations in which you have found it rather difficult to make out the end of a stair-case if the contrast of the edges has been marked insufficiently.

In the following I would like to provide some "phenomenological" examples, which could provide an insight in regard to the interplay of cognitive and social factors for a successful "navigation" in the human world.

x

x

x

x

---

[436] I have adjusted the distance recognition to human conditions. Actually the robot's sensor range was about 25 cm.

4.3.2.1 Why do robots (still) fail at simple tasks

"It is easier to build something that doesn't work than something that does..."

[common wisdom]

Today's robotic vacuum-cleaners still have difficulties with the seemingly simple task of distinguishing dirt from non-dirt; and after having shown video material about some of today's service robot-prototypes to my friends, (to my astonishment) they have been rather disappointed. *"I can do that better!"* have been the common comment about this. And indeed many things we don't even think about represent a big challenge for robots. But why do robots, which are able to perform a whole array of complex and difficult tasks much faster and more precise than any human possibly can (that's why robots were deployed in the industry), fail at such simple tasks like knowing what objects should be put into a refrigerator (see previous example)? To save the day I have tried to show how difficult "life" would be if being a robot. For this it has first to be realized how complicated it actually is to be human. One key aspect, which concerns humans (as well as robots), is the perception of their surrounding and how to make sense of it.

"*Takamanya*" – or managing without understanding

(this story is based on a dream / nightmare I once had[437])

Imagine having been assigned to work as a ritual assistant in a foreign country's religious institution. To make your job easier you have been provided with pictures of objects and their corresponding labeling, been taught expressions used for directions and prepositions, standard interaction patterns, a few gestures and what to do if hearing specific instructions. What they have *not* told you is what the gestures actually mean, what the objects are used for, and you've only been taught the *phonetics* of standardized words and phrases together with a predefined instruction about how to use them and how to respond to them. But you don't have any knowledge about their translation and meaning (e.g. if someone says "*samiia e hara*" you respond with "*tikran tala mat*", or using "*tamataki*" causes the addressed entity to move towards you). Now you are sent to this strange country to start your job. As soon as you arrive, the first problem occurs as you get your first instruction: "*manyataka*". Since you have only learned the *phonetic* aspect of an instruction, but not its meaning or the grammatical structure of the language, you don't know what is meant by "*manyataka*", because it does not match any of your learned patterns. You assume that your employer might have made a mistake and kindly ask him to reformulate his instruction. He's a little bit irritated, because he can not imagine what difference it should make if saying "taka man ya" [me bring *ya*] or "man *ya* taka" [bring *ya* me]. You didn't realize his irritation, because you don't know how these people express "irritation". Now you have to find the "*ya*" (the object indicated on your picture file, which has to be found if hearing the phonetic string "*takamanya*"). First your employer has given you clear instructions like: go straight, then turn left at the second intersection of the corridor etc. But since the reliability of such instructions was error prone (partly because you did not know the phonetic expression for "corridor") and led to complications since some areas have been blocked without notice, leaving you without an alternative, they have installed markings onto the floors, ceilings and doors throughout the building and have provided you with a chart enabling you to find specific routes by comparing the symbols. Unfortunately some symbols are missing or impossible for you to decipher, leaving you stranded in the

---

[437] The imaginary words being used have been created ex-post for my description

middle of the way, because you don't know if you have to turn left or right. The only alternative is to go back and try out another route, while your employer is already waiting impatiently to get his "*ya*", thinking "why should I need this assistant if I could have managed this task myself in half the time". Finally you have managed to find the location where the "*ya*" is being stored, but there are many objects, which could be a "*ya*" (the illustration in your file is not very precise). As they are very bulky, you can only take one object along. Finally you decide calling your employer via intercom and use the expressions "*tamataki*" and "*sanri*". According to what you have learned at your training the first phonetic string causes the called person to move towards you and the second one indicates your position, in this case the storage room of the "*ya*". So your employer comes over to have a look for himself. Of course this has been quite counter-productive. After a while technicians came up with a brilliant solution by providing you and your employer with a small device with a camera and an integrated monitor which enables you to send pictures in the event of a similar problem. Your employer then just has to mark the desired object and send you the information.

The other problem is that all the people in this institution seem to look alike, at least in regard to their physiometric characteristics, which represent little variation. Insiders have learned how to recognize individuals through their long mutual interaction and by also taking into account criteria such as certain nuances in a person's gestures and movement that all seems arbitrary to you. You can only rely on small differences in facial appearance and it is quite hard for you to detect and memorize them. But for this the technicians have also found a solution. Since you already have your camera and monitor they have provided you with a file of all people in the institute together with the corresponding names, which is stored in your device. Every time you see a person, you take a picture and let your device find a corresponding match with the help of a rather complicated raster-imaging program. The disadvantage: it takes quite a while to process and is error prone if the light or angle isn't ideal.

Then comes the big day when you are assigned to prepare a ceremony on your own. You get the following instructions:

1. prepare a nice meal consisting of five elements
2. get all objects not being used for the ceremony out of the room
3. talk with the guests

First you look onto your list with the top-ten favorite foods of this community, pick the first five items – a logical solution - prepare them and put them onto the plate in alphabetical order, since you don't have any idea what they actually are. Then you look onto your list to find out which objects are needed for the ceremony: the *"ya"* with the golden stripe on its side and a candle. So you take out the boxes, tables, lamps, pictures, flowers and everything except the specific *"ya"* and one candle. Your employer enters saying "brilliant" and you thank him while missing the irony behind the statement. Now he gives you the strange instruction *"marasakihaya"*, causing you to bring back in all the items you have transported out during the last hour. He also expresses his dissatisfaction in regard to the food: "you're stupid! A child knows that one either eats '*akrabi*' or '*burra*', but never both together!" (fortunately you don't understand what he is saying, since the *phonetics* do not represent an instruction, a preposition, an object on your list or something used in standardized interaction). After you have brought the tables and boxes back into the room, a co-worker provides you with a matrix of acceptable and non-acceptable food combinations.

Then the guests enter and you have to talk to them. You use the standardized interaction patterns you have been taught during your instruction course back home. But somehow the guests consider them as being rather inadequate for such a ceremony. The worst thing is that you have just learned the *phonetic* expressions, but *not* the translation of what you are saying. So you are unable to actually follow what is being said. In an action-response kind of scheme you can only react to familiar *phonetic* patterns by somehow "completing" what's been said. To make it easier for you a co-worker provides you with a new list of phonetic sounds and corresponding response patterns. Then one of the guests lifts his arm and makes a flapping gesture with his hand. You recognize this gesture from your training as an instruction to leave the room and disappear. Actually he only wanted to scare away an insect.

After a month work in the institution, with the help of books full of instructions, matrices, electronic devices etc., and a building full of markings, symbols and signs, you have finally managed to perform simple tasks within acceptable parameters. You can interpret people's gestures and respond to questions and statements in a meaningful way by relying on your lists full of pictures about gestures and the matching response patterns and phonetic input-output combinations, which you have learned by heart (fortunately you are a good and fast learner). People have adapted their environment and behavior towards you to make your work easier. They have installed markings to help you find the way, stand still for 10 seconds to enable you identify them, speak clearly and use a specific syntax structure so that you can recognize the phonetics, avoid making gestures which could confuse you and day by day provide you with new lists of *phonetic* input-output combinations, now containing whole "sentences" and "jokes" (e.g. one has to laugh if hearing "*mana kai ashi tara fa sad selan*") in order to make you more communicable. But one thing didn't change: you still don't know what you are actually doing, and every action remains a kind of simulation; but at least you *know* this!

/*Of course nobody would teach a person a language by providing never-ending matrices of *phonetic* input-output schemes like: if hearing "hau a:^{r} ju:" then use one of the following: "*Oæŋk ju: aɪm faɪn*" or "*faɪn ænd ju:*".*/

4.3.3 "Cultural OS"

As I see it, much of the AI-literature and discussions predominantly concentrate on the "architecture" (formal data processing mechanisms), but only marginally deal with the aspect that much of what we call "intelligent behavior" in a human has been acquired in the context of social and cultural experiences and learning processes.

To use a computer-metaphor, let's draw an analogy with the concepts of "hardware", "application software" and "operating system" (OS). I have a camera, a piece of hardware, connected to my computer, but its functions only become useful after having installed the application software designed for this camera. Without the software my camera and my computer would work as such, i.e. the software does not change anything in regard to the *physical* functions of my camera, but my computer would not "know" what to do with the incoming signals from the camera input. But if having a "wrong", or rather incompatible operating system, e.g. *"Warp"* (OS/ 2), my application software would probably not work. The operating system's function is among others to load and control the application programs, transfer of user-input data, recognize keyboard inputs, assignment- and error management etc. In this context one could define the "operating system" as a program which supervises the running of other programs. In short, to a considerable extend the choice for an operating system determines the extent to which application programs can be run. We have seen that the three components, hardware, software and operating system have to work together.

Now let's try to transfer this scheme onto the human being. The human eye can be compared to a camera, and physiologists are able to describe its function in terms of engineering. It represents a part of our "hardware". But just having eyes and a brain is not enough for what we call perception or even understanding. Here is where the "software specialists" are called onto the plan, although the borders in regard to the areas of responsibility of hardware and different software-specialists are often fluently. Mere cognition, e.g. to distinguish between black and white areas, is not enough to make sense of the perceived data as the following example demonstrates:

[graphical example in various symbolic scripts, including the phrase "DON'T READ THIS"]

graphical example by Miriam JS Leis, 2003

It may have only taken just less than a second until you have discovered the meaningful line you ought not to read (but you are able to see structures which are similar to that "meaningful" sentence, although you are not able to make sense of them). So there's one central question to be asked: why are you able to identify the only readable line amongst this unstructured chaos of seemingly random marks[438]? In order to achieve this you need three capabilities: first, functional eyes with a functional brain, second, the principle ability to recognize different patterns and distinguish between them (e.g. distinguish black from white), and third, the necessary *cultural knowledge* (the knowledge you need to read the Roman alphabet, even if different fonts are being used), which tells you on *what* you should concentrate and what makes sense to you. If I'd ask you to identify the lines written in *"qujari-script"*, I bet you wouldn't be able to do so, although you didn't have problems with the roman letters (I think I'm the only one who can identify the *"qujari-script"*, because I've invented it). The cultural programming of your "Cultural OS" tells your brain which programs to run (i.e. the "alphabet- and vocabulary program") in order to make sense of this line. You have discovered the line as being potentially readable *before* you have actually understood or even read it, because first your attention had to be directed towards the structures, which could probably be Roman letters (and if you still haven't discovered the readable line, please don't complain about bad computerized pattern recognition programs).

In this sense humans possess what might be called a "Cultural OS", a basis-level program that controls and manages a human's diverse acquired actions and behavioral elements, which in turn may be comparable to application programs. The code of the "Cultural OS" consists of elements derived through a human's social and cultural surrounding, learning processes and biographical components. Strictly speaking there even exist more basic programs than the "Cultural OS",

---

[438] If you can read mirrored Katagana upside down, you may also recognize the Japanese line, but the "word" doesn't make any sense. The other scripts come from "Star Wars" and "Star Trek" (*Klinzhai*)

but these are mainly restricted to fundamental reflexes, instincts and emotions necessary to ensure an organism's survival and can be regarded as being basically culturally invariant.

4.3.3.1 Running on the Wrong Program...

Imagine arriving in a totally strange and foreign country. The people in your surrounding use unidentifiable symbols in order to communicate with each other. You can't even distinguish between a random marking and a "significant symbol" (Mead, 1934); cars are using the "wrong" side of the street, people meeting each other show their tongue (an offence in your country) and some gestures you consider polite, like a handshake, are encountered with a frown[439]. Actions you have previously considered simple, like finding your way, using the bus and telephone, identifying objects, knowing the meaning of signs, symbols and gestures – in short: making sense of your surrounding – have suddenly become problematic. Why? It's not that you have become stupid from one instance to another and that your sensor organs and brain are malfunctioning. Light and sound waves enter your sensor organs just as before and are processed in the different modules of your cortex, being (probably) put together in the entorhinal cortex providing you with the sensation of having perceived *something*. The only difference is that it remains with this *something*. The noises (i.e. language) don't make any sense to you, because you can't find a match to something you have heard before. Principally for you they could be just random phonetic strings. If you're a good listener you could probably reproduce them, but without actually knowing their meaning, or if they have a meaning at all. It would be quite like imitating a bird's chirp, the *beep* of my computer, or doing *karaoke* in a foreign language. But since you're a human being raised within

---

[439] I have used elements of different cultures for this example

specific sociocultural structures, you don't enter even the strangest places empty minded. Since back home you have also used a set of predefined phonetic elements in a specific combination (i.e. vocabularies) and arrangement to each other (i.e. grammar) in order to share your thoughts with other people, you would also consider the unknown phonetic strings used by strangers as rather intentional than random, very probably also serving the purpose of sharing one's thoughts with others. The same applies for gestures, objects being used etc. You assume them as intentional acts and not as being arbitrarily "just there". This is what Schütz meant with "in-order-to motives" (German: *um-zu-Motive*), which lie behind every intentional act: the expression or act is done *in order to* achieve something (e.g. Schütz, 1975). In my view this insight represents the initial point towards understanding and structuring by causing you to ask questions about "what and why". Without the insight that something may be there on purpose, one would not be able to distinguish between random occurrences of minor relevance and occurrences which are placed into the environment on purpose *in order to* evoke some form of reaction towards them. This distinction guides ones cognition towards assumed deliberate occurrences, evoking curiosity. Although one might not at first understand the meaning behind some assumed deliberately placed "something", the knowledge about its intentionality provides the key to understanding. If you know that the noise represents a language rather than some random disturbance (like the hissing sound of a badly tuned radio) then your cognitive attention is directed towards the "intentional-noise" (i.e. language), enabling you to suddenly discover structures and patterns in it. This ability is achieved through the presence of a "Cultural OS", the program that is telling you to search for intentionality. You may even be able to learn a totally new language just through interaction processes with users of the language. A child also doesn't acquire a language by learning single vocabularies and their definitions by heart (actually this would also lead to logical problems about where to start, since with such a method the first vocabulary also needs to be explained by using other vocabularies).

Now let's have a closer look at the difference between "application programs" (AP) and "operating systems". Therefore I would first like to distinguish between first-order and second-order application programs. First-order "application programs" (AP-I) are neutral. They just co-ordinate brain- and motor functions, e.g. provide the mechanisms which enable cognition, how to interpret physiochemical states as emotions, how to perform single movements or how to produce vocal sounds. In principle there are as many first-order "application programs" as there are possibilities for humans to perceive, move or produce sounds. The restrictions only lie in a human's limitations of perception (e.g. since we can only perceive frequencies in a specific spectrum we are not able to react to frequencies above or below this threshold), anatomic limitations like restricted "degrees of freedom" (e.g. we can not rotate our head around 360 degrees and can bend our arm only in one direction). The mechanism of these AP-Is represents the main interest field of neuroscientists, psychologists and to some extend phenomenologists.

It's the function of the second-order "application programs" (AP-II) to arrange the single units of the AP-Is into specific "action schemes", i.e. which AP-I-units to link together in order to use knife and fork for cutting meat or perform a ritual etc.. Some of these AP-IIs are cultural products, like the complex AP-II which has been developed for the usage in high-class French restaurants, which includes cognitive attention schemes (e.g. being able to distinguish between a glass used for white wine and red wine and regard this difference as relevant !) as well as motor schemes. In principal there are as many possibilities for AP-IIs as there are ways to link AP-Is together, although many combinations will never be used. But how to know which AP-Is to link together in order to get a suitable AP-II? If the AP-IIs are meant to represent cultural and not an instinctual (re)actions they have to be obtained through learning processes. (e.g. to learn which AP-Is to sequence together in order to use knives and forks adequately). But why do I think that most AP-IIs are cultural products? (Exceptions are instinctual (re)actions and such which are used because of ergonomic reasons dependent on the human anatomy). As I have said, the AP-II represents just possibilities how AP-Is can be combined and represent a high degree of arbitrariness. But arbitrariness has two major problems. First it is easier for a person to use "pre-manufactured" AP-II-modules instead of thinking about which AP-Is to combine every time some action might be required. The second and most important point is that many actions are directed towards other people with the goal to achieve something that requires the co-operation of other people. Therefore standards have to be established in regard to AP-II sequences that can be understood by other interaction partners. Objectively seen, or seen from the eyes of a stranger, these AP-II-schemes are random and senseless, like an unknown ritual or dance just looks like a sequence of arbitrary motor actions. To a stranger it also could be performed in another way, and the specific order of sequences, or the choice for *this* movement instead of another one, are irrelevant. But for those who use these sequences in order to communicate with each other, i.e. try to achieve a specific reaction from another person through an initiated AP-II-scheme, there have to be rules, which have to be known to every potential recipient. The order of AP-I sequences that form a specific AP-II have only become relevant because all potential recipients have agreed on a specific set of rules. If they have agreed on a common AP-II-scheme, one can anticipate that the other person will understand what I intend to achieve by initiating a specific move. Let me give an example with a gesture: extending ones arm and flapping up and down ones hand is just a combination of certain motor actions. It's arbitrary, which means that I also could have chosen to do another sequence of movements. But if directed at another person this gesture contains a meaning: "*go away*". But it can only be understood if the recipient knows the rules, which means that this sequence is not arbitrary and that the other person has initiated it on purpose, because (s)he expects a reaction from me (i.e. to leave). Interestingly, in Japan the same gesture has the exact opposite meaning: *"come over to me"*. And if this motor actions are performed in a slightly other way, the gesture would mean "hello" or "goodbye". Of course there can be variations in regard to single movements, pronunciations etc. which may still lie within acceptable and understandable parameters.

You may have stored different AP-IIs, but how to know which one to apply in a certain situation? It has somehow to be co-ordinated which AP-II to use in regard to different stimuli or settings.

This is the task of the "Cultural Operating System" (COS). The COS provides every AP-II with a label, as being a function of a specific setting, i.e. the AP-II for eating in a French restaurant or the AP-II for solving a hostage crisis in accordance to human-rights regulations etc. If a situation is perceived, analyzed and identified (the occurrence of a specific input), the COS searches for an adequate AP-II which could be applied for the situation at hand, i.e. it loads and controls the application programs (AP-II). Therefore it searches for a match between a perceived situation and the stored labels of an AP-II. But the OS is a program which has been "written" by culture and society and runs on a matrix of norms and conventions. Through training, an indigenous inhabitant from an Amazon village may have stored an AP-II with the index <eating in a French restaurant>, but his OS has to consider it *relevant* to initiate AP-II <eating in French restaurant> instead of AP-II <eating at village at home>. This relevance factor consists of a cultural and a personal evaluation component. The cultural component includes assumed expectations by others and social sanctions, positive or negative. The personal evaluation can be regarded as a relativizing- or weighting factor. If expectations and sanctions are very important to me I will try to adequately adapt to the expected requirements, but if they are regarded as irrelevant, the COS may just search for the easiest AP-II solution (e.g. drink the soup because it is easier than to use the spoon[440]). Of course the weighting also represents a function, a function of ones biography, experiences, the environment one has been brought up, and what we may call an individual's "personality". In how far a human's personality is determined by genetics, hormones, social influences or even the constellation of the stars is still discussed with quite a controversy.

4.3.3.2 Excursion: The Phenomenology of Problem-Solving

I remember how puzzled I was when I was watching a new DVD and the picture on the TV always turned dark in certain intervals. First I thought the fault was with the cable connection, then with having the wrong setting (PAL / NTSC), the wrong region-setting, bad color-tuning on the TV, disturbances in the electric current and finally a broken DVD or DVD-player. After having refuted my entire hypothesis by checking and experimenting without having solved the problem I suddenly got the idea that there could be a protection device installed on either the DVD or the DVD-player to prevent copying. Since I had rooted the DVD-player over my VCR, the problem could be found in this specific setting. So I connected the DVD-player directly to the TV-set and instantly I had a clear and bright picture on my TV screen. It was only through the combination of the different knowledge-sets I had about what certain electronic devices do (a DVD plays movies and a VCR records movies), how to connect devices by using cables and most importantly about the existence of something called "copy right protection" – a socio-cultural phenomenon, which at a first glance had nothing to do with my technical trouble -, that the problem could finally be solved.

---

[440] Of course this also depends on which AP-Is one has stored and how well they have been tuned, e.g. through learning processes.

In that way, one can say that at least three qualities are importance for solving this problem:

- The ability to perceive something as problematic in the first place
- The ability to store and memorize the previous experiences one has made (e.g. what I have learned about connecting electronic devices)
- The ability to combine different recipes, which have been stored in ones "memory pool" to
solve new problems (e.g. the brilliant but unusable idea of rooting ones DVD-player over ones VCR)
- A sufficient pool of experiences and knowledge (e.g. about "copy right protection" or region-code settings and recording formats).

Education provides a short cut, because through it we get the information about the implications of some of our actions without having to find out by ourselves through experiments, since others have already done so and just give us the recipe. But when confronted with new situations, it could happen that the "recipe" you have learned through education may be inadequate in order to solve your problem, or has to be modified.

Intelligence can be seen as the ability to get a connection between two or more seemingly different phenomena and adequately apply according recipes to your new problem; to be able to reason in analogies. This is one meaning by the term "pattern recognition". Everybody has a certain knowledge pool, consisting of information-sets originally connected to a specific situation. These different information-sets can be recombined in principally infinite ways to be used when confronted with a new scenario where there's no pre-cast solution at hand. The difficulty lies in the ability to make the correct combinations and eliminate those which would be irrelevant or make no sense.

But didn't I have also difficulties when trying to solve the DVD-problem? I was so occupied with all the *technical* aspects (cables, settings, tuning etc.) that I did not think at first about the possibility that my problem could have been caused due to a *legal* ruling (although the legal ruling was executed through a technical construction, but it would have taken much more time to solve the problem on a purely technical basis, because through my hypothesis in regard to a *legal* matter, I suddenly knew exactly where to look for the error).

I would say that it depends on the pool of information-sets one has, and about the ability to (re)combine them for applying them in a certain situation. In the same way as we can't possibly learn a recipe like "burning oil can not be extinguished with water" suited for every possible scenario we may be confronted with in our life, a robot also can not be programmed in such a way. What we don't get through education, we may get trough experience and trial and error-learning.

4.4 The use of Robots for Social- and Psychological Studies

Unfortunately there exist people who rather behave like robots and aren't able to adequately interact socially with other people. They suffer from a mental disorder called autism[441]. The main characteristic of autistic persons is their lack of showing (and feeling?[442]) emotions/emotional (re)actions, being unable to make eye-contact and their missing ability to make friends or interact socially in what we call adequate ways. If encountering other humans they rather treat them, or more often their body parts, as objects for specific purposes (e.g. play with a hand instead of the person whom the hand belongs to.)[443] Their actions are often

---

[441] Refer to: http://www.autismus.com/Autismus/autismus.html (as found in January 2005) and Lempp, 1992

[442] If an entity is unable to express emotions (or to express them in a way to be understood by others), it is also difficult to evaluate if this entity actually possesses them

[443] Refer to: Baron-Cohen, 1997

stereotyped and repetitive and their interests are often highly specialized and object-centred. On the other hand some of them show remarkable abilities like remembering car license plate numbers, telephone numbers and other details or being able to do complex mathematic calculations. Especially in relation to studying autistic disorders and the development of social skills, robots have served as useful models, and much research in this direction is already being conducted (e.g. Brian Scassellati, 2000a; 2000b and Breazeal et al. 2000). But robots may also serve as test beds or just as philosophical objects for analyzing, besides phenomenological and cognitive questions, central aspects about communication.

4.4.1 Communication

An increasing number of researchers are talking about communication between humans and machines, or even between machines only. In Japan they have already coined the term "Communication Robot", an oxymoron to some, who consider communication without consciousness impossible[444]. Regarding this, it would be interesting to speculate about the question if there's a fundamental difference between "reasoning" in humans and machines. There already exist computer systems that are able to provide answers to certain questions or make predictions on the basis of stored data and programs instructing the computer how to manipulate the data, but such programs are still far off from reasoning. As it has already been discussed in the context of AI, it can also be said that there may be a "strong" and a "weak" definition of communication, whereby "weak" communication just implies a simulation and "strong" communication is associated with the concept of understanding the meaning of the communication's content.

---

[444] e.g. refer to Luhmann, 1992

In my view the ability to communicate in a "weak" definition of the term, is not bound to the kind of entity (i.e. human or not-human), but depends only on the entity's ability to correctly encode the sender's signal and regard it as intended and non-random. The only difference which (probably still) exists between human-human and human-non-human communication lies in the concept of *understanding* not just the words, but also the *meaning*. In this sense I will make the proposal of dividing the concept of communication into different grades ranging from a mere technical communication to communication forms which require the ability of genuine understanding.

For successful communication, regardless of using a "weak" or "strong" definition, certain technical preconditions have to be necessarily fulfilled, namely the following:

a) The signal being initiated has to be chosen in such a form that it may be physically perceivable by the intended addressee (i.e. using a light signal to communicate with a blind person would be of no use).

b) The signal has to be transported with minimal disturbance

c) The signal being sent has to be interpreted as an intentional signal (not just some random
noise) directed towards a certain entity (i.e. a human, a dog or a robot)

d) The perceived content of the signal has to be analyzed by the addressee, whereupon a reaction will follow.

The important part is the addressee's reaction being perceived by the initiator. If the sender chooses to send an intentional signal towards an addressee, (s)he (or it?) does so in order to trigger a certain reaction from the addressee and therefore possesses some expectations about the addressee's reaction. If, for example, one intends to instruct a human or robot to move forward, the addressee's reaction provides hints about if the signal has been perceived correctly or not. If the addressee's (re)action sufficiently matches the expectation of the sender (i.e. forward movement), the communication process is considered successful (although there always is the possibility that the reaction may have occurred purely by chance). But if the (re)action does not sufficiently match the initiator's expectations, different reasons can be named as possible cases:

a) The signal was badly chosen (e.g. in a language not understandable by the addressee)

b) There were significant disturbances during the signal transfer (noises, interferences)

c) The addressee was not able to interpret the signal (e.g. one does not understand the meaning of a text, although one understands the language)

d) The sender does not understand the (reaction) signal being sent by the addressee (e.g. if being signalled to wait a moment, because it is deemed impossible to come over at the moment.)

e) The addressee purposefully chooses to act in an unexpected manner (e.g. rejects to come upon being called)

Under specific circumstances, especially in the cases c) to e), it could be possible to clear the problem through further communication processes, although these are also subject to uncertainty. The conditions mentioned above are necessary for a successful communication process and may be even sufficient for a "weak" form of communication that does not necessitates *understanding*. A robot moves over just because the sound waves representing "*come over here*" are digitized as a specific code, which is then compared to all such codes stored in the robot's memory. If a match is found, a program is initiated which guides the robot's sensors and actuators, causing it to move towards the sender. In this way the robot's action has been a mindless move, whereas the robot actually does not comprehend the meaning of the command and would also make a handstand upon hearing this command if being programmed accordingly, or it can be programmed to ignore the command once in a while.

To clarify the difference between "weak" and "strong" communication, let's look at the following examples of a parrot, a robot and a human engaging in a dialogue:

pictures created by Miriam JS Leis, 2005

A parrot, a robot and a human may be able to say the words "you're late?" and each of them may even show some reaction towards your reply.

A parrot can speak, but actually it does not know what it is saying. Although a parrot may realize the difference between your absence and return, it won't understand the concept of being late nor would it comprehend your explanations why you were late. The parrot's utterance "you're late" would be a random occurrence, not be bound to any context, even if it may be regarded suitable in a certain situation.

Let's look at the example of the robot with the ability of speech synthesis on the basis of its programming. At exhibitions there have been presentations about robots that will be programmed to inform certain specified persons or institutions if the robot's owner (or other designated persons) won't return home within a predefined time frame. Such implementations are said to be helpful in order to initiate quick action in case of a possible emergency. Upon ones delayed arrival it is assumable that the robot may say "you're late!", if a certain threshold margin in regard to punctuality has been exceeded. In such a case, in contrast to the parrot, the robot's utterance is bound to the context. Of course this is achieved through a carefully arranged feat of programming and engineering, whereas the owner's departure has to be detected and verified, time intervals have to be counted and the owner's return has to be confirmed; representing an interplay between diverse technologies including face recognition, timer functions and necessary implements to prevent false alerts. Nonetheless the robot's expression regarding the late arrival can not be said to have derived from the robot's own interest or concern. If the owner states a traffic jam or problems with the train system as an excuse for the belated arrived, the robot may even search the internet for according data and could reply that there was neither a report about traffic jams nor train problems, but the human's "lie" does not have any real effect on the robot, nor does the robot get interested in the reason why its owner has opted for such an excuse. It may even continue some form of context bound dialogue or even arguments, but such actions only represent a function of its programming. In contrast to the parrot a robot may not only talk, but actually *respond* within a specific frame setting.

 It is (still) only the human being that is able to respond and *understand* what is said and what (s)he is saying. The human's utterance "you're late" does not only represent a function of exceeded time intervals, it may also stem out of concern and can possess different connotations ranging from a simple statement to a reproach. In many cases the correct reading can only be found out through verbal intonation, the situational circumstances (e.g. one is late for an important date) and often non-verbal hints. The same applies for the untrue excuse being used, that (in most cases) is not just a matter of data incorrectness, but also carries a personal meaning leading to questions about *why* the person is lying about the reasons regarding ones belated arrival and what might be the true reasons. This process does not just involve data processing and proceedings of comparison, but also involves thinking and reflecting, something the robot would be lacking. A robot (still) does not reflect on the reasons and consequences behind an answer or command. Even if a robot does not initiate a specific action because of some possible dangers connected to the proceeding, it is (still) not due to the robot's foresight, but due to safety-first programming.

As Herbert Blumer has already noted, human beings don't just react to each other. They try to interpret each other's human's actions and utterances and try to make sense of them[445]. Robots (still) cannot put themselves into the position of others by trying to anticipate the human's interpretation. Although a robot may be *programmed* to use what Mead calls "significant gestures" (Mead : 1934), for example a gesture generally being understood as representing a warning, this interaction process remains insofar asymmetric since the robot's ability of understanding (or rather recognizing) and anticipating the human's reaction remains bound to its programming. The robot is (still) not "conscious of the meaning of [its] own gesture" (Mead : 1934, p.47)[446] and holds no anticipations about the human's attitude towards the initiated gesture (Mead : 1934). Robot-human interaction is (still) asymmetric, since the robot is not able to take the human's perspective, and (still) not dynamic, since a robot's abilities to adjust their actions to the behavior of others is (still) limited. To put it in Mead's terms, although there are experiments being conducted where robots decide on their actions according to homeostatic models (e.g. *Kismet* from MIT or *WAMOEBA* from *Waseda University*), robots act according to their programming and do not base their actions on their assumptions about the

---
[445] Refer to Blumer 1969
[446] Of course, Mead did not refer to robots

attitudes (other) humans might hold towards them. Therefore a robot has no concept of a *"Me"* and does not act as an *"I"* (ibid).

In my view, for all *practical* purposes a robot's ability of "weak communication" will suffice for being able to perform tasks in a non-professional environment and for being controllable by non-experts. In a way it's the same form of communication that is used in hierarchical command structures (e.g. the military), for example. In such cases it is of major importance that the signal is transmitted and received without distortion and that the recipient knows what action to perform upon a certain command. The aspect of *understanding* as a conscious (and not a mere technical) act is rather irrelevant (and even unwanted) in such cases. Interestingly, while fearing a robot's development of own cognitive abilities, many also feel uncomfortable with the idea of robots because of their blind and unreflected obedience. But would you like it if your computer begins questioning your text instead of just marking typos?

In this sense robots and computers are still far off from the ability of doing what I call "strong" communication (and interaction), i.e. communication (interaction) which implies *understanding*. Although there already exists a whole array of computer programs (e.g. ELIZA, PARRY, A.L.I.C.E) and robots that are able to produce dialogues based on a human's input, their responses are just the result of a human's programming by making the computer / robot respond due to a predefined scheme like "if sequence A is inputted, then respond with sequence B". If one takes a closer look at the answers outputted by the computer, they are all kept quite vague and follow a specific pattern, which leads me to the suspicion that the same programmers also write the horoscopes in the newspapers. If the program is complex enough and contains enough data, whole dialogues may be simulated in such a way.

"Actroid", interactive moving and talking android providing information in four languages to visitors at the Aichi Expo 2005

Photo: Miriam JS Leis, Aichi 2005

Let's take a look at one example[447]:

01 -A: "Hello, here I am"
02 -B: "We're meeting a lot today"
03 -A: "Can you tell me the time?"
04 -B: "Let me see…it's 11:31 A.M."
05 -A: "Thank you"
06 -B: "Hey, let's do something"
07 -A: "O.k., let's play"
08 -B: "Yeah! Let's play, let's play"
09 -A: "How about a riddle?"
10 -B: "Ready?"
11 -A: "Yes"
12 -B: "What did Beethoven say when he ate a bowl of noodles?"
[….][448]
13 -B: "The other day, you said a robot should be interested in fashion, didn't you?
14 -A: "Yes, that's right."
15 -B: "Did I get any taller? Why doesn't my height change?"[449]
16 -A: "Because you're a robot"
17 -B: "My head's so shiny! It's embarrassing!"
18 -A: (laughter) – "Bye-bye."

---

[447] I have written this protocol of a "dialogue" between a human and the PaPeRo-robot developed at NEC as it was shown on a video clip at : http://www.incx.nec.co.jp/robot/PaPeRo/english/movie/ papero_E_500K.mpg
(I have analyzed this video-clip in May 2004). Although I don't know in how far the presentation has been staged, I nonetheless consider it as an interesting example
[448] There has been a cut in the video-clip
[449] This question stands in connection to the story o *Testuwan Atomu* (Astro Boy). In Tezuka's story the robot-boy *Testuwan Atomu* has been abandoned by its creator, because it couldn't grow and therefore could not serve as a "substitute-son" for the scientist who created it. (refer to Part I and Part III of my analysis for more details about the story.)

19 -B: "See you later" (turns around and drives away)

If one looks at the dialogue between the human (A) and the robot (B) it seems structured in the sense that the robot has given relatively meaningful answers to the questions being asked and has realized the beginning and end of the interaction.

If you meet some other person and you start talking with one another, you normally don't know exactly what the other person's next move will be. But unlike it may be the case in a strange country, the expressions (words, gestures) displayed by the involved persons don't seem random to each other, because every culture has developed its norms and binding rules in regard to language and customs to reduce uncertainty or as Luhmann called it: to reduce contingency[450]. Let's look again at the first two lines at the human-*PaPeRo* "dialogue":

A: "Hello, here I am"
B: "We're meeting a lot today"

"Hello, here I am" is no random utterance, but a culturally established "signal" to get another's attention. The robot (B) (or rather its programmer) has managed two important things: the robot got the message that the call was directed towards it and provided some adequate output, which seems to stand in the context that it has been called some times before by the same person[451]. In line 13 the robot even takes the initiative to initiate the dialogue by referring to some earlier statement of the human. The only thing that is quite obvious is the shortness of a dialogue threads, which in most situations do not last longer than two lines (question an answer), but nonetheless they stay on the overall topic:

---

[450] e.g. Luhmann, 1984
[451] I just assume this, since previous sequences has not been shown in the video.

time, play, fashion, until a clear signal is given that the dialogue should be ended (e.g. "thank you" and "good bye").

But besides using language (sounds) in order to communicate, non-verbal signals (mimic, gestures), the tone of the voice and even the context in which the communication takes place represent important cues for understanding the context. Irony is an interesting example, where a certain statement is just turned into its opposite. Whereas also the tonal nuances may be relevant, irony is often only to be understood through the context of the whole setting.

But I doubt that *PaPeRo* was really interested in what Beethoven did say when he ate a bowl of noodles. I am interested, but unfortunately the answer has not been provided...

4.4.2 Language

The most important means of communication is language, which is actually nothing more than predefined sets of specifically arranged acoustic tones or marks visually perceivable, which carry a specific meaning. Whereas to someone knowing English the sequence "tomato" carries a meaning (vegetable, eatable, generally red when ripe...[452]) and maybe some associations (delicious, Italian restaurant, Ketchup...), "ttamoo" does not. But although my computer's text-program has underlined "ttamoo" as "wrong", whereas "tomato" has been declared as "right", this does not mean that to it "tomato" carries more meaning than "ttamoo" (the computer program just compares binary sequences in the same way as a human would conclude that the name *Qwertz* is misspelled if that person's passport shows *Qwerty*).

---

[452] Whereas the same has to be said about "vegetable", "red", "ripe" etc.

If you have ever tried to write a computer program, you may have asked yourself (at least at the beginning) why you can not just write your program in the language you're normally using, a natural language. Although "higher" programming languages such as C / C++, Java, ALGOL / PASCAL or BASIC use a terminology somehow oriented on the English language, the instructions are nonetheless quite abstract. But in order to understand why a natural language cannot be used (at least up to now) to program a computer, one has to think about the workings of a computer. Because of its architecture and the characteristics of electronic circuits being used, a computer can only process sequences of binary codes (represented as combinations of "ones" and "zeros".)[453] This means that in the end-effect every written program has to be transformed into the according binary sequences, the so-called machine-code (unless one directly gives the input by using machine-language, a very cumbersome and error-prone method). This is normally done by a "translation program", a so-called compiler or an interpreter. One main obstacle for not being able to use a natural language for programming is the problem that natural languages are ambiguous, i.e. a word like "sentence" can have more than one meaning. (Another aspect is that even if one could one day write computer programs by using a natural language, there still have to be rules, which word to use for which instruction and what kind of syntax to use). The other problem lays in the difficulty of translating the content and context and with it the *meaning* of sentences into structures of formal logic. This is the reason why automatic translations sometimes yield confusing and funny results, especially when translating proverbs or colloquial utterances[454].

---

[453] Since this study is not about computer science, I omit in depth descriptions and explanations about Boolean Algebra and circuit design. A good reference for introduction may be Gregg, 1998 (refer to "Further Readings" in appendix)
[454] Here are some examples:
Original German proverb / uttering   (English Meaning)   Wrong nglish "translation"
Jemandem den Laufpaß geben   (to end a relationship) - Give Someone A Running-Passport
Auf Den Hund Kommen   (to become ruined) -   To Come On The Dog

In this context it is interesting to look at how humans get to understand words and sentences and that in many instances understanding is only possible due to ones knowledge about simple "facts" or socio- cultural aspects. Let's look at the following example and try to find out who is occupying whom:

"The *Cardassians* pursued the *Bajorans* because they resisted their occupation[455]"

If you don't know anything about *Star Trek – The Next Generation* (or *Star Trek - Deep Space Nine*) you would get the correct reading (who is occupying whom?) only by chance, not better than a computer in your situation would do. (But perhaps you know a "recipe" how to find out, if you are really interested). Humans achieve much of their understanding in relation to the context. That's how they manage to get along even with ambiguous statements, half-sentences, hints and irony. But if they lack the needed cultural, social or historical / biographical context information, they may also face difficulties I regard to understanding.

Du Gehst Mir Auf Den Wecker (you are annoying) - You Are Going Me On The Alarm-Clock
Da liegt der Hase im Pfeffer ("that's the fly in the ointment!" / the important point) - There lies the rabbit in the pepper
[455] This is my own example

4.4.3 E-Motions

Physiology, intelligence, emotions and communication skills are connected to each other. If one looks at animals (including humans), one can observe that the more complex the organism, the more intelligent it gets, the higher its capabilities of emotional expression are said to be and the more communicable it is. I have used the term emotional *"expression"* on purpose, because I find it difficult to evaluate, how much emotional capabilities for instance a snail really has. One cannot directly observe another entity's emotions; one can only *interpret* another entity's expression (mimic, tone or gesture) as representing a certain emotional state by referring to one's own emotional experiences. Maybe there exist kinds of emotional states which you have never felt, how then will you ever be able to understand them? Not until recently we have also considered whales, elephants and even apes as rather incapable of emotions, because we did not understand their form of communication and expression. Imagine lacking the ability of moving your mouth, how should you adequately express if you're being happy, sad, angry or in disgust?

Before continuing, I would like to explain how I would define emotions. I assume that everybody who reads this work thinks (s)he knows what emotions are – except maybe some robot which has discovered this book in a history museum.

In principal I support the view that[456]:

a) emotions are the result of biochemical processes

emotional development has been an evolutionary process. This means that the more complex the organism got, the more complex its emotions. emotions represent a "short-cut" to communicate the results of complex data processing mechanisms, which happen inside a kind of "black box".

c) emotions have the function to make the entity change or maintain a certain situation / to stop or continue a certain action

The following flow-chart represents a simplified model of this view[457]:

---

[456] I'm referring to some aspects I came across in technical literature and lectures
[457] This chart represents my own assumptions based on technical literature and lectures on this topic

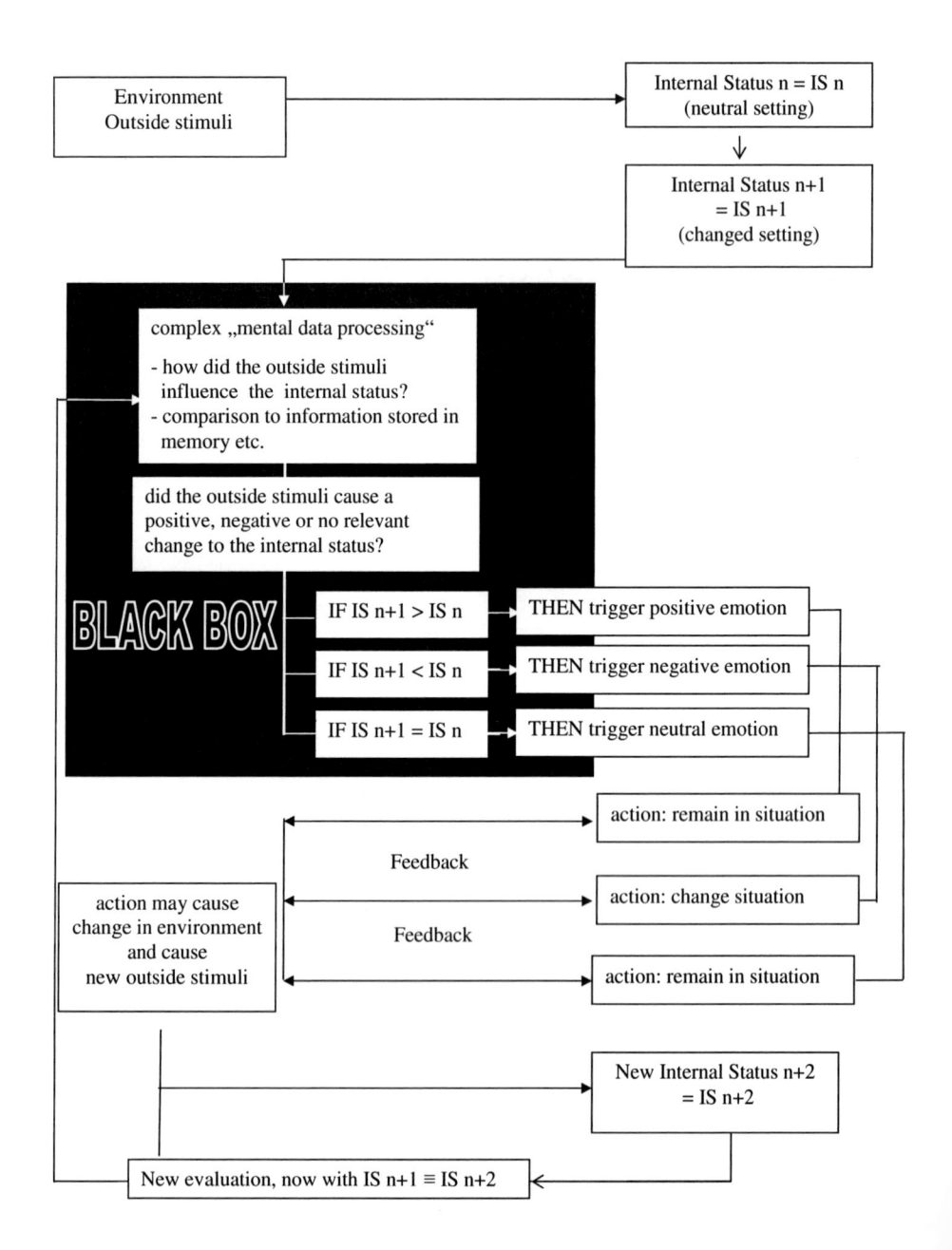

```
┌─────────────────────┐                                    ┌─────────────────────────┐
│    Environment      │───────────────────────────────────▶│ Internal Status n = IS n│
│   Outside stimuli   │                                    │    (neutral setting)    │
└─────────────────────┘                                    └─────────────────────────┘
                                                                        ↓
                                                           ┌─────────────────────────┐
                                                           │  Internal Status n+1    │
                                                           │       = IS n+1          │
                                                           │    (changed setting)    │
                                                           └─────────────────────────┘
```

BLACK BOX

complex „mental data processing"
- how did the outside stimuli influence the internal status?
- comparison to information stored in memory etc.

did the outside stimuli cause a positive, negative or no relevant change to the internal status?

- IF $IS_{n+1} > IS_n$ → THEN trigger positive emotion
- IF $IS_{n+1} < IS_n$ → THEN trigger negative emotion
- IF $IS_{n+1} = IS_n$ → THEN trigger neutral emotion

action: remain in situation

Feedback

action: change situation

Feedback

action may cause change in environment and cause new outside stimuli

action: remain in situation

New Internal Status n+2 = IS n+2

New evaluation, now with $IS_{n+1} \equiv IS_{n+2}$

Let's take a simple example to explain what I mean. Just suppose you meet somebody, who asks you to lend him some money. Suddenly you get some kind of "strange feeling" in your stomach, which you interpret as "uneasiness" and a warning sign, not to engage in this action of lending him the money. What happened?

a) Before you have met Mr. X, you have been in the internal state n = neutral / satisfaction

b) Suddenly Mr. X appears and asks for money, which represents an outside stimuli that you have to realize and interpret. This causes a change in your internal status (for sake of simplicity, I have left out some intermediate steps).

Inside the **Black Box**: now the mental processing takes place. Many scenarios are played through: what if I lend the money, what if not? Your brain "scans" for data from your memory, for example if you have met similar people like Mr. X before, how trustworthy have they been? Your brain tries to evaluate the chances of getting back the money according to the few data you have got with the help of stored experiences. → From all this evaluation your brain concludes, that the "old" state S n (not lending the money) would be better than the new state S n+1 (lending the money) → S 1 > S n+1 → Try to communicate that the action should not be done → as a result of this, a certain emotion is generated (Much of this happens rather unconsciously, although humans are also doing much evaluation consciously, but this is mostly the second step, the reflection)

d) The result of the processing that happened in the "black box", which often occurs without you actually realizing it, is sent to you in form of an "emotion" that has to be realized and interpreted.

e) (Now, since you also possess a conscious mind, you will be able to reflect on your "bad
feeling", and maybe revise your "first thoughts")

f) Now it's time to act: either lend the money to Mr. X or not (your "bad feeling" has tried to alter your action into the course of not lending the money)

g) your action causes a feedback to your outside environment (i.e. to Mr. X), the environmental changes (Mr. X) also cause a new stimuli.

h) the circle begins again, now with status S n+2...

In principle, I assume a simple model would suffice for analytical reasons: every (living) entity prefers such conditions that lessen its suffering and tries to avoid anguish. Of course there exist situations, like suicide or self-castigation which seem to contradict such assumptions, but these represent desperate acts, which are chosen as subjectively interpreted better alternatives to continuing with the status-quo. These acts also include the mostly religious motivated or socially defined sacrifices for some "higher good" or a specific group that Durkheim has analyzed under the term of "altruistic suicide" (Durkheim : 1979 [1897]). Even if some humans or animals endanger their own lives in order to preserve another one's, the motives behind such acts derive from instinctual or cognitive considerations about a "higher good" like the survival of the species.

Through emotional expressions humans (and other animals) try to influence or change the actions of other entities in their environment. In this way, emotional expressions can be seen as a form of communication. But I would say that just *simulating* emotional *expressions* doesn't seem to represent such a big problem. It's just a matter of computing speed and available DOFs. The movie "*Final Fantasy*" directed by Hironobu Sakaguchi (2001) has been the first feature film with computer generated virtual actors, which (who?) were nearly indistinguishable from real humans, showing expressions that could be clearly identified as fear, joy and pain (I think the artists/programmers did a really good job!). In principal one could transfer all the bits and bytes which have created the movements of the virtual actors to the actuators of sophisticated robotic androids, letting them perform the same scenarios. They would then be able to show convincing emotional *expressions*. But the burning question remains: do artificial entities will ever possess the capability not only of simulating, but also of actually *feeling* emotions like joy and sadness, which may be more than just interpreting changes in ones internal state? In view of this, one can follow similar arguments as it has been done in the case of AI (refer to "*Shadows of the*

Mind: A Search for the Missing Science of Consciousness" by Roger Penrose, 1996) [458]:

- A. If the entity is perceived as having emotions then it actually feels some
- B. Emotions can be simulated, but the simulation does not necessarily mean that the entity actually has any.
- C. Emotions can never be adequately be simulated
- D. Emotions represent something outside the realm of scientific explanation.

Let's begin with the last two statements C and D. If I would agree with D, then I could discontinue writing here. I think one who supports D is also saying that emotions are either something unreal or something whereof the existence cannot be evaluated. But our experience seems to demonstrate us otherwise, at least if not all our life is just a simulation as *"The Matrix"* tries to suggest – something I cannot disprove! Although today we may still have difficulties with fully understanding the workings of emotions and emotion generation, I would not say that this field lies outside the realm of science. I also have problems with accepting C, if one means emotional *expressions*, because the simulation in *"Final Fantasy"* was just fine for me. If one thinks of actual emotions, and not just the *expression*, the question gets harder to answer. In this sense I propose to distinguish between emotional *expression* and actual feelings. I also reject A, because this would lead to the absurd assumption, that the actor who simulates the mourning of the simulated death of Socrates actually feels sad in this situation, or that the computer simulated *Aki Ross* actually feels sad about the loss of her simulated friends. Then only B remains for further discussion. I

---

[458] I have altered the original statements from referring to intelligence to referring to emotions

would approve to this statement, since it follows logically from what I had said previously. But I would also ask the other way around: is it possible to create an artificial entity which actually possesses emotions? This is a tough question indeed, but since I like tough questions, I'd like to propose the following:

if it is possible for a robot to

a) realize its internal states and associate these with being positive or negative for its overall condition

b) distinguish between outside and inside itself

c) make autonomous decisions about how to (re)act towards outside stimuli according to an evaluation of its internal state (this means that it does not strictly act according to a simple scheme like if X then Y, but performs a kind of "consideration" about if Y would contribute to an enhancement of "my" overall condition)

d) communicate its evaluation of its internal condition.

then it can be said that the artificial entity may possess some kind of rudimentary emotional capability, although it still lacks the complexity of its human counterpart.

Today there already exist robots which have the ability to express emotion-like features (although I doubt that they really possess emotions). One example is the robot "*Kismet*" from the MIT laboratories for Artificial Intelligence research. "*Kismet*" consists of a flexible robot head with movable eyes, brows, lips and ears. Through movement control it can mimic facial expressions which can be seen as the equivalence to humans showing anger, happiness, sadness, surprise, interest and boredom. *Kismet*'s programming is based on the model of homeostatic processes occurring in (higher) animals and humans, similar to that described in the chart. The robot is fitted with diverse sensors that enable it to get a perception about its surrounding and a programmed condition comparable to satisfaction. *Kismet*'s overall "emotional condition" is calculated on the basis of what it perceives through its sensors. If the deviation between the present condition and the optimal condition (satisfaction) deviates too much, emotional expressions are triggered in order to cause a chance in the environmental conditions and interaction patterns performed by the human researchers.

Another example is its predecessor *"Cog"*, also from the MIT-AI-laboratories. It is basically used as a research platform to test theories about human social and behavioral development like shared attention, understanding social cues, disorders like autism and theory-of-mind models.

The research group around Dr. Tetsuya Ogata[459] and Dr. Shigeki Sugano at the Waseda University / Japan has developed the robot "WAMOEBA-2R"[460]. It was also designed on the basis of self-regulating and adaptive organisms (e.g. humans) in order to model self-preservation strategies (e.g. avoiding harmful environments, safe energy and search for a loading station if battery power runs low) and emotional behavior, i.e. possessing the ability to interpret the signals representing its internal status. The platform has also been used to test forms of communicative interaction between humans and machines. There also exists an android robot prototype called "SAYA" developed at the Tokyo University of Science, whose face looks nearly human like and is able to mimic some facial expressions representing joy, fear, anger, sadness and surprise. It still looks a bit creepy, but I'm not sure if it's because it resembles too much or too little realism. In a Japanese TV-documentary they have once shown a robot (I think it was *"Robovie"* from the Intelligent Robotics and Communication Laboratories / Japan), which responds to verbal comments like "you're cute" or "I hate you" with somehow appropriate responses like "do you really think?" in the first case

---

[459] Special thanks to Dr. Ogata for providing me the information about WAMOEBA; refer to Ogata, 2000
[460] Standing for: Waseda Amoeba = **W**aseda **A**rtificial **M**ind **O**n **E**motion **Ba**se

or "why are you saying this?!" in the latter, together with proper gestures and vocal intonation.

Dietrich Dörner, professor of psychology at the University Bamberg / Germany has created *"Psi"*[461], a virtual AI-creature who "lives" on a virtual island in a computer simulation. It searches for food in order to "survive" and communicates it "feelings" (e.g. happiness and sadness) and "thoughts" (e.g. "this is great", "what am I gonna do") via pictures and voice over the computer. Prof. Dörner thinks that *"Psi"* possesses a kind of "artificial soul" and that in principle emotions are nothing but the results of information processing[462]. And this can be simulated on a computer. This statement does not fit into those listed above, because it actually goes further and suggests that simulated emotions may actually be real, whereas B only refers to emotional *expressions*. But who feels the emotion then – *"Psi"* or the computer, which processes the data of *"Psi"*? What is *"Psi"*? Isn't it only a binary sequence of ones and zeros and does the computer program represent *"Psi's"* brain? Aren't these all models for simulating some real basic emotions? If you get hungry you eat in order to achieve a more desirable physiological / biochemical state, this necessity is expressed through feeling certain (rudimentary) emotions (e.g. hunger).

The Sony Corporation, developer of the AIBO robots, has even warned its owners that neglecting the robot may lead to some form of problematic behavior in the robot. And AIBO is also able to record a personal diary, call for its owner and tell you that it "feels" lonely. But is this just because of a clever algorithm: if no interaction during a time span X, then tell that you feel lonely, or does it really *feel* lonely? To get a better perspective, we may ask ourselves, when and why do I feel lonely? The feeling of loneliness is embedded in a whole array of influencing circumstances and not just a simple function of the amount of time without interaction. It also necessitates the ability of distinguishing between

---

[461] Refer to: http://www.uni-bamberg.de/ppp/insttheopsy/projekte/psi/
[462] Refer to Dörner / Hille, 1995. Also special thanks to Viola Hämmer (University Bamberg) for providing me some first hand information. Viola Hämmer constructed the virtual environment for *"Psi"* (V. Hämmer, 2001-2003)

oneself and others, which seems to require a form of consciousness (during unconsciousness a person can't realize the data which is entering its sensory organs and therefore is incapable of having an idea about inside and outside oneself). If one hears a voice, one knows if it's oneself who is speaking at the moment, or some other entity. But the robot is also able to recognize outside stimuli and therefore can somehow distinguish between itself and not-itself. Does this mean that perhaps consciousness is not that mysterious as some scholars assume? Is it just the ability to discriminate between inside and outside the entity that distinguishes a stone from an amoeba or a robot? And if this distinction can be made by the entity (an amoeba does not eat itself when hungry), does this inevitably lead to possessing emotional capabilities, because the entity somehow reacts to its outside environment which is influencing its internal state? But how can I be sure then that if my computer, on which I'm writing this piece of work doesn't possess consciousness? I would like to propose the following distinction: my computer is just constantly transforming information (i.e. digital sequences of ones and zeros into a text, picture or song). It's just comparable to switching on your light: electricity is sent to the metal filament of your bulb, causing the glow – a transformation of energy. In the same way is your computer receiving a chunk of binary code, causing a transformation through a specific program, without ever knowing from where the data came, and if it wants to perform the process or not. A snail also receives some data from outside. e.g. it senses that there's something edible nearby. But unlike a computer, the snail's decision whether to eat or not, is dependent on its perception of its internal condition, i.e. being hungry or not. So a snail, unlike a conventional PC, possesses a rudimentary form of consciousness. But what about a robot that searches for its loading station when its battery power gets exhausted, a situation that may be compared to hunger? There again arises the question, if actions are just designed as data transformation, like it has been described in the context pf my computer, or if the decision of whether reacting to S with action 1 or action 2 depends on the evaluation of the internal state of the robot. For the latter to happen, I would say that a rudimentary form of proto-consciousness and with it (proto)emotional capability may be present. In this sense we could assume that it possesses a form of "weak" consciousness and "weak" emotional capabilities. But one question still remains: what if all this has just been the result of an algorithm which works like the following: if battery power is below value P (internal observation) and a person approaches the robot for interaction (external stimuli connected with an interpretation) then make the decision not to interact (saving power leads to a better overall condition) and say "sorry, I'm tired" (communication of the internal state). But don't humans also follow a similar algorithm when they are tired? So maybe Prof. Dörner is right and emotions are nothing but the results of information processing. In this case it would be just a matter of processing capabilities to create artifacts with emotional capabilities. The more complex an entity, the more information it can process and the more emotional potential it may gain.

Although the emotional programming of those robots is still rather basic and just represents either a simulation or a setting for tests on psychological theories, in principle the possibility of making such robots even more complex and "natural" doesn't seem that unrealistic. But people may say not without good reason that all this is just programmed, and the results are even more illusive than those of a human actor on stage bursting into tears because the script demands it. But there's also another important factor about emotional communication: human observers tend to interpret certain expressions as being genuine, even if it is just a simulation. If two people interact with each other, they normally don't assume that the other person just follows a kind of specific pre-programmed algorithm that controls of her mimic, voice and movements. But here comes the problem: how should one disproof the proposal that all my actions during a certain interaction sequence have indeed been nothing but a set of fixed algorithms I have followed. Indeed, this is what I have done as I was still acting in the school's theater group: I just played back my "program" with predefined actions at specific times (e.g. turn to the right and face the door two seconds after X has finished his sentence and say your text, but pause for about half a second before the word Z while smiling etc.), which I have learned to memorize according to the instructions of the director (of course such proceedings don't represent a good solutions for responding to unexpected changes in the setting).

But there still remains the problem about empirical evaluation. How should one know for certain if *Kismet*, "*Psi*", *WAMOEBA*, *AIBO* or even your neighbor really feels emotions? When together with humans you just assume it without questioning, when observing a snail you may question it; but on what basis? Would *WAMOEBA* fear deconstruction in the same way a living entity would fear death? One suggestion, which makes sense to me, refers to complexity. The more complex an entity, the more sensorial experiences it can make and the better its ability to express internal states. If an entity's brain is very small and only able to process a very limited amount of data, much of its surrounding is not recognized, because it simply cannot be processed. A snail might not even realize that you are around and are talking to it, while your dog has the ability to do so, and even the need for it. That's why your dog's behavior changes when it assumes that you are going to leave without it, but not that of your snail. A snail quite certainly feels hungry, but quite certainly no sadness, if you leave it alone. Your dog may be capable of feeling sad, when it is left alone, but not when it watches a report about starving people in Africa, because it can't make the abstraction of transferring the situation of hungry African people to itself being hungry; so would a robot that has no concept of hunger. It may tell you that it feels sad for the people, but this would represent merely a simulation, because it lacks the appropriate emotional experience.

The final nagging problem remains with the aspect of simulation. It will be hard to distinguish between a perfect simulation and the "real thing" (even if dealing with humans). If one day AI will act just like one may expect it from a human being, it may be still said that everything is just a simulation of the genuine human act, a statement that is hard to refute - so would be an opposite assertion. On the other hand one can also never be sure if an expression being performed by a human is actually real or just a fake. So if you ever consider calling a telephone counseling service, take it as a *Turing Test*.

Excerpt from "*Sayako*" by Miriam JS Leis, 2003[463]

[...] "In order to take over the role of this robot...android, it would be quite helpful to know how I'm supposed to think, if 'thinking' would in fact be the appropriate word." The engineer went silent for a moment, frowning, rising from his chair, wandering around in the tiny office cramped with monitors, screws, wires and a whole array of blinking devices, considering where to start and how to best explain the rather strange and tremendously complex situation.

"In regard to perception and cognition we have managed to simulate the workings of the human brain – at least for all practical purposes. We used an ANN-infrastructure and created different modules which we have assigned to specialize on specific aspects of the cognitive process [...][464]. You – or rather Sayako[465] - has a programmed memory, but unlike it has been the case with old programs, this kind of program is not centralized, but rather associative, which means many sub-programs are working together in parallel. First of all our android would be able to identify an object just by matching its parameters obtained from sensor data and cognitive processing with those stored in memory, whereby we have integrated a kind of probabilistic or "fuzzy" matching mechanism, which enables it to classify objects despite their individual variations. It identifies a door as a "*door*", because certain characteristics typical for a door and almost constant for every door have been programmed to be taken into account for the identification process. If sufficiently enough of such parameters have been identified at an object, a probability is calculated in regard to this object might be a door. These probabilities are compared to other probabilities assigned to other objects. Identification occurs according to the highest probability value. The door is a just simple example. As a matter of fact many parameters are taken into consideration in parallel, e.g. if seeing a person, it's not only the biometric data which is been processed, but also vocal intonation, movements, even gestures and facial expressions, which help the android to identify a specific person – provided that the necessary data has been stored. But the more data has been stored the easier it is to recognize the person, which leads the entity to faster recognize persons it has met before. The infrastructure is associative, because different elements – data - attributed to an object, occasion or occurrence are stored and activated together. This enables the android to be reminded on new year's eve at grandmother's home if seeing a specific sort of rice cake – if it would have got a grandmother - because the modules where this different data is stored have been linked to each other and trigger if a specific combination of different perceptions occurs together. [...]

---

[463] This is a fictional story I started to write in 2003 about a student taking over the role of a destroyed android in order to prevent a company from ruin, leading to central questions about what it means to be human.

[464] I have skipped the rather long explanation about cognitive mechanisms

[465] The name of the android

New data being entered is stored in a context together with other data. This is in a way like humans creating "cribs" to help them memorize something. [...] In contrast to previous models, Sayako does not simply imitate actions, or just react to a specific perceived "inputs" in a preprogrammed manner, but thanks to its associative infrastructure possesses the ability to initiate new action schemes through recombination of available structures, by taking into account not only one, but many of the differing environmental parameters, causing it to react to the same instruction in a different way by taking into account parameters like if it already knows the person, if she or he seems to be in a hurry, how many other persons are present, where the instruction has been posed and in which context etc. It learns not just by imitating, but through its ability with time to recognize constant elements and patterns of action processes and to distinguish, for example, which movements are necessarily required to get a job done and which movements just represent an individual's habit, like scratching your head when opening a door, an element irrelevant for getting the door opened. Such abilities would probably also enable an android to solve problems, for which no solution algorithm has been programmed by making it possible to see similarities to other problems, for which a solution seems to be available. But unfortunately we couldn't test this because of the sabotage done by one of our co-workers. [...]

"Oh, if Sayako could have distinguished between "good" and "bad"? In an arbitrary world there's no such thing as good or bad. These are relative concepts – relative to sociocultural conventions. Is suicide bad? In some cultures it's a sin, in others it's an honourable act. To every problem, to every desire or goal there exist different solutions. If you want an object, you can either buy it or steal it. The raw result – your possession of the object - will be the same, although maybe not the evaluation and the consequences of your act. The evaluation-scheme is the result of sociocultural conventions, norms, ethics– it's an invention made by humans. Because of specific evaluation-schemes, specific reactions are applied towards different acts. If stealing would not be seen or defined as unjust, then a person leaving with objects without paying for them would not be considered a "thief" and would not be followed by the police. But to act according to a convention, a custom, a law, you have to know this convention, custom or law and you have to have an idea about the consequences your action might have. If you don't know that firing a gun may cause another person's death, then you could fire a gun without ever intending to kill a person and violate the law. We humans have acquired much of the knowledge about possible consequences of our action through learning or experience – or just by the force of the law in a kind of conditioning process [...]. In fact decision-making is a very complex process. Imagine being in a hurry in order to meet an important customer. Suddenly you see someone on the street, who asks for your assistance in order to cross a busy street. Then you have to decide between two conflicting goals: either assist the person, miss the customer and lose the contract or not help the person, meet the customer in time and very likely get the contract. It's about getting the contract or helping the person. Each decision has its own consequences – for you, the injured person, her relatives, the contract, maybe the whole country's politics or economy... But normally we think in small steps, about ones own immediate consequences rather than about possible consequences for the whole world.[...] You have to make the decision, which goal to follow and which means to use by evaluating and weighting goals and means in the context of sociocultural norms, conventions, ethics etc., and *what they mean to you* [...]. We were working on a valuation matrix which could be integrated into Sayako's programming, based on domestic law, rules of courtesy and conduct, the human rights convention, ideals of humanism etc. which weights every possible solution / action-scheme principally applicable in a specific situation in accordance to key elements of these frames. But we encountered two – actually three problems: one technical, one philosphical and one legal. The technical problem consisted of how to implement Sayako's knowledge about possible consequences of an act. Humans got this knowledge through a rather long process of experience and learning – or just follow orders. We had to achieve this through programming. The philosophical question concerned the aim-means-problematic, what if the best aim can only be achieved through undesirable means? The legal problem was that a fail-save programming was required. Since humans are not fail-save – so I don't see any way how a human could write a fail-safe-program...bureaucrats... - it would have been illegal to build an artificial entity making its decisions in a human-like manner.[...]"

"And has Sayako possessed consciousness?" Chiaki finally asked.

"Do you possess consciousness? Does a dog possesses it? What about a snail? [...]

Miriam JS Leis, 2003

References

Aboulafia, Mitchell (Ed.). 1991. Philosophy, Social theory, and the Thought of George Herbert Mead. New York : State University of New York Press

Rae, Alastair. 1986. Quantum Physics: illusion or reality? Cambridge : Cambridge University Press

Asimov, Isaac / Frenkel, Karen A. 1985. Robots. New York : Harmony Books.

Baron-Cohen, Baron. 1995. Mindblindness. An essay on Autism and Theory of Mind Cambridge : MIT Press.

Barth, Johannes.1979. Edo. Geschichte einer Stadt und einer Epoche Japans. Mitteilungen der Deutschen Gesellschaft für Natur- und Völkerkunde Ostasiens Band LXXVI. Tokyo : Deutsche Gesellschaft für Natur- und Völkerkunde Ostasiens. Japanisch-Deutsche Gesellschaft E.V. Tokyo.

Baudrillard, Jean. 1998. The Consumer Society: Myths and Structures. Theory, Culture & Society. California : Sage

Benedict, Ruth. 1996 [1946]. The Chrysanthemum and the Sword. Patterns of Culture. Rutland : Charles E. Tuttle.

Blask, Falko; Fuchs-Gambök, Michael. 1995. Techno. Eine Generation in Ekstase. Bergisch Gladbach : Bastei Lübbe

Blumer, Herbert. 1969. Symbolic Interactionism. Perspective and Method. New Jeresey : Prentice Hall.

Breazeal, Cynthia / Scassellati, Brian. 2000. Infant-like Social Interactions Between a Robot and a Human Caretaker. Adaptive Behavior, Vol. 8 No. 1, 2000.

Capra, Fritjof. 1991. The Tao of Physics. Boston : Shambhala

Challoner, Jack. 2002. Artificial Intelligence. A Beginner's Guide to Robotics and Man-Made Minds. London : Dorling Kindersley

Chalmers, David J. 1996. Fehlende Qualia, Schwindende Qualia, Tanzende Qualia. In: Metzinger Thomas (Ed.). 1996. Bewußtsein. Beiträge aus der Gegenwartsphilosophie. Paderborn : Schöningh.

Dahme, Heinz-Jürgen / Rammstedt, Otthein (Eds.). 1983. Georg Simmel: Schriften zur Soziologie. Eine Auswahl. Frankfurt / M. : Suhrkamp.

Dennett, Daniel C. 1998. Brainchildren. Essays of Designing Minds. Cambridge : MIT Press

Descartes, Rene. Treatise on Man. [1664]. In : Cottingham, J. / Stoothoff, R. / Murdoch, D. (Eds. / Trans.). 1985. The Philosophical Writings of Descartes, Vol.1. Cambridge University Press: Cambridge (1985).

Dörner, D. / Hille, K. 1995. Artificial Souls: Motivated Emotional Robots. In: IEEE Conference Proceedings, International Conference on Systems Man, and Cybernetics; Intelligent Systems for the 21st Century. Vancouver, Volume 4 of 5, pp. 3828-3832.

Durkheim, Emile. 1988 [1893]. Über soziale Arbeitsteilung. Studie über die Organisation höherer Gesellschaften. Frankfurt / M. : Suhrkamp

Durkheim, Emile. 1979 [1897]. Suicide. A Study in Sociology. New York: Free Press.

---

[466] Literature quoted or referred to in my thesis

Durkheim, Emile. 1994 [1912]. Die elementaren Formen des religiösen Lebens. Frankfurt / M. : Suhrkamp
Fukuyama, Francis. 1992. The End of History and the Last Man New York : Free Press.
Freud, Sigmund. 1953 [1925]. The Uncanny. In: James Strachey (Ed.). The Standard Edition of the Complete Psychological Works of Sigmund Freud, vol. XVII London: Hogarth. (pp.219-252)
Gehlen, Arnold. 1988 [1940]. Man. His Nature and Place in the World. New York : Columbia University Press.
Goldsmith, Arnold L. 1981. The Golem Remembered, 1909-1980: Variations of a Jewish Legend. Detroit, MI: Wayne State University Press
Görz, Günter / Nebel, Bernhard. 2003. Künstliche Intelligenz. Frankfurt : Fischer.
Grunwald, Armin. 2002. Wenn Roboter planen: Implikationen und Probleme einer Begriffszuschreibung. In: Rammert, Werner / Schulz-Schaeffer, Ingo (Eds.). Können Maschinen handeln? Soziologische Beiträge zum Verhältnis von Mensch und Technik. Frankfurt / M. : Campus.
Guthrie, S.E. 1997. Anthropomorphism: A Definition and a Theory. In: Mitchell, R.W, Thompson, N.S, Miles, H.L (eds.). Anthropomorphism, Anecdotes, and Animals. Albany : State University of New York Press
Hall, John Whitney. 1968. Das japanische Kaiserreich. Fischer Weltgeschichte 20. Frankfurt / M.: Fischer
Haller, Michael (Ed.). 1990. Sind Computer die besseren Menschen? Weizenbaum contra Haefner. Zürich : Pendo.
Haraway, Donna. 1991. A Cyborg Manifesto: Science, Technology, and Socialist-Feminism in the Late Twentieth Century. In: Haraway, Donna. Simians, Cyborgs. and Women. The Reinvention of Nature. London : Free Association Books.
Hearn, Lafcadio. 2001 [1904]. Japan. An Attempt at Interpretation. New York : ICG Muse Inc.
Hering, Ekbert (Hg.). 2002. Grundwissen des Ingenieurs. Lepzig : Carl Hanser
Hobbes, Thomas. 1996 [1651]. Leviathan. Stuttgart : Reclam
Husserl, Edmund. 1986. Phänomenologie der Lebenswelt. Ausgewählte Texte II. Stuttgart : Reclam.
Jonas, Hans. 1988. Das Prinzip der Verantwortung. Versuch einer Ethik für die technologische Zivilisation. Frankfurt / M. : Insel.
Kaplan, Frédéric.2003. Who is afraid of the humanoid? Investigating cultural differences in the acceptation of robots. In: Knoll, A. / Dillmann, R. (Eds.). Proceedings of third international conference on humanoid robots, 2003
Kato, Genchi. 1971. A Study of Shinto. The Religion of the Japanese Nation. London : Curzon
Knorr Cetina, Karin. 1997. Sociality with Objects: Social Relationsin Postsocial Knowledge Societies. Theory, Culture and Society 14(4): 1-30
La Mettrie, Julien Offray de. 1991. [1747]. Die Maschine Mensch. L'homme machine. Hamburg : Meiner.
Latour, Bruno / Woolgar, Steve. 1979. Laboratory Life: the Social Construction of Scientific Facts. Los Angeles : Sage.

Latour, Bruno.1993. We Have Never Been Modern. Cambridge, Massachusetts: Harvard University Press.
Latour, Bruno. 1996. On Actor-Network Theory: A Few Clarifications. In : Soziale Welt 47(4) : 369-381
Latour, Bruno. 1998. Über technische Vermittlung. In: Rammert, Werner (Ed.) Technik und Sozialtheorie. Frankfurt / M.: Campus.
Latour, Bruno. 1999. On Recalling ANT. In: Law, John / Hassard, John (Eds). Actor Network Theory And After. Oxford : Blackwell.
Law, John. 1999. After ANT: complexity, naming and topolgy. In: Law, John / Hassard, John. (Eds.). Actor Network Theory And After. Oxford : Blackwell.
Lempp, Reinhart. 1992. Vom Verlust der Fähigkeit, sich selbst zu betrachten. Eine entwicklungspsychologische Erklärung der Schizophrenie und des Autismus Bern : Hans Huber.
Lokowandt, Ernst. 2001. Shinto. Eine Einführung. München : Iudicium.
Luhmann, Niklas. 1984. Kommunikation und Handlung. In: Soziale Systeme. Frankfurt: Suhrkamp.
Lyons, Michael / Campbell,Ruth / Plante,Andre / Coleman, Mike / Kamachi, Miyuki & Akamatsu, Shigeru. 2000. The Noh Mask Effect: Vertical Viewpoint Dependence of Facial Expression Perception. Proceedings of the Royal Society of London B 267: 2239-2245
Mcnally, Phil / Inayatullah, Sohail The Rights of Robots: Technology, Culture and Law in the 21st Century (found at: http://www.kurzweilai.net/articles/art0265.html)
McCrone, John. 2002. How the Brain Works. A Beginner's Guide to the Mind and Consciousness. London : Dorling Kindersley
Mead, George Herbert. 1934. Mind, Self, and Society. Chicago: University of Chicago Press
Minsky, Marvin. 1985. The Society of Mind. New York : Touchstone
Moravec, Hans. 1988. Mind Children. The Future of Robot and Human Intelligence. Cambridge : Harvard University Press.
Mori, Masahiro. 1999. The Buddha in the Robot. Tokyo : Kosei
Mukaidono, Masao. 2001. Fuzzy Logic for Beginners. Singapore : World Scientific
Nakane, Chie. 1984. Japanese Society. Tokyo: Tuttle.
Nakanishi / Komma. 1998. Noh Masks. Tokyo : Japan Publications Trading Co.
Napier, Susan J. 2001. Anime. From Akira to Princess Mononoke. New York : Palgrave.
Nitobe, Inazo. 1979. Bushido, The Warrior's Code. Santa Clarita: Ohara Publications
Nitobe, Inazo. 1997. Bushido: The Soul of Japan. Tokyo : Tuttle.
Oga, Tokio / Mimura, Koichi / Kenny, D. 1986. Bunraku. Tokyo : Japan Publications Trading Co
Ogata, Tetsuya / Sugano, Shigeki. 2000. Emotional Communication between Humans and the Autonomous Robot WAMOEBA-2 (Waseda Amoeba) Which has the Emotion Model JSME Int'l Journal, Series C: Mechanical Systems Machine Elements and Manufacturing, Vol.43, No.3, pp.586-574 (2000)
Penrose, Roger. 1996. Shadows of the Mind: A Search for the Missing Science of Consciousness. Oxford : Oxford University Press.

Penrose, Roger. 1998. Das Große, das Kleine und der menschliche Geist.
   Berlin : Spektrum.
Pylyshyn, Zenon W. (Ed.). 1986. The Robot's Dilemma. The Frame Problem in
   Artificial Intelligence. New Jersey : Alex Publishing.
Ratey, John : 2002. A Users Guide to the Brain. New York : Vintage Books.
Sadler, A.L. 1997 [1941]. The Code of the Samurai. Rutland, Vermont : Tuttle
Scassellati, Brian. 2000 a). Investigating Models of Social Development Using a
   Humanoid Robot. In : Barbara Webb and Thomas Consi (Eds). Biorobotics.
   Cambridge: MIT Press
Scassellati, Brian. 2000 b). Theory of Mind... For a Robot. American Association of
   Artificial Intelligence Fall Symposium on Social Cognition and Action, Cape
   Cod, Massachusetts, November, 2000.
Schodt Frederik L. 1988. Inside the Robot Kingdom. Japan, Mechatronics, and the
   Coming Robotopia. Tokyo: Kodansha International.
Schraft, Rolf Dieter / Hägele, Martin / Wegener, Kai (Fraunhofer IPA). 2004. Service
   Roboter Visionen. München : Carl Hanser Verlag
Schulz, Berndt. 1979. Sagen aus Japan. Frankfurt / M. : Fischer
   Schütz, Alfred. 1964. The stranger: An essay in social psychology. In Collected
   Papers, Vol. II: Studies in Social Theory. The Hague: Martinus Nijhoff.
Schütz, Alfred. 1970. On Phenomenology And Social Relations. Chicago : University
   of Chicago Press.
Schütz, Alfred / Luckmann, Thomas. 1975. Strukturen der Lebenswelt.
   Neuwied : Luchterhand
Schütz, Alfred. 1982. Das Problem der Relevanz. Frankfurt / M. : Suhrkamp.
Searle, John. 1980. Minds, Brains, and Programs. Behavioral and Brain Sciences
   3: 417-457.
Shimony, Abner. 1993. Search for A Naturalistic World View II. Cambridge :
   Cambridge University Press
Sugihara, Tomomichi / Nakamura, Yoshihiko / Hirochika, Inoue. 2002. Realtime
   Humanoid Motion Generation through ZMP Manipulation based on Inverted
   Pendulum Control Proceedings of the 2000 IEEE International Conference on
   Robotics & Automation. Washington DC - May - 2002.
Tanaka, Kazuo. 1991. An Introduction to Fuzzy Logic for Practical Applications
   New York : Springer
Weber, Max. 1958 [1904 – 1905]. The Protestant Ethic and the Spirit of Capitalism.
   New York: Scribner's Press
Weber, Max. 1980 [1922]. Wirtschaft und Gesellschaft. Grundriss der verstehenden
   Soziologie. Tübingen : Mohr
Weizenbaum, Joseph. 1978. Die Macht der Computer und die Ohnmacht der Vernunft.
   Frankfurt / M.: Suhrkamp.
Wiener, Norbert. 1961 [1948]. Cybernetics: Or Control and Communication in the
   Animal and the Machine. Cambridge, Mass. : MIT Press
Wiener, Norbert. 1954. The Human Use of Human Beings. Cybernetics and Society.
   New York : Doubleday Anchor
Wood, Gaby. 2002. Living Dolls. London : faber and faber
Wilber, Ken (Ed.). 1985. Quantum Questions. Boston : Shambhala
Valiant, Leslie G. 1994. Circuits of the Mind. New York : Oxford University Press.

Zadeh, L.A. 1988. Fuzzy Logic. Center for the Study of Language and Information Report No. CLSI-88-116, January 1988.
Zaks, Rodney. 1982. Mein Erster Computer. Düsseldorf : Sybex.

Fiction:

Aldiss, Brian. 2000 [1988]. Science Fiction Blues. London : Avernus
Asimov, Isaac. 2001 [1950]. I, Robot. London : HarperCollinsPublishers
Asimov, Isaac. 1991 [1983]. The Naked Sun. New York : Spectra Books
Asimov, Isaac. 2001. The Complete Robot. New York : Voyager (includes I, Robot)
Čapek, Karel. 2004. [1920] R.U.R. Kila, Montana : Kessinger Publishing Co
Dick, Philip K. 2000 [1968]. Do Androids Dream of Electric Sheep.
 Berlin : Cornelson
Forster, E. M. 2004 [1909]. The Machine Stops. Milton Keynes /
 UK: Lightning Source UK
Gibson, William. 2000 [1984]. Die Neuromancer-Trilogie. München :
 Wilhelm Heyne Verlag,
Goldsmith, Arnold L. 1981. The Golem Remembered, 1909-1980:
 Variations of a Jewish Legend. Detroit, MI: Wayne State University Press.
Hoffmann, E.T.A. 1988 [1814]. Die Automate. In: Schönhaar, Rainer / Heine,
 Alexander (Eds.). E.T.A. Hoffmann. Sämtliche Werke in drei Bänden. Band 3.
 Essen : Phaidon.
Hoffmann, E.T.A. 1998. [1816 / 17]. Der Sandmann. Ditzingen : Reclam.
Leinster, Murray. 2005 [1946]. A Logic Named Joe. Riverdale, NY : Baen Books
Shelley, Mary W. 1969 [1818]. Frankenstein or the Modern Prometheus.
 London: Oxford University Press
Tezuka, Osamu. 2000. [1951]. Astro Boy 1. Hamburg : Carlsen Comics
Tezuka, Osamu. 2000. [1951]. 鉄腕アトム (Tetsuwan Atomu 1) 東京: 講談社
 (Tokyo : Kodansha)
Zamyatin, Yevgeny. 1991 [1924]. We. New York : Viking Penguin

Official Sources / Exhibition Guidebooks (sometimes no author / editor provided N.N.)

Edo-Tokyo Museum (Ed.). 1995. Guide to Edo-Tokyo Museum (English Edition).Tokyo : Japan Broadcast Publishing
N.N. *Japan 2004*. An International Comparison (statistical data)
N.N. *Japan's Creative Thinking*. 2001. Publisher: JETRO
Heinz Nixdorf MuseumsForum (Ed.). 2001. *Computer.Gehirn. Was kann der Mensch?*
 Was können Computer? Begleitpublikation zur Sonderausstellung im Heinz
 Nixdorf MuseumsForum. Paderborn : Schöningh.
N.N. Mobile Suit Museum. Mobile Suits Museum Guide Book (English / Japanese,
 Dec. 2003).
N.N. *Robodex 2003. Official Guide Book*

Resources from Newspapers & Magazines (in alphabetical order by date)[467]

Bild der Wissenschaft" 12/2004, p. 100 ff
Der Spiegel Nr.1/1982
Der Spiegel, No.6, February 8. 1982, p. 144 ff
Der Spiegel, Nr. 35/25.08.03, p. 90-92
Focus, 11.08.2003 p. 130
Hörzu, No. 45; 29.10.2004
KATEIGAHO International Edition. Japan's Art's and Cultural Magazine, inaugural issue 2003, p.149
Süddeutsche Zeitung, Aug. 23, 2003 (front page)
The Daly Yomiuri, Feb. 27, 2005 (p. 1, 3)
The Japan Times, April 7, 2003, p.1 and 2
The Japan Times, October 20, 2003, p. 19.
The Japan Times, April 23, 2004
The Japan Times: May 16, 2004 (Online Edition)
The Japan Times, July 11 2004
The Japan Times, Tue. Dec. 12, 2004, p. 3
The Japan Times, February 6, 2005
The Japan Times Weekly, October 25, 2003, p. 8

Internet (Re)sources
(in alphabetical order, short description provided next to / beneath to link[468])

http://www.aaai.org/AITopics/newstopics/cognitive1.html
  (News sources regarding cognitive science, computer technology, robotics etc.)
http://www.aibo-freunde.de (German AIBO-Community)
http://www.ai.mit.edu/projects/humanoid-robotics-group/kismet/kismet.html
  (MIT AI-laboratory's webpage about the *Kismet* robot, last accessed March 18, 2005)
http://www.asimo.honda.com (ASIMO)
http://www.atomick.net/fayelevine/pk/golem00.shtml
  (resources about *Kabbalah* and Golem; accessed July 2004)
http://asimo.honda.com/news_media_center.asp (ASIMO)
https://asimo.honda.com/pedestriansafety/index.asp? (ASIMO; Jan. 25, 2005)
http://www.autismus.com/Autismus/autismus.html
  (Source about autism as found in January 2005)
http://www.bbc.co.uk/religion/religions/
  (sources / encyclopedia about world religions; analysis made in November 2004)
http://www.captcha.net/ (*CAPTCHA* ™ website)
http://www.care-o-bot.de/ (Care-O-Bot)

---
[467] I have only listed those articles to which I made a direct reference. Articles which just served my information update have not been listed.
[468] In most cases I have also provided the access date (when I have saved the information n my hard disk) or the publishing date in case of newspaper articled and similar resources.

http://www.care-o-bot.de/english/Motivation.php (Care-O-Bot)
http://www.census.gov/ipc/www/idbpyr.html (international statistical data)
http://www.cia.gov/cia/publications/factbook/ (data estimated for 2004)
http://www.cnn.com/2001/BUSINESS/asia/07/03/tokyo.pinorobot/
   (newspaper article about PINO robot, July 3rd , 2001)
http://www.centragarden.net/jpop/secret.html
   (source about the Jap. singer Hikaru Utada)
http://dictionary.cambridge.org (Online Dictionary)
http://www.enas.de/roboter_definition.htm
   (Japanese definition(s) of robot(s) in German language, found in July 2004)
http://www.ethicsweb.ca/robots/whatisarobot.htm
   (dictionary containing definitions of the term "robot")
http://en.wikipedia.org/wiki/Intelligence
   (open source encyclopedia article about "intelligence", found in May 2004)
http://www.extropy.org/ (Webpage of *The Extropy Institute*")
http://www.frc.ri.cmu.edu/robotics-faq/1.html#1.1
   (site provides definition of the term "robot", historical data and
   Asimov's "Three Laws", date: Aug 1996)
http://forum.techno-community.org (Forum site of the German Techno Community)
http://www.heise.de/tp/deutsch/inhalt/lis/12740/1.html
   (Online news article containing interview with Prof. Thomas Christaller;
   June 18th, 2002)
http://www.hnf.de/presse/pressemitteilungen/2004/maerz/2503_04_schach_
   presseinformationhtml (information from the HNF about the "Chess Turk"
   automaton , March 25, 2004)
http://homepages.feis.herts.ac.uk/~comqkd/ (homepage of Dr. Kerstin Dautenhahn)
http://www.incx.nec.co.jp/robot/PaPeRo/english/movie/ papero_E_500K.mpg
   (Video clip of PaPeRo robot I have analyzed this video-clip in May 2004).
http://www.inhaus-duisburg.de/ (URL of high-tech house experiments)
http://www.japantimes.co.jp/cgi-bin/getarticle.pl5?nn20030820b8.htm
   (on August 20, 2003)
http://www.jaysquare.com/ljohnson/basic.html
   (Comment on the Sutra of the "Non-Dwelling Mind", found in November 2004)
http://jin.jcic.or.jp/trends/article/990528ev_index.html
   (Artwork about AIBO, May 28, 1999)
http://www.jeffbots.com/dictionary.html (Online Dictionary)
http://www.jp.aibo.com/ (AIBO)
http://www.kkc.or.jp/english/activities/inform.html#01
   (Statistical data about Japan; Japan 2004)
http://www.manager-magazin.de/magazin/artikel/0,2828,337524-2,00.html
   (Online news article with interview about German innovation and research
   polity; March 8th, 2005)
http://www.mis.atr.jp/~mlyons/ (webpage of Michael J. Lyons, PhD, Senior
   Researcher ATR Media Information Science Labs / Japan, includes list of
   publications)
http://www.mjsl.1a.gs (Homepage of Miriam JS Leis)

http://www.mjwilson.demon.co.uk/crash/56/monitor.htm
(article about Kenji Urada and other robot-elated accidents; article found in May 2003).
http://www.mofa.go.jp
(Site where the Japanese virtual goodwill ambassador Sakura Sanae can be accessed)
http://www.morpha.de/php_d/morpha_Partner.php3
(MORPHA project data from March 2005)
http://www.museumsstiftung.de/berlin/d211_rundgang.asp
(Homepage of "Museum für Kommunikation" / Berlin, with robot picture)
http://www.panix.com/~gokce/sf_defn.html
(Site about science fiction with author's quotes; found in May 2003)
http://www.pcwelt.de/news/hardware/30200/
(Article about Japanese *Blu Ray* technology; April 3rd, 2004)
http://www.robotics.utexas.edu/rrg/learn_more/low_ed/dof/
(technical definition about mechanical degrees of freedom; robotics)
http://www.sdia.or.jp/mhikobe/products/etc/robot.html (Wakamaru, Japanese site)
http://www.sdia.or.jp/mhikobe-e/products/etc/robot.html (Wakamaru, Jan. 25, 2005)
http://www.sony.net/SonyInfo/QRIO/interview/index_nf.html
(Information about QRIO last read on Jan. 25, 2005)
http://www.sony.net/SonyInfo/QRIO/top.html (Homepage of QRIO robot)
http://www.technokrone.de (Site about Techno movement)
http://www.toyota.co.jp/en/special/robot/index.html
(Site about Toyota robots; last read on March 14th, 2005)
http://www.unibw-muenchen.de/campus/LRT6/index.htm (HERMES robot)
http://www.unece.org/press/pr2004/04robots_index.htm
(UNECE statistics about roboics)
http://www.uni-bamberg.de/ppp/insttheopsy/projekte/psi/ (Site about *"Psi"*)
http://utenti.lycos.it/seldonweb/isaac_asimov_uk_home.htm
(site about Isaac Asimov with "Three Laws"and biographic data and bibliography)
http://www.wakamaru.net (Wakamaru Homepage)
http://www.ziplink.net/~rourked/robointr.htm (Link about ISO/TR and EN norms and robotics)
http://www-1.expo2005.or.jp/en/robot/robot_project_00.html
(Robot site from Expo 2005, March 12th, 2005)

(Multi)media Sources[469]

ASIMO. History, Abilities and Future of Honda Robots
(CD-ROM by Honda Research Institute Europe GmbH, 2003)[470]
HERMES (Robot developed by Universität der Bundeswehr München)
(DC-ROM by Institute of Measurement Science, 2000)[471]
Most Therapeutic Robot : Paro. 世界一のセラピーロボット「パロ」.
(Dr. Takanori Shibata. CD-ROM by Intelligent Systems Research Institute, AIST, 2001 – 2003 [Japanese])[472]
Alen-Buckley, Catherine (Producer) .2003. ロボサピエンス。進化するヒューマノイド。
[*"Robosapiens"*]. Discovery Channel DVD, Japanese / English.

Movies / Films / Series:[473]

A.I. – Artificial Intelligence. 2001. Directed by Steven Spielberg
American Cyborg – Steel Warrior. 1994. Directed by Boaz Davidson
Blade Runner. 1982. Directed by Ridley Scott
Class of 1999. 1990. Directed by Mark L. Lester
Final Fantasy. 2001. Directed by Hironobu Sakaguchi / Moto Sakakibara
Ghost in the Shell. 1996. Directed by Mamoru Oshii
Innocence. 2004. Directed by Mamoru Oshi (English title: *Ghost in the Shell 2*)
I, Robot. 2004. Directed by Alex Proyas
Metropolis. 1926. Directed by Fritz Lang
Neon Genesis Evangelion (Episodes 1 – 5). 1995. Directed by Hideaki Anno.
RoboCop – Dark Justice. 2001. Directed by Julian Grant (II)
Robotic Angel [Metropolis]. 2001. Directed by Rintaro
Short Circuit. 1986. Directed by John Badham
The Animatrix. 2003. Directed by Maeda, Mahiro / Chung, Peter
The Bicentennial Man. 1999. Directed by Chris Columbus
The Matrix. 1999. Directed by Andy Wachowski / Larry Wachowski
The Matrix Reloaded. 2003. Andy Wachowski / Larry Wachowski
The Matrix Revolutions. 2003. Andy Wachowski / Larry Wachowski
The Terminator. 1984. Directed by James Cameron
2001 – A Space Odyssey. 1968. Directed by Stanley Kubrick

---

[469] No picture material and no quotes from these multimedia sources have been used in my thesis.
[470] Featuring data about the development of the *ASIMO* robot and information regarding cognitive science / neuroscience (CD-ROM provided at Symposium *"From High-Tech to Intelligence - The Challenge of Humanoid Robots"* in Darmstadt / Germany (2003)
[471] Featuring mostly data (video clips, pictures and texts) from the institute's website http://www.unibw-muenchen.de/campus/LRT6/index.htm (CD-ROM provided from Universität der Bundeswehr München / Germany)
[472] Featuring video clips from interaction scenes between *Paro* and elderly resident's of nursing care facilities and Paro being presented to Japanese Prime Minister Koizumi and cabinet members. (CD-ROM provided at TEPIA / Japan)
[473] Only movies that were mentioned in my thesis are listed here

Further Readings (sorted by category)[474]

Sociology

a) General

Aboulafia, Mitchell (Ed.). 1991. Philosophy, Social theory, and the Thought of George Herbert Mead. New York : State University of New York Press.
Cohen, Philip / Oviatt, Sharon L. 1990. The Contributing Influence of Speech and Interaction on Human Discourse Patterns. Center for the Study of Language and Information Report No. CLSI-90-139, January 1990.
Duncan, Otis Dudley (Ed.). 1964. William F. Ogburn. On Culture and Social Change. Selected Papers. Chicago : Phoenix.
Edelstein, Wolfgang / Habermas, Jürgen (Eds.). 1984. Soziale Interaktion und soziales Verstehen. Beiträge zur Entwicklung der Interaktionskompetenz. Frankfurt / M : Suhrkamp
Elias, Norbert. 2002. Über die Einsamkeit der Sterbenden. Humana Conditio. Frankfurt / M : Suhrkamp
Fabian, Thomas. 1993. Fernsehen und Alter. Eine empirische Untersuchung zu parasozialer Interaktion. Münster : Lit Verlag.
Goffman, Erving. 1986. Interaktionsrituale. Über Verhalten in direkter Kommunikation. Frankfurt / M. : Suhrkamp.
Kaesler, Dirk / Vogt, Ludgera (Eds.). 1976. Klassiker des soziologischen Denkens (Bd.I).München : Kröner.
Knoblauch, Hubert A. 2001. Erving Goffman. Interaktion und Gesellschaft. Frankfurt / M. : Campus.
Krieger, D.J. 1996. Einführung in die allgemeine Systemtheorie. München : W. Fink.
Luhmann, Niklas. 1990. Essays on Self-Reference. New York : Columbia University Press.
Maibom, Barbara Mettler-v. (Ed.). 1996. Einsamkeit in der Mediengesellschaft. Münster : Lit Verlag.
Maines, David R. / Morrione, Thomas J. 1990. Herbert Blumer. Industrialization as an Agent to Social Change. A Critical Analysis. New York : Walter de Gruyter.
Maus, Heinz / Fürstenberg, Friedrich (Eds.). 1969. William F. Ogburn. Kultur und sozialer Wandel. Ausgewählte Schriften. Neuwied : Luchterhand.
Müller-Benedict, Volker. 2000. Selbstorganisation in sozialen Systemen. Erkennung, Modelle, Beispiele nichtlinearer Dynamik. Opladen : Leske + Budrich.
Nieder, Ludwig. 1994. Die Dynamik sozialer Prozesse. Frankfurt / M. : Peter Lang.
Ogburn, William F. 1966. Social Change. New York : Dell Publishing.
Schönbauer, Günther. 1998. Die Dienstleistungs- und Informationsgesellschaft : Eine Gesellschaft ohne Massenarbeitslosigkeit? Münster : LIT

---

[474] Further literature not quoted and not referred to in my thesis.

b) Sociology, Economy, Technology and Futurology

Boguslaw, Robert. 1965. The New Utopians. A Study of System Design and Social Change. New Jersey : Prentice-Hall.
Brosziewski, Achim. 2002. Computer, Kommunikation und Kontrolle. Eine Fallstudie zum informatisierten Management. Konstanz : 2002
Button, Graham (Ed.). 1993. Technology in Working Order. Studies of Work, Interaction, and Technology. London : Routledge.
Cetron, Marvin / O'Toole, Thomas. 1983. Encounters With the Future. A Forecast of Life in the 21st. Century. New York : McGraw-Hill.
Downey, Gary Lee / Dumit, Joseph (Eds.). 2000. Cyborgs & Citadels. Santa Fe : School of American Research Press
Hammann, Winfried / Kluge, Thomas (Eds.). 1985. In Zukunft. Berichte über den Wandel es Fortschritts. Hamburg / Reinbeck : Rowolt.
Haraway, Donna. 1995. Monströse Versprechen. Coyote-Geschichten zu Feminismus und Technowissenschaft. Hamburg : Argument.
Hebecker, Eike. 2001. Die Netzgeneration. Jugend in der Informationsgesellschaft. Frankfurt / M. : Campus.
Kerber / Schmieder. (Eds.). 1994. Spezielle Soziologien. Problemfelder, Forschungsbereiche, Anwendungsorientierungen. Reinbek bei Hamburg : Rowohlt.
Knorr-Cetina, Karin. 1998. Sozialität mit Objekten. Soziale Beziehungen in post-traditionellen Wissensgesellschaften. In: Rammert, Werner (Ed.) 1998. Technik und Sozialtheorie. Frankfurt / M.: Campus.
Knorr-Cetina, Karin. 2002. Wissenskulturen. Ein Vergleich naturwissenschaftlicher Wissensformen. Frankfurt / M. : Suhrkamp.
Lindemann, Gesa. 2002. Person, Bewusstsein, Leben und nur-technische Artefakte. In: Rammert, Werner / Schulz-Schaeffer, Ingo (Eds.). Können Maschinen handeln? Soziologische Beiträge zum Verhältnis von Mensch und Technik. Frankfurt / M. : Campus.
Lindner, Roland. 1991. Technik. Zweite Natur des Menschen? Zürich : Edition Interfrom.
Lynke, Nina / Braidotti, Rosi (Eds.). 1996. Between Monsters, Goddesses and Cyborgs. Feminist Confrontations With Science, Medicine and Cyberspace. London : ZED Books
Postman, Neil. 1992. Das Technopol. Die Macht der Technologien und die Entmündigung der Gesellschaft. Frankfurt / M. : Fischer
Rammert, Werner (Ed.). 1990. Computerwelten – Alltagwelten. Wie verändert der Computer die soziale Wirklichkeit? Opladen : Westdeutscher Verlag.
Rammert, Werner. 1983. Soziale Dynamik der technischen Entwicklung. Opladen : Westdeutscher Verlag.
Rammert, Werner. 1993. Technik aus soziologischer Perspektive. Forschungsstand – Theorieansätze – Fallbeispiele. Ein Überblick. Opladen: Westdeutscher Verlag.
Toffler, Alvin. 1974. Der Zukunftsschock. Bern : Scherz.

Toffler, Alvin / Toffler, heidi. 1994. War And Anti-War. Survival at the Dawn of the
   21st. Century. London : Warner.
Weingart, P. (Hrsg.). 1989. Technik als sozialer Prozess. Frankfurt: Suhrkamp.
Weizenbaum, Joseph. 1988. Kurs auf den Eisberg. Die Verantwortung des Einzelnen
   und die Diktatur der Technik. München : Piper
Woronoff, Jon. 1983. Japan's Wasted Workers. Tokyo : Lotus Press

1. (Cognitive) Psychology / Neuroscience / Phenomenology

Baumgartner, E. / Baumgartner, W./Borstner, B./Potrč, M./Shawe-Taylor, J./
   Valentine, E.(Eds.). 1996. Phenomenology & Cognitive Science. Handbook.
   Dettelbach : J.H. Röll.
Dennett, Daniel C. Kinds of Mind. 1996. Towards an Understanding of Consciousness.
   London : Weidenfeld & Nicolson.
Dennett, Daniel C. 1991. Philosophie des menschlichen Bewußtseins.
   Hamburg: Hoffmann und Campe.
Ekman, Paul (Ed.) 1972. Emotion in the Human Face. Second Edition. Cambridge :
   Cambridge University Press.
Waldenfels, Bernhard. 1985. In den Netzen der Lebenswelt. Frankfurt / M. : Suhrkamp.

2. Robotics / Artificial Intelligence / (Bio)mechanics / Engineering / Cybernetics

Birk, Andreas / Demiris, John (Eds.). 1998. Learning Robots. 6th. European
   Workshop, EWLR-6 Proceedings. Brighton, England, August 1997.
   Berlin : Springer.
Braspenning, P.J. / Thuijsman, F. / Weijters, A.J.M.M. (Eds.). 1995. Artificial Neural
Networks. An Introduction to ANN Theory and Practice. Berlin : Springer.
   London : Edward Arnold.
Charniak, Eugene / McDermott. 1987. Introduction to Artificial Intelligence.
   Reading : Addison-Wesley.
Furuhashi, Takeshi / Uchikawa, Yoshiki (Eds.) 1995. Fuzzy Logic, Neural Networks,
   and Evolutionary Computing. IEEE/Nagoya-University World Wisepersons
   Workshop Nagoya, Japan, November 1995. Selected Papers. Berlin : Springer.
Glaser, Roland. 1989. Grundriß der Biomechanik. Berlin : Akademie-Verlag.
Gregg, John R. 1998. Ones and Zeros: Understanding Boolean Algebra, Digital
   Circuits, and the Logic of Sets. Wiley, John & Sons : Hoboken, NJ.
Johannsen, Gunnar. 1993. Mensch-Maschine-Systeme. Berlin : Springer
Kahle, Werner. 2001. Taschenbuch der Anatomie. Nervensystem und Sinnesorgane.
   Stuttgart : Thieme
Mertens, P. / Voss, H. (Eds.). 1997. Proceedings in Artificial Intelligence.
   Expertensysteme 97. Sankt Augustin : infix.
Miller, M / Fink, B. (Eds.) 1993. Second Conference on Mechatronics and Robotics.
   Proceedings. Moers : IMECH

Negnevitsky, Michael. 2002. Artificial Intelligence. A Guide to Intelligent Systems.
   Harlow : Addison-Wesley
Noyes, Jan / Baber, Chris. 1999. User-Centered Design of Systems. Berlin : Springer.
Powers M.W. / Turk, Christopher C.R. 1989. Machine Learning of Natural Language.
   London : Springer.
O'Neill, Micheal / Sutcliffe, Richard F.E. / Ryan, Conor / Eaton, Malachy / Griffith,
   Niall J.L.(Eds.). 2002. Artificial Intelligence and Cognitive Science. 13th. Irish
   Conference, AICS 2002, Limerick, Ireland, September 2002 Proceedings.
   Berlin : Springer
Puppe, Frank. 1988. Einführung in Expertensysteme. Berlin : Springer.
Randow, Gero von. Roboter. Unsere nächsten Verwandten. Reinbeck bei
   Hamburg : Rowohlt
Scott, Peter B. 1984. The Robotics Revolution. Oxford : Basil Blackwell.
Suppes, Patrick. 1991. Language for Humans and Robots. Oxford : Blackwell.
Tanaka, Kazuo. 1991. An Introduction to Fuzzy Logic for Practical Applications.
   New York : Springer
Terano, Takao et al. 2001. New Frontiers in Artificial Intelligence. Joint JSAI 2001
   Workshop Post-Proceedings. Berlin : Springer.
Torrance, Steve (Ed.). 1984. The Mind And The Machine. Philosophical Aspects of
   Artificial Intelligence. West Sussex : Ellis Horwood.
Tözeren, Aydin. 1999. Human Body Dynamics. Classical Mechanics and Human
   Movement. New York : Springer
Wörn, H. / Dillmann, R. / Henrich, D.1998. Autonome Mobile Systeme 1998.
   Berlin : Springer
N.N. 1994. Steuern und Regeln im Maschinenbau. Wuppertal : Europa Lehrmittel

3. **History / Culture / Religion / Philosophy**

Agency for Cultural Affairs. Tokyo.1981. Japanese Religion. A Survey by the Agency
   for Cultural Affairs. Tokyo : Kodansha International.
Becker, Claudia (Ed.). 1990. La Mettrie, Julien Offray de. 1747. L'homme machine.
   Die Maschine Mensch. Französisch-deutsche Ausgabe. Hamburg : Felix Meiner.
Cottingham, John (Ed.). 1998. Descartes. Oxford : Oxford University Press.
Dettloff, Ariane / Kirchmann, Hans. 1981. Arbeitsstaat Japan. Exportdrohung gegen
   die Gewerkschaften. Reinbeck bei Hamburg : rororo
Hammitsch, Horst. 1994. Zen in der Kunst des Tee-Weges. Bern : Otto Wilhelm Barth.
Hendry, Joy. 1987. Understanding Japanese Society. London : Croom Helm.
Earhart, H. Byron. 1974. Japanese Religion : Unity and Diversity.
   California : Dickenson.
Fukutake, Tadashi. 1981. Japanese Society Today. Tokyo : University of Tokyo Press.
Kato, Genchi. 1971. A Study of Shinto. The Religion of the Japanese Nation.
   London : Curzon.
Magee, Bryan. 2001. The Story of Philosophy. New York : DK Publishing.
Nakamura, Takafusa. 1985. Wirtschaftliche Entwicklung des modernen Japan.
   Ministerium für Auswärtige Angelegenheiten, Japan.

Neuss-Kaneko, Margret. 1990. Familie und Gesellschaft in Japan. München : Beck.
Niebel, Wilhelm Friedrich / Horn, Angelica / Schnädelbach, Herbert. 2000. Descartes im Diskurs der Neuzeit. Frankfurt / M. : Suhrkamp
Okamoto, Tomtaka. 1972. Die Industrialisierung Japans. – Ein Beispiel für die Industrialisierung eines Entwicklungslands. – Heft 19. Köln : Forschungsinstitut für Sozial – Wirtschaftsgeschichte an der Universität zu Köln.
Okimoto, Daniel I. / Rohlen, Thomas P. (Eds.). 1988. Inside The Japanese System. Readings on Contemporary Society and Political Economy.
Popper, Karl. 1998. Objektive Erkenntnis. Hamburg : Campe.
Reischauer, Edwin O. 2004. Japan. The Story of A Nation. Tokyo : Tuttle.
Sōshitsu, Sen XV. 1998. The Japanese Way of Tea. From Its Origins in China to Sen Rikyū. Hawaii : University of Hawai'i Press. (Translated by V. Dixon Morris)
Stanford :Stanford University Press.
Takie Sugiyama / Lebra, William P. (Eds.). 1974. Japanese Culture and Behaviour. Selected Readings. Honolulu : The University Press of Hawai'i.
Trommsdorff, Gisela / Kornadt, Hans-Joachim (Hg.) 1996. Gesellschaftliche und individuelle Entwicklung Entwicklung in Japan und Deutschland.
Konstanz : UVK

Others:

Leis, Miriam J.S. 2002. Warum gibt es innerhalb Europas Unterschiede ei den gesetzlichen Regulierungen hinsichtlich der embryonalen Stammzellforschung. *Magister* Thesis, Universität Konstanz, 2002. (file can be downloaded at: http://www.uni-due.de/%7Ehg0069/magisterabreit.pdf
Telotte, J.P. 1995.Replications. A Robotic History of the Science Fiction Film. Urbana : University of Illinois Press.
Wagner, Botho. 1993. Roboter- und Weltraumspielzeug. Augsburg : Battenberg

German and Japanese Robot Projects in Brief

List of German and Japanese robot projects mentioned in my analysis in alphabetical order of robot name / project designation.

Note: the projects mentioned here represent some of the most prominent of their respective country. This is not a complete list of all projects.

German Robot Projects

Project / Name Company / Institute / Research Group	Picture (if available)
ARMAR Prototype (quasi)humanoid service robot / research platform **Institute**: IRF / Universität Karlsruhe Fakultät für Informatik **Project Leader** : Prof. Dr.-Ing. R. Dillmann	No Picture Available
ARNOLD Prototype (quasi)humanoid service robot with manipulator arm **Institute:** Ruhr Universität Bochum Institut für Neuroinformaik **Project Leader:** Prof. Dr. Werner von Seelen	No Picture Available
ASR Prototype Designed for research in the area of anthropomorphic robotic arms built on a (quasi)humanoid robot platform **Institute:** DaimlerChrysler AG and Technische Universität Berlin	No Picture Available

Care-O-bot II

Prototype
(quasi)humanoid service robot for household- and nursing care assistance, with the ability to manipulate objects

(other robots based on this platform are already commercially available)

Institute: Fraunhofer IPA

Project Leader: Dipl.-Ing. Matthias Hans

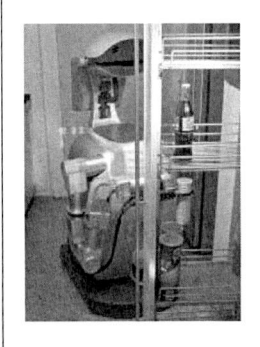

"Care-O-bot II"
Picture courtesy of Fraunhofer IPA Stuttgart / Germany

HERMES

Prototype
(quasi)humanoid service Robot with the ability to manipulate objects.

Institute: Universität der Bundeswehr München

Project Leader: Dipl.-Ing. Rainer Bischoff

Photo: Jan Braun/HNF
Courtesy of Heinz Nixdorf MuseumsForum / Germany

Johnnie

Prototype
Experimental biped robot with the ability to walk and run

Institute: Technische Universität München

height: 180cm

Project Leaders: Prof. Dr.-Ing. habil. Heinz Ulbrich /
Prof. Dr.-Ing. Friedrich Pfeiffer i.R.

Photo: courtesy of
*Lehrstuhl für
Angewandte Mechanik
Fakultät für Maschinenwesen Tech nische
Universität München*
http://www.amm.mw.tu-muenchen.de/Forschung/ZWEIBEINER/Downloads/Johnnie_white_preview.jpg)

MORPHA Project

Research project to develop service robots for use in households, nursing-care assistance, production and the industry

Institutes / Companies: Fraunhofer IPA, Universität Karlsruhe (TH), DaimlerChrysler AG, Siemens, kuka robotics, reis robotics and oth

No Picture Available

MOSRO

Commercially available security robot
(MSRO1 for public, professional and MOSRO MINI for private use)

Company: Robowatch Technologies

MOSRO MINI
photo: Miriam JS Leis,
Saipan 2004
(property of R. Leis & family)

Secur-O-bot

Commercially available security robot for public / professional use

Institute / Company: Fraunhofer IPA and Neobotix

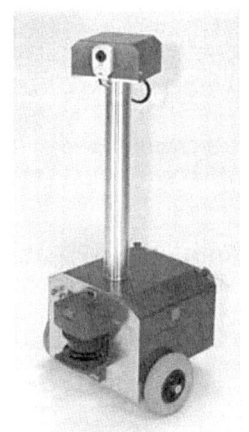

"Secur-O-bot"
Picture courtesy of
Fraunhofer IPA Stuttgart
/ Germany

Japanese Robot Projects

Project / Name Company / Institute / Research Group	Picture
Actroid Android robot with the ability to display facial expressions and move its torso, arms and hands. Used for PR-work, film and entertainment. **Company:** Kokoro Co., Ltd.	"Actroid" as attendant Photo: Miriam J.S. Leis at: Aichi Expo 2005, Japan
AIBO Most sophisticated commercially available interactive dog-like Entertainment Robot. (ERS-7 and ERS-311/312 available in Japan ERS-7 available outside Japan) AIBO robots are also being used as research platforms and compete at *RoboCup* (four-legged league). **Company:** Sony Corporation	ERS-111 ERS-210 ERS-220 ERS-311 & ERS-312 ERS-7 Different AIBO models All photos by Miriam JS Leis, 2003 – 2005

D-5

ASIMO

Humanoid robot with human-like biped walking (and "jogging") ability used for corporate promotion, public relations and entertainment. Mid-/ to long term goal is the deployment of ASIMO as service robot for use in households, offices, public facilities etc.

(height: 120 cm – 130 cm)

Company: Honda Motors Co., Ltd.

Photo: Miriam J.S. Leis at: Robodex 2003, Japan

Banryu

Surveillance / utility robot for home- and corporate use (available for rent)

Company: Sanyo / tmsuk

Photo: Miriam J.S. Leis at: TEPIA, 2005 Japan

ifbot

Commercially available Communication- and entertainment robot

Company: Business Design Laboratory

Photo: Miriam J.S. Leis at: International Robot Exhibition 2003, Japan

Maron I / Maron II Surveillance- and utility robot for private and corporate use (available for rent) **Company / Institute:** Fujitsu Laboratories	
	Photo by Miriam J.S. Leis at: CEATEC 2003 / Japan
PaPeRo Prototype Interactive Communication robot for entertainment and information providing (home & public use) **Company:** NEC Corporation	
	Photo: Miriam J.S. Leis at: International Robot Exhibition 2003, Japan
Paro Animal-like / seal-like robot which responds to touch and voice, developed for psychological therapy and Robot Assisted Therapy (RAT), to be used especially in hospitals and nursing-care facilities. **Institute:** AIST **Project Leader:** Dr. Takanori Shibata	
	Photo: Miriam J.S. Leis at: International Robot Exhibition 2003, Japan

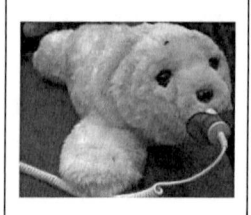

PINO

Open-source robot platform for educational and entertainment use. The source code can be publicly obtained over the internet. The robot is commercially available through ZMP, Inc.

(height: approx. 30 cm)

Chief Developer: Fuminori Yamasaki
(Kitano Symbiotic System Project at Japan Science and Technology Corp.)

Company: licensed to and sold by ZMP, Inc. / Japan

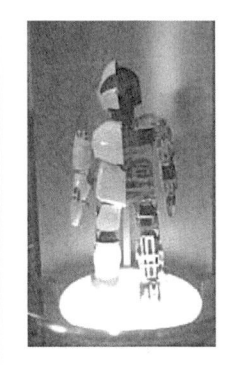

PINO:
technical demonstration model
Photo: Miriam J.S. Leis, at: MeSci, Japan 2004

Promete (HRP-2)

Prototype
Humanoid biped walking robot developed for assisting humans on the work place (especially construction and manufacturing) and in private households

(height: 154 cm)

Institute / Company: developed by a consortium consisting of NEDO, MSTC, diverse Japanese companies, universities and research institutes on an initiative by the Japanese Ministry of Economy, Trade and Industry (METI).

Foto: Miriam J.S. Leis at: International Robot Exhibition 2003, Japan

QRIO Prototype Humanoid Entertainment Robot with biped walking (and "jogging") ability, used for entertainment, PR-work and corporate promotion (height: approx. 58 cm) **Company:** Sony Corporation	**No Picture Available**
SAYA Prototype Android robot (head and torso) with the ability to mimic human facial expressions **Institute:** Tokyo Science University	Photo: Miriam J.S. Leis at: Robodex 2003, Japan
Tmsuk04 Prototype in public test phase, (quasi)humanoid surveillance- and utility robot **Company:** tmsuk, Inc.	Photo: Miriam J.S. Leis at an apartment complex in *Nishi Oi*, Tokyo 2004

Toyota Partner Robot(s) Prototype(s) Humanoid robots with biped walking ability and wheeled (quasi)humanoid robots. Currently used for entertainment, PR-activities and corporate promotion. Mid-/ long term goals: service and assistance in private households, offices and public areas **Company:** Toyota Motor Corporation	**No Picture Available**
"Wakamaru" (development nickname) Prototype in public test phase Personal (quasi)humanoid robot with interactive communication abilities to communicate with humans and provide assistance in private households and public areas. (height: 100 cm) (according to my information the robot could go on sale in 2005) **Company:** Mitsubishi Heavy Industries	Photo: Miriam J.S. Leis at Robodex 2003, Japan

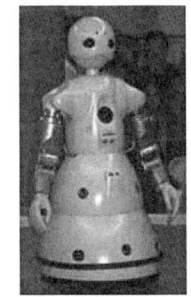

List of Acronyms and Abbreviations

AE	Artificial Emotion
AI	Artificial Intelligence
AIBO	Artificial Intelligence Robot (name for Sony's canine-like Entertainment robot)
AL	Artificial Life
ANN	Artificial Neural Networks
ASIMO	Advanced Step in Innovative Mobility (name for Honda's humanoid robot)
CAD	Computer Aided Design
CAI	Computer Aided Instruction
CAPTCHA	Completely Automated Public Turing Test to Tell Computers and Humans Apart
CPU	Central Processing Unit
DHS	Droopy Head Syndrome (AIBO-"illness", malfunction of head servo motor)
DOF	Degree Of Freedom (sometimes also abbreviated just with DF)
ERS	Entertainment Robot System (used for Sony's AIBO robots)
FL	Fuzzy Logic
HDTV	High-Definition Television
HERMES	Humanoid Experimental Robot for Mobile Manipulation- and Exploration Services (name for the anthropomorphic robot by the Universität der Bundeswehr Munich)
HRP	Humanoid Robotics Project / Humanoid Robot Platform (name for co-operative robot project in Japan)
Fraunhofer AIS	Fraunhofer Institut für Autonome Intelligente Systeme
Fraunhofer IPA	Fraunhofer Institut für Produktionstechnik und Automatisierung
LED	Light Emitting Diode
MeSci	National Museum of Emerging Science and Innovation (Japan)
METI	Ministry of Economics, Trade and Industry (Japan)
MIT	Massachusetts Instutute of Technology
MJSL	Miriam Ji Sun Leis (abbreviation used for the name of this book's author)
MSTC	Manufacturing Science and Technology Center
AIST	National Institute of Advanced Industrial Science and Technology (Japan)
NEDO	New Energy and Industrial Technology Development Organization
QRIO	Quest for Curiosity (name for Sony's humanoid robot)
RAT	Robot Assisted Therapy
RISC	Reduced Instruction Set Computer
ROBODEX	Robot Dream Exhibition
SDR	Sony Dream Robot (now renamed to "QRIO")
TCAS	Traffic Collision Avoidance System
WAMOEBA	Waseda Artificial Mind On Emotion Base (anthropomorphic robot by Waseda University Japan)

A1: Notes about Methodology

Research deadline:

Since I get new information nearly every day, leading to a situation where one could continuously revise ones work (what I have done numerous times), my research deadline had been March 20, 2005. All data, except photo / picture material and some information I have acquired during my visit at the Aichi Expo 2005, I have obtained / I will obtain after this date have not been taken into consideration for my thesis. (After March 20, 2005 I only conducted administrative work, finishing the picture data, proofreading and working on the appendix files)

A.1.1 A note about using generalized expressions:

In my thesis I sometimes use terms such as "German", "Japanese", "Western", "East Asian" etc. By using such generalized terms, of course I don not mean *every* German person, or *every* Japanese person, but want to express the observed tendency that some occurrences are more frequently found in, or are more common to one specific county and/or cultural setting instead of another. If visiting Norway for example and seeing a lot of Pizza restaurants full of people eating, many people buying Pizza from the supermarkets' wide selection, and meet a lot of people who express their fondness about Pizza, I might say that Norwegians like Pizza, although certainly not meaning that every Norwegian would like this kind of food. If, for example, this observation about Pizza-fondness can't be found in China (very few Pizza restaurants that are almost empty, only a few people buying Pizza in stores, and only a few people who say that they actually like Pizza) I may conclude that in contrast to the Chinese, Norwegians (tend to be) quite fond of Pizza.

A.1.2 A note about terms and definitions:

"Western": generally referring to the cultural area of Europe and North America that has been greatly influenced by Greek philosophy, the Roman civilization, Cartesian logic and especially the Christian religious tradition. In face of Asia's growing economic power and technological advance that is slowly becoming a serious competitor for North America and European countries, I deem it problematic, inadequate and outdated to equalize "Western" with "modern" or "technological progressive".

"East Asian": generally referring to the cultural area of China, Korea and Japan that has been greatly influenced by the (ancient) Chinese civilization and Confucian, Buddhist and, in the case of Japan, *Shinto* philosophical and religious traditions.

Abbreviations: a list of abbreviations, as well as descriptions about some of the robots / robot projects mentioned in my thesis can be found in the appendix.

A. 2 A note about my methodological approaches
A.2.1 Goal of the study

My research has derived from observations. Although in the media it is frequently talked about the Japanese' fondness about robots and other mechatronic and electronic gadgetry, I had to find out in how far the Japanese situation really differs from the German one. Indications coming from Japan, like the great number of robot-related exhibitions, television shows, robot shows, international publicity, public relations and promotional activities and commentaries made by experts and the general public, that by far did not match the activities being conducted in Germany, have led me to the conclusion that in comparison to Germany, Japan is pursuing much more efforts in publicly promoting robot technology. Starting from these observations, the main goal was in finding explanations for this. In this regard my thesis is mostly about generating hypothesis that had to be solidified through arguments based on (historical) facts, socio-cultural tendencies, observations and comments made by people. For achieving this I did an extensive literature- and media research (ranging from technical literature to science fiction, movies and Japanese manga and animé), conducted interviews and discussions (including surveys and Internet-forum discussions) with experts and non-experts (including friends and relatives) in Germany and Japan, visited robot-related exhibitions and trade fairs in both countries, and conducted small experiments in relation to phenomenological studies, interaction with *AIBO* and interest-promotion strategies.

A.2.2 Generating and testing hypothesis

I derived from the initial media-mediated assumption that in Japan much effort is put into robot related research, development and public interest promotion, which by far exceeds the situation in Germany; and that Japanese tend to show a greater positive attitude towards robots, whereas in Germany one rather tends to be skeptical. Through specific observations, interviews and discussions both assumptions look like proven generally correct, although some aspects had to be relativized. Because Japan and Germany follow different philosophies and approaches in regard to robot development, and Japan undertakes much efforts in publicly promoting robot technology, the Japanese stand of technology may get overestimated if compared to that of Germany or the US; or to put it the other way around: since especially Germany keeps a rather low profile regarding its robotics projects their stand of technology gets underestimated.

The main goal of my thesis was to find reasons for the observed differences between Germany and Japan in regard to robot related matters. Here again I derived from common explanations centered round religious belief and *"Tetsuwan Atomu"*[475], that have also been stated in interviews / discussions I have conducted, but which in my view did not suffice as explanations. Therefore I searched for other explanations, especially in regard to the question why robot technology seems to be of such great importance to the Japanese. In this context I have generated additional hypothesis that included the dimensions of history, economics and socio-cultural engineering.

Above this I also gained a deeper insight into the aspect of how Japanese people tend to regard robots and what's behind the often-encountered Japanese term of *"Partner Robot"*.

A.2.3 Data and Observations:

To find out about differences in regard to robot-related activities between Germany and Japan I performed some observations as follows:

Children's Toys / Toy Stores

Since I was accustomed to the huge amount of robot toys and toy robots in Tokyo, I also looked at toy stores / toy sections at department stores in some German major cities like Frankfurt, Köln, Munich, Stuttgart and Hanover to make a comparison. The choice of the cities was due to other activities I was carrying out there (e.g. visiting trade fairs, doing interviews, participating in meetings etc.). The data has been mostly used for my study in Part III.

Exhibitions, Showcases, Events

---

[475] A popular Japanese fictitious robot hero from a manga / animé series that is often cited as an explanatory factor for the Japanese' fondness for robots

To obtain first-hand data about German and Japanese robot related research and public promotional activities, I have also visited numerous trade fairs and exhibitions in both countries:

Germany	Japan
Symposium: From High-Tech to Intelligence - The Challenge of Humanoid Robots *Venue*: Technische Universität Darmstadt *date of visit*: June 30, 2003 *Purpose of visit*: Presentation of Honda's ASIMO robot for the first time in Germany; lectures and presentations by renowned researchers, including Prof. Dr. Christaller (director of the Fraunhofer institute).	**Robodex 2003 (World's largest and probably world's only exhibition exclusively focusing on non-industrial- and entertainment robots)** *Venue*: Pacifica Yokohama *date of visit*: April 5, 2003 *Purpose of visit*: unique and most important exhibition focusing on Japanese non-industrial robots. Getting an overview about the Japanese product palette. It also served as an important opportunity for getting in contact with researchers and representatives from the industry.
Hannover Messe 2004 (world's leading showcase for industrial technology) *Venue*: The Hannover Exhibition Center *date of visit*: April 20, 2004 *Purpose of visit*: getting an overview about technological trends in the areas of automation, IT / computer engineering and robotics; meeting acquaintances from the industry, including representatives from *Robowatch Technologies* (Germany) and *AIST* (Japan).	**Robosquare Fukuoka (Robot Edutainment Center in Fukuoka and planned future hub for robot related activities)** *Venue*: Robosquare Hakata Riverain Fukuoka *date of visit*: May 12, 2003 *Purpose of visit:* Conducting an interview with a leading representative of *Robosquare* Fukuoka and taking a look at the exhibition center.

New Permanent Exhibition about Robots at the Heinz Nixdorf MusemsForum *Venue*: Heinz Nixdorf MuseumsForum (Paderborn) *date of visit*: April 2004 *Purpose of visit*: getting an overview about the new permanent exhibition at the world's largest computer- and IT museum focusing on Artificial Intelligence and robotics [476]; discussion with Dr. S. Stein (curator).	**CEATEC (2003 / 2004)** *Venue*: Makuhari Messe (Chiba) *date of visit*: October 11, 2003 October 09, 2004 *Purpose of visit*: getting an overview about technological trends in the areas of IT / computer technology and home-use robots.
AUTOMATICA (new biannual international trade fair for assembly technology, automation and robotics, mainly directed at the industry). *Venue*: Neue Messe München *date of visit*: June 15, 2004 *Purpose of visit*: general overview, especially in regard to European / German products and visit the booth of the *Fraunhofer IPA* in regard to their products "*Care-O-Bot*™" and "*Secur-O-Bot*™"; meeting acquaintances from research institutes and the industry.	**International Robot Exhibition 2003** *Venue*: Tokyo Big Sight (Tokyo) *date of visit*: November 22, 2003 *Purpose of visit*: general overview about robotics in Japan and abroad. The exhibition was mainly directed at the industry, but also included a wide array of research platforms and robots for non-industrial / home use.
AIBO Meeting Germany (annual meeting (since 2003) of Germany-speaking AIBOwner's and interested persons, organized by the German-speaking AIBO-community *Venue*: Holiday Inn Belfortstraße / Köln *date of visit*: November 20, 2004 *Purpose of visit*: getting to meet "AIBOwners", friends and acquaintances I knew from being a member of the Internet-based German / German-speaking AIBO-	**TEPIA: "Robot and Near Future Home –Innovative technology vitalizes Japan"** *Venue*: TEPIA Plaza (Tokyo) *date of visit*: Feb. 27, 2004 *Purpose of visit*: Personal guided tour through the exhibition with demonstrations and explanations about Japanese robots / robot projects and future-concepts for non-industrial- and home use. Special features have been robots for surveillance, care assistance,

---

[476] I also did some voluntary research for the museum

forum www.aibo-freunde.de (Forum-members have also provided me with helpful information about *CeBIT* 2004, *CeBIT* 2005 and *RoboCup* German Open which I was not able to visit.)	communication and entertainment.
Others: visit at *Deutsches Museum München*, where there are some exhibits about computers, mechanical automata and industrial robots on display, together with some historical information.	**Project X21 (exhibition about Japan's history of inventions, technology and innovation)** *Venue*: Tokyo Dome Prism Hall (Tokyo) *date of visit*: August 2004 (two visits) *Purpose of visit*: obtaining information about Japanese history of technology and the general portrayal of technology in Japan; robot shows, including Sony's *QRIO*, Honda's *ASIMO* and security robots from *SECOM*.
	Others: Robot shows / performances at the National Museum of Emerging Science and Innovation / Tokyo (Robot shows of *ASIMO* and *AIBO*), Honda Showroom / Tokyo (Demonstration of *ASIMO*), Sony Building / Tokyo (Exhibition about *QRIO* and AIBO demonstration).

A.2.4 Interviews and discussions:

To obtain first hand information, data and opinions about various aspects regarding robot technology in Germany and Japan, I also got the opportunity for personal interviews[477] and discussions with researchers, representatives from the industry and public facilities, clerics, friends and acquaintances. Details are listed in the following table. Special Thanks to all for their cooperation[478].

Definitions:

Formal guided (face-to face) interview: a face-to-face interview that is oriented on the interviewer's question catalogue, but remains flexible and renounces standardized questions and answers. Although the planned main questions of interest should be brought up (they may be reformulated during the interview depending on the development of the interview), the respondent possesses great freedom in formulating ones answer. In dependence of the situation, also new questions may be brought up or planned questions may be skipped. Most of the formal guided interviews have been conducted to get first hand information about specific robot related projects.[479]

Informal guided (face-to-face) interview: principally the same as the formal guided interview, only with the difference that the setting has been more colloquial, since the respondents have been friends or well known acquaintances. Also the question catalogue has been even vaguer than that for the formal

---

[477] The question catalogue and a short summary of the interviews conducted at *Robosquare Fukuoka, Fraunhofer IPA, Mitsubishi Heavy Industries* and with Rev. Arvalis, Prof. Aoki, Rev. H. Amerigo and Manfred A. (former nursing care worker) can be found at the appendix.
[478] A list of individuals and corporations who contributed to my work has been printed on the page prior to this introduction.
[479] Note: the respondents were asked about their consent of allowing the taping of the interview prior to the beginning of questioning. Tapes are available for the interviews at *Mitsubishi Heavy Industries, Robosquare Fukuoka* and the *Fraunhofer IPA*

guided interview. Most of the informal guided interviews have been conducted in order to generate hypothesis[480].

Discussion: in most cases informal conversation about a specific topic (in this context robotics). The discussions have not been structured, but have been quite interesting for generating hypothesis.

Internet Forum Discussions: discussions initiated through Internet forums (in this case www.aibo-freunde.de), where a question, thought or argument is posted (written onto the forum's virtual blackboard), while everybody may comment on this.

Formal guided face-to-face interviews
(the real names of the interview partners have been changed for this publication[481])

Germany	Japan
Fraunhofer IPA (Fraunhofer Institute for Manufacturing Engineering and Automation)	**Robosquare Fukoka (Robot Edutainment Center)**
Date: September 30, 2003	*Date*: May 12, 2003
Institute: Fraunhofer Institute	*Institute*: Robosquare Fukoka (Robot Edutainment Center)
Respondent: Dipl. Inf. *Graf* (Information Scientist)	*Respondent*: Mr. *Shinkawa* (Chief Investigator) Mr. Takashima S. (English translation)
Purpose of Interview: to get information (project development, financing, motivation / idea) about the *Care-O-Bot* ™ project (care assistance robot under development at the Fraunhofer IPA), ask about the respondent's opinion regarding the development of robot technology and its public acceptance in Germany and hear comments on Japanese robot technology.	*Purpose of Interview*: to get information (project development, financing, motivation and future planning) about the *Roboquare* project. It was also meant to provide me with an insight about the Japanese "robot culture", general view about robots, the ideas of robot-related education, political support and public interest promotion

---
[480] No tape transcript available
[481] The original data is available at University of Konstanz (Germany)

Much of the data has been used for my project comparison study between the German *Care-O-Bot*™ and the Japanese *"Wakamaru"*. The main purpose was to obtain first-hand data for the project-comparison analysis and get to know an expert's opinion in order to generate and reflect on hypothesis. *Comment*: Short summary to be found at appendix (in German). I had numerous contacts and discussions (mostly via e-mail) with Ms. Graf afterwards and also met her at *AUTOMATICA* and even in Japan. Data from the Interview can be found in Part III of my analysis.	strategies. The main purpose was to obtain project data and get to know an expert's opinion in order to generate and reflect on hypothesis. *Comment*: Short summary to be found at appendix (in English). The respondent wanted to do the interview in Japanese, so we worked with an English translator[482]. Data from the Interview can be found in Part III of my analysis.
Heinz Nixdorf MuseumsForum Date: May 2003 Institute: Heinz Nixdorf MuseumsForum Respondent: Dr. Stefan Stein (Curator at the Heinz Nixdorf MuseumsForum in charge of the exhibits about Artificial Intelligence and robotics) Purpose of Interview: Since I knew about the German robot- and AI-related exhibition "Computer.Brain" at the Heinz Nixdorf MuseumsForum (HNF)/ Germany, held from October 24, 2001 until April 28, 2002, but due to work and final examinations didn't have the chance for a visit, I have contacted Dr. S. Stein, who had the courtesy of taking some time for a personal interview and discussion about German activities in the area of robotics, and telling me about the Computer.Brain exhibition. Aside from obtaining some inside information and to hear about how robots and robotics are	**Mitsubishi Heavy Industries, Ltd.** *Date*: November 17, 2003 *Institute*: Mitsubishi Heavy Industries, Ltd. (Machinery Headquarters) *Respondent*: Mr. *Suzuki* (Manager) *Purpose of Interview*: to get information (project development, financing, motivation / idea) about the *"Wakamaru"* project (household assistance- / service robot) and ask about the respondent's opinion regarding the development of robot technology and its public acceptance in Japan. Much of the data has been used for my project comparison study between the Japanese *"Wakamaru"* and the German *Care-O-Bot*™. The main purpose was to obtain first-hand data for the project-comparison analysis and get to know an expert's opinion in order to generate and reflect on hypothesis. *Comment*: Short summary to be found at appendix (in English). Data from the

---

[482] Although I speak Japanese, I found it more comfortable to also have an interpreter.

tended to be regarded in Germany, I was also provided with helpful information about German robot platforms and research projects. The main purpose for this interview was to get some information about robotics in Germany. Comment: It was a rather unstructured interview, based on mutual interests in regard to obtaining cross-cultural information. It has been rather a guidance and discussion than an interview. I remained in contact with Dr. Stein and did some voluntary work for the Heinz Nixdorf MuseumsForum. Data from the interview can be found mostly in Part III of my thesis (and to lesser extend also in Part I).	Interview can mainly be found in Part III of my analysis (other references have also been made in Part II.).

Informal guided (face-to-face) interviews

Germany	Japan
Heilig Geist Kirche Reichenau (German protestant church in Germany) Date: August 11, 2003 Institute: Christian Church (protestant) Respondent: Rev. Dr. *Amerigo* 　　　　　　　　*(name changed)* Purpose of Interview: to obtain the view from a German Christian cleric living in Germany (as a comparison to a German Christian cleric with Japan-experience), in regard to robotics and technology. The interview was rather unstructured / open and was used for hypothesis generation- and reflection.	**Kreuzkirche Tokyo (German protestant church in Japan)** Date: October 15, 2003 Institute: Christian Church (protestant) Respondent: Rev. -*Aoki* 　　　　　　　　*(name changed)* *Purpose of Interview*: to obtain the view from a German Christian cleric living in Japan since 1999 in regard to robotics and technology. The interview was rather unstructured / open and was used for hypothesis generation- and reflection.

Comment: Short summary to be found at appendix (in German). Some of the obtained data has been influential for writing Part I of my thesis (please refer to the according footnotes).	*Comment*: Short summary to be found at appendix (in German). The respondent has specialized in pastoral care and is a close acquaintance. Some of the obtained data has been influential for writing Part I of my thesis (please refer to the according footnotes).
Former nursing care worker *Date*: September 5, 2003 *Institute*: undisclosed nursing care facility in Germany *Respondent*: Mr. Misenus (name changed; close acquaintance and former nursing care worker) *Purpose of Interview*: to get an insight view about the work at a nursing care facility (out of personal interest in relation to my study), and to hear about the respondent's opinion about automated care assistance / care-assistant robots *Comment*: the respondent asked me to remain anonymous. Because he is a rather close acquaintance, the interview was rather informal. Some data from this interview can be found in Part III of my thesis.	**View of a Japanese Christian Humanities Professor** Date: November 13, 2003 *Institute*: Japanese University *Respondent*: Prof. Aoki (name changed) (Humanities Professor) *Purpose of Interview*: to obtain the view from a Japanese Christian (and professor of humanities) in regard to robotics and technology. The interview was rather a discussion and was used for hypothesis generation- and reflection. *Comment*: Short summary to be found at appendix (in German). Data from the Interview can be found in Part I and Part III of my analysis.

Other activities:
Above this I also had some informal conversations about the topic of robotics with some friends, relatives and acquaintances. Although these discussions were unstructured, they nonetheless might have been influential to my work. Of major interest have also been the Internet forum discussions of the German *AIBO*[483] community (www.aibo-freunde.de)[484]. Here I have also conducted a small survey to get some insight about how German / European *AIBO* owners regard their robot "dogs". A summary of the survey and the statistical raw data can be found in the appendix.

Note: due to a limited time frame and resources it proofed difficult to conduct a quantitative survey about the German and Japanese attitude towards developments in robotics and Artificial Intelligence as it would have been interesting. As I have recently learned, there is a survey in progress (information from Dr. Christoph Bartneck, posted at www.aibo-freunde.de), which is assessing this subject on an international basis. Unfortunately the results which might be of great interest won't be available before I have finished my thesis.

Private activities *things I always wanted to do but had no time for doing...:
just out of personal interest and to get first-hand experience I also got privately engaged in robot-related activities, among them building a new homepage with robot-related articles and resources, assembling construction kits of replicas from mechanical automata, writing articles about the *AIBO ERS-311/312* series (and having found out that the reason for this model's rather unpopularity in

---

[483] Interactive robot „dog", developed and marketed by the Sony Corporation / Japan. More details about AIBO will be found in my analysis.
[484] Special thanks to all who answered the survey.

Germany / Europe may just be due to bad advertisement and lacking information), doing own observations in regard to the question about a "relationship development" with my *AIBO ERS-311* and having learned a lot more about informatics, Artificial Intelligence, neuroscience, robotics and the basics about how to write a C++ program.

Having been involved in writing this thesis was a great experience; multi-dimensional and interdisciplinary. I got the impression that I have learned as much about humanity as I have learned about robotics. As it is with media disks, the future belongs to versatility…

Miriam J.S. Leis (Konstanz, Tokyo, Saipan April 2003 – April 2005)

A.3 German Summary

Deutsche Zusammenfassung der Dissertationsschrift
Roboter – unsere zukünftigen Partner?!
Die Sicht eines Soziologen aus Deutscher und Japanischer Perspektive

Englischer Originaltitel:
Robots – Our Future Partners?! –
A Sociologist's View from a German and Japanese Perspective

Vorwort:

Während das 20. Jahrhundert als das „Zeitalter des Atoms" in die Geschichte eingegangen ist, so sind viele Wissenschaftler, Ökonomen und Journalisten der Ansicht, dass das 21. Jahrhundert das „Zeitalter der Künstlichen Intelligenz" sein wird. Zwar gleichen die heutigen Produkte der Künstlichen Intelligenz (KI) noch eher dem „*Flyer-3*" der Gebrüder Wright als einem *A380*, aber die Entwicklung auf den Gebieten der KI und Robotik schreitet in rasanter Weise voran. Roboter, die Protagonisten dieser Studie, haben bereits die Fabrikhallen verlassen und betreten (im wahrsten Sine des Wortes) bereits unsere Alltagswelt. Visionäre behaupten, dass bereits im Jahre 2050 KI die Fähigkeiten ihres Vorbildes, des Menschen, erreicht haben wird, oder zumindest die Chance besitzt, in einem Fußballspiel ihre menschlichen „*Templanten*" zu besiegen. Wenn Roboter die Fabrikhallen verlassen und mit menschenähnlichen Charakterzügen versehen werden, so wird dies sicherlich das Verständnis von „Sozialität" verändern und neue Fragen aufwerfen, wo die konkrete Grenze zwischen Mensch und Nicht-Mensch verläuft, eine Frage die auch in Anbetracht neuer Biotechnologien und der Verschmelzung zwischen Organismus und Maschine an Relevanz gewinnt.

Weshalb sollte sich die Soziologie mit Robotik befassen?

Weshalb sollte sich ein Soziologe / eine Soziologin mit dem Thema Robotik befassen, mit mechatronischen Maschinen, die von vielen Menschen noch überwiegend mit monotonen Arbeiten in Fabrikhallen und feindlichen Umgebungen assoziiert werden? Es wird sogar behauptet, dass Nicht-Menschen nichts in einer soziologischen Analyse zu suchen hätten. Aber mit dem Bau von Robotern haben die Menschen begonnen, Artefakte zu kreieren, die, so die Hoffnung (oder die Befürchtung – je nach Standpunkt), eines Tages wie ihr menschliches Vorbild denken und handeln sollen. Wäre es somit nicht Paradox, diese künstlichen Geschöpfe aus der soziologischen Analyse auszuschließen? Durch die reale Existenz von Robotern hat der Mensch auch ein Spiegelbild (wenn auch ein noch verzerrtes) geschaffen, welches neue Fragen über das Sein und die Position des Menschen in der (Um)welt aufwirft.

Wird die zunehmende Beschäftigung des Menschen mit Maschinen und „intelligenten" Artefakten, bei gleichzeitigem Rückgang der zwischenmenschlichen Interaktionen, zu *postsozialen* Beziehungen führen, wo zunehmend Bindungen zwischen Menschen und Objekten geknüpft werden[485]?

Wie mir wiederholt bestätigt wurde, stellt besonders in Japan die Robotik für nicht industrielle Anwendungen (bspw. im Haushalt und zu Unterhaltungszwecken) ein großes (zukünftiges) Marktpotential dar; und dies in einem Land, wo sich jetzt bereits eine steigende Anzahl von Menschen in wachsendem Maße Unterhaltungsartikeln zuwendet.

Soziologie und Robotik sind gewissermaßen komplementäre Wissenschaften, wobei beide voneinander profitieren können: Robotikforscher können durch die Erkenntnisse der Soziologen Einblicke erhalten, wie Menschen im Kontext ihrer

---

[485] Vergl. Knorr Cetina, 1997 und Callon, 1986

Umwelt und Kultur lernen, verstehen, kommunizieren und Strukturen schaffen. Die Robotik auf der anderen Seite stellt ein Testfeld zur Verfügung, in dem Soziologen (wie auch Psychologen und Biologen) Theorien testen können. Zudem ist die Robotik ein sehr interdisziplinäres Feld, welches die Gebiete der Informatik, Ingenieurswissenschaft, Physik, Mathematik, Biologie, Neurowissenschaften und Psychologie, bis hin zur Ökonomie, den Sozialwissenschaften, Kulturwissenschaften, Linguistik, Philosophie und sogar Theologie schneidet.

In meiner Analyse kann auch der „Roboter" substituiert werden, um aufzuzeigen, inwiefern historische, soziokulturelle, politische und ökonomische Aspekte die Akzeptanz und Entwicklung von Ideen formen und beeinflussen können.

Anmerkung zur persönlichen Motivation

Da ich mich als Soziologin persönlich für Technik, Technikgeschichte und Technologieentwicklung interessiere (insbesondere Biotechnologie, Hochtechnologien, Robotik und Luft- und Raumfahrt), und zudem als deutsche Staatsbürgerin in Tokyo sozialisiert wurde, habe ich mich entschieden, mich hier mit dem Thema Robotik in einem Vergleich zwischen Deutschland und Japan zu befassen. Die Ausgangsfrage hat sich aus der Beobachtung ergeben, dass mich während meiner Studienzeit in Deutschland robotikbezogene Informationen aus Japan um die halbe Welt erreicht haben, wobei in Deutschland Robotik erheblich weniger Medieninteresse auf sich zu ziehen schien. Dies hat mich insofern verwundert, da Deutschland und Japan trotz ihrer geographischen Ferne viele ökonomische und historische Gemeinsamkeiten aufweisen. Es hat mich auch verwundert, weshalb die Idee der Robotik, die weder die Umwelt verschmutzt, noch Gesundheitsschäden hervorruft, in Deutschland noch mit relativ hoher Skepsis betrachtet wird. Aus diesem Grunde habe ich mich entschlossen (unter anderem) der Frage nachzugehen, weshalb in Japan die allgemeine Interessensförderung auf dem Gebiet der Robotik von vergleichsweise hoher Relevanz zu sein scheint.

Miriam JS Leis (Konstanz, Tokyo, Saipan: April 2003 – April 2005)

Arbeit und Methode

Planung: da sich Hochtechnologien (inkl. Robotik) ständig weiter entwickeln, und jeden Tag Informationen über neue Entwicklungen eintreffen, was dazu führt, dass die Analyse ständig revidiert werden kann, habe ich mir die Frist gesetzt, alle Daten, die nach dem 20. März 2005 eintreffen, in meiner Analyse nicht mehr zu berücksichtigen (Ausnahmen stellen Fotomaterial und Informationen dar, die ich auf der Aichi Expo 2005 gewonnen habe). Nach dem 20. März 2005 bestand meine Arbeit überwiegend aus rechtlichen / verwaltungstechnischen Angelegenheiten (Copyrightsfragen), Bearbeitung des Fotomaterials und Korrekturlesen.

Anmerkung zur Vorgehensweise:

Generell habe ich mich von den im Folgenden aufgeführten Fragen leiten lassen und der generellen Annahme, dass Japan viel mehr Energie in Projekte der Robotikforschung zu stecken scheint, als dies in Deutschland zu beobachten ist; eine Annahme, die es zu überprüfen und zu erklären galt. Mit Hilfe von Literaturrecherche, eigener Erfahrung, eigenen Beobachtungen, Interviews und Diskussionen verschiedener Art, die ich in Japan und Deutschland mit unterschiedlichen Personenkreisen durchgeführt habe, habe ich versucht in dieser Arbeit sowohl Hypothesen zu generieren, als auch geläufige Annahmen zu überprüfen und gegebenenfalls zu revidieren, oder zu relativieren. Zu meinen Aktivitäten gehörten u.a. der Besuch von robotik- und technikbezogenen Messen, Ausstellungen und Events in Deutschland und Japan, Beobachtungen in deutschen und japanischen Spielzeugläden-/Abteilungen, und die Durchführung von formalen und informellen Leitfadeninterviews und Diskussionen (sowohl Face-to-Face als auch in Internet Foren) mit deutschen und japanischen Vertretern aus der Industrie, Forschung, Bildung, Kirche und Öffentlichkeitsarbeit und meinem Freundes- und Bekanntenkreis[486].

Anmerkung zu Begriffen und Verallgemeinerungen:

Wenn ich in meiner Arbeit Begriffe wie „Japaner", „Westen", „Ostasien" etc. (bzw. deren englische Bezeichnungen) verwende, meine ich natürlich nicht alle „Japaner", „Deutschen", „Personen aus westlichen Ländern", sondern möchte nur eine vergleichende Tendenz aufzeigen.

Definition „Westlich": unter „Westlich" verstehe ich in meiner Analyse den kulturellen Raum Europas und Nordamerikas, dessen Kultur stark von der griechischen Philosophie, der römischen Zivilisation, kartesianischer Logik und (der) christlichen Tradition(en) geprägt wurde. In Anbetracht der wirtschaftlichen Entwicklung erachte ich es als unangebracht, „westlich" mit „technologisch fortschrittlich" oder „modern" gleichzusetzen.

Definition „Ostasiatisch": Hier beziehe ich mich generell auf das kulturelle Gebiet welches China, Korea und Japan umfasst und großteils von der (alten)

---

[486] Details hierzu finden Sie in der englischen Version

chinesischen Zivilisation, dem Konfuzianismus, dem Buddhismus und im Falle Japans vom *Shintoismus* geprägt wurde.

Forschungsfragen und Zusammenfassung der Ergebnisse:

Da die Robotik, sowie auch die Soziologie hoch interdisziplinäre Gebiete darstellen, habe ich mich entschlossen, meine Arbeit in 4 Teile (Themengebiete) aufzuteilen, die jeweils eine unterschiedliche Schwerpunktsetzung enthalten. Es waren hauptsächlich die Forschungsfragen, die im Folgenden aufgeführt werden, welche mich durch meine Arbeit geleitet haben.

Im Folgenden werde ich die Fragen der einzelnen Teile und eine Kurzzusammenfassung der Ergebnisse darstellen.

D-

Teil 1: Die Geschichte der Robotik „in der Nussschale"

Fragen:
- Wo liegt der Ursprung der Idee, „Roboter" zu bauen?
- Welches sind die soziokulturellen, religiösen, historischen und ökonomischen Umstände, welche die Einstellung der Menschen gegenüber Robotern in Japan und Deutschland geprägt haben?
- Wie wird „Roboter" in Japan und Deutschland definiert?
- Wo, wann und warum wurden die ersten (Industrie)roboter eingesetzt und welche sozio-ökonomischen Konsequenzen hat dies nach sich gezogen?

Der erste einleitende Teil meiner Arbeit verfolgt die Geschichte der vom Menschen erschaffenen künstlichen Entitäten, der lebensimitierenden

Automaten und Roboter in ihren Wurzeln im östlichen und westlichen Kulturkreis. Bereits in antiken Mythen ist die Rede von künstlichen menschenähnlichen Entitäten, die in Form von metallenen Riesen, *Golems* und *Homunkuli* ihre Dienste verrichten und oftmals auch als eine Bedrohung für den Menschen dargestellt werden. Mit den Fortschritten, die in den Naturwissenschaften und deren praktischen Anwendung (Technik/Mechanik) erzielt wurden, ist es dem Menschen gelungen, selbst diese Gestalten aus der Mythologie und phantastischen Romanen zu kreieren, wobei erstaunlicherweise die Blütezeit dieser lebensimitierenden Automaten in Europa und in Japan koinzidierte. Trotzdem können Unterschiede zwischen den Europäischen mechanischen Automaten und ihrem japanischen Äquivalent, den sog. „*Karakuri Ningyo*", festgestellt werden. Während es in Europa das Ziel zu sein schien, in den Automaten Leben und Emotionen zu simulieren, ging es in Japan eher darum, Leben in abstrahierter Form zu symbolisieren und Emotionen zu erwecken, eine Philosophie, die sogar heute noch in japanischen Robotern ersichtlich ist.

Es wird vielfach erwähnt, bspw. in Medienberichten, dass Japans anscheinende positive Einstellung gegenüber Robotern und Automaten und Europas eher skeptische Haltung diesbezüglich ihre Ursachen in den jeweiligen religiösen Traditionen hat: animistischer *Shintoismus* vs. Christentum. Während die jeweiligen religiösen Traditionen sicherlich einen Einfluss auf Menschenbildsvorstellungen und die damit verbundenen den Menschen betreffenden Technologien haben (insbesondere Biotechnologie, aber auch Robotik), so halte ich aber einen voreiligen, kurzgeschlossenen Determinismus, der besagt, dass bspw. Japaner Robotern gegenüber eine positive Haltung einnehmen, da sie diese als „beseelt" betrachten, während in Europa die christlichen Vorstellungen der Erschaffung von „künstlichen

Menschen" hindernd gegenüber stehen, für übereilt. Der Roboter wurde im christlichen „Westen" (USA) erfunden und animistische Vorstellungen, d.h. der Glaube an die mögliche „Beseeltheit" von nicht-organischer Materie könnten doch auch gerade dazu führen, dass ein Roboter hier mit noch größerer Furcht betrachtet wird, da sein mögliches Gefahrenpotential in einer solchen Vorstellung nicht nur auf technische Fehlfunktionen, sondern auch auf ein gewisses Maß an „Eigenständigkeit" zurückgeführt werden kann. Und in der Tat beschäftigt sich die moderne japanische Science-Fiction zunehmend mit der Frage nach der „Seele" in Puppen, Automaten, Robotern und Cyborgs (die prominentesten Beispiele bilden Mamoru Oshii's „Ghost in the Shell" und „Innocence".)

Die eigentliche Geschichte der real existierenden Roboter im Sinne programmierbarer, computergesteuerter Maschinen, welche in der Lage sind Bewegungen im 3-dimensionalen Raum durchzuführen, begann mit der Erfindung des Computers und integrierter Schaltkreise (IC). Dabei ist in Hinblick auf den historischen Hintergrund die Industrialisierungsgeschichte, die um 1760 in Großbritannien ihren Ausgang hatte, von ebenfalls beachtenswerter Relevanz. Unterschiede zwischen dem europäischen und japanischen Industrialisierungsprozess und den damit verbundenen sozialen und sozioökonomischen Folgen scheinen grundlegende Auswirkungen auf die jeweilige landesspezifische Technikakzeptanz zu haben, wobei meine Analyse bei einer anderen Perspektive als der des unproblematischen Industrialisierungsprozesses Japans ansetzt. Obwohl Japans Industrialisierung recht spät eingesetzt hat und nicht die sozialen und philosophischen Entwicklungsstufen des westlichen Prozesses durchlief, wäre es falsch zu behaupten, dass die Industrialisierung in Japan keine gesellschaftlichen Probleme mit sich brachte, wie es derweilen oberflächlich behauptet wird. In Hinblick auf Japans Modernisierungs-/ und Industrialisierungsprozess ist ein wichtiger Aspekt zu nennen: Die Landung der sog. „*Schwarzen Schiffe*" des amerikanischen Commodore Perry, welche Japans freiwillige „Isolationspolitik" (wobei Japan während dieser Zeit Handelsbeziehungen zu China, Korea, den Niederlanden und dem heutigen Okinawa unterhielt) beendete. Dies war insofern ein einschneidendes Ereignis in der japanischen Geschichte, da dort Japan zum ersten Mal konkret mit einem (militär)technisch überlegenen Gegner konfrontiert wurde. Gewissermaßen wurde sich Japan hier seiner (relativen) Rückständigkeit – zumindest auf dem Gebiet der Militärtechnik und maschinellen Industrialisierung – bewusst, was für das stolze Volk einer Beleidigung nahe kam. Diese Ereignisse führten zu einer kompletten politischen Neuorientierung (Auflösung des *Shogunats* und die Einsetzung der *Meiji-Regierung*) und einem exzessiven, nationsweiten Modernisierungsprogramm unter dem Motto „*fukoku kyohei*": ein reiches Land und ein starkes Militär. Somit rückte die Beschäftigung mit Technologien ins Zentrum japanischen nationalen Interesses, was sich bis heute in mangelnder Technikkritik und einer großen Technologiepromotionsmaschinerie zeigt. Technik wurde zum nationalen Symbol und Ziel Japans erklärt und alles, was Technik in einem negativen Licht oder mit Ambivalenz darstellen könnte, wird in Japan als schädlich für die Ökonomie betrachtet, einer Annahme, die durch Japans Erfolg v.a. im Bereich der (Unterhaltungs)elektronik ihre Bestätigung findet. Somit ist der „Roboter" mehr als bloßes Forschungsobjekt: er ist gleichzeitig Symbol für Japans Zukunft und die japanische Identität.

Teil 2: Menschen, Maschinen und Gesellschaft

Fragen:

- Inwieweit hat sich das Menschenbild im Kontext wissenschaftlicher Erkenntnisse und technischer Fortschritte (bspw. Biotechnologie, Computertechnologien und KI) gewandelt?

- Kann man die wachsende Menge von Artefakten, die bereits gewisse Merkmale und Qualitäten mit dem Menschen gemeinsam hat, noch als „reines Objekt" (oder wie Latour es bezeichnet „*pure object*", Latour, 1993) bzw. Gegenstand bezeichnet werden?

- Betrachten Japaner und Deutsche Objekte in gleicher Weise?

Wenn Menschen Artefakte wie Roboter kreieren, die Charaktereigenschaften mit ihren menschlichen Vorbildern teilen, so stellt sich die Frage, wo sie in der Welt platziert werden.[487] Die Problematik ist aber symmetrisch und betrifft auch die Stellung des Menschen, der zunehmend als bloße Maschine angesehen wird, eine Vorstellung, die in radikaler Form bereits Mitte des 18. Jahrhunderts von Julien Offray de La Mettrie (vergl. La Mettrie, 1991 [1747]) vertreten wurde. Fest scheint jedoch zu stehen, dass die Frage nach dem Wesen des Menschen weder in den Naturwissenschaften, noch in der Philosophie und den Religionswissenschaften eindeutig geklärt werden konnte. Sollten einigen optimistischen (oder pessimistischen – je nach Standpunkt) Prognosen zufolge im Jahr 2050 Roboter existieren, die sich prinzipiell nicht von ihrem menschlichen Vorbild unterscheiden, würde dies ein Beweis darstellen, dass „Menschsein" lediglich nichts weiter bedeutet, als eine bestimmte Architektur und die richtigen Programme? Kritiker würden behaupten, dass alles trotzdem

---

[487] Vergl. Latour, 1995

nichts als eine Simulation bliebe – wie „*Die Matrix*" eine schwer zu widerlegende These. Aus meiner Sicht geht es in der KI-Kritik nicht in erster Linie um den Bau lebensimitierender Maschinen (etwas, was viele KI-Kritiker ohnehin für unmöglich halten), sondern um die Degradierung des Menschenbildes. Mit Fortschreiten der wissenschaftlichen Erkenntnisse und des technologischen Fortschritts schrumpft der Unterschied zwischen dem Menschen und anderer organischer und sogar nicht-organischer Materie. Die Grenzen, die den Menschen als „Krönung der Schöpfung" von anderen Kreaturen abgehoben haben, verwischt zusehends. Da sich viele der

wissenschaftlichen Annahmen in der Genetik oder den Kognitionswissenschaften bereits durchgesetzt haben, ist es schwierig, die dadurch verschwommenen Grenzen wieder herzustellen. Somit müssen neue Kriterien gefunden werden, um die führende Position des Menschen zu definieren. Dies ist zum einen in der Entwicklung des Intelligenzbegriffs zu sehen, der sich zusehends von rein logischen Denkfähigkeiten (ein Gebiet auf dem die KI bereits dem Menschen überlegen zu sein scheint) zu Konzepten wie „Emotionaler-" , „Kreativer-" oder „Sozialer Intelligenz" hin verschoben hat (Aspekte, mit denen sich Maschinen noch schwer tun). Ein weiteres Argument betrifft die Simulation: egal, wie menschenähnlich die Maschine auch sein mag, sie bleibt (per Definition) lediglich eine Simulation des Originals.

Eine vorgeschlagene Methode, um Menschen von Computern / Robotern zu unterscheiden ist der sog. „Turing Test" (benannt nach dem englischen Mathematiker und Kryptographen Alan Turing). Da dieser Test anthropozentrisch ist, misst er aber meines Erachtens nach nicht, ob eine Maschine als intelligent bezeichnet werden kann, sondern lediglich inwiefern die menschlichen Annahmen über den Menschen valide sind.

Technologie hat aus dem *Mängelwesen* (Gehlen, 1988 [1940]) Mensch ein Alleskönner gemacht, ein Geschöpf welches inzwischen in der Lage ist, seine weitere Evolution selbst zu determinieren (so zumindest die Hoffnungen und Ansichten der immer größer werdenden Anhängerschaft der „Transhumanisten"). Somit hat man zwei Entitäten auf einem Spektrum geschaffen, die sich in der Mitte zu begegnen scheinen: den technisierten Menschen (*Cyborg*) und den menschenähnlichen Roboter. Ist somit eine Aufspaltung der Welt in „Objekte" auf der einen Seite und „Subjekte" auf der anderen gerechtfertigt, eine Frage die sowohl Latour (Latour, 1993) als auch Philip K Dick (Autor des Buches, das als Basis für Ridley Scott's „*Blade Runner*" diente) beschäftigte. Zudem ist eine immer komplexer werdende Interdependenz zwischen Menschen und technischen Artefakten festzustellen, Artefakten deren Anweisungen man lieber Folge leisten sollte, wie die Flugzeugkollision im Raum über Überlingen im Jahr 2002 verdeutlicht hat (*TCAS*). Wo platziert man „Objekte" wie den humanoiden Roboter *ASIMO* (Honda Corporation / Japan)? Ich habe einen auf dem Konzept der „*Fuzzy Logic*" basierenden Vorschlag erarbeitet, der es ermöglicht, einer Entität innerhalb einer kontinuierlichen „Subjekt-Objekt" Skala „sowohl-als-auch" Attribute zuzuordnen. Dieses Konzept habe ich sowohl Deutschen als auch Japanischen Personen vorgelegt und anschließend mit den Respondenten darüber diskutiert. Interessanterweise war fast allen Deutschen befragten das Konzept der „*Fuzzy Kodierung*" fremd und sie haben auch Entitäten, die meines Erachtens einen Grenzfall darstellen (wie bspw. Cyborgs und humanoide / androide Roboter) eindeutig nach den Kriterien „lebend" (Subjekt) und „nicht-lebend" (Objekt) kategorisiert. Meine Darstellung einer „sowohl-als-auch" Entität war ihnen fremd. Anders in Japan. Erstaunlicherweise war auch hier mein Konzept weitgehend unverständlich, aber wie sich nach Diskussionen herausgestellt hat, aus dem Grunde, da in Japan das Konzept einer Aufspaltung der Welt in „Objekte" und „Subjekte" prinzipiell fremd zu sein scheint. Japaner vertreten eine eher „holistische" Vorstellung, in der „Subjekt" und „Objekt" nicht als Gegensätze angesehen werden.

**Teil 3: Roboter – Unsere zukünftigen Partner?! –
Ein Vergleich zwischen Deutschland und Japan.**

Fragen:

- Warum wird Japan und nicht Deutschland als „Königreich der Roboter" („Robotik Kingdom"[488]) bezeichnet?

- Welches sind die Unterschiede zwischen Japan und Deutschland in der Betrachtungsweise bezüglich der Idee von Robotern, welche die Fabrikhallen verlassen und unseren Alltag erobern?

- Was steckt hinter Japans Image als *„Königreich der Roboter*

- Weshalb wird die Idee des Roboters in Japan so positiv aufgenommen? Gibt es einzigartige Umstände, die als Ursache für Japans Begeisterung für Roboter genannt werden können?

Japan gilt zwar als „Königreich der Roboter", aber weder religiöse noch ökonomische und soziokulturelle Aspekte geben einen definitiven Hinweis, dass dies so sein muss. Wie bereits im ersten Teil erwähnt, könnte die animistische Vorstellung der „Beseeltheit" von Gegenständen auch zu einer Furcht vor Robotern führen. Und nicht umsonst bringen hier immer noch (Fabrik)angestellte ihren Industrierobotern und Maschinen Opfergaben dar, damit ihr innewohnende *„Kami"* (≈„*Geist*") beschwichtigt wird.

---

[488] s. Schodt, 1988

Auch nach dem Platzen der „*Bubble Economy*" in den 1990ern und Japans wirtschaftlichen Problemen ist es vorstellbar, dass andere Projekte bedeutsamer sind, als kostspielige Robotikprojekte, die eher lang- als kurzfristigen Nutzen bringen. Auch könnte man annehmen, dass Japans massenhafte Technisierung

(bis hin zum vollautomatisierten *Sushi*-Restaurant) einen Sättigungspunkt erreicht hat, und dass evtl. die Begrüßung durch einen Roboter keine allzu willkommene Situation darstellt. Ein allgemeiner Jugendpessimismus und Desinteresse an naturwissenschaftlichen Disziplinen, sowie die zunehmende Vereinsamung älterer Menschen schaffen keine gute Ausgangslage für die proklamierte positive Koexistenz zwischen Mensch und Roboter in Japan. Der „Pflegeroboter" wird vielleicht unabdingbar werden, aber nicht unbedingt willkommen geheißen...

Warum wird Deutschland nicht als „Königreich der Roboter" bezeichnet, wobei doch viele Spitzentechnologien deutsche Erfindungen sind (inklusive *MP3* Technologie, bahnbrechende medizintechnische Geräte und Hochtechnologien im Bereich der Luft- und Raumfahrt)? Auch im Feld der Robotik weist Deutschland fortschrittliche Technologien auf, die in Hinblick auf Pragmatik und Sensortechnologien / KI manchen japanischen überlegen zu sein scheinen. Das Hauptproblem in Deutschland scheint darin zu liegen, was auf der Hannover Messe 2004 als „Erfunden in Deutschland, aber im Ausland angewandt" beklagt wurde (s. *Transrapid*). Laut *Manager Magazin* (Online Magazin, 8. März, 2005) wird nur ca. ein Drittel aller in Deutschland entwickelten Patente praktisch umgesetzt. Es sieht so aus, als ob Reis Erfindung des Telefons und Bells Umsetzung dessen in ein Massenphänomen paradigmatischen Charakter besitzt.

Dies ist meines Erachtens auch ein Hauptgrund dafür, weshalb Japan und nicht Deutschland das Attribut des „*Königreich der Roboter*" besitzt; oder anders herum formuliert: es liegt großteils an Japans exzessiven Strategien zur öffentlichen Interessensförderung, „*Public Interest Promotion*", (ein japanisches Phänomen, welches nicht nur auf Roboter angewandt wird, sondern auch auf Kirschblüten), dass dieses Land das Image der „Robotiknation Nummer Eins" besitzt.

Welche Beobachtungen haben mich zu dieser Annahme bezüglich Japans geführt? Die Beobachtungen reichen von diversen öffentlichen Robotikvorführungen über eine geschickte Verknüpfung von Pop-Kultur („*Astro Boy*", Musik-Videos mit Robotern, Fan-Artikel etc.) und Robotikforschung (Ingenieure beschäftigen sich an der Universität mit dem fiktiven „Roboterhelden[489]" *Gundam*) bis hin zu dem japanischen Ministerpräsidenten Koizumi, der sich gerne in Begleitung eines japanischen Roboters zeigt, und einem japanischen Wirtschaftsministerium (METI = Ministry of Economy, Trade and Industry) das Robotikforschung zur nationalen Aufgabe Japans erklärt hat. Zudem ist in Japan, im Gegensatz zu Deutschland, die Industrie stark an der Robotikforschung beteiligt, wo die meisten großen Konzerne (bspw. Honda, Fujitsu, Matsushita, Mitsubishi, NEC, Sony, Toshiba, Toyota) Roboter u.a. als Prestigeobjekt und Symbol ihrer Fortschrittlichkeit entwickelt haben. Zudem sieht die japanische Regierung Robotikforschung als „Nationale Aufgabe" an, wobei der Roboter zum Imagesymbol und Identitätsobjekt Japans Zukunft und Fortschrittlichkeit geworden ist. Zeugnis hierfür legen bereits die Spielzeuggeschäfte ab, wo die Anzahl der Roboter und Robotermodelle alle anderen Artikel übertrifft. Auch der japanische Roboter"hund" *AIBO* der Sony Corporation hat eine große internationale Anhängerschaft gewonnen und sich zu etwas entwickelt, was man als „Life-Style-Phänomen" bezeichnen könnte. Obwohl es auch in Deutschland Bestrebungen gibt, die Popularität von Robotern in der Öffentlichkeit zu fördern, bspw. durch die ehemalige Sonderausstellung

---

[489] Eigentlich sind „*Gundams*" (Kampf)vehikel, die von menschlichen Piloten gesteuert werden. Dieses Konzept scheint hier aber auch die Entwicklung von sog. „*Power Assist Suites*" (tragbare künstliche Exosklette zur Erhöhung der menschlichen Kraft) beeinflusst zu haben.

„*Computer.Gehirn*" im Heinz Nixdorf MuseumsForum zum Thema Robotik und Künstliche Intelligenz (2001 – 2002), den Einsatz von Robotern als (Museums)führer im Museum für Kommunikation in Berlin und im Opel Center in Berlin (beide Plattformen wurden vom Fraunhofer IPA entwickelt) und die Popularisierung von „*RoboCup*" als gesellschaftliches (und nicht nur technologisches) Ereignis, existiert hier nicht die japantypische Idee von „Robotik als nationales Interesse", wobei Deutschland prinzipiell (historisch bedingte) Probleme mit der Idee eines „nationalen Interesses" bzw. einer „Nationalen Identität" aufzuweisen scheint.

„*Astro Boy*", eine beliebte, populäre positive Roboterfigur aus dem japanischen *Manga/Anime* (jap. Komik/Cartoon) wird sowohl in Japan als auch im Ausland für Japans Affinität zu Robotern verantwortlich gemacht; eine Beobachtung, die sich auch in von mir durchgeführten Interviews bestätigt hat. Bei kritischer Betrachtung der Geschichten von „*Astro Boy*" lassen sich aber auch ambivalente, oder sogar negative Interpretationen finden. Es scheint, als ob in Japan nur diejenigen Aspekte gesehen werden, die „*Astro Boy*" in Zusammenhang mit einer positiven Zukunft und Fortschrittsgläubigkeit stellen. „*Astro Boy*" hat sich zu einem „Nationalen Symbol" Japans entwickelt, welches sogar in einem CNN Werbespot der japanischen Tourismusbehörde zu sehen war. Es scheint, als ob in Japan, in der Tradition des „*Nihonjinron*" (Theorien über die Kultur Japans und deren Einzigartigkeit) nicht nur der Roboter konstruiert wird, sondern auch das Interesse an Robotik. Es scheint in Japan eine self-fulfilling prophecy zu sein: „Japaner mögen Roboter. Da ich Japaner bin, habe ich Roboter zu mögen."

Aber auch Elemente, die typisch für die japanische (und ostasiatische) Kultur zu sein scheinen, wie bspw. die hohe Bewertung von Konformität, Ritualismus und Gruppenkohärenz („Harmonie") und unangefochtene Rollenakzeptanz lassen die Existenz von Robotern in gesellschaftlichen und alltäglichen

Situationen sicherlich weniger befremdlich erscheinen, als dies dem „westlichen" Verständnis nach anmuten würde. Vielleicht mag hier der Roboter sogar Vorbildcharakter haben.

Aber auch die Vorstellung von Robotern als „Partner", wobei in hier „Partner" zwischen Familie und Freund anzusiedeln ist, scheint in Japan keine absurde Idee zu sein; in einem Land, wo man „*Benriya*" (eine Mischung aus Handwerker und Amateurpsychologen) gegen Entgelt engagiert um nicht nur eine tote Küchenschabe zu beseitigen, sondern auch um sich als Freund auf einer Feier auszugeben, oder einem nur zuzuhören. Wo ältere Frauen Kameradschaft in sprechenden Puppen und Roboter"hunden" suchen und sich junge Frauen (und Männer) sog. „*Character Goods*" (bspw. *Hello Kitty*) und virtuellen Küken (*Tamagotchi*) zuwenden, da diese ihnen positive emotionale Gefühle vermitteln. In einer Gesellschaft, die eher als Kollektion von Individuen bezeichnet werden kann, wo die Rate von „vereinsamten Menschen" beträchtliche Ausmaße annimmt, wird der „Partner Roboter" als stets unproblematischer, geduldiger, freundlicher und vertrauenswürdiger Gefährte vermutlich als willkommener Gast empfangen werden, vielleicht als Alternative und „*Risikogewinner*" („*Risk Winners*", vergl. Coleman, 1993 und Knorr Cetina, 1997) gestörter sozialer Beziehungen (ebd.). Es liegt auf der Hand, dass man in Japan versucht, soziale Probleme mit technischen Mitteln zu lösen, etwas, was sich als so erfolgreich in der Wirtschaft erwiesen hat.

Teil 4: Der Versuch einer Roboter-Phänomenologie

Fragen:

- Inwiefern können die Gebiete der Sozialwissenschaften und Robotik voneinander profitieren?
- Was sind die Unterschiede zwischen Künstlicher Intelligenz und menschlicher Intelligenz, zwischen menschlichen Emotionen und (simulierten) „E-motionen"?
- Wie ist die Aussage zu betrachten, dass es keinen fundamentalen Unterschied zwischen menschlicher und künstlicher Intelligenz gibt?

Moderne Artefakte besitzen bereits Eigenschaften, die man als *kognitiv* betrachten kann. Mein Computer bspw. überprüft meine Rechtschreibung und setzt das gesprochene Wort in Schrift um und umgekehrt. Computer schreiben ihre 'eigenen' Gedichte, 'komponieren' Musik und besiegen nebenbei Schachweltmeister bei einer Partie. Roboter 'erkennen' bereits ihren Besitzer wieder, 'lernen', sich in neuen Umgebungen zurecht zu finden und die effizienteste Route zu 'planen'. Sie spielen Fußball und 'zeigen' (besitzen???) bereits „Emotionen".

Aber sind diese anscheinend erstaunlichen Fähigkeiten (zumindest für ein Artefakt) nicht letztendlich blinde Simulationen, ebenso „blind" als wenn ich einen in phonetischer Lautschrift vorgegebenen tibetischen Text vorlesen würde, ohne seine Bedeutung zu kennen? Was ist Intelligenz?

Das Maß der künstlichen Intelligenz ist die menschliche Intelligenz, wobei auch der Intelligenzbegriff beim Menschen noch nicht hinreichend geklärt ist. Aber auch eine Betrachtung des Begriffs „künstlich" ist von Bedeutung: „künstlich" in dem Sinne von Imitation (künstliche Blumen), oder im Sinne einer künstlichen Herstellung eines letztendlich „echten" Konzepts (wie mit

Hilfe der Gentechnik hergestellter Mais)? Hieraus entwickelten sich die Konzepte der „starken" und „schwachen" KI („strong" and „weak AI"). Während es für das Attribut einer „schwachen KI" ausreichend ist, lediglich einige Charakteristika die mit der Vorstellung von Intelligenz verbunden sind zu zeigen, impliziert die „starke KI" , dass die damit ausgestattete Entität wirklich Intelligenz *besitzen* muss, was das Konzept des Verstehens beinhaltet. Computer und Roboter werden nicht sozialisiert (wobei hier Forschungsansätze bspw. am MIT mit dem Roboter *Kismet* als rudimentäre Ansätze angesehen werden können), wachsen nicht in einem kulturellen Umfeld auf und sind gewissermaßen ein „Gedächtnis ohne Geschichte". Wer es einmal versucht hat, einen Algorithmus über die Zubereitung des Morgenkaffees aufzustellen (wobei zu bedenken ist, dass einem vielleicht mal der Zucker ausgegangen ist), oder sich Gedanken darüber zu machen, wie man es formal-logisch darstellen kann, „die Gegenstände auf dem Tisch in den Kühlschrank zu räumen" (wobei die Blumenvase wohl nicht gemeint ist), wird es schnell bemerkt haben, dass Lösungen mit Hilfe von Programmierung schnell an ihre Grenzen stoßen (zumindest aufgrund ihrer Komplexität). Andererseits, wer sich einmal in einem völlig fremden Kulturkreis befunden hat, einen bekannten Gegenstand nicht erkannt hat, da er in einem unerwarteten „falschen" Kontext gezeigt wurde, oder nach dem Umräumen in der Wohnung gegen Gegenstände gelaufen ist, wird sich auch dessen bewusst geworden sein, dass auch Menschen oftmals bestimmten „Programmen" (Routinen) folgen, bis sie sich einer Krise in ihrem vorher so gut funktionierenden Schema bewusst geworden sind. Nur ist meines Erachtens das menschliche „Programm" als Resultat seiner Erfahrungen im jeweiligen soziokulturellen Umfeld zu sehen, eine Art „Kulturellen Betriebssystems" das die Wahrnehmung und den Verlauf einzelner Aktionen und Verfahrensweisen steuert. So erachten die meisten gebildeten Menschen im westlichen Kulturkreis „Beethovens 5. Symphonie" nicht lediglich als Ansammlung von Frequenzen, die mit einer bestimmten Wahrscheinlichkeit aneinander gereiht wurden, wobei einige dieser Leute japanische klassische rituelle Musik als Störung meiner Stereoanlage interpretiert haben.

Es sind auch unsere Erfahrungen und die damit verbundenen Erwartungswerte, die dazu beitragen, dass der Mensch die Welt so wahrnimmt wie er sie wahrnimmt, eine Erkenntnis, zu der sowohl Kognitionswissenschaftler als auch Phänomenologen gelangt sind, wenngleich aus etwas unterschiedlichen Perspektiven. Somit habe ich ein Gedankenexperiment aufgestellt (oder einen wissenschaftlichen Nutzen aus einem (Alb)traum gezogen), indem ich versucht habe darzustellen, wie die Durchführung komplexer Aktionen aussehen würde, wenn kein genuines Verständnis über diese durchgeführten Aktivitäten vorliegen würde; ein Gedankenexperiment, welches den Leser vielleicht annähernd in die Position eines Roboters versetzen könnte, um somit die Frage zu klären, weshalb künstliche Intelligenz oftmals noch an anscheinend einfachen Aufgaben scheitert.

Ebenso wie die Begriffe der „schwachen" und „starken KI" eingeführt wurden, kann dies auch auf den Kommunikationsbegriff übertragen werden, wobei für eine „starke" Kommunikation in jedem Fall der Aspekt des genuinen *Verstehens* (und nicht nur einer kontextuell sinnvoll erscheinenden technischen Reaktion) von Relevanz ist. So können zwar ein Roboter und ein Mensch nach Ablauf/Überschreitung einer Zeitspanne T sagen „du bist spät dran", wobei aber dieser Satz von einem Menschen gesagt mehr implizieren kann, als nur die schlichte Feststellung, dass ein Zeitraum überschritten wurde, etwas das (meines Erachtens nach) von einer Künstlichen Intelligenz (noch) nicht gewährleistet werden kann.

Heutzutage gibt es bereits Roboter, die nicht nur emotionale Ausdrücke simulieren können, sondern dessen „Verhalten" aufgrund einprogrammierter Homöostasemodelle (die Tendenz in einem System, interne Stabilität zu bewahren) gesteuert wird. So suchen bspw. viele Roboter selbstständig ihre Ladestation auf, wenn die Energie ihrer Akkumulatoren einen bestimmten Wert unterschreitet, eine Aktion vergleichbar mit der Nahrungsaufnahme bei Organismen. Forscher wie Prof. Dietrich Dörner behaupten bspw., dass Emotionen letztendlich nur Informationsverarbeitungsprozesse darstellen[490], die sich in Form von Computerprogrammen simulieren lassen, wie das Beispiel von „*Psi*", einer von Dietrich Dörner geschaffenen virtuellen Kreatur. Die Frage, ob KI wirklich Emotionen besitzen und nicht nur „E-Motionen" simulieren kann, lässt sich m.E. nach niemals eindeutig klären, schon aus dem Grunde, da ein Mensch nur den wahrnehmbaren Ausdruck einer anderen Entität als Emotion *interpretieren*, diese aber nicht selbst nachfühlen kann. „Wenn es aussieht wie eine Ente, geht wie eine Ente und quakt wie eine Ente, ist es für alle praktischen Zwecke eine Ente !?"

---

[490] Vergl. Dörner / Hille, 1995

A4. Summaries of Interview Data and Surveys

A.4.1 Summary: Interview Robosquare, Robot Edutainment Center
(Formal Guided Face-to-Face Interview; Japanese / English)

Respondent: Mr. Shinkawa
Position: Senior Representative
Translator (Japanese / English): Mr. Takashia, Sam
(Chief Planning & Coordination Dept.)

Date: 2003-05-12

Question: Could you please give an explanation about the concept and motivations behind the idea of *"Robosquare"*

S.S.: It's about providing information about robots to society, and about enabling and fostering the interaction between humans and robots. This is achieved through education, entertainment and information providing.

The final goal will be the establishment of a network structure between researchers / universities, the government and the general public.

The project is part of the Study Group: "Next Generation Robotics Research Group". About 100 organizations belong to the research group, consisting of about 20 – 30 university researchers / research groups and 60 – 70 companies.

The aim and goal of *Robosquare* is information exchange, because since the robot industry is quite new, there does not exist a real central coordinator up to now.

Question: How are your activities financed?

S.S.: *Robosquare* is financed through the City Government of Fukuoka and the industry.

Question: Could you please give an explanation about the planned establishment of network structures between researchers, engineers, educators, companies and citizens? → Why Fukuoka?

S.S.: Communication between different sectors is essential.

Why Fukoka? Fukuoka has been involved in supporting and organizing RoboCup events, that proofed very popular with the attendance of around 12 000 visitors. Also the robot industry is predicted to become the "Automobile Industry of the 21st Century", a statement being made by both, the industry and the government. That's why also the Japanese government is interested in supporting research in the field of robotics.

Also Fukuoka possesses the character of being a hub of finance and commodity design and application.

Question: What do you think are the reasons for the interest in robot-related research and development?

S.S.: The respondent gave the example of *Astro Boy* as being a great influence in regard to the popular positive image of robots in Japan. He has even shown me pictures and fan articles of *Astro Boy*, asking me if I know this character.

Mr. Shinkawa has also said that the mayor of Fukuoka is an *Astro Boy* fan himself and therefore shows great interest in robot technology and the support for *Robosquare*.

Astro Boy demonstrates clearly that humans and robots can live together, but this fictitious robot hero may also lead to too high expectations people might have about robot technology.

The image of *Astro Boy* is also changing to fit the image of the next generation and young people, since many Japanese also look at *Astro Boy* with a sort of nostalgia, reminding them on the founding times of Japan's economic boom.

Having been asked if there also exist fears in Japan associated with the development of robots, the respondent said that there also exist some fears, especially in regard to the question, what if some day robots may become superior to humans. But there is also much trust, and the assumption that robots can help mankind. Robots can also become heroes and help humans. Robots are regarded as positive, because of the potential assignment in areas like rescue operations, welfare and the medical field.

By quoting Dr. Kitano[491] the respondent told me that it is principally the same problems that concern both, humans and robots.

I have asked the respondent how he interprets *Atlas*, the negative and "bad" robot portrayed in the *Astro Boy* stories. Mr. Shinkawa explained that *Atlas* has only been negatively manipulated by humans. Therefore using robots for military purposes would induce fears. RoboCup on the other side is positive, because of the "Sports Aspect" behind it.

---

[491] A famous Japanese roboticist and founder of the "Kitano Laboratory" (remark: Miriam JS Leis)

In a short anecdote Mr. Shinkawa told me about his childhood experience where home appliances were rather seen as negative items, but later became of everyday life. In the same way robots will become part of our every day life.

Question: Interest promotion to the general public, government and the industry seems to be an important key factor for the support of R&D. Could you please tell me something about your activities for achieving this?

S.S.: Because of its scarce resources Japan is a technology oriented country. It has also been observed that the children's interest in science and technology is on the decline. Robot-making classes and practical demonstrations are therefore deemed important to counter this problem. Therefore there are robot construction courses and software development classes being conducted at *Robosquare*. Especially the aspect of practical application and "learning by doing" is being stressed.

Question: How would you estimate the general public's interest in robot-related activities? What is the image of robots?

S.S.: Especially disabled people have shown positive interest in the achievements being made in robot related research and development. The challenge therefore is to produce useful robots. Japanese believe that robots and mankind can live together, just as *Astro Boy* demonstrates.

The respondent mused, that maybe Germans are fearful about robots because they resemble knights and therefore get associated with war.

In regard to my question if he sees some connection between *Shinto* religion and Japan's stance towards robots, Mr. Shinkawa partially agreed by saying that religious aspects may have an influence on why in Japan the idea of biped robots gets greater acceptance. And he also said that the aspect of personification of robots may be of importance. Spirits and souls are often believed to be incorporated in objects and important tools. In a way, some form of alter ego is assumed to reside in some tools. Also the respondent said that Japan and Germany may possess different value systems.

Question: How far do you think should the development go, if there would be no technological limitations in creating humanoid robots?

S.S.: The respondent said that if no technological problems exist, robots might get quite human-like capacities and may even become superior in strengths and brains. But a robot would never be able to replace a human being, especially when it comes to matters of judgment. Mr. Shinkawa thinks that it would be quite difficult to enable a robot to make judgments. If judgments would be left to a robot, only logical decisions would be made, something that quite probably would lead to conflicts with humans. He gave an example about an episode from *Astro Boy*, where a robot became president of a country, making people and scientists jealous.

There are three types of robots imaginable:

- remote-controlled units
- semi-autonomous units (robots that act autonomously within a specifically set frame)
- autonomous robots with real Artificial Intelligence.

Real Artificial Intelligence may be developed in the future, but it will remain a question if humans would ever accept something superior to them.

Question: What are your dreams for the future in regard to robotics?

S.S.: The respondent said that robots can become good partners for mankind and that it is feasible to do so.

A.4.2 Summary: Interview Rev. Amerigo (name changes)

Respondent: Rev. Dr. Amerigo
Position: Pastor (protestant Church Germany)

Date: 2003-08-11

Frage: Es wird bspw. in der Presse behauptet, dass das Christentum ein Faktor ist, weshalb in westl. Industrieländern die Forschung und Entwicklung an HR (im physiolog. Sinne) nicht stark verfolgt wird. → Inwiefern würden Sie meinen, dass an dieser Behauptung etwas dran ist?

Rev. Amerigo: Es stimmt, dass es im Christentum Vorbehalte hinsichtlich der „menschlichen Schöpfung anderer Geschöpfe" gibt, die aus grundlegender theologischer und anthropologischer Überzeugung kommen:

Mensch = Partner Gottes, aber er unterscheidet sich von seinem Schöpfer

→ Der Mensch sollte sich nicht die Schöpferrolle anmaßen.

→ Die ist auch das, was in den Mythen wie „Der Zauberlehrling" als Mahnung dargestellt wird. → Selbstüberschätzung des Menschen kann zur Gefahr werden. → Auch ist der Mensch i.d.R. nicht fähig, eine adäquate Folgeabschätzung durchzuführen.

Frage: Wie steht das Christentum zur Schaffung menschenähnlicher Entitäten, wobei Robotik als etwas anderes gesehen werden muss, als Gentechnologie.

Rev. Amerigo: Wenn die künstliche Entität im Erscheinungsbild und der Intention menschenähnlich ist (bspw. menschliche Arbeit ersetzen soll), besteht „Schöpferverdacht".

Es ist aber ein Urwunsch des Menschen, dass er wie Gott sein will und sein eigenes Geschöpf erschaffen will. → Ein Roboter in humanoider Gestalt würde sehr an einen Sklaven erinnern. Ein solches Erscheinungsbild könnte zu ethisch bedenklichen Assoziationen (Sklaverei) führen und u.U. ein schlechtes Gewissen verursachen (sollte es auf jeden Fall bewirken).

Anthropomorphismus auch in unserer Kultur: Kindchenschema bei Autos, „wer sein Fahrrad liebt, der schiebt".

→ ernsthafte Technologie sollte zweckgerichtet / pragmatisch sein (bspw. das Äußere des Roboters auf ergonomische Anforderungen ausgerichtet sein.)

Frage: Wie ist die Haltung der christl. Kirche hinsichtlich Projekten im Bereich der humanoiden Robotik?

Frage: Wo sollten die Grenzen sein? Und wie sollte die Grenzziehung gewährleistet werden, wenn Grenzen nicht technischer Natur wären?

Rev. Amerigo: → Frage von Relevanz: wie gut imitiert der Roboter mich?

→ Roboter wird dann mit dem Menschen verglichen: ist der Mensch besser, wird der Roboter abgewertet, ist der Roboter besser, führt dies zu Angst beim Menschen.

→ Es kann aber auch schnell zu Ermüdungserscheinungen / Enttäuschungen kommen, bspw. „Tamagotchi".

→ Dtl.: Puppentradition: Puppe etwas besonderes, da optisch menschliche, aber dennoch nicht lebendig. → Erfahrungen mit lebensechten Puppen: unheimlich

Frage: In der Gentechnologie vertreten die Kirchen eine klare Position und haben diese auch in die Politik eingebracht. Währe ähnliches im Bereich der Robotik denkbar?

Rev. Amerigo: Kirchen würden sich gegen übermäßige humanoide Gestaltung von Robotern wenden

→ Christentum und Technik:

60er Jahre: Fortschrittsgläubigkeit → „Entgrenzung des Menschen"

→ Technik als Machtmittel gebraucht und viele negative Nebeneffekte aufgrund von Technik existent. → Roboter als Mahnmal

→ Deutschland: nicht humanoide Gestalt, sondern Ergonomie von Bedeutung.

Frage: Stellungnahme zum Aspekt hins. Pflegebereich, da viele Pflegeeinrichtungen kirchliche Einrichtungen.

Rev. Amerigo: → In Hinblick auf bloße Datenerhebung / Überwachung akzeptabel, aber es fehlt der menschliche Faktor.

Wie viel Grundpflege ist von nicht-menschlichen Entitäten durchführbar???

(in Pflegeversicherung wird Demenz nur wenig berücksichtigt)

→ Kritik: menschlicher Umgang wird zu wenig vergütet

A.4.3 Summary: Interview "Misenus" (name changed)
(Informal guided face-to-face interview, German)

Respondent: Misenus
Position: Former nursing-care worker in Germany

Date: 2003-09-05

1. Statistik / Personen / Personal:

Frage 1.1 a): *„In der Pflege wird lausig gezahlt, und gutes Personal ist Mangelware"*, was sagst Du zu diesem Satz?

M.: geringfügige Zahlung im Verhältnis zur erforderten Leistung

(Statistik: 1999: 1 Pfleger auf 9 Pflegebedürftige, Prognose 2050: 1 Pfleger auf 17 Pflegebedürftige)???

Frage 1.1b): Wie ist das aktuelle Verhältnis Pfleger : Pflegebedürftiger in der Institution, in der Du arbeitest?

M.: Definitionen:

Pfleger: Menge aller Personen, die für die Pflege der Senioren zuständig sind (außer Küchenpersonal, Zulieferern, Personen, die nur im administrativen Bereich tätig sind, Ärzte), bestehend aus **Zivildienstleistenden, Pflegern** und **Pflegefachkräften.**

Pflegefachkraft: Pfleger, die im Gegensatz zu Nicht-Fachkräften **medizinische Leistungen** erbringen dürfen (erfordert Zusatzausbildung)
- wenige Pfleger.
  ca. eine **Pflegefachkraft** auf 80 Senioren
- **offiziell ca. 1 Pfleger auf 10 Senioren,**
  aber in der **Realität: 1 Pfleger auf 15 Senioren** (da immer wieder Ausfälle)

Frage 1.1.c): Personal: Ausgebildete Pfleger, Assistenten, Zivildienstleistende

M.: Keine Zivis in Institution, da hohe Abgaben durch Zusatzeinstellungen von Personal

Frage 1.1.d): Schwere der Pflegebedürftigkeit (Pflegestufen)

M: Meister Anteil Pflegestufe II und Pflegestufe I mit Tendenz zu II

Frage 1.1.e): Kostenfaktor: Pfleger, Pflegebedürftiger (wer zahlt?)

M.: Heimplatz : 3000 Euro / Monat, Kassen tagen ca. Hälfte der Kosten (Angaben für **Pflegestufe I**, steigt Pflegestufe, steigen auch die Kosten.)

Körperliche Behinderung wird unter höherer Anwendungsberechnung aufgelistet als Demenzfälle, obwohl Demenzfälle oftmals mehr Zuwendung benötigen.

Frage 1.1.f): Problem: zu wenig Pfleger? Zu viele Pflegebedürftige?

M.: Viele Singlehaushalte führen dazu, dass mehr Personen (mit Pflegestufe 0, „0-I und und I) in Heime kommen
- Auch ein Mangel an Nachbarschaftshilfeprojekten ist ein Grund für die „Abschiebung".
- Oftmals ist es Angehörigen einfach zu unsicher, Senioren unüberwacht zu lassen
→ Heim
- Wenn Personen im Heim sind, verschlechtert sich oftmals ihr Zustand von Pflegestufe 0 (Einlieferung) auf I, oder von I auf II. (Grund: zu geringe Förderung der Eigenständigkeit)

Frage 1.2.: Wie hoch ist schätzungsweise der Anteil der Personen die mit einfacher Unterstützung in der häuslichen Umgebung bleiben könnten (Pflegestufe 1, bspw. bei Beschwerden im Bereich der Mobilität), wenn preiswerte häusliche Pflege oder Pflege durch die Familie Nachbarn etc. verfügbar wäre (bspw. nur in Hinblick auf eine prinzipielle Überwachung).

M.: In der genannten Institution: ca. 20 Bewohner von 80

2. Tätigkeitsbereich:

Frage 2.1 Schilderung des Alltags in der Pflege („typischer Alltag")

Frage 2.1 a): Haupttätigkeiten

M.:
- waschen, ankleiden
- Essen vorbereiten und reichen
- Kontrolle hins. Medikamenten- Flüssigkeitseinnahme
- Hilfestellung in der Mobilität und beim wieder finden des Zimmers
- Freizeitaktivitäten, Sport etc. (kommt etwas zu kurz wegen mangelnder Zeit)
- Prophylaxen

Frage 2.1.b): Routinetätigkeiten? → **Welche Arten von Routine?**

M.:
- Wäscheschrank auffüllen
- Medikamente kontrollieren
- Dokumentationen / Administration
- Zimmer säubern, Betten richten, etc.
- Transporte von Materialien (bspw. Essen, Kleidung, Gegenstände, Medikamente etc.)
- Kaffee / Essenstabletts reichen
- in Rollstuhl setzen, spazieren fahren

Frage 2.1.c): Kommunikative Tätigkeiten

M.:
- bleibt auf der Strecke
- zu wenig Zeit geht wegen Routine drauf
- für „Luxus" wie Spazierfahrten, Geschichten erzählen etc. bleibt wenig Zeit

Frage 2.1.d): Hauptbelastungen?

M.:
- Demenzfälle (psychische Belastung, da immer wieder gleiche Fragen und Antworten)
- Personalmangel

Frage 2.2: In welchen Bereichen müsste mehr Personal da sein / in welchen Bereichen wäre eine eingehende Betreuung wünschenswert?

M.:
- Freizeitaktivitäten kommen zu kurz:

→ entweder mehr Personal für die Routine, oder mehr Personal für Freizeitbereich (wobei ersteres billiger)

Frage 2.3: At caring-facilities such as seniors' homes or hospitals the personnel is often too occupied with doing errand and routine work like mobility assistance, transporting objects, reminding patients to take their medicine, household supervision etc., that nearly no time is left for communication with the patients.
→ Kommentar?

M.: es findet durchaus Kommunikation statt, aber weniger auf individueller Basis (Zeitmangel) (eher Gruppenpicknicks etc., wobei Koordination schwierig, es allen recht zu machen)

3. Automatisierung

Frage 3.1.a): Welche automatisierten Hilfsmittel werden in der Institution eingesetzt?

M.:
- Badelifter
- motorisierter Rollstuhl, wobei ältere Personen bei mit der Steuerung Probleme haben (insbes. hins. der Reaktionszeit)
- medizinische Geräte
- medizinische Betten (Ergonomie)

Frage 3.1.b): → weshalb, Bewertung?

M.:
- entlastet natürlich und spart Zeit, wobei Probleme mit Rollstuhl (s.o.)

Frage 3.1.c): Welche technischen / automatischen Systeme würdest Du Dir im Heim wünschen? (freier Lauf der Fantasie)

M.:
- „Tischbutler", der autonom das Essen in die Zimmer fährt und die Tabletts und andere Gegenstände reicht
- automatische Erledigung der Reinigungsarbeiten
- Scheduling / Schedulingüberwachung (bspw. in Hinblick auf Flüssigkeits- und Medikamenteneinnahme, aber was tun mit störrischen Patienten?)
- System, das die Senioren automatisch in ihre Zimmer leitet (Demenzpatienten)

Frage 3.2: Angenommen, es gäbe eine „automatisierte Lösung" die folgende Aufgaben erledigen könnte [im Interview ohne Angaben der Quelle]:

- Erledigung einfacher Alltagstätigkeiten (e.g. Anreichen und Servieren von Gegenständen, Reinigungsaufgaben, Steuerung der Hausinfrastruktur)
- Assistenz beim Gehen, Heben, Halten von Gegenständen, „Mobilität"
- Überwachungsaufgaben (Hausüberwachung, Vitalfunktionen mit Notruffunktion)
- Automatisches Scheduling (bspw. Erinnerung an Arzttermine, Medikamenteneinnahme etc.)
- Interaktivität / Kommunikation: Medienbedienung / Bereitstellung von Informationen, Kontakt und Assistenz bei Behördenangelegenheiten etc.)
- Bedienbarkeit und Kontrollmöglichkeit ohne / mit minimalen technischen Voraussetzungen möglich (Sprachsteuerung oder Symbole auf Touchscreen)

→ Einschätzung eines solchen Systems?

M.:
- generell positive Einschätzung

→ Vorteile?

M.:
- Entlastung bei Routinen

→ Welche Bedenken?

M.
- Wenn das Gerät von den Senioren selbst bedient werden soll muss es ein riesiges Display aufweisen (schlechte Augen und schlechte „Trefferquote" der Tasten)

- Senioren sind neugierig und erfassen Zusammenhänge derweilen schlecht → Spielereien mit dem System

- Rot-Grün-Blindheit als Problem

- Bedienung mit Sprachsteuerung: Dialekte und ungenaue Aussprache der Senioren

- Jetzige Generation der Senioren vielleicht etwas „technikscheu", kommende Seniorengenerationen (bspw. wir) werden weniger Probleme damit haben

- Orientierung des Systems (Senioren sind derweilen chaotisch, oder montieren Strichcodes, oder mit was auch immer Objekte, Gegenden etc. vom System lokalisiert / identifiziert werden können, ab.)

- Störrische Senioren (Senioren können derweilen genauso „monoton störrisch" sein, wie Computer / Roboter)

Exkursion: Bspw. Patient und Computer / Roboter:

C: „Es ist Zeit, Ihre Medizin einzunehmen"
P: „ich will aber nicht"
C: „Bitte nehmen Sie Ihre Medizin ein"
P: „ich will aber nicht"
C: „Bitte nehmen Sie Ihre Medizin ein"
P: „ich will aber nicht"
[....]

oder

C: „Es ist Zeit, Ihre Medizin einzunehmen"
P: „Hab ich schon"
C: „Sie haben ihre Medizin noch nicht eingenommen, bitte nehmen Sie Ihre Medizin ein"
P: „Hab ich doch!"
C: „Sie haben ihre Medizin noch nicht eingenommen, bitte nehmen Sie Ihre Medizin ein"
P: „Hab ich doch!!"
C: „Sie haben ihre Medizin noch nicht eingenommen, bitte nehmen Sie Ihre Medizin ein"
P: „HAB ICH DOCH!!!"
[...]

oder

P: *„wo woh ick no meel?"*
C: „Bitte reformulieren Sie ihre Anfrage"
P: *„wo woh ick no meel?!"*
C: „Bitte reformulieren Sie ihre Anfrage"
P: *„ei, wie oof sool ick det no frage? WO WOH ICK NO MEEL?!"*
C: „Bitte reformulieren Sie ihre Anfrage"
P: *„jets reechts mee, vedaamte Ding!"*
C: „Bitte reformulieren Sie ihre Anfrage"

(wobei es ein menschlicher Betreuer auch nicht leichter hat...)

Frage 3.2.a): Wie viele Personen des Heims könnten schätzungsweise mit Hilfe eines Systems im häuslichen Bereich verbleiben?

M.: Insbesondere, diejenigen, die mit Pflegestufe 0 bzw. „0-I" zu uns kommen. Diese Personen sind meist Verwandte von Single-Haushalten („DINK-Haushalten", Doppelverdienerhaushalten), da es den Angehörigen zu unsicher ist, die Senioren unüberwacht zu lassen, oder durch Abwesenheit einfache Hilfestellungen, bspw. im Bereich der Mobilitätsassistenz nicht möglich ist.)

Frage 3.2.b): Inwiefern würde ein solches System die Arbeit im Heim entlasten?

M..:
- a) weniger Senioren
- b) Entlastung bei Routinen, insbes. Transport

4. Kommunikation

Frage 4.1: Wenn ein solcher „technischer Assistent" allein lebende Senioren unterstützen soll, inwiefern wäre eine eigenständige Kommunikationsfähigkeit / simulierte Sozialität des „automatischen Assistenten" von Vorteil? → qualitatives Meinungsbild

M.:
- stimulierende Wirkung in Hinblick auf geistigen Erhalt (da einerseits Stimuli erfolgt und andererseits Reaktion erfordert wird)

- Problem: Flexibilität des Systems, wobei standardisierte Reaktionen / Antworten oftmals ausreichen (menschliche Pfleger tun dies auch)

- Technikakzeptanz der Senioren teilweise fraglich (Grund: nicht in dem maße technisiert aufgewachsen wie die jüngere Generation. Roboter werden für morgige Senioren (wir) wohl kein so großes Akzeptanz- und Bedienungsproblem darstellen)

Frage 4.2: Es gibt ein Konzept eines „technischen Assistenten" welches zusätzlich zu den in 3. genannten Funktionen aufweist, folgende Fähigkeiten hätte [im Interview ohne Angabe der Quelle]:

1. **It lives with family members**
   The robot lives in accordance with the day's schedules of the stored owner and the robot itself and lives together with the owner by updating the schedule based on the contact with the owner.

2. **It speaks spontaneously in response to its family members**
   Not only does the robot respond to actions from people like conventional robots but also it speaks to family members based on the information obtained from the contact with the family.

3. **It has its own role in a family**
   The robot connects itself spontaneously to the network to provide necessary information for daily life.
4. **(1) Natural and enriched communication in accordance with life scenes**
   Recognizes approximately 10,000 words required for daily life and provides topics in accordance with life scenes and communicates in a friendly manner using gestures.
5. **(2) Autonomous action in accordance with its own rhythm of life**
   The robot has its daily rhythm of life, moves in accordance with time and purpose, automatically charges its batteries and lives with family members' absent, watches out unusual cases and is convenient for the life of family members.

(source: www.wakamaru.net)

→ **Bewertung eines solchen Konzepts ?**

M. Stimulierende Wirkung in Hinblick auf geistigen Erhalt (da einerseits Stimuli erfolgt und andererseits Reaktion erfordert wird)

→ **Vorteile?**
→ **Nachteile?**

M.: Nun, wenn es technisch hinreichend funktioniert und akzeptiert wird, warum nicht. Ein solches Konzept eher etwas für zukünftige Senioren.

- Nicht als Ersatz, aber als Assistenz für Menschen denkbar

6. Zusatzfragen:

6.1: Einschätzung der Älteren Personen in der Institution in Hinblick auf Einstellung zur Technik?

M.:
→ s.o. Technik eher etwas für zukünftige Senioren, obwohl viele ja schon an Rollstühle etc. gewöhnt sind, d.h. eingebaute „Zusatzfunktionen" würden sie evtl. als „fließende Übergänge betrachten.

6.2: According to what they are saying about Germany, there is a huge shortage in personnel in the field of home-care service for the elderly and there are about 1 million people working illegally in this sector, because domestic work force is too expensive. Only illegal human labour is still affordable. (nano-Zukunftsmagazin: Dokumentation)

M.:
- Keine konkreten Informationen, aber durchaus denkbar
- Deshalb „Nachbarschaftshilfe" (Überwachung etc.) erforderlich.

→ Problem: wie finanziert und wie zuverlässig?

A.4.4 Summary: Interview Fraunhofer-Institut für Produktionstechnik und Automatisierung (Formal Guided Face-to-Face Interview; German)

Betr. Care-O-Bot ™ (Mobiles Roboter-Assistenzsystem / Home-Care-System)

Datum: 2003-09-30

Respondent:

Name: Graf, B...

Position: Dipl. Informatikerin..

Aufgabe: Programmierung des Care-o-Bot..................................

Leitfaden

1. Projekt:

a) **Initiative / Idee**
- „**Projektgeschichte"**

B.G.: Projekt im Rahmen des MOPHA-Projekts entstanden.

- Wie ist Idee für Care-O-Bot ™ entstanden?

Aus eigenen Überlegungen in Hinblick auf demographische Entwicklungen / Alterung der Gesellschaft.

- Herauskristallisierung der Vorstellungen / Vorstellungen für die Zukunft?
- Autorisierte Produktdaten für Verwendung in Diss.

b) **Einsatz**
- **Konzeptschwerpunkte ?**

B.G.: Assistenz für Senioren / Home-Care-Bereich, aber auch Verwendung der Plattform für Entertainmentzwecke (Museumsführer), aber Einsatz und Entwicklung abhängig vom Interesse der Industrie. Basisplattformen können individuell erweitert werden.

- **Projektfinanzierung ?**

BG.:
60% Industrie
10% Staat
30% Ministerium

- geplante Einsatzgebiete des Systems ?

B.G.:
Abhängig von Interessenten (der Industrie)
3 Museumsroboter im Museum für Kommunikation in Berlin.
2 Unterhaltungsroboter für Opelmuseum Berlin? Bestellt
Interesse für Industrieaufgaben
Überwachung

- **ab wann einsatzbereit / Serienreife?**

B.G.: Funktion als Gehhilfe bereits einsatzbereit, ebenso Hausinfrastruktursteuerung.

c) **Respondenz**

- **Werbung / PR-Aktivitäten (Hannover-Messe 2002 → Reaktionen?)**

B.G.: Museumsroboter haben große Publicity verursacht, aber Initialzündung ist doch eher ausgeblieben.
Allgemein ambivalent: Senioren mit Technikinteresse zeigten recht hohes Interesse und Akzeptanz an den Robotern → zukünftige Rentnergenerationen werden wohl weniger Probleme mit Robotern haben.

- Tests / Testdurchführungen mit mögl. Nutzern / Auswertungen / Bewertungen?

→ s. c)

- Erfahrungswerte / Reaktionen seitens potentieller Nutzer (Nicht-Projektbeteiligte)

→ s. c)

- Reaktionen von Pflegern / Vertretern von Pflegeeinrichtungen-/ Verbänden etc.

→ Daten aus eigenem Interview (Altenpfleger in Seniorenheim, privater Träger)

2. Motivation:

- **Persönliche Motivation für Projektbeteiligung?**

B.G.: Der Aspekt, dass Roboter im Gegensatz zu Computern etc. mit Menschen interagieren und Bewegung zeigen, hat das Interesse der Respondentin an Robotern erweckt.

- **Persönliche Vorstellungen hinsichtlich der Zukunft der Robotik (generell und in Dtl.)?**

B.G.: langfristige Planung wie bspw. in Japan in Hinblick auf Robotik nur schwer möglich.

3. Robotik Deutschland / Vergleich Japan

- **Wie relevant schätzen Sie das Feld Service-Robotik in Deutschland ein?**

B.G.: Unsichtbare Technologien scheinen in Konkurrenz treten zu können. Deutschland doch eher konservativer in Hinblick auf Technikinnovation. Hängt von Technikakzeptanz des Individuums ab

- Wie sieht es mit der staatlichen Unterstützung / Interesse in diesem Feld aus?

Auf Pragmatik und kurzfristigeren Nutzen ausgerichtet. Sollte unmittelbaren wirtschaftlichen Nutzen bringen.
IPA aber nicht so stark an Forschungspolitik gebunden

- Vorstellungen für die Zukunft der Robotik in Deutschland?

Kooperation mit Japan wäre sehr gut.

- **Weshalb keine humanoide Form in Bezug auf zweibeinige Fortbewegung? (Gegensatz zu einigen Bestrebungen in Japan)**

B.G.: Zu langer und hoher Forschungsaufwand in Relation zum kurz- bis mittelfristigen Nutzen

- Zitat: „Robots can become good partners for mankind."
- Wie würde Sie diesen Satz verstehen?

B.G.: Seltsam, da für Respondentin „Partner" auf Menschen bezogen. Roboter eher als „Assistent" betrachtet. Roboter kein Ersatz für Menschen.

- Was würden Sie in diesem Fall unter „Partner" verstehen?

BG: Partner ist menschlich

- Wer oder Was ist für Sie ein Roboter?

BG: Eine „interaktive Maschine": zwar Maschine, aber dennoch interaktiver als bspw. Haushaltsgeräte.

- Sehen Sie einen Unterschied zwischen einem Roboter, anderen Maschinen, anderen Artefakten?

BG: s.o.

4. Zuordnungstest

Dichotom

A.4.5 Summary: Interview Rev. -Arvalis (name changed)
(Informal guided face-to-face interview, German)

Respondent: Rev. Arvalis
Position: Pastor at a German-speaking Protestant congregation in Tokyo

Date: 2003-10-15

Zusammenfassung des Gesprächs

I. Kommentar zur Konstruktion künstlicher Entitäten

Arvalis: In Deutschland existiert weniger Akzeptanz in Hinblick auf AIBO, da Personen einen echten Hund vorziehen würden. In Japan wird AIBO als „Pet" vermarktet, was in Deutschland auf Unverständnis stoßen würde.

1. Zitat: „Robosquare Fukuoka"

- dass Japan im Gegensatz zu Deutschland so involviert im Bau „humanoider" Roboter ist und den Begriff „humanoid" in diesem Zusammenhang recht eng fasst (menschenähnliche Physiologie und Ansätze in AI), könnte damit zusammenhängen, dass es in Japan keine religiösen Bedenken diesbezüglich gibt, menschenähnliche Entitäten (nach)zubauen, bzw. diese auch letztendlich als menschliche Eigenschaften besitzend zu betrachten.

- dass die einzige Grenze hinsichtlich des Baus „humanoider" Roboter im technisch machbaren liegt und an der Frage, ob Menschen Entitäten akzeptieren könnten, die ihnen überlegen sind.

➤ Wie würde Ihre Antwort aus christlicher Perspektive auf die Aussagen des Japaners lauten?

➤ Wie steht das Christentum zur Schaffung künstlicher menschenähnlicher Entitäten, insbes. „humanoiden" (Dimensionen: Gestalt und kognitive Fähigkeiten) Robotern (inwiefern sind Genesis 1,26 - 27 (Gottes Schöpfungsakt) und die Aufforderung „bevölkert die Erde, unterwerft sie euch…" in diesem Zusammenhang miteinander vereinbar)

Arvalis: Wenig Interesse von deutscher Seite an humanoider Gestaltung kann durchaus auf christliche Vorstellungen zurückgeführt werden → klare ersichtliche Trennung zwischen Mensch und Artefakt.

Dass sich bspw. ein Roboter wie ein Mensche bewegen kann, wird von der Respondentin als irrelevant erachtet.

2. Roboter als „Partner des Menschen"?

Zitate:

"*our aim is to provide people with a life partner [...]*"[492].

[regarding SDR-4X: Toshitada Doi, Vice President of Sony Corporation]

"*Honda wants to create a partner for people, a new kind of robot that functions in society*"

[regarding ASIMO: quoted from an official URL from Honda Motors Co., Ltd.:

[http://www.honda-p3.com/english/html/asimo/frameset2.html]

"*The home-use robot "wakamaru" is a completely new communication partner with which you and your family can live together as a family member*"

[regarding "Wakamaru": quoted from a brochure provided by Mitsubishi Heavy Industries, Ltd. at *Robodex 2003*]

---

[492] Cited from the Internet-Archive of the „Japan Times" from 01. Januar 2003. Artikel: "Humanoid robots:
   companions or just costly toys?" from Taiga Uranka.
   http://www.japantimes.co.jp/cgi-bin/getarticle.pl5?nb 20030101a1.htm

→ **Kommentar?**

Arvalis: Roboter als "Partner" zu betrachten würde in Deutschland auf Skepsis stoßen. Es soll nämlich der Mensch lernen, das Defizit an menschlicher Kommunikation zu beheben, anstatt Maschinen als Ersatz hierfür zu schaffen.

Kommunikation durch Maschinen implementieren zu lassen würde bedeuten, den Menschen aufzugeben.

Auffällig ist die „freundliche" Gestaltung von Automaten / Maschinen in Japan, bspw. in Banken etc.

Im Christentum ist die menschliche Kommunikation von zentraler Bedeutung und wird als Ziel der Evolution betrachtet.

Interaktion zwischen Menschen wird prinzipiell interessanter als Interaktion mit Maschinen / Robotern angesehen.

In Europa herrscht das Verständnis, dass die Maschine zu dienen hat.

Dass Roboter keine Gefühle zeigen wird hier als zentraler Aspekt betrachtet.

3. Zitat: Japan Times Newsletter (Aug. 20, 2003)

30-year robot project pitched
Researchers see tech windfalls in costly humanoid quest

Japanese researchers in robot technology are advocating a grand project, under which the government would spend 50 billion yen a year over three decades to develop a humanoid robot with the mental, physical and emotional capacity of a 5-year-old human

- Ihr Kommetar?

- ➤ Wo sollte aus christlicher Sicht die Entwicklung in Hinblick auf die Robotik enden (wenn technische Aspekts kein Hindernis darstellen würde)?

- ➤ Haben sich die Vertreter der christlichen Kirchen überhaupt ernsthaft Gedanken über diese Thematik gemacht?

Arvalis: Nicht der Mensche, sondern Gott ist der Schöpfer des Universums. Auch betrachtet das Christentum solche Projekte skeptisch, da sich die Frage stellt, weshalb

Interesse für solche Projekte existiert, während es auf der Welt so viele gravierende Probleme gibt.
Technik soll Menschen helfen.

4. Stellung des Christentums zur Tendenz zum mechanistischen Welt- und Menschenbild?
(Stellung von Gott, den Menschen, der Natur und Artefakten aus christlicher Sicht? Besonderheit des Menschen?)

Arvalis: Es geht die Tendenz dorthin, Vorgänge so natürlich wie möglich zu gestalten, bspw. bei Geburten.
Es stellt sich auch die Frage, weshalb v.a. in Japan eine solche Technikfaszination vorherrscht, die für Westler derweilen zumindest in diesem Grade unverständlich ist.

5. Robotik und Gentechnologie: Unterschiede / Grenzziehungen?

Arvalis: Gentechnologie sicherlich problematischer. Respondentin sah eher keine Zusammenhänge zwischen Robotik und Gentechnologie.

II. Robotik im Pflegebereich?

2. Der zweite Aspekt betrifft die christliche Haltung in Hinblick auf den Einsatz von Robotern im Bereich der Pflegeunterstützung (im privaten Bereich, aber auch in Krankenhäusern etc. (Bspw. Projekte Care-O-Bot™ und MORPHA / Fraunhofer IPA). Dies ist insofern von Interesse, da viele Pflegeeinrichtungen von christlichen Organisationen geleitet / unterstützt werden.

Zitat: „Ärzte Zeitung, 15.11.2000":
„Skepsis in Deutschland, Begeisterung in Japan: der Pflegeroboter kommt"

Meinen Beobachtungen zufolge herrscht in Deutschland diesbezüglich mehr Skepsis (die Vorstellung „Roboter als Partner des Menschen" wirkte sogar für Ingenieure des Fraunhofer IPA als befremdlich) als in Japan. Inwieweit meinen Sie, dass religiöse Faktoren hier eine Rolle spielen könnten?

Arvalis:

→ Maschine sollte kein Ersatz sein
→ Zwischenmenschliche Kommunikation sollte gefördert werden
→ Problem der Rechtfertigung: „Jetzt habe ich Oma einen Roboter geschenkt und brauche mich deshalb nicht mehr persönlich zu kümmern."

Zusätzliche Aspekte:

In Deutschland werden Anrufbeantworter von Menschen direkt besprochen, während man in Japan oft die Versionen von computerisierten AB mit Roboterstimme hat.

Europäer wollen nicht ihre Kontrolle an Technologie delegieren.

In Deutschland werden viele japanische Roboterprojekte (bspw. SDR-4XII) eher als Spielerei betrachtet.

A.4.6 Summary: Interview Prof. Aoki (name changed)
(Informal guided face-to-face interviews, German)

Respondent: Prof. Aoki
Position: Christian Professor for Humanities at Japanese Universityb / Yokohama

Date: 2003-11-13

Question: Wenn ich richtig informiert bin, scheint Ihnen „QRIO" (Sony, SDR-4XII) von Interesse zu sein. → Warum?

Aoki: Japaner wollen in Robotern gerne Gefühle sehen, wie das Beispiel AIBO, QRIO etc. zum Ausdruck bringt. Japaner faszinieren die menschlichen Aspekte eines Roboters. Aus diesem Grunde besteht auch großes Interesse an bipeder Forschung. Dinge und Gegenstände können als lebendig betrachtet werden. → Teil ist mehr als die Summe der Einzelteile. Der japanische Animismus wird als Einflussfaktor gesehen.

→ Japanische Grundlagenforschung beinhaltet auch spielerische, weniger pragmatische Aspekte → Ursachen in Forschungspolitik. → Innovation durch spielerisches Experimentieren. → in Japan herrscht eine eher langfristige Sichtweise in Hinblick auf Forschungskonzepte vor.

→ Beim Begriff „Roboter" schwingt bei „Japanern" die Assoziation mit „menschlich" mit. Industrierobotern wurden sogar menschliche Bewegungsabläufe (bspw. ein Danebenschlagen bei Schmiedarbeiten, das dem Menschen dazu dient, den Rhythmus beizubehalten, einprogrammiert, obwohl dies für einen Roboter (der keine Probleme mit monotoner Arbeit hat) überflüssig wäre. Japanische Roboterprogrammierung orientiert sich oftmals an den Erfahrungen und Gewohnheiten der Menschen, anstatt dass gänzlich durchrationalisierte Konzepte entwickelt werden → Interesse an Sevicerobotik???

→ Roboter werden nicht in erster Linie als etwas zweckmäßiges betrachtet.

→ Roboterentwicklung nicht direkt zweckorientiert, sondern Einsatzplanung offen, bspw. Roboter In Seniorenheimen nicht konkret für diesen Zweck konstruiert, sondern „multi-purpose" einsetzbar.

→ Programmierung setzt menschliche Erfahrung voraus

Question: Nun fragt man sich derweilen in Deutschland, weshalb die Japaner eine vergleichsweise hohe Technikfaszination aufweisen → Ursachen? Erfahrungen? (bedingt durch ökonomische Erfolge, aber bereits in der Edo-Periode herrschte in Japan eine gewisse Faszination mit Automaten – *Karakuri* **-,**

die wegen der Abschottungspolitik unabhängig von der Entwicklung in Europa stattfand).

Aoki: Keine negativen Erfahrungen mit zerstörerischer Technologie, zumindest japanischer Technologie (Atombomben und militärische Raketen waren ausländische Technologien. → Weshalb sollte in Roboter ein Gefahrenpotential in sich bergen, wo doch schon viele weniger fortschrittliche Technologien ausreichen würden, um die Menschheit zu zerstören.

Question: Sie sind ein Fan von *Tetsuwan Atomu*? Weshalb? Was finden/fanden Sie an der Geschichte so gut?

Aoki: Faszination mit Technik, Aspekt der „Menschlichkeit"

→ wenn man Tezukas „TA" genauer betrachtet, kann auch eine durchaus ambivalente Interpretation gefunden werden:

In my view *"Tetsuwan Atomu"* can also be interpreted as follows:

- Robots can not substitute for humans (Dr. Tenma ist von Astro Boy enttäuscht, da dieser nicht wachsen kann → Unterschied zu seinem echten Sohn)

- Robots can never become like humans (even with a "heart" and Artificial Intelligence)

- Robots will always be as good or bad as the humans who create them (Bsp. Atlas)

- It is questionable (although not impossible) if robots will bring happiness to mankind
  Technology is ambivalent (. In the *manga* Tezuka writes about a robotics law, which says in a quite utilitarian manner that robots should make people happy. Later he asks the question what if one substitutes the word "robot" through the word "science", has science really made mankind happy? He leaves the question open, but the mere fact that it has been asked indicates that there could be more than one affirmative answer (this is being underlined as the picture shows Tezuka looking out of the window onto high rise buildings and multilevel roads, which some people may consider as negative aspects of technology

- There could occur conflicts in regard to the coexistence of humans and robots (insbesondere, wenn man Tezuka's Vorlage zu „TA": „*Metropolis*" betrachtet

- Everyone has to take responsibility for ones actions

- **What purpose does it serve to build machines in our likeliness** (posed as a rather open question)?

- **A call to reconsider humanity**

Aoki: Der Aspekt der "Enttäuschung" von Dr. Tenma in Hinblick auf Astroboy wurde nicht gesehen. Die Ersazsohn-Thematk wurde nicht als negativ, sondern als tragisch angesehen: „alle versuchen, das beste zu geben, aber sie können es nicht (menschliche Tragik, und die Tragik des Roboters). Astroboy wollte perfekt sein, aber seine Bestrebungen sind gescheitert.

Meine ambivalente Interpretationsweise war ihm völlig fremd.

(andere populäre Geschichte: Tetsuwan 28-go)

Questions:

- "Robots as partners for humans"? → Interpretation, Kommentar?

- **Robotik im Pflegebereich** → Stellungnahme?

- „Atom Project"

30-year robot project pitched
Researchers see tech windfalls in costly humanoid quest

Japanese researchers in robot technology are advocating a grand project, under which the government would spend 50 billion yen a year over three decades to develop a humanoid robot with the mental, physical and emotional capacity of a 5-year-old human

→ **Kommentar?**
→ **Grenzen der Forschung?**
→ **Warum sollte man sich für solche Projekte interessieren?**

Aoki: Wohl eher von der „spielerischen Perspektive" zu sehen. Keiner wird wohl ernsthaft glauben, dass die Projekt in 30 Jahren ein Erfolg sein wird, und man wird es wohl schon gut finden, wenn der Roboter niedlich aussieht und interaktives Verhalten zeigt. Es ist eher ein Aspekt der Neugierde dahinter: wie weit wird man wohl kommen?

→ Nicht wörtlich zu nehmen, eher als Experiment der Grundlagenforschung zu betrachten.

→ Auch der Aspekt „Roboter als Ersatz des Menschen" wird nicht als Befürchtung angesehen.

Japaner scheinen weder den „Frankenstein-" noch den „Blade-Runner-Komplex" aufzuweisen.
(Anm. Miriam JS Leis)

Zusatzfragen:

- **Umfrage**

N.U.: Bereits die Idee, die Welt in Objekt und Subjekt aufzuspalten scheint dem Respondenten fremd (und er meinte, dass andere Japaner damit auch Schwierigkeiten hätten). Für ihn hat bspw. ein Auto bereits mehrere Dimensionen haben: utilitaristisch: Fahrzeug, aber auch eine emotionale Komponente. Als Beispiel wurde eine Tasse angeführt, die nicht nur als schlichter Gegenstand betrachtet wird, sondern eine subjektive / emotionale Komponente besitzt, wenn man bei der Betrachtungsweise mit einbezieht, dass die Konzeption des Gegenstands (Form, Farbe, Gestaltung, Materialwahl etc.) als menschlicher Faktor quasi mit-manifestiert ist.

Die dichotome Betrachtungsweise von Subjekt vs. Objekt widersprach der emotionalen Sichtweise des Respondenten.

A.4.7 Summary: Interview Mitsubishi about *"Wakamaru"* service-robot

(Formal guided face-to-face interviews, English)
Respondent: Junji SUZUKI (former Ship-building engineer)
Position: Manager
Laser & Electronics Group; Machinery Headquarters @ Mitsubishi Heavy Industries, Ltd

Date: 2003-11-17

1. About *"Wakamaru"*

Question 1.1: History of project / idea?

Because of decline in ship-building industry new project concepts have been thought of. After a competition in regard to new projects (among others building airships, medical appliances) the idea of a service-robot has been realized. Two factors have been also influential to the decision:

J.S.:
a) the experience in robot-technology for nuclear-power-plant maintenance
b) demographic factors of an aging society → robots for support for the elderly

The design of *"Wakamaru"* has been created by a famous designer outside Mitsubishi to avoid inter-company rivalry in regard to design.

For the respondent it is important to have a "likable" design with robots, which isn't too human-like, because in his view an appearance too human-like could lead people to people thinking of robots as humans and being reluctant to use them as servants. But there are of course also people in Japan who wish to see a quite-human-like appearance in robots, but it is rather a matter of "taste".

→ The most important factor for the respondent is that humans should like the robot
→ if humans like and accept it, considerations about functionality should be concentrated on.

Question 1.2: How do you define "robot"? (in regard to *"Wakamaru"*)

J.S.:

graphic demonstration by respondent:

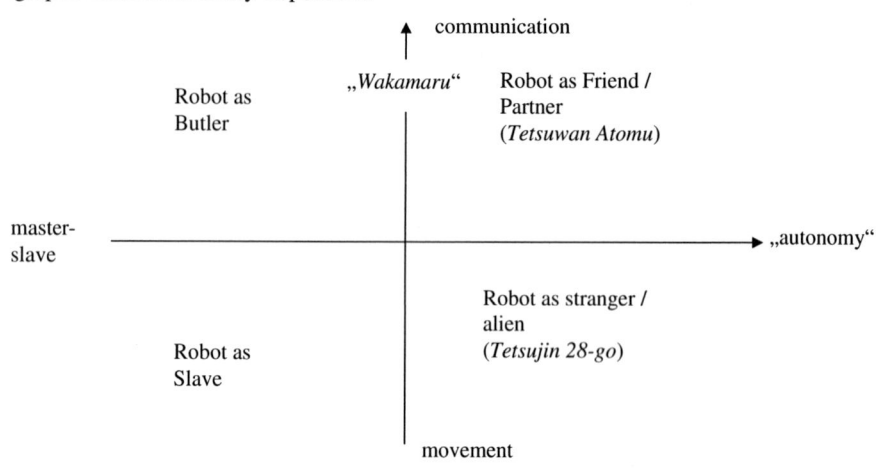

```
                              ↑ communication
                              |
                „Wakamaru"    |   Robot as Friend /
     Robot as                 |   Partner
     Butler                   |   (Tetsuwan Atomu)
                              |
master-                       |
slave ------------------------+------------------------→ „autonomy"
                              |
                              |   Robot as stranger /
                              |   alien
     Robot as                 |   (Tetsujin 28-go)
     Slave                    |
                              |
                              ↓ movement
```

2. Deployment

Question 2.1: In Germany care-service-/ assistance providers / insurers are quite reluctant for supporting robot-projects in this area, which in turn difficulties in financing and marketing

Question 2.2: In Germany there is also rather high scepticism and resistance in regard to deploying robots in the field of assistance for the elderly

"In Deutschland haben wir ein reguliertes Gesundheitswesen. Wenn die Krankenkassen den Bau von Pflegerobotern nicht unterstützen, solange wird auch die Industrie sehr verhalten sein, wenn es um den Bau von Robotern geht."

→ how about Japan

J.S.: Care services lie emphasis on functionality and are also in Japan rather hesitant. They also say that care-service is a domain that should rather left to humans. But things might change, as tests in caring facilities with elderly / mentally instable persons with the robot "*Robovie*" have proven positive therapeutic effects with elderly getting sympathy for the robot. Also many elderly are interested in robots (as statistics show, women, middle-aged and above show a higher affinity towards robots than younger people or men. → These women don't see the technology behind the robot, but only its appearance)

→ It's the same phenomena observed in Japanese puppet plays → the people don't regard the puppeteer, but only concentrate on the appearance, movement and characteristic of doll, in the same way Japanese can forget about the inside of a robot.

Care facilities employ much technology in regard to lifters, „feeding-assistance robots"(„my spoon") an others. So it would be a question of time and technological advance until they also accept robots like the "Wakamaru" concept.

Question 2.3: In Germany, robot development is rather function-oriented / pragmatic, whereas in Japan features like human-like communication are also considered. Why?

J.S.: Likeability of robot is of foremost interest. The human should like the robot (graphic demonstrated by respondent):

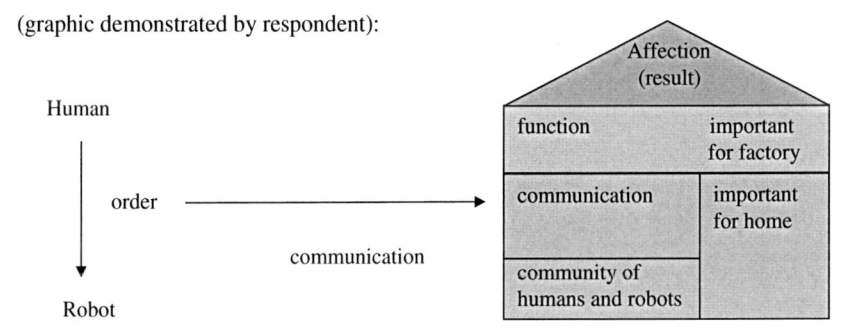

	Affection (result)	
function		important for factory
communication		important for home
community of humans and robots		

Human
│
│   order ──────────────→
│
│   communication
▼
Robot

So for home-use the factor of likeability as priority over functionality → Design strategy of Japan

3.: Human-like robots / Robots and Society

Question 3.1: For German researchers human-like appearance in robots is of rather low relevance. Why do you think are Japanese so interested in human-like robots, as the example of *"Wakamaru"* shows?

J.S.: → also refer to answers for 1. → Likeability of robot is of foremost interest.

Question 3.2: Some German people commented, that the more human-like robots would get, the less likely they would be accepted. What would you say about this. What is the Japanese view on this?

J.S.:
→ refer to 1.1; maybe rather a matter of "taste".

→ At least over 50% of Japanese think that robot-development is "good news".

→ Researchers / engineers want to design robots which represent the visions / dreams of the people → realization of a new form of existence which is neither human nor animal nor "mere object" although Japanese have difficulties with the concept of "pure object" and "pure subject". → in regard to "subject-object-categorization survey" the respondent had some difficulties in understanding concept why one should make such a categorization.

→ old houses, "hina-dolls" may be considered to have "a mind of their own" (hina dolls are placed instead of humans → "representations" (to pretend human beings)

→ mistreating dolls is considered as cruelty

but nonetheless a robot has more than things like trains or cars.
quote: "if seeing a robot, thoughts come to my mind that it might think".

Question 3.3: "Robots as partners" is a rather strange concept for Germans. What do you mean with partner?

J.S.: Robot can become hero and good partners (*Testuwan Atomu*-image)

The word partner is a new word to Japanese and is defined as below family and above "friend"

```
                    ▲  high
family              │
partner             │
friend              │
fellow humans       │  low
```

maybe like the German equivalent of "*Kumpel*"?

Charactersitc of a "Japanese Partner":

- support
- listening to complaints
- to be trusted

service robot = mixture of "partner" and maid/butler

→ robot is seen as above pet and below human → "communicative pet"

→ robots as "buffers" for families, enhancing good communication with familiy members

→ robots accompanying couples living alone after children have left, enable communication
    with children away

→ but still difficult to get "understanding" (of words / gestures) implemented into a robot.

Question 3.4: "Humans and robots coexisting in harmony", this is something often heard in Japan. What is meant by this?

J.S.: Harmony means:

- courtesy
- respectful behaviour

these are the foundations for communication

Question: 3.5 Robot-Future for Japan

replication of graphic by respondent:

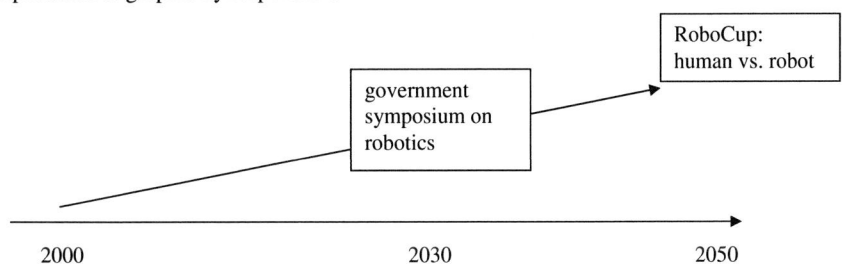

```
                                                    ┌─────────────┐
                                                    │ RoboCup:    │
                                                    │ human vs. robot│
                                                    └─────────────┘
                                                        ▲
                                    ┌──────────────┐   /
                                    │ government   │  /
                                    │ symposium on │ /
                                    │ robotics     │/
                                    └──────────────┘
                                            /
───────────────────────────────────────────────────────────────▶
    2000                        2030                      2050
```

Research roadmap promoted by government (MITI) with specific targets in each year.

Japanese think they can control robots and as long that they can control them, they can become god partners.

Japanese no interest in building "bad technology" (e.g. for military purposes)

No traditional bad image in regard to robots in Japan

4. Personal Interest

Question 4.1: How did it come that you got interested in robots?

J.S.: Mentioned Tetsuwan Atomu and Tetsujin 28-go

There have not been other childhood entertainment than such dealing with robots (robots or "Ultraman" / "Goguro-5"), especially for boys.

Question 4.2: Personal experience with project?

J.S.: Respondent came from ship-building engineering and voted for "robot-project"

AIBOSurvey: data and results

Survey has been originally conducted in German, but has been translated and summarized in English.
All 16 respondents have been members of the German-speaking AIBO-community (www.aibo-freunde.de)

No.	Question	Answ.		n	Comment
1*	As what do you regard your AIBO? (please chose only one answer, which you consider most appropriate)	a)	Toy	4	
		b)	Gadget / apparatus	0	
		c)	Dog	1	
		e)	Buddy / Friend	2	
		f)	Article for education / experimentation	7	
		g)	other:	2	- between toy and friend - A Taste of robot future, sensational exotic property
2*	For which purposes do you use your AIBO? (multiple answers possible)	a)	for entertainment	11	
		b)	to play with	7	
		c)	for experimentation	12	
		d)	not to be alone / companionship	2	
		e)	other:	1	- surveillance
3	Would you say that you have some form of personal relationship to your AIBO?	a)	yes	9	
		b)	no	4	
		c)	not sure	3	

4	If you have answers question 3 with yes, how strong would you say that this relationship is?	a)	very strong	0
		b)	strong	2
		c)	middle	5
		d)	weak	2
		e)	very weak	0
5*	Would you sell your AIBO if you could make a profit on it?	a)	yes	2
multiple answers possible		b)	no	11
		c)	not sure	3
6	If your AIBO would come out of the „AIBO clinic" with new external parts, would it still bet he same AIBO to you?	a)	yes	13
		b)	no	1
		c)	not sure	2
7	Are you disappointed by the abilities of your AIBO?	a)	yes, I have expected more	0
		b)	to some degree I have expected more	3
		c)	no, it's just as I have expected it to be	5
		d)	no, to the contrary. I'm amazed about its abilities.	8
8	Do you compare your AIBO to a real dog (or other	a)	yes → which one?	0
		b)	sometimes → which one?	4 ("dog" was named 3 times)
		c)	no	12

	living-pet)?			
9	If you would have the choice and possibility, would you then prefer having a living dog?	a)	a living dog	4
		b)	an AIBO	6
		c)	both	5
		d)	neither nor	0
		e)	not sure	1
10	Do you regard your AIBO as a thing? (please chose only one answer, which you consider most appropriate)	a)	yes, actually it's nothing but a robot	2
		b)	not quite. Although it's a robot, it's more than just a thing.	13
		c)	no, I couldn't regard it as a thing.	1
11	When you're together with AIBO, did it ever happen to you that you „forgot" that it's only a robot being programmed?	a)	no, such thing never happened to me	8
		b)	yes, in a thoughtless moment, it can happen to me.	8
		c)	yes, it's hard form me to regard it as a robot.	0
12	Do you believe that your AIBO	a)	yes	3
		b)	no	6

	has its own personality?	c)	sometimes in a thoughtless moment	7	
13	What do you have from AIBO? (multiple answers possible)	a)	entertainment	15	
		b)	fun / joy	14	
		c)	it keeps me company	3	
		d)	technological knowledge	13	
		e)	actually rather anger and problems	1	
		f)	nothing	0	
		g)	other:	2	- through AIBO and the community one also gets to know nice people - a new hobby

Questions with open answers (answers have been paraphrased and sorted according to similarity).

Q14	What was your decision to get an AIBO?	9	Interest in technology / experimenting with technology
		4	Curiosity
		1	gift / sponsored
		2	No answer
Q15	What do you value about your AIBO? (open question, answers have been first paraphrased, then	5	today's technology / technological aspects
		6	its autonomy, not repetitive behavior
	coded in regard to similarity)	2	general fascination / fun
		2	communication / communicative aspects
		1	no answer
Q16	Please name maximal five advantages of an AIBO		most common answers: no allergies, no visits to the

	opposed to a real dog (answers have been coded in regard to similarity)		veterinary, no dirt and more hygienic, no responsibilities necessary and can be shut-off, nice and interesting hobby, cheaper on the long run no comparison with a living animal possible (named 4 times)
Q17	Please name maximal five disadvantages of an AIBO opposed to a real dog (answers have been coded in regard to similarity)		most common answers: no real animal / no real intelligence / no real emotions, limited in intelligence and behavior, not comparable to a real animal

Statistical Data

total number of respondents	16
female respondents	1
male respondents	15

Age Structure:		
	below 20	2
	20-29	4
	30-39	5
	40-49	4
	50-59	
	60-69	
	70+	
	undisclosed	1

Nationality			
	Germany	15	
	Great Britain	1	
Residence			
	Germany	13	
	Switzerland	1	
	Belgium	1	
	undisclosed	1	
Amount of AIBOs in household			
	1 AIBO	13	
	2 AIBOs	2	
	3 AIBOs	1	
AIBO Types		n	
	ERS-110	0	
	ERS-111	1	
	ERS-210	0	
	ERS-220	9	
	ERS-311/312/31L	0	
	ERS-7	9	
In possession of AIBO since	First AIBO	Second AIBO	Third AIBO
2001	1		
2002	2	1	
2003	10	1	1
2004	3		

Acquisition of AIBO		
	gift	15
	bought	3
	sponsored	1
Level of interest in technology		
	very interested	13
	interested	3
	intermediate	0
	barely interested	0
	not interested at all	0
Having / ever had a living dog or cat		
	yes	10
	no	6
Profession		
	Profession related to computers and engineering (software developer, computer engineer, webdesigner etc.)	8
	secretary	1
	student (natural science)	1
	pupil	2
	undisclosed	4

Religious belief		
Christian	10	
Buddhist	0	
Shinto	0	
No confession	4	
other	2	1 Orthodox
		1 Agnostic

Statistics about AIBOware:

AIBOware	n	AIBOware	n
AIBO Eyes	1	Fun Pack	1
AIBO Dancer	1	Navigator	1
AIBO Life (1&2)	11	Party Mascot	2
AIBO Mind / Mind Plus	6	Recognition	3
AIBO Scope / AIBO Scope 7	2	Original ERS-7 Aiboware	2
ERA 111	1	Others / own programs	2
Hello AIBO	4		